FIRE IN

The Dynamic Buddhism
of Nichiren

Daniel B. Montgomery

Mandala
An Imprint of HarperCollins*Publishers*

Mandala
An Imprint of GraftonBooks
A Division of HarperCollins*Publishers*
77-85 Fulham Palace Road,
Hammersmith, London W6 8JB

Published by Mandala 1991
1 3 5 7 9 10 8 6 4 2

A catalogue record for this book
is available from the British Library

ISBN 1-85274-091-4

Typeset by Harper Phototypesetters Limited,
Northampton, England
Printed in Great Britain by
Mackays of Chatham, Kent

Contents

Daniel B. Montgomery
has been studying Buddhism and
comparative religion for over 40
years, and lectures throughout
America and Japan. He has written
extensively on Nichirenism,
including an English translation of
the Lotus Sutra.

Acknowledgements _____

Grateful acknowledgement is made to the following for copyrighted material:

Bukkyo Dendo Kyokai
Excerpts from *The Teaching of Buddha*, 93rd revised edition, 1984. © 1966. Reprinted by permission of the publisher.

Columbia University Press
Excerpts from *Kukai: Major Works* translated by Yoshito S. Hakeda, © (1972) Columbia University Press; *Scripture of the Lotus Blossom of the Fine Dharma* translated by Leon Hurvitz, © (1976) Columbia University Press. Used by permission.

Dover Publications Inc.
Excerpts from *The Gods of Northern Buddhism* by Alice Getty (1988 reprint of the 2nd edition, 1928). Reprinted by permission of the publisher.

Harvard University Press
Excerpts from *Nichiren the Buddhist Prophet* by Masaharu Anesaki (Gloucester, Mass.: Peter Smith, 1966); © (1916) Harvard University Press. Used by permission.

Kosei Publishing Company
Excerpts from *Dharma World*; *Kosei Times*; *Buddhist Sutras* by Kozen Mizuno. © 1980, 1982; *The Beginnings of Buddhism* by Kozen Mizuno. © 1974, 1980; *My Father, My Teacher* by Nichiko Niwano. © 1980, 1982. *Travel to Infinity*, by Nikkyo Niwano. © 1968; *Lifetime Beginner* by Nikkyo Niwano. © 1976, 1977, 1978. *Honzon* by Nikkyo

Niwano. © 1969; *A Guide to the Threefold Lotus Sutra* by Nikkyo Niwano. © 1968, 1975, 1981; *The Lotus Sutra: Life and Soul of Buddhism* by Nikkyo Niwano. © 1970; *The Threefold Lotus Sutra.* © 1971, 1974, 1975; *Rissho Kosei-kai.* © 1966; *Rissho Kosei-kai: For Our New Members.* © 1972. Reprinted by permission of the publisher.

Daiichi Shobo
Excerpts from *T'ien T'ai Buddhism: An Outline of the Fourfold Teachings.* © 1983. Reprinted by permission of the publisher and Masao Ichishima, compiler.

Senchu Murano
Excerpts from *The Sutra of the Lotus Flower of the Wonderful Law.* © 1974; *The Lotus Sutra and Nichiren* by Eisen Hoshino. Reprinted by permission of the translator. *An Outline of the Lotus Sutra.* Reprinted by permission of the author.

Nichiren Order of North America
Excerpts from *St. Nichiren* by J. A. Christensen. © 1981 by The Nichiren Buddhist Order of America. Reprinted by permission of the publisher.

Nichiren Shu Headquarters
Excerpts from *Shingyo Hikkei* (1978) and *Nichiren Shu News.* Reprinted by permission of the publisher.

Nichiren Shu Overseas Propagation Promotion Association
Excerpts from Nichiren's *Ho-on-jo.* © 1980; *Kaimoku-sho.* © 1987; *Senji-sho.* © 1989. *A Phrase a Day* © 1986. Reprinted by permission of the publisher.

Office Appliance Co. Ltd.
Excerpts from *The Essentials of Buddhist Philosophy* by Junjiro Takakusu, third edition (1956). Reprinted with permission of the publisher.

Pantheon Books, a division of Random House, Inc.
Excerpt from *Nature, Man and Woman* by Alan W. Watts. © 1958. Reprinted by permission of the publisher.

Princeton University Press
Excerpts from *Lay Buddhism in Contemporary Japan: Reiyukai Kyodan* by Helen Hardacre. © 1984. Reprinted by permission of the publisher.

Reiyukai
Excerpts from *The Development of Japanese Lay Buddhism* by Tsugunari Kubo. © 1986; *The Reiyukai Movement: Buddhism as an Interreligious Philosophy* by Tsugunari Kubo. © 1987; *Looking for the Spirit of Buddha?*; *Reiyukai Today*; *Reiyukai and Social Services*;

Reiyukai: People Promoting Friendship and Awareness; *Buddha's World*; *Circle*; *Inner Trip Friends*. Reprinted by permission of the publisher.

Shambhala Publications, Inc.
Excerpts from *Bodhisattva of Compassion* by John Blofeld, © 1977. Reprinted by arrangement with Shambhala Publications, 300 Massachusetts Avenue, Boston, MA 02115. Excerpts from *Mandala* by José and Miriam Argüelles, © 1972. Reprinted by arrangement with Shambhala Publications, 300 Massachusetts Avenue, Boston, MA 02115.

Soka Gakkai
Excerpts from *The Major Writings of Nichiren Daishonin*; © 1979, 1981, 1985, 1986 by Nichiren Shoshu International Center; *A Dictionary of Buddhist Terms and Concepts*. © 1983 by Nichiren Shoshu International Center; *The Human Revolution*, Vol. IV, by Daisaku Ikeda. © 1968 by The Seikyo Press; *Lectures on Buddhism*, Vol. IV, by Daisaku Ikeda. © 1967 by The Seikyo Press; *Science and Religion* by Daisaku Ikeda. © 1965 by Daisaku Ikeda; *Lecture on the Sutra*. 3rd edition, by Josei Toda. © 1968 by The Seikyo Press; *Outline of Buddhism* by Yasuji Kirimura. © 1981 by Nichiren Shoshu International Center; *Seikyo Times*; *World Tribune*. Reprinted by permission of the publisher.

Unitarian Universalist Association
Quote from *A Religion for Greatness* by Clarence R. Skinner (Bost: Universalist Publishing House, 1945) used by permission of the Unitarian Universalist Association, Boston, MA.

University of California Center for South and Southeast Asia Studies
Excerpt from *Saicho: The Establishment of the Japanese Tendai School* by Paul Groner (Berkeley Buddhist Studies Series, 1984). Reprinted by permission of the publisher.

University of Pennsylvania Press
Excerpt from *Buddhism in Japan* by Dale Saunders. © 1964 by the Trustees of the University of Pennsylvania. Reprinted by permission of the publisher.

Wadsworth Publishing Company
Excerpts from *American Buddhism* by Charles S. Prebish © 1979 by Wadsworth, Inc. Reprinted by permission of the publisher.

Introduction _____

Many believe that the twenty-first century will be the Century of Japan. The East is said to be beating the West at its own game. Its business conglomerates, which lay in ruins only a few decades ago, now outperform those of Europe and America. This has happened and will continue to happen because Japanese firms enjoy a better rapport between labour and management, take seriously the contributions to quality and production offered by workers, and make their marketing programmes more responsive to the wishes of consumers. In order to compete with the Japanese economic onslaught, American and European businessmen need to become humble students, adopt Japanese methods, learn to think in the long term rather than in terms of immediate profits, and become more concerned with the success of their companies than with their own individual careers. In other words, in order to remain competitive they must imitate the Japanese.

Japanese products now flood the world markets. Japanese ideas, on the other hand, are little known outside their land of origin. The Japanese are thought to be adapters, not originators. First they copied the Chinese; now they copy the West. Indeed, the Japanese themselves tend to underestimate their own intellectual originality. They are more likely to study the thoughts of Plato, Nietzsche, or Marx than those of their own intellectual forefathers. The modern world was built by the West, not the East, and most Japanese feel they must learn its way in order to master it.

During the 1950s and '60s, before the Japanese economic boom had reached its present level, the West expressed an interest in some of the more picturesque aspects of Japanese culture — martial arts, flower arranging, and Zen. However, these fruits of old Japan hardly explain the new Japan. What is the origin of this driving work ethic, this sense of loyalty between employer and employee, this confidence in innate Japanese abilities? It certainly comes neither from the Greek Plato nor from Chinese Zen. Rather it derives from something very deep within the Japanese psyche.

It is not my intention to analyse what this 'something' might be. However, this inner force has been tapped and put into an intelligible form. There is a philosophy of action which is purely Japanese. It was born on Japanese soil and formulated by a native son. Although it is based on a foreign import, Buddhism, in its final form it is exclusively Japanese. It is the one purely original Japanese contribution to world thought. From its inception it has been committed to a mission — a mission to enlighten and save not only its native country but the world beyond. It claims to be the universal truth, manifested in Japan but applicable everywhere. It is called Nichirenism.

Nichirenism bears the name of its founder, the 13th century Japanese religious reformer Nichiren. During the first two centuries of its existence, it spread among all classes of Japanese society in spite of sometimes violent official opposition. It even travelled abroad to Manchuria and China — the only Japanese philosophy ever to do so. But then it split into competing sects, and was effectively boxed in by the Tokugawa dictatorship (1600–1868). It degenerated into formalism, revived in the 20th century as an ally of militant Japanese nationalism, and then surged ahead after the Second World War as it broke free from all government entanglements.

Nichirenism was first introduced to America around 1913 by Professor Masaharu Anesaki at Harvard. Ten years later it was presented to England by Kishio Satomi, son of Chigaku Tanaka, who had invented the term, 'Nichirenism'. Tanaka, one of the leaders in the Nichiren revival in Japan, had coined the name to distinguish the general philosophy from sectarian Nichiren Buddhism. These Japanese scholars, however, seem not to have aroused much enthusiasm in the West, which was then eyeing Japanese nationalism with increasing apprehension.

After the Second World War, the Nichiren revival became a torrent. Nichiren sects, fuelled by ardent lay enthusiasts using the latest evangelical techniques of mass communications, grew so explosively that together they now number more adherents than any other religion in Japan. Some groups have felt strong enough to organize their own political societies and in one case even their own political party. Several have extended their missionary outreach abroad, where they have enjoyed considerable success among non-Japanese.

In October 1960 President Daisaku Ikeda of Sokagakkai, a Nichiren lay organization, arrived in California and was greeted by a handful of Japanese-American followers. He announced modestly that his arrival in America would be as significant to the history of the world as the arrival of Columbus in 1492. Like other Eastern *gurus* who had come before him, he declared that he would build a temple in the New World from which his religion would spread across the continent. But unlike his predecessors, he solicited no funds. All expenses would be borne in Japan. Today his organization has indeed spread over the United States, Canada, Mexico, Panama, and Peru. It has crossed the Atlantic to Europe and Africa and spread southwards to Australia and southern Asia. Thirty years after Ikeda's first missionary excursion, Sokagakkai International claimed twenty million members in 115 countries.

Still no funds have been solicited abroad. All major bills are paid from Japan. The world is its mission field, an investment in the future. By the twenty-first century, Sokagakkai expects to be the most powerful political–religious force in the world. It alone claims to preach the truth, and the truth means success. The Japanese economic miracle is believed to have its origin in the spirit of Japan as elucidated by Nichiren. To prosper further it must renovate the world.

For the first time in centuries, the West finds itself the receiver of cultural values rather than the maker of them. Spiritual values from the East have been coming westward for a long time. But none have had the intensity of Nichiren Buddhism, fuelled as it is by the explosive Japanese economic power.

We may not concur with Ikeda that the secret of this power is Nichirenism. The Japanese themselves do not all adhere to Nichirenism, and some, indeed, are strongly opposed to it. Nevertheless, it remains the most important indigenous expression of the Japanese national spirit and one which has recruited enthusiastic adherents among non-Japanese as well. It is time we looked at it more closely.

Chapter 1

Prince of India _____

The sixth century before Christ was one of the great watersheds of human history. Never before or since have so many men of genius appeared on our planet. Their words and deeds inspired generations who came after them and looked back to them as the final arbiters of right and wrong. It was centuries, even millennia, before the influence of any of them began to be replaced by that of newer sages.

In China there were Kung Fu-tzu (Confucius), who taught people how to live in society, and Lao Tzu, who taught them how to live with nature. In Persia, Zoroaster proclaimed an eternal struggle between good and evil. In India Mahavira taught non-violence and extreme asceticism, while Gautama the Buddha countered with the Middle Way. In Mesopotamia and Palestine, Jeremiah, Isaiah, Ezekiel, and Daniel proclaimed one God who rules all nations. In Greece, there were philosophers, poets, and scientists such as Solon, Thales, Pythagoras, Zeno, and Heraclitus. The whole civilized world seemed to catch fire in a blaze of inspiration.

The light of some of these great teachers has faded with the passing of time. But one of them, Siddhartha Gautama, the Buddha, still commands the veneration of hundreds of millions around the globe. The details of his life, like those of most of the others, are sketchy. There are references to him interspersed among records of his teachings, but no detailed biography appeared until five or six hundred years after his death, when Ashvaghosha (1st/2nd centuries A.D.) wrote his master-piece, *Buddhacarita*, 'Acts of the Buddha'. By that time it was in the form of a 'gospel', a sacred narrative designed to carry a religious message. Nevertheless it is here we must begin if we want to see the man of flesh and blood, even though much of what we discern may be the invention of later generations.

The exact dates of the Buddha are uncertain, although most modern authorities believe that he lived from 563 to 483 B.C. A traditional dating from China places him back in the 10th century B.C., but this was probably contrived to make him appear older than Confucius or Lao Tzu, his 'ideological rivals'.

We do not have any portraits of him. The thousands of statues and paintings of the Buddha, which are found throughout the East, are as unreliable as his biography. At first it was considered impious to depict him at all. Buddhist art used symbols to show his presence — a throne for his teaching authority or a footprint to show where he had trod. However the conquests of Alexander the Great linked India to Greece. It was Greek artists from the Graeco–Indian kingdom of Gandhara who broke the taboo and sculptured the Buddha in the form of a Greek hero.

Although the Buddha's ancient followers were not interested in knowing what he had looked like, they were very concerned to know what he had said and where he had travelled. They went to great pains to keep each of his sermons in its proper geographical and temporal setting. Buddhist scriptures always begin with a description of the occasion on which the sermon had originally been preached by the master. Only later did his followers become curious about details in his life not associated with any particular sermon. The more they venerated his words, the more they wanted to know about the one who had spoken such words.

Gautama had warned them against this: 'Do not seek for me in a physical form. If you understand my words and put them into practice, then you have seen me as I am.' But those who loved him could not be restrained forever from wanting to find out as much about him as they possibly could, and where details were lacking, they did not hesitate to invent them. The life of the Buddha became itself a sermon, one which eventually became better known than the words he had actually spoken.

He was born, it was said, in the Lumbini Gardens, just over the Indian border in modern Nepal, while his mother was on a journey from the local capital of Kapilavastu in northern India. He may not have been a member of the dominant Aryan race. His teachings have more in common with the anthropocentric pre-Aryan systems of yoga, Sankhya, and Jainism, than with the theocentric legends of the Aryans. By caste he was a Kshatriya (warrior), by clan a Shakya (hence the later title, Shakyamuni, 'Sage of the Shakyas'), and his family name was Gautama. His father Suddhodana Gautama was king of the area and raja of the Shakya clan. His mother Maya died within a week of giving him birth.

The grieving father determined to give his child every advantage which money and power could obtain. He named the child Siddhartha and placed him in the custody of Queen Maya's sister, Prajapati. The young prince of the Shakyas grew up in the palace of Kapilavastu within sight of the world's mightiest mountain range, the Himalayas. Although motherless, he never lacked parental affection either from his father or his step-mother. They did everything possible to shield him from the sorrows of the outside world. Rarely, indeed, was the boy permitted to stray beyond the palace grounds. The king, still mourning his lost bride, had premonitions that someday his son, too, would leave him. This he would prevent at any cost, and he anticipated his son's every desire.

In spite of so much pampering, the boy remained strangely unspoiled. Everyone loved him, even the animals. One day while he was playing in the garden, a white swan, its wing pierced by an arrow, fluttered to the ground near his feet. Calming the frightened creature, the prince gently removed the arrow and massaged the wounded wing. As he sat there with the bird on his lap, his cousin Devadatta burst into the garden.

'There is my bird!' he said, 'Give it to me! It was I who shot it.'

'No,' answered Siddhartha. 'If it were dead, perhaps you could claim it. But it is alive and a free creature.'

'Alive or dead,' protested the hunter, 'what is the difference? It was free when it flew above, but now it is mine, for I brought it down.'

The argument was logical, but Siddhartha only pressed the wounded swan to his breast and answered solemnly, 'No. It is mine, the first of many things which shall be mine by right of mercy. And I shall teach compassion to all men, and speak for those who have no speech.'

Much annoyed, Devadatta took his case to the learned doctors and lawyers of the court. 'If I shot the bird, isn't it mine by rights?'

However, the court sided with Prince Siddhartha: 'Life belongs not to him who takes it, but to him who saves it.'

Devadatta never forgave Siddhartha for having humiliated him before the court. He would eventually become the Buddha's most implacable enemy.

It is significant that Siddhartha Gautama's first recorded act of mercy was towards an animal. It was not to be the last such act, by any means. Later in his life he was to speak out strongly against cruelty to animals, especially the age-old practice of sacrificing animals to appease the gods. 'If man expects mercy from the gods,' he asked, 'should he not himself be merciful to those creatures that look upon him as a god?'

As Siddhartha Gautama grew to young manhood, he continued to lead a sheltered, peaceful, and happy life. From time to time he would be momentarily disturbed by rumours of evils and tragedies in the world outside, but the distant rolls of thunder would soon fade away and be forgotten. His father now tried to interest him in the opposite sex, and saw to it that the palace had frequent visits from eligible princesses. Siddhartha was only mildly interested until he met the lovely Princess Yashodhara; then his world turned upside-down. He could think of nothing except her. He must marry her or die.

His father was delighted, but her father was not so sure. How could this pampered prince carry on the traditions of the warlike Shakya clan? He wanted no dreamer for a son-in-law, but a warrior worthy of their ancestors. Let him prove himself in a tournament on the field of valour.

He had underestimated his daughter's suitor. Siddhartha at 19 was a natural athlete of agility and strength — strength which would later carry him through physical trials that would kill an ordinary man. Previously he had avoided competing with his peers because he always felt sorry for the loser, but for Yashodhara he would do whatever was necessary. He would challenge all comers.

In the tourney, Siddhartha easily defeated his rivals at archery, swordplay, and horsemanship. Mounted on his great white charger, Kantaka, he looked the very picture of a Kshatriya, the mighty men from the west who in those days were conquering all of India. Crowds gathered about him for a closer look, and even his future father-in-law knew that with such a leader the Shakya clan could never know defeat. What more could he ask for than a son-in-law like this one?

And so the prince was wed. King Suddhodana constructed a pleasure palace for the young lovers, sparing no expense. If his paternal affection were not enough to keep the prince by his side, surely the love of Yashodhara would do so. When Yashodhara bore Siddhartha a son, the king's joy knew no bounds. It seemed that all his plans were working out. He had sired a noble progeny who would increase the fortunes of his family, clan, and caste.

Ten years passed happily for Siddhartha. However, the rolls of distant thunder were growing more ominous. Was the world really such a happy place? Was his pleasure garden the real world, or was it just a dream which might burst at any time? Were other people as content with life as he was? Were his beloved wife and child really secure? What sustained their paradise? What was the outside world really like?

He decided to find out. One fateful morning he announced that he would take his chariot into the city. His father was expecting this, but reasoned that perhaps if the prince could see how happy the people were, he would stop worrying about matters which need not concern him. Therefore he ordered the streets to be cleaned and garlanded for a festival, and all beggars and other undesirables to remain out of sight. Siddhartha would see the town at its best.

So it was that when the prince rode into the city, he saw only smiling happy faces. The people were enjoying the unexpected holiday and the rare opportunity to view their beloved but seldom seen prince. They waved and cheered him as he waved back, delighted with all that he saw. He wished that the day would never end, and when finally he reached the town limits, he instructed the charioteer to keep going. He wanted to see everything.

But outside the city there was no festival. Here life went on as usual. And here Siddhartha saw four sights which changed his life.

The first sight was an old man, tottering and feeble. 'What's wrong with him?' asked the prince. 'Why does he drag himself so painfully?'

'He is just old, sir,' replied the charioteer, 'as we all will be if the gods will have us live so long.'

'Will I, too, come to that?' thought Siddhartha, 'And Yashodhara and even the baby? Is that our destination in life?'

The second sight was a sick man lying by the roadside and crying for alms. His body was a mass of sores.

'Don't let it disturb you, sir,' said the charioteer. 'He is sick. Just look away.'

Look away? Where?

The third sight was a funeral procession — death, the inevitable end of us all. Suddenly Siddhartha was depressed. 'Turn back,' he said. 'I don't want to see any more.'

On the way home, they passed a fourth man, a wandering mendicant such as are common in India to this day, a man who had given up all his worldly goods and set off to seek the meaning of life. 'That man,' thought the prince, 'is the only one who has seen the world as it really is — a dance of death.'

Thereafter, the pleasures of home and family were hollow to Siddhartha Gautama. The world had lost its flavour. He was haunted by the three deadly curses of old age, sickness, and death from which there was no escape and which would sooner or later assault not only himself, but his beloved wife and child as well. Was there really no escape? Perhaps not. But if there was, he would find it. He must find it!

Thus he came to the hardest moment of his life. With a great wrench, he tore himself away from everything that he held most dear. One night, he stole quietly into the bedroom to look for the last time at his sleeping wife and child. Then he left, mounted his favourite horse, and quietly rode out of the palace accompanied only by one attendant. When they had ridden some distance from Kapilavastu, he stopped, dismounted, took off his jewels, and presented them to the unhappy servant. He took a sword and cut off his long black hair. Finally he exchanged his fine clothes with those of a beggar who had been observing the strange scene.

His last words to his attendant were, 'Tell the people of Kapilavastu that either I will soon return, the conqueror of age and death, or that I myself, will fail and perish.' With a final pat to his horse Kantaka, he turned and vanished into the forest.

Siddhartha was 29 years old when he left home to become a mendicant. For the next six years he drove himself mercilessly, racking his brain and punishing his body. At first he visited famous teachers and philosophers, but found that each one was anxious only to refute the other. They generally agreed on one thing, however: the soul is a prisoner of the body. The body must be subjugated so that the soul can liberate itself and unite with the Over-soul, Brahman. While this theory did not quite satisfy him, it did suggest a practical method he could try for himself. He became an ascetic and reduced his physical needs to the bare minimum.

There is a remarkable Indian statue which depicts him at this stage of his life. Called 'Buddha Fasting', it shows him seated in thought. The body of the once stalwart Shakya prince is wasted away to a living skeleton. Bones and veins stand out against his nearly transparent skin. For Shakyamuni — as we will now call him — was determined that if deliverance could come by fasting and physical austerity, he would outfast everyone. His fame spread, and five fellow-ascetics became his disciples. They marvelled at his endurance and wondered how he stayed alive.

But he pushed himself too far. One day while he was bathing in a river, he reached up for an overhanging branch, only to discover to his horror that he scarcely had strength enough to drag himself from the water. It seemed to take him forever to get out, and the effort left him limp and exhausted. For hours afterwards he lay on the river bank, bitterly disappointed with himself. He knew then that he had been on the wrong track. Seeking the meaning of life, he had been pursuing death, instead.

Finally a shepherd girl came by, took pity on him, and offered him some goat's milk. Shakyamuni accepted gratefully, forgetting his fast. As the milk coursed through his body, he felt new life surging up inside him. How good it was to be alive! When he had recovered his strength, he got up and began to eat and drink normally again, much to the disgust of his fellow-ascetics, who promptly abandoned him as a renegade.

Shakyamuni did not care. He felt more relaxed and happier than he had for years. He found that he could think clearly and calmly. He knew that he was very close to something wonderful, something that would come of its own accord without his having to strain for it.

In the weeks that followed he experienced a peace of mind that he had never known before. Gradually he approached the town of Gaya in Bihar, where the Great Enlightenment was to take place. He accepted food if it was offered to him. He spoke little, and then to the most unlikely people. He was deeply touched one day when a young housewife told him of her simple faith in the gods and her love for her husband and child. 'You teach the teachers,' he told her. 'In you I see why there is hope for mankind.'

Arriving finally at Gaya, he knew that his time had come. One evening he seated himself calmly beneath a fig tree, called later the Bodhi-tree, the Tree of Enlightenment, knowing that when next he rose, he would be Buddha, the Enlightened One.

The story says that during that long night Shakyamuni was assaulted by three temptations: lust, fear, and social obligations. But he resolutely rejected them all until at last 'there arose insight, knowledge, understanding, wisdom, light.' His mind penetrated to the heart of all compounded things; he clearly perceived the inner reality of everything. He was enlightened; he was the Buddha, the Enlightened One.

With the Buddha's enlightenment, we pass over from the mundane to the beyond. Until this point we could perceive Shakyamuni as a mortal man on a quest. His questions were like our questions and his hypothetical answers were like our own imaginings. As the enlightened Buddha, however, this was no longer so. He was now in a different dimension from the rest of us and spoke from a different perspective. He even called himself by a new name, the Tathagata (Tut-hah-guh-tuh).

The first people he spoke to after his enlightenment were his five former companions, whom he found in the Deer Park near Varanasi. At first they received him coldly, resentful that he had abandoned rigid asceticism. But there was something about him now which commanded their attention, and before the day was done they had become his first disciples. Later he went to Rajagriha and converted an old friend, King Bimbisara. Other important converts were the teachers Maudgalyayana and Shariputra, who brought all their followers into his fold. After that his movement increased rapidly.

His curious title, *tathagata*, was as much of a puzzle to the ancient Buddhists as it is to us today. 'Without much doubt,' says Leon Hurvitz, '*tathagata* is a non-Indic word refurbished to have an Indic appearance long after it had come into current use among India's Buddhists' (Hurvitz 1976, xxiii); What did Shakyamuni mean by it? We cannot say for sure. Perhaps it was an old pre-Aryan term still comprehensible to his people. Later generations, thinking it must be of Sanskrit derivation, etymologized *thata gata*, 'thus gone', and *tatha agata*, 'thus come'. In any case, by giving himself this singular title in a foreign tongue, Shakyamuni further emphasized that now he was no longer Prince Siddhartha Gautama, the seeker after truth, but himself the bearer of the truth and manifestation of the Absolute.

For the next 45 years, he travelled round north-eastern India preaching his doctrine, the Dharma. He did return home as he had promised, and taught Dharma to his father, his stepmother, his wife, and his young son Rahula. Then he moved on. His teachings were for the world, not just for his family. His son Rahula joined his father's band of disciples, and even Devadatta followed him for a while. In time, however, Devadatta, who was always jealous of his cousin, withdrew to found a rival religious order of his own. Devadatta's smouldering jealousy grew into implacable hatred, and until his death he was a thorn in the side of the Buddha.

There are hundreds of stories about Shakyamuni and his many colourful followers. He lived to the age of 80, moving from place to place as he taught the Dharma and settling down for extended stays only during the rainy seasons. But one day, sick from having eaten spoiled meat which had been offered to him by a well-meaning black-smith (although he was a vegetarian, he made it a general policy never to refuse a gift made in good faith), Shakyamuni lay down between two sala trees near Kusinagara and prepared to breathe his last.

'My disciples,' he said, 'my end is approaching; our parting is near, but do not lament. Life is ever-changing; none can escape the dissolution of the body. This I am now to show by my own death, my body falling apart like a dilapidated cart. Do not vainly lament, but realize that nothing is permanent and learn from it the emptiness of human life. Do not cherish the unworthy desire that the changeable might become unchanging.

'My disciples, the last moment has come, but do not forget that death is only the end of the physical body. The body was born from parents and was nourished by food; just as inevitable are sickness and death.

'But the true Buddha is not a human body: it is Enlightenment. A human body must die, but the Wisdom of Enlightenment will exist forever in the truth of the Dharma. He who sees merely my body does not truly see me. Only he who accepts my teaching truly sees me.

'After my death, the Dharma shall be your teacher. Follow the Dharma and you will be true to me.

'During the last forty-five years of my life, I have withheld nothing from my teachings. There is no secret teaching, no hidden meaning; everything has been taught openly and clearly. My dear disciples, this is the end. In a moment, I shall be passing into Nirvana. This is my instruction' (*The Teaching of Buddha*, 14–15).

He died quietly reclining on his right side. In spite of his final words of comfort, it is said that all the beasts of the forest and even the twin sala trees bowed their heads and wept. But worse was yet to come. The disciples cremated his body and were preparing to inter the ashes, when some chiefs and petty rulers began to arrive and demand that the ashes be buried in their respective domains. Serious quarrels broke out, and swords were drawn in anger. There were even threats of war. The disciples were horrified at this unexpected turn of events. Finally one of them, Dona, was able to convince the eight quarrelling mon-archs to divide the ashes into equal shares placed in identical urns. Even the embers of the fire and the earthen jar which had held the ashes were ground up and given to two other princelings who arrived late on the scene.

One of these urns, which was once revered by the Shakyas, themselves, and contained relics of Shakyamuni, was discovered in Piprahwa, India, late in the nineteenth century. It bears the inscription: 'This is the urn of the relics of the Bhagavat (Blessed One), the Buddha of the Shakya tribe, that is enshrined (by honorable brothers and sisters, wives and children)' (Mizuno 1980, 14, 85).

In his 45 years as a teacher, Shakyamuni had preached an enormous number of sermons to a great variety of listeners. None of these sermons were put into writing, but instead they were passed down orally from the listeners to succeeding generations. This avoidance of the written word was probably deliberate. In those days literacy meant power. The early Buddhists were well aware of the power the Brahmin priesthood exercised over the illiterate masses. Buddhism, which criticized the haughty Brahmins and their caste system, wanted to be open to all. It therefore transmitted the Dharma in the spoken tongues of the people.

On the other hand, this meant that if someone wanted to learn the Dharma, he had to 'join the club' where the Dharma was retained. This was the Sangha, the brotherhood of disciples. If the student could not join the Sangha, at least he could go to it for instruction and support it by his donations. Thus Buddhism was built on three bases which it named the Three Treasures: the Buddha (the teacher), the Dharma (the teaching) and the Sangha (the fellowship of those who observed and transmitted the teachings).

Since Buddhism is not so much a doctrine to be believed in as a path to be travelled, individual followers had much latitude in which to emphasize which steps on the way were the more important and even to interject ideas and interpretations of their own. By the first century BC, Buddhism was in danger of fragmenting into small sects. It became imperative to set down the 'true' teachings in writing before they were lost beyond all recognition. But it was already too late. By the time the writings began to appear, differing schools of thought had long been in existence. There were two major streams of interpretation and various sub-divisions of each. The two major branches were the narrowly monastic Lesser Vehicle (Hinayana) and the broader-based Great Vehicle (Mahayana).

The Chinese, who received Buddhism mostly in the Mahayana form, were bewildered by the quantity and variety of scriptures which came pouring in from India. How could they tell which ones were authentic and which were not? In the sixth century, Chih-i (Zhi-yi), who was probably the greatest of all Chinese Buddhist scholars, came up with an ingenious solution. *All* the received scriptures, he said, were authentic. Their styles and contents differed only because they had been preached at different times and to different audiences. They only seemed to contradict each other. In reality, they harmonized in one grand Dharma taught by the Buddha over a period of 45 years. The one Dharma, he said, could be found in four types of teachings to four kinds of listeners (thus making eight teachings) during five periods of Shakyamuni's public life. [1]

Modern philology and textual criticism can no longer accept the details of Chih-i's classification. However, as Bruno Petzold has pointed out, if we dismantle the Buddhist Canon according to the latest philological methods, we are left with the task of creating a new classification of our own, one which will then be open to new criticisms as the latest discoveries and interpretations come into being.

> All dismemberment of the Buddhist Canon by modern text-criticism will not lead to a definite dissolution of Buddhism; it will only lead to a new synthesis of the texts and teachings. When this new synthesis is tried, then the genius of Chisha Daishi (Chih-i) will once more become clear to the world. He had made his classification of the whole of Buddhism on purely ideological grounds, possessing none of the auxiliary means of scholarship, which are now at the disposal of every young student of philology. And yet his classification, from the point of view of his own time, was as cogent and convincing as it could possibly be; it has moreover exercised its influence for no less than 1,500 years . . . What makes this classification so great, what makes its real importance, is not so much its details, but the spirit pervading it . . . We may characterize it as the idealistic tendency of the mind, which tries to harmonize all seeming contractions into one logical unity.
>
> (*Tendai Buddhism* 283-4)

The first teaching period, according to Chih-i, was what he called the Time of the Garland.[2] It was of very short duration, only 21 days. Here Shakyamuni meditates on the meaning of his enlightenment. These are transcendent teachings belonging to the world of the Absolute. Many people consider them the most profound and comprehensive teachings to be found in all of world literature. Chih-i almost agrees, but not quite. They are *too* profound, he says, incomprehensible to most people. Moreover, they do not include the teachings of the Three Baskets (Hinayana), which the Buddha preached immediately after his Enlightenment. The perfect teaching, which will include everything, is to come later in the form of the *Dharma Flower*. The Garland is like a dramatic prelude opening the opera, sounding forth mighty themes that will be elaborated and developed later.

Indian legends say that the gods now came and begged Shakyamuni to share his light with all, but he did not need to be persuaded. It is a central principle of the Garland teachings that all life, all existence, is interrelated. Living beings are like blossoms on a garland or knots in a net. All are connected. When any single knot is raised up, it pulls the others along with it. Just as a Hitler can drag millions of people down to misery and destruction, so a Buddha can lift up millions to a nobler and happier life. Nothing exists in isolation. If a sparrow dies in China, the ecological balance of the cosmos is altered. When a baby smiles, the clouds laugh. The reverse is also true: when the clouds laugh, a baby smiles. We are like jewels in the net of the god Indra: each jewel reflects all the others.

The three weeks of meditation on the Garland lead naturally into the next period, public ministry. The Dharma is not only to be understood; it must be shared. Buddha's first students were his old companions from his years of austerities, the same ones who had deserted him when he began to eat and drink normally. He found them in the Deer Park near Benares, and it was to them that he preached his famous first sermon. It is the best known of his sermons and often considered to be the summary of the Dharma. Chih-i says it is the summary only of a distinct type of teaching which takes its name from the locale of this first sermon, the Deer Park. Sometimes these teachings are called the Three Baskets after their three categories: sermons (*sutras*), monastic rules (*vinaya*), and later commentaries (*abhidharma*). They are essentially the same as the teachings of Hinayana Buddhism, (the Lesser Vehicle).

These teachings, says Chih-i, were directed primarily at seekers after the truth such as he himself had been — to those who had left home and family to search out life's deepest mysteries. Some of these men wandered alone in the forests, others lived in little groups. The latter became the nucleus of the Sangha (the Buddhist brotherhood).

Gradually the Buddha broadened his teachings to include men and women from all walks of life. As the circle extended, the teachings had to change accordingly. What was good advice for a lonely hermit would not necessarily apply to monks living in a community. And what was true for monks would not be of much help to a housewife, a farmer, a merchant, or a king. Chih-i says that this extension is the origin of the Mahayana sutras.

From Chih-i's point of view, the 'lower' teachings were those applicable to the most limited audiences and to those taking their first steps along the path. This makes the Deer Park not the one 'true' teaching but the beginning teaching, the teaching for monks only. The 'perfect' teachings would be those with the most universal application and outreach. These would be for all of humanity, humble as well as noble. However, such teachings, if presented too abruptly, could be misinterpreted; they had to be preceded by careful preparation.

The Deer Park teachings are generally given in numerical groups for easy memorization. Thus we have the two extremes to be avoided (self-indulgence and self-denial), the Three Signs of Being, the Three Kinds of Concentration, the Three Roots of Evil (ignorance, greed, and aversion), the Three Treasures (Buddha, Dharma, and Sangha), the Four Noble Truths, the Four Levels of Meditation, the Eightfold Noble Path, the Twelve Links of Conditioned Co-production, and other such classifications. All of them are logical and above all practical. The student is invited to test each item for himself by means of specific techniques.

First, said Shakyamuni, there are the Three Signs of Being, or Seal of the Three Laws:

1. Change is universal; nothing is permanent.
2. Just as everything changes in the outer world, so is the inner world in constant flux. There is no permanent 'thing' inside us called an 'immortal soul'.
3. There is, nevertheless, an immovable centre: Nirvana.

The second point does not mean that there is no individuality or self. It means that there is no permanent individuality, no *unchanging* self. (Malalasekera. *Aspects of Reality*, 14) We, like everything else, are a process, an ever-flowing stream, which could be broken down into Five Aggregates: 1) physical form, 2) sense reactions to contacts, 3) awareness and assimilation of sensations, 4) conditioned reflexes and volitions, and 5) consciousness. We can separate them in analysis but not in fact, although if any one is more important than the others, it is the penultimate, volition (the thirst to exist and to expand). It is the greatest energy in the world, the power that propels the evolution of all life.

On these bases are built the Four Noble Truths:

1. Suffering is universal.
2. The cause of suffering is craving for what we cannot get or keep, since all is impermanent.
3. Suffering can be eliminated if its cause is eliminated.
4. The method for eliminating blind craving is by practising the Middle Way of the Eightfold Path.

The Eightfold Path consists of: 1) right view of life, 2) right aim in life, 3) right speech (courteous and truthful), 4) right action (harming neither oneself nor others), 5) right livelihood (not to harm self or others while earning one's living), 6) right effort, 7) right mindfulness, and 8) right contemplation on reality.

The Eightfold Path is not eight consecutive steps because all eight components are to be practised concurrently. Their symbol is a wheel, wherein each spoke is a necessary part of the whole. Without morality there can be no peace of mind, and without peace of mind there can be no insight into reality.

Great emphasis is put on calming the mind in order to be able to gain true insight into reality. Shakyamuni taught various techniques to do this. One is to sit quietly and concentrate on the natural function of breathing by counting the breaths up to ten, and then repeating the process over and over until the mind is fully aware of what is happening. A Hinayana manual for laymen by Narada Thera and Bikkhu Kassapa (*The Mirror of the Dhamma*) says, 'This harmless concentration may be practised by any person irrespective of religious belief' (23).[3]

The Twelve Links of Conditioned Co-Production explain that all life arises from a series of causes. The series, sometimes called the Wheel of Life, is often depicted in Buddhist art. Turning the wheel backwards, we find that each link on the chain depends on the preceding one. Beginning at the end, death, it implies that death was preceded by birth. Birth implies that something came into being. Coming into being implies clinging together. Clinging together implies desire, and there can be no desire without perception. Perception implies sense contact, which could not have happened without the organs of sense, which are enumerated as six (the five physical senses plus mind). The six senses imply 'name and form', that is, mind and matter. Mind implies the subconscious mind, which again implies coming into being, clinging, desire, perception, and so on back all over again.

At a deeper level, the unconscious implies blind activity, which could only result from the unconscious state. The unconscious is a continuation of death, so death does not release us from the wheel. Unconsciousness (or the subconscious) leads to blind actions resulting in coming into being all over again.

As the wheel turns forward, the energy of each preceding stage brings the next stage into being. Even at death, the action of one being will cease, but the action–influence (*karma*) remains to propel a new being towards birth. This does not mean reincarnation as popularly understood, for there is no 'soul' to incarnate. But it does mean that so long as there is energy, it is going to work. The Wheel of Life keeps turning, blindly and unconsciously, forever.

A living being determines its own nature by its own actions. In other words, we are self-created. We consist of the effect of our past actions and the cause of our future. In the words of U Chan Htoon of Burma:

> The act of creation is one that is taking place continually within ourselves. The idea is one that will be familiar to all who are acquainted with Bergson's theory of creative evolution; the Buddha expressed it succinctly and with profound meaning when he said, 'Within this fathom-long body, equipped with mind and sense perceptions, O Monks, I declare to you is the world, the origin of the world, and the path to its cessation.' If the human mind with its limitations cannot envisage an infinity of time, neither can it form any picture of a state outside its temporal and spatial situation. Nevertheless, the third of the Four Noble Truths asserts the reality of Nibbana (Nirvana), which is precisely the release from the bondage of time, space and conditioned existence.
>
> (*Buddhism and the Age of Science*, 9)

This brings us to the culmination of these teachings: Nirvana. The Buddha stated that there is a way out of this terrible wheel of birth and death.

There is an Unborn, Unoriginated, Uncreated, Unformed. If there were not this Unborn . . . escape from the world of the born, the originated, the created, the formed, would not be possible. But since there is an Unborn, Unoriginated, Uncreated, Unformed, therefore is escape possible from the world of the born, the originated, the created, the formed.

(Udana VIII, 3)

Nevertheless, if we stop here — as, indeed, many have done — we are left with a problem. There seems to be only sorrow on the one hand and escape from it into the Unborn on the other. If this is the case, what motivates the Buddha to participate in this world of pain? Why does he not — why did he not — just give up? There is something vital still missing here among all these analytical systems. if the negative forces of greed, aversion, and ignorance cause the negative result of suffering, what positive force motivates the beautiful life of Shakyamuni?

It was Mahayana, the Great Vehicle, which undertook to answer this question. It pointed beyond the Buddha's words to his heart, the same heart which beats at the core of the universe. This it called the Great Compassion.

Chapter 2

Mahayana: The Great Vehicle

One of the Buddha's favourite disciples was his cousin Ananda. Ananda had an enquiring mind and a good heart. He had an excellent memory, and the others often relied upon him to recount the exact words of the master. But he liked women and found it difficult to be a celibate monk. The lengthy sermon known as the Great Crown Sutra was delivered by the Buddha to the conscience-stricken Ananda after he had succumbed to the charms of a beautiful woman. Shakyamuni did not scold him for breaking his vows of chastity. Instead, he introduced him to new perspectives.

By then large crowds of people were turning out to hear Buddha's sermons, and the monks found it almost impossible to live in complete isolation from them. There were many women among the listeners, and to some monks, such as Ananda, they were a distraction. But he was not just tempted in the flesh; he also noticed that many married couples were truly devoted to each other. Their mutual love deeply moved the young monk, who saw something spiritual in their relationship. They seemed to develop beautiful qualities that even the holy monks sometimes lacked. How could that be?

One day he decided to challenge the Buddha on this matter. 'I think,' he said to his teacher, 'that such loving concern as they show for each other is half the holy life'.

'Not so, Ananda, not so!' came the reply. 'Beneficent friendship is the whole of the holy life' (*Samyutta Nikaya, Kosala Vaga*).

How the other monks must have raised their eyebrows when they heard that! They took it for granted that in leaving behind the entanglements of domestic life they had embarked on the narrow path to sainthood. Had they been doing something wrong or was this some new teaching?

This brings us to what Chih-i called the third period (or flavour) of Shakyamuni's teachings, the Expanded Teachings. In later times, when the Buddha's words were set down in writing, most of these new sermons were recorded in literary Sanskrit rather than in vernacular language, like Pali. They do not form a part of the Pali collection of sacred texts ('The Three Baskets'), but belong instead to a group called Mahayana scriptures, or *Vaipulya*, 'Expanded Teachings'.

Gradually Buddhism divided into two distinct types: the Lesser Vehicle (Hinayana), which accepted only the primitive teachings, and the Greater Vehicle (Mahayana), which accepted both the old and the Expanded Teachings. Today the former type predominates in southern Asia (Ceylon, Burma, Thailand), and the latter in northern Asia (Tibet, China, Korea, and Japan). For many centuries the two schools existed side by side in India, sometimes even being taught in the same monasteries or universities.

The two schools share many teachings in common, so much so that Chih-i considered that these teachings might sometimes have been taught at the same time but to different students. Mahayana, however, puts a particular emphasis on the laity rather than the monastic brotherhood and on a new definition of sainthood. In Mahayana Buddhism the goal is no longer to become an *Arhat* (one who obtains deliverance for himself), but a *Bodhisattva*, (one who obtains deliverance for others).[4]

Nirvana, too, is given a new meaning. It is now no longer defined negatively as the extinction of defilements. This is said to have been an expedient teaching 'for dull people . . . who were attached to birth and death, and who were troubled by many sufferings' (Lotus Sutra, Chap. 2). Instead it is defined positively as 'an inner explosion of light' (to use the definition of some modern Japanese scholars).

> There arises some new positive force which was not hitherto experienced. Nay, it may be said that this positive force is indeed the origin of the inner explosion, and due to this force the last remaining passions and lusts are extinguished. This may be shown clearly by the fact that the Buddha spent six years in the attempt to extinguish his passions only to end in failure, while he received the explosion leading to Enlightenment after a week's meditation under the Bodhi tree. This was due to the fact that he engaged himself during this time in especially developing this positive force. Furthermore, the Buddha's active life for 45 years following his enlightenment cannot be explained without recognizing this positive force. Again, from a theoretical standpoint, the Buddha made the getting away from old age, illness and death his ultimate object; but actually even when he reached enlightenment, i.e., when he attained Nirvana, he could not get away from these three curses of mankind. However, even

though he couldn't get away from the above bondages, he always declared that he had already reached a state of non-death. By this we feel he meant that, besides having no longer any fear of old age, illness and death and being assured that he would not have to undergo further rebirths in the future, he had attained some inner force that was not affected by these three curses.

(Tsunoda 1955, 67–8)

The Japanese term for this period, *Hodo*, means 'equality', and points to the principle of the middle path or reality, which we will discuss in a later chapter. Breaking the term down, *Ho* signifies sentient beings to be taught, and *To* the various doctrines to be taught (JEBD, 108). There is something here for everyone.

To take a few examples, the *Shrimala Sutra* which belongs to this period, features Lady Shrimala, a daughter of King Prasenajit of Kosala and a contemporary of Shakyamuni. It presents Buddhism as understood by a woman — not a nun, but an educated laywoman. It stresses that the 'Buddha nature' is inherent in all sentient beings, not just monks or men or even humans.

The *Nirvana Sutra*, which is said to be the last sutra preached by the Buddha, makes the same point, also giving positive qualities to Nirvana: true selfhood, eternity, purity, and happiness.

The *Lankavatara Sutra* explains 'Buddha nature' in more detail with an elaborate discussion of the workings of the mind, especially the subconscious. The Buddha nature lies below the subconscious; it is universal. A similar discussion is found in the 'Sutra of the Revelation of the Profound and Secret Teaching' (*Gejimmitsu-kyo; Samdhinir-mochana-sutra*), this time in a question-and-answer form similar to Plato's method of teaching. It is found, too, in a later but very popular writing, 'Awakening of Faith in Mahayana'.

Some of these sutras are even more explicit in their appeal to the laity rather than to monks. The 'Sutra of the Golden Light' (*Konkomyo-kyo; Suvarnaprabhasa-sutra*) is addressed particularly to reigning monarchs and people in authority. Their duty, it says, is to protect those who proclaim the true Dharma. The *Nirvana Sutra* contains similar passages.

The *Vimalakirti Sutra*, which features the adventures of a wealthy layman named Vimalakirti (Yuima in Japanese), is decidedly anti-monastic. Vimalakirti is critical of the monks, whom he considers narrow-minded and self-righteous. He loves nothing better than to get into a spirited debate with one of Shakyamuni's leading disciples, and then leave him sputtering in confusion. In Vimalakirti we see a sharp break between the disciples, who are following the Hinayana 'Way of the Elders', and many laymen, who tend to prefer the more broad-based Mahayana.

In the Lesser Vehicle, Hinayana, the duty of the laity is to practise basic morality and support the monks. Lay Buddhists cannot attain enlightenment, because they are not devoting all their time and effort to the task. In the Great Vehicle, Mahayana, lay men and women play an active role. Vimalakirti criticizes the monks for being attached to their own special path. They will never find enlightenment — total liberation — that way, he tells them. They are so attached to their 'way of perfection' that they are incapable of making the sacrifices required of an ordinary householder. At a deeper level, they do not understand freedom from attachments at all. The *Vimalakirti-nirdesha*, especially in its Chinese translation by Kumarajiva, became one of the most widely read books in the Far East, second in popularity only to the Lotus Sutra.

Aiming to 'save' everyone, Mahayana left no stone unturned. There are two more types of sutras, which came late into prominence but may have existed from the beginning; they each have a special appeal of their own. The first is a set of three esoteric sutras for those who prefer the path of ritual, mystery, and magic. Esoteric Buddhism began in India, where it flourished for many centuries until it was gradually merged with Hindu Tantrism and/or was wiped out by the Moslem conquerors. One branch survives in the almost inaccessible mountains of Nepal and Tibet, where it is still the predominant form of Buddhism. Another branch moved to China, where it flourished briefly but was later suppressed. It passed over to Japan, and exists there to this day under the generic name of *Shingon* ('True Words' or 'Mantra'). Esotericism has secret teachings and practices which can be learned only through a series of initiations. It became very popular among Japanese courtiers, who enjoyed its elaborate and mysterious rituals.

Three basic sutras set forth its leading ideas: the *Mahavairochana Sutra*, the 'Diamond Crown Sutra', and the 'Sutra of the Accomplishment of Perfection'.[5]

Modern textual critics believe that the esoteric sutras were the last Buddhist texts to be put into writing. Certainly they were the last to arrive in China. Chih-i, who lived in the sixth century, has no place for them in his classification because he had never heard of them. His later followers put them in here, at the Third Period, but not without serious opposition from those who were attracted to esotericism. These people maintained that the texts were even older than the Buddha himself, were the source of his enlightenment, and then were hidden away for centuries until recovered by the esoteric masters.

Another set of Mahayana sutras had an even broader appeal. For those who considered themselves neither clever enough to imitate Vimalakirti, wise enough to understand esotericism, or even good enough to be simple believers, there was still hope. Three 'Pure Land' sutras stress that the Buddha is so compassionate that he saves living beings as naturally and spontaneously as the sun shines in the sky. Shakyamuni tells how another Buddha, Amida, has sworn that he will not enter enlightenment unless all other beings can accompany him. Since he has, indeed, attained 'infinite light and infinite life' (the meaning of the name Amida), his task has been accomplished. All you have to do is rely on him wholeheartedly, and he will ensure that after this life you will be reborn in a Pure Land, where there are no hindrances to ultimate enlightenment. If you can make no progress in this life, you need not despair; your salvation is assured in the life to come. The three sutras which set forth these teachings are the *Eternal Life Sutra, Meditation on Eternal Life Sutra*, and *Amida Sutra*.[6]

With the Pure Land teachings, Buddhism seems to have gone as far as it could go in the direction of popularization. Having started as a narrow way for dedicated students, it has ended as a broad, easy path for anyone, wise or ignorant, male or female, saint or sinner. Beginning with scepticism and self-reliance, it has ended with a complete 'salvation by faith alone'. Aiming originally at deliverance in this life, it has ended with its focus on heaven and the life of the world to come. Is this really the same religion we started out with?

Chih-i says 'Yes, it is.' There are central themes which have been running through all these variations, and these will all be tied together in the Buddha's ultimate teachings, which are expounded in the 'Dharma Flower Sutra'. But first there remains one final preparatory teaching, the teaching of the Void or Emptiness.

Chih-i considers this the fourth of the Five Periods (or flavours), and calls it the 'Time of Wisdom'. Whereas the previous teachings were in sharp contrast to what had gone before, these are termed 'inclusive', for their discussions of non-substantiality and dependent co-origination are 'inclusive' of all things (Chappell, *T'ien T'ai Buddhism* 77). Again their purpose is to free people from attachments. Just as the Expanded Teachings were designed to free monks from their attachment to the narrow way of disciplinary rules, so the Wisdom Teachings aim to free the Mahayanists from attachment to any theories of their own. They preach the Void: non-attachment to anything.

What is the Void? No concept in Buddhism is more difficult to understand, and yet none is richer in levels of meaning. Volumes have been written about it. The Buddha is said to have devoted 22 years to explaining it. But in the final analysis, nothing can be said about it at all; its very essence is beyond definitions, beyond words.

Void does not mean 'nothingness', but devoid of special conditions — 'unconditioned' is the term used by Dr Junjiro Takakusu, editor of the 100-volume Japanese edition of the Buddhist scriptures (*Buddhist Philosophy*, 47). He finds the final solution to the problem of the Void in the writings of Chih-i (69), and we will return to him later. Meanwhile partial explanations are found throughout the Buddhist scriptures and especially in those known as Transcendental Wisdom.

Two concepts might help us here: relativity and the mathematical zero. Relativity is discussed in a paraphrase of Transcendental Wisdom in *The Teaching of Buddha*:

There are causes for all human suffering, and there is a way by which they may be ended, because everything in the world is the result of a vast concurrence of causes and conditions, and everything disappears as these causes and conditions change and pass away. Rain falls, wind blows, plants bloom, leaves mature and blow away. These phenomena are all interrelated with causes and conditions, are brought about by them, and disappear as the causes and conditions change.

One is born by the conditions of parentage. His body is nourished by food; his spirit is nourished by teaching and experience. Therefore, both flesh and spirit are related to conditions and are changed as conditions change.

A net is made up by a series of knots, so everything in this world is connected by a series of knots. If anyone thinks that a mesh of the net is an independent, isolated thing, he is mistaken. It is called a net because it is made up of a series of connected meshes, and each mesh has its place and responsibilities in relation to other meshes.

Blossoms come about because of a series of conditions that lead up to their blooming; leaves are blown away because a series of conditions lead up to it. Blossoms do not appear independently, nor does a leaf fall of itself. So everything has its coming forth and passing away; nothing can be independent without any change.

(46–7)

This absolute relativity is called Void. In the words of Dr Takakusu again: 'To see the true nature of the true state of all things is not to find one in many or one before many, nor is it to distinguish unity from diversity or the static from the dynamic. *The true state is the state without any special condition.* It is, in fact, "the true reality without a reality", i.e., without any specific character or nature. It is very difficult for the human mind to understand this idea of a reality in which there is no "sub-stance" at all.' (45–6)

Because of interdependent causation, subject and object are void in themselves. Remove one, and the other goes with it. The same applies to action: there is an actor, an act, and an acted-upon. Each implies the other two; none exists by itself. Instead there is a dynamic and freely revolving circle. For the Void is not nothingness, it is potentially everything.

The mathematical zero is a Buddhist invention. The Sanskrit word *shunya* (void) became *shifr* in Arabic, *cifra* in Latin, and finally *cipher* in English. The ancient Greeks and Romans, preoccupied with 'being', never conceived of the cipher. The cipher is void, but what a vital role it plays in mathematics! It contains all possible numerical combinations; it is both the smallest and the largest.

Einstein's idea of space is similar to the Buddhist doctrine of Void. It used to be thought that space was 'nothingness', a vacuum. Therefore physicists invented a 'stuff', which they called ether, to fill space and carry light. Otherwise, they reasoned, how could light travel at all? But Einstein said that space is 'alive'; it acts and reacts; it is a field of potential energy. Matter, on the other hand, is nothing more than a concentration of energy in a very small space. There is no essential difference between matter and field. 'Matter is where concentration of energy is great, field where the concentration of energy is small' (Einstein and Infeld, *The Evolution of Physics*, 257). In the words of the Buddha, 'Form is void and void is form; whatever is form, that is void; whatever is void, that is form' (*Prajnaparamita-hridaya*).

It is a difficult concept. But today, nearly three thousand years later, it is accepted as basic by scientists the world over.

From a practical point of view (and it is always the practical point of view that matters in Buddhism), if field and matter are the same, so are Nirvana and this world of *samsara*, 'constant flow'. The *Lankavatara Sutra*, one of the favourite scriptures of the Great Vehicle, expresses it this way:

> Enlightenment has no definite form or nature by which it can manifest itself; so in enlightenment itself, there is nothing to be enlightened. Enlightenment exists solely because of delusion and ignorance; if they disappear, so will Enlightenment. And the opposite is true also: there is no Enlightenment apart from delusion and ignorance; no delusion and ignorance apart from Enlightenment. Therefore be on guard against thinking of enlightenment as a 'thing' to be grasped at, lest it, too, should become an obstruction. When the mind that was in darkness becomes enlightened, it passes away, and with its passing, the thing which we call Enlightenment passes also.
>
> As long as people desire Enlightenment and grasp after it, it means that delusion is still with them; therefore, they who are following the way to Enlightenment must not grasp at it, and if they reach Enlightenment they must not linger in it. When people attain Enlightenment in this sense, it means that everything is Enlightenment itself as it is; therefore, people should follow the path to Enlightenment until in their thoughts, worldly passions and Enlightenment become identical as they are.
>
> This concept of universal oneness — that things in their essential nature have no distinguishing marks — is called *Shunyata*. *Shunyata* means non-substantiality, the un-born, having no self-nature, no duality. It is because things in themselves have no form or characteristics that we can speak of them as neither being born nor being destroyed. There is

nothing about the essential nature of things that can be described in terms of discrimination; that is why things are called non-substantial.

As has been pointed out, all things appear and disappear because of causes and conditions. Nothing ever exists entirely alone; everything is in relation to everything else. Wherever there is light, there is shadow; wherever there is length, there is shortness; wherever, there is white there is black. Just like these, as the self-nature of things cannot exist alone, they are called non-substantial.

By the same reasoning, enlightenment cannot exist apart from ignorance, nor ignorance apart from enlightenment. Since things do not differ in their essential nature, there can be no duality. Buddha's teaching leads us to non-duality, from the discriminating concept of two conflicting points of view. It is a mistake for people to seek a thing supposed to be good and right, and to flee from another supposed to be bad and evil.

If people insist that all things are empty and transitory, it is just as great a mistake as to insist that all things are real and do not change. If a person becomes attached to his ego-personality, it is a mistake because it cannot save him from suffering. If he believes that there is no ego, it is also a mistake and it would be useless for him to practice the Way of Truth. If people assert that everything is suffering, it is also a mistake; if they assert that everything is happiness, that is a mistake, too. Buddha teaches the Middle Way transcending these prejudiced concepts, where duality merges into oneness.

(Teaching 65–7, 70–1)

It seems that the Buddha is repudiating everything that he has said thus far. In a way, he is; he is shattering our attachments to any ideas or dogmas that may have formed in our minds and have now become obstructions. He has said these things from the beginning, but now he is driving them home with a special emphasis. Even in the Deer Park teachings, we find words like these:

The world, for the most part, holds either to a belief in being or to a belief in non-being. But for one who, in the light of perfect insight, considers how the world arises, belief in the non-being of the world passes away. And for one who, in the light of perfect insight, considers how the world ceases, belief in the being of the world passes away . . . That all is existent is one extreme; that all is non-existent is another extreme. The Thus-come (the Buddha), avoiding the two extremes, preaches his truth, which is the Middle Path.

(Samyutta Nikaya 12–15)

The human mind has a tendency to veer off towards one of two extremes. Either it reduces everything to 'the One', calling it Truth, or Spirit, or God, or Over-Soul, or the Original Idea, or the Absolute, or something of the sort; or else it sees only isolated facts. The first way of thinking is called monism; the second is pluralism, existentialism, or materialism. Buddhist philosophy has not always escaped these two extremes, either. The schools of the Little Vehicle lean towards pluralism; those of the Great Vehicle sometimes slip into monism or pantheism.

Human conduct has also tended to go to the extremes. Either it is 'good' (perhaps 'goody-goody'), and therefore self-conscious and self-righteous, or it is 'bad', looking out for Number One at the expense of everybody else. 'Religious' people tend to be 'other-worldly'; 'this-worldly' people can be harmful to others. Most people try to adopt a compromise: they are moral as long as it is expedient; they will behave themselves in society as long as society gives them a fifty–fifty chance. But this is obviously just a more subtle form of 'looking out for Number One'. Number One is a good citizen as long as it is in his own interest.

Clearly when the Buddha speaks of the Middle Way, he is not talking about any kind of moral compromise; his system is strongly ethical:

> Those who are seeking the Way of Enlightenment must always bear in mind the necessity of constantly keeping pure in body, lips, and mind. To keep the body pure, one must not kill any living creature, steal, or act immorally. To keep the lips pure, one must not lie, abuse, deceive, or indulge in idle chatter. To keep the mind pure, one must remove all greed, anger, and false judgment.
>   If the mind becomes impure, the following deeds will be impure; if the deeds are impure, there will be mental suffering; so it is of greatest importance that the mind be kept pure.
>   (*Anguttara Nikaya* 3:117)

Morality springs spontaneously from a pure mind. To purify the mind by removing greed, aversion, and ignorance is the whole point of Buddhism. However, this is not easily done; it is difficult to keep on the Middle Path and not tip over into a 'holier-than-thou' attitude on the one side or a cynical, utilitarian 'ethic' on the other. So the disciple is constantly warned not to become attached to popular causes, no matter how worthy they may appear. He must find solutions in his own self, not in the ideas of others. He must free his mind from attachments to either the good or the evil, which, after all, are merely his own opinions about what is good and what is evil.

So far the Buddha has said a great deal about what the Middle Way is not, but he has not yet said what it is. We are still missing the final capstone. Is it entirely beyond words? Many Buddhists believe so.

Around the year A.D. 150, a powerful dialectician named Nagarjuna systemized the Buddhas's teachings into a philosophy of negations. The Middle Way, he said, is beyond words. Life itself is beyond words; it is also beyond thought. As soon as one idea arises, an opposite idea can be brought forward to refute it.

Nevertheless, Nagarjuna said that there is, indeed, a capstone to Buddhism. There is an important missing element, which has constantly been implied but not yet stated openly. It is to be found, he said, in the Buddha's final teaching, called the *Lotus of the Wonderful Dharma*, or Dharma Flower Sutra. Nagarjuna, true to his system of absolute negation, never said what 'it' is, but he did tell us where to look. Millions of people in India, China, Japan, and throughout the Orient have been following his advice ever since. Let us now do likewise.

Chapter 3

The Lotus Flower of the Wonderful Dharma

No book in the East has so inspired its adherents and so puzzled outsiders as the *Saddharma-Pundarika Sutra*, 'The Sutra of the Lotus Flower of the Wonderful Dharma'. Believers in the Great Vehicle are almost unanimous in singing its praises. Although every sect has its own favourite scripture, all agree that the *Dharma Flower* (Lotus Sutra) is especially important. The Middle Way School of Nagarjuna (Madhyamika) and its Chinese and Japanese successors, the Three Treatises School, the Heavenly Terrace School of China (T'ien-Tai) and Japan (Tendai), and the Nichiren School are all based on the *Dharma Flower*. The Flower Garland School (Kegon) calls the *Dharma Flower* 'the final doctrine of the Great Vehicle' (Takakusu, *Essentials of Buddhist Philosophy* 115), while the Esoteric School (Shingon) ranks it near the top — eighth on a scale of ten.[7] Other schools, such as the Yuzunembutsu of Japan, synthesize the *Dharma Flower* with their own tenets. Volumes and volumes of commentaries have been written on it, including one by Prince Shotoku, 'the father of Japanese Buddhism'. The Chinese philosopher Chi-tsang (Ji-zang) wrote no fewer than seven books on the *Dharma Flower*. However, none are as authoritative as two works by Chih-i, 'Profound Meaning of the Dharma Flower' and 'Words and Phrases of the Dharma Flower', which were themselves the subjects of later commentaries.

The importance of this sutra to the Chinese and Japanese can be better appreciated if we abbreviate its title, not to the usual English form of *Lotus Sutra*, but by saying as they do, 'Dharma Flower Sutra' (*Hokekyo*). (The word 'lotus' does not appear in the title.) This puts it in a proper perspective. To its adherents, it is not just one more book attributed to the Buddha, a book called *The Lotus*. It is the flowering, the culmination, of the entire Buddha-dharma; it is the Dharma Flower.

Yet the average reader, having heard such extravagant praises, is apt to put the book down with a feeling of disappointment. First, until recently, there was no really satisfactory English translation. For many years the only complete English version was that by the Dutch Sanskrit scholar, H. Kern, done in 1884 for the *Sacred Books of the East* series.[8] Edward Conze, an outstanding modern translator, commented in the journal of the British Buddhist Association, *The Middle Way*, that the Kern version 'abounds in misunderstandings' (November 1962, 95). Copious footnotes compare the text with Greek and Hindu mythology.

In 1930 W.E. Soothill, an Englishman, published an abbreviated translation from the Chinese.[9] This is a revised version of an unpublished manuscript by the Japanese Nichiren Buddhist priest, Bunno Kato. Soothill had reservations about the value of the text, and explained that he had cut it short so that it would not be 'unavoidably cumbrous and inspirationally innocuous.' Dr Conze does not think too highly of this version, either. Both of them 'are now quite inadequate and frequently misleading on doctrinal matters.'[10] He published new translations of several chapters, and even rewrote some of his own previously published versions. Careful scholar that he was, he found difficulty in transferring 'the rarefied language of the original' into prosaic English.

With the new interest in this sutra, three good translations appeared in the 1970s. All of them were made not from the Sanskrit, but from Kumarajiva's popular Chinese version. Two of them were published in Japan and the third in the United States. In 1971 Rissho Kosei-kai, an organization we shall discuss later in this book, published an improved and complete version of the Kato/Soothill work under the title, *Myoho-Renge-Kyo: The Sutra of the Lotus Flower of the Wonderful Law*. In 1975 other translators revised this work and added to it the traditional 'opening' and 'closing' sutras: 'The Sutra of Innumerable Meanings' (*Muryogi-kyo*) and 'The Sutra of Meditation on the Bodhisattva Universal-Virtue' (*Kanfugen-gyo*). The three together make up 'The Threefold Lotus Sutra'. In 1974 the Nichiren Buddhist Professor (later Bishop) Senchu Murano published *The Sutra of the Lotus Flower of the Wonderful Law* with an excellent glossary of Sanskrit and Chinese terms. It was revised in 1990 with the help of the present writer. Finally, Professor Leon Hurvitz, an internationally known expert in the sutra, presented a lively idiomatic translation entitled *Scripture of the Lotus Blossom of the Fine Dharma* (1976). It, too, is translated from the Chinese, but makes detailed comparisons with extant Sanskrit documents.

Translation, however, is not the only problem. This is not an ordinary book, and the profundity of its message easily eludes the reader. Two centuries ago the Zen master Hakuin related how disappointed he was when he read the book for the first time; he found there nothing of any value at all. 'All my great hopes were smashed.' But later, after he had experienced awakening, he 'perceived the perfect, true, and ultimate significance of the *Dharma Flower*.'

Another Zen story tells of a monk named Fa-ta, who knew the book so well that he could recite it from memory, but even he did not really understand it. Finally an enlightened master had to open his eyes to the inner meaning of the work.

If devout and learned Buddhist monks sometimes find that the book leaves them cold, modern Westerners cannot expect much better until they learn to 'read it between the lines', as Nichiren used to say. For it speaks to us in the language of ancient mythologies which no longer communicate with us directly. It takes effort on our part to reach the perspective of Joseph Campbell and see that 'myth is the secret opening through which the inexhaustible energies of the cosmos pour into human cultural manifestation' (*The Hero with a Thousand Faces*, 3).

From a literary point of view the *Dharma Flower* is of very mixed quality. There are passages of majestic beauty, but there are others of tedious dullness. There is a great deal of repetition; after every few pages of prose (much of it repetitious in itself) come two or three pages of verse on the same subject. Strangely enough, the prose and poetry in the original are in different languages. The prose is in Sanskrit, the literary language of ancient India; the verse is in an Indian vernacular derived from Sanskrit, called Buddhist Hybrid Sanskrit, or the *Gatha* dialect, since it is found in the *gathas* (verses). In their present form the verses are older than the prose. Kogen Mizuno, an authority on Buddhist literature, points out that ancient editors put the holy books into classical Sanskrit to make them appear more elegant, but they had trouble with the rhymes and rhythms of the verses, so they left them alone. Sanskrit is the older language, but the verses are the older writings (*Buddhist Sutras* 32–3).

This gives us another hint as to why our English translations are often so unsatisfying. The book is full of poetry. It reaches beyond the rational mind to something deeper within us — to the subconscious. It is not meant to be read silently; it is supposed to be chanted or recited to the beat of a drum.

Kumarajiva's Chinese version (A.D. 406), which was really the work of a team of Chinese scholars under his direction, captured the original spirit. Even the prose sections swing along to a hypnotic beat. To this day *Dharma Flower* devotees prefer his version to any other. D.T. Suzuki points out that:

All the Mahayana sutras . . . are not meant to appeal to our reasoning faculties, that is, to our intellectual understanding, but to a different kind of understanding, which we may call intuition. When the *Prajnaparamita* [or the *Dharma Flower*] is recited in Sanskrit or Chinese or Tibetan, without trying to extract its

logical meaning, but with a devotional turn of mind and with the
determination to go through the masses of repetitions, the
Prajna-eye (Wisdom-eye) grows gradually more and more
penetrating. Finally it will see, through all the contradictions,
obscurities, abstractions, and mystifications, something
extraordinarily transparent, which reveals the 'other side'
together with 'this side.' This is the awakening of the Prajna . . .
Herein lies the secret of sutra recitation.

(*Indian Mahayana Buddhism* 97)

This is what is meant by 'reading between the lines'. If the *Dharma
Flower* is really the flowering of the Buddha-dharma, as its name
implies, then it should account for the many contradictions found in
other sutras. The Deer Park teachings criticized all philosophical
systems and advocated strict monastic discipline. The Expanded
Teachings criticized the Deer Park, claiming that its adherents were
attached to their egocentric search for enlightenment. The Wisdom
sutras demolished any delusions of attachment, even attachment to the
Great Vehicle, and left us only Emptiness. Certainly from the viewpoint
of the *Dharma Flower* a most thorough groundwork has been laid
down. All that is unreal has been demolished. Can the Dharma now
burst into bloom on a positive note?

Before answering this question, let us pause parenthetically as
Shakyamuni himself is said to have done while he was preaching this
sermon. The scene takes place on top of a mountain known as the
Vulture Peak, or Eagle Peak, outside the city of Rajagriha. The whole
area contains numerous stupas (monuments erected by early
Buddhists), one of which is claimed to shelter part of the ashes of
Shakyamuni. Other stupas mark places of significance during his
lifetime. 'Right at the summit,' says S.F. de Silva, 'is the cave wherein the
Blessed One often stayed. The yard where he preached, where he
walked up and down, the cliff where Devadatta rolled a boulder to kill
him, are all identifiable. Truly this is where in the words of Sir Edwin
Arnold:

Lo, thou who comest here, bare thy feet
And bow thy head, for all this spacious earth
Hath not a spot more dear and hallowed.[11]

The Lotus Sutra opens like a Wagnerian opera to a great prelude which
E.A. Burtt calls 'one of the most dramatic and stupendous scenes in all
religious literature' (*Teachings of Buddha*, 157). A serene light emits
from the Buddha, who is seated in contemplation. In the radiant air is
seen a great host of Bodhisattvas, deities, saints, humans, and non-
humans. Heavenly blossoms rain upon the assembly. All are gripped
with wonder, waiting in awe for what is about to happen.

But one important disciple is missing. He is Bimbisara, the king of Rajagriha and an old friend of the Buddha. For while this heavenly scene is taking place on the mountain top, a grim drama is unfolding in the city below.

The story of King Bimbisara is one of the most poignant in all religious literature. There is the ring of truth about it, for unlike most pious tales, this one does not have a happy ending.

In his youth, Bimbisara had been a typical oriental despot. He wanted a son and heir by his beloved wife Vaidehi, but when none was forthcoming he consulted a fortune-teller to see if he should take another wife. The fortune-teller, like most Indians, believed in reincarnation. He told the king that he would, indeed, have a son by Vaidehi, but not quite yet. The son's soul was then inhabiting the body of a certain aged hermit. When the hermit died, the son would be reborn as the long-awaited prince.

Impatient, Bimbisara decided he would speed things up by having the hermit put to death right away. The horrified fortune-teller then told the king that in this case his son would be a curse, because sooner or later he would avenge his cruel murder.

The king went ahead and ordered the murder anyway, but then he began having second thoughts. When in due course the child was born, Bimbisara ordered it cast out and exposed to the elements to die. Somehow the child survived; the scriptures do not tell us how. Perhaps he was saved by the unhappy mother. In any case he was rescued, brought back to the palace, and raised as the king's son and heir. Eventually, however, the boy learned the story of his childhood brush with death. His filial feelings turned to resentment and finally to hatred for his father.

When the Buddha visited the city for the first time, King Bimbisara was greatly impressed by his words. He converted to the Dharma, and thereafter did his best to live a pure life. Gradually he let go of his civic responsibilites as he devoted more and more time to religious contemplation and pious acts of charity. He was not aware that power was slipping from his hands into those of his son, Ajatasatru. The nobles and bureaucrats found themselves turning to the prince rather than to the king in important affairs of state. There was much muttering that the king should abdicate, join the Sangha, which he seemed so fond of, and leave the business of governing to his son.

At this point Devadatta, the Buddha's cousin and arch-rival, saw his opportunity. The king had spent a fortune supporting Shakyamuni and his hordes of followers. Some of these people were noble arhats, but many must have been idle loafers, who enjoyed living at public expense. It was time to eject the whole lot of them and establish a new state cult under the direction of the charismatic Devadatta.

The clever conspirator managed to gain the confidence of the ambitious prince. Some say that it was he who invented the whole story about the fortune-teller and the murdered hermit. As 'proof', he pointed to a scar on Ajatasatru's finger. 'That scar,' he said, 'has been there since that awful day when your father had you cast out of the palace as a helpless babe.' He bent over and piously kissed the scar, swearing everlasting fidelity to the wronged prince. (Fujimoto *Triple Sutra* 2:18).

This was all that Ajatasatru wanted to hear. Already he wielded the state power in practice; now he would take it in name also, justified in avenging an ancient wrong, and supported by a respected religious leader. It might be wrong to kill his father, but not wrong to have him put out of the way. It was not difficult to convince the courtiers to join him. In a sudden *coup d'état*, he had his father seized and thrown into a dungeon, there to rot until he died of starvation.

Queen Vaidehi pleaded with her son, but to no avail. She did everything possible to keep her husband alive. First, she tried smuggling him food. When the guards prevented her, 'she purified her body by bathing and washing. She mixed ghee and honey with the flour of roasted wheat, and with these she painted her body. In the various pendant ornaments which she wore, she concealed the juice of grapes. These she gave to the king without being noticed (*Bussetsu Kanmuryoju-kyo*).

When Ajatasatru found out what his mother was doing, he was furious. He drew his sword and would have rushed out to kill her, but two of his ministers, hands on their sword hilts, barred his way.

'O great king,' said one of them, 'we ministers hear the Vedas say that since the beginning of the ages, as many as eighteen thousand princes have killed their own fathers in order to gain a throne. But never have we heard of one killing his own mother. If you do this, you will bring disgrace upon the blood of the Kshatriyas. We will not allow it.'

Their determination started Ajatasatru. 'Aren't you my faithful ministers?' he asked. 'Didn't you promise to support me in this matter?'

'We will support you,' they replied, 'only if you do not harm your mother.'

Ajatasatru dropped his sword and promised to do as they said, but he also gave strict orders that his mother was to be confined to her quarters and no longer permitted to visit the king in prison.

The poor queen was in despair. Her husband was wasting away to a painful death, and she could do no more. She sent a messenger to ask the Buddha if he would send Ananda and Maudgalyayana, two of his most distinguished disciples, to come and comfort her. The Buddha not only sent the two disciples, but came himself. Queen Vaidehi greeted him with a flood of tears.

'What evil have I done to deserve such a fate? I have tried to be a good wife and a good mother. Now my son has turned on his father and threatened to kill me as well. My husband, a good man who has long protected and served you, now wastes away in agony. You have taught us that everything happens because of a cause. What have we done to cause this? For years now, we have tried to do nothing but good as you taught us. And look what has happened!

'If I earned my cruel son because of some evil deed I did in a past life, then you, too, Lord Buddha, must have sinned to have earned a cousin like Devadatta!

'There is no justice in this world! I am sick of it! I don't want to remain here any longer! Just tell me one thing, please. Is there another world where everything is as it ought to be, where a good cause will yield a good fruit, where there is no wickedness, no pain, no hunger, no beastliness?'

She knelt at his feet, sobbing helplessly.

Shakyamuni did not answer her hysterical questions about past lives. She was in no mood for rationalizations, and he had always said that such speculations were a waste of time. What mattered was not the past but the present and the future. Nor did he rebuke her for her pointed remark that he, too, must have done some evil to have deserved a cousin like Devadatta. (This matter would be taken up later in the *Dharma Flower*.)

Instead of preaching a sermon, he opened her eyes. Spiritual illumination often comes at moments of great stress. Shakyamuni had attained enlightenment after he had almost died of starvation and drowned in a river while bathing. Many centuries later Nichiren was to open his inner eye as the executioner raised a sword above his head to strike the life from his body. Now Bimbisara in his gloomy cell, and Vaidehi, weak and defeated at the Buddha's feet — one facing a slow death and the other facing despair — had been stretched back like bent bows ready to snap.

'Then,' says the *Meditation on Eternal Life Sutra*, 'the World-Honored One flashed forth a light from between his eyebrows. It was of golden hue, which extended to all the innumerable worlds of the ten quarters and which, returning, rested on top of the Buddha's head, transforming itself into a golden seat, looking like Mount Sumeru. There the pure and wonderful countries of the Buddhas of the ten quarters were seen. A country there was of seven gems; another all full of lotus flowers. One was like the palace of Maheshvara-deva, and another like a mirror of crystal. Here the countries of the ten quarters were all reflected. And all such innumerable Buddha-countries were resplendent and delightful to see. Vaidehi was made to see all this.'

King Bimbisara also saw this. 'Advancement in wisdom came to him spontaneously, and he attained the fruition of one who never returns to this earth.'

Shakyamuni later explained to the queen that 'when you perceive the Buddha, it is indeed that mind of yours that at once possesses those 32 signs of perfection and the eight minor marks of excellence. This mind makes the Buddha. This mind is the Buddha himself.'

Tan-luan (476–542), explaining the above passage, says that the mind is like water. 'If it is clear, it will reflect true reality. It will at once perceive the Buddha and his Pure Land' ('Ojoronchu', *Shinshu Seiten* 125).

The scripture from which the above story is taken, known as 'Meditation on Eternal Life Sutra', together with other sutras dealing with the Pure Land, became the favourite texts of the Pure Land school of Buddhism. Its devotees attempted to attain the vision of Queen Vaidehi, especially at the hour of death. The school flourished in China and was taken to its logical limits in Japan during the thirteenth century by Honen (1133–1212) and Shinran (1173–1262). They taught that such visualizations are superfluous. One need only call with faith upon the name of Amida, the Buddha of the Pure Land, and he will receive anyone into his paradise whether or not he has spiritual insight (Honen), or one can enter by faith alone, even without calling on the name (Shinran). The compassionate Buddha wishes to exclude no one.

According to the *Dharma Flower* devotees, however, these are one-sided interpretations that have strayed from the original intent of the 'Meditation on Eternal Life Sutra'. Several other writings mention that the enlightenment of Queen Vaidehi was an interlude during the teaching of the Lotus Sutra [12] Its grim tale of palace intrigue and murder serves as a gloomy contrast to the brilliance and luminous light of the *Dharma Flower*. Queen Vaidehi's spiritual awakening is a vision of the same radiance surrounding the Buddha on the Vulture Peak.

The *Dharma Flower* dazzles the imagination with its endless processes of Buddhas, Bodhisattvas, gods, demons, garudas, nagas, and other wonderful beings far removed from our everyday life. The tragic story of Queen Vaidehi is a necessary antidote to such unworldly splendour. It reminds us that the Pure Land of all the Buddhas can arise in our minds from the ashes of life's most crushing defeats. But the Buddha-land is not just 'over there' beyond the grave. It is right here. This was to be a central message of the greatest champion of the *Dharma Flower*, Nichiren of Japan.

Chapter 4

The Eternal Buddha _____

As the *Dharma Flower* opens, the Buddha emerges from deep concentration and turns to address Shariputra, who is reputed to be the wisest of his followers. 'The wisdom of the present Buddhas cannot be understood by the Shravakas (disciples, specifically those of the Lesser Vehicle) or the Pratyekabuddhas (those who attain enlightenment by themselves) because the present Buddhas attained the most profound Dharma by practising the teachings of the past Buddhas in their previous existences, and because they are expounding the Dharma in various ways according to the capacities of living beings.

'I also attained the Wonderful Dharma and became a Buddha by practising the teachings of the past Buddhas in my previous existence. Since I attained Buddhahood, I have been expounding the Dharma with various stories of previous lives, parables, and similes. The Wonderful Dharma is the secret lore of the Buddhas. It can be understood only by the Buddhas and Bodhisattvas who are firm in faith. By my Wonderful Dharma, I mean the truth of the reality of all things in regard to their appearances as such, their natures as such, their embodiments as such, their powers as such, their activities as such, their primary causes as such, their environmental causes as such, their effects as such, their rewards and retributions as such, and the equality of these nine factors of theirs as such.'

He elucidates this point, and then goes on to say that although the Disciples, the Solitaries, and the altruistic Bodhisattvas seem to be following different paths, this is not really true. The Buddha taught them different methods only as expedients to help each one at his own level of understanding and ability.

I expounded the teaching of Nirvana to the dull people,

Who wished to hear the teachings of the Lesser Vehicle,
Who were attached to birth and death,
And who were troubled by many sufferings
Inflicted on them because they had not practiced
The profound and wonderful teachings
Under innumerable Buddhas

I expounded this expedient teaching in order to cause
    them
To enter the way to the wisdom of the Buddha.
I never said to them:
'You can attain the enlightenment of the Buddha.'
I never said this
Because the time was not yet ripe for it.

Now is the time to say this.
I will expound the Great Vehicle definitely.
I expound various sutras of the nine elements
According to the capacities of living beings.
I expounded the different sutras
Because they were a basis for the Great Vehicle.

(Murano *Lotus Sutra* 32)

To illustrate, he tells a story of a wealthy father who returns home one day to find his house burning while all his children are playing thoughtlessly within. They are either not aware of the fire or not alarmed by it. In any case they are too involved in their games to consider leaving the house. The father wants them out as quickly as possible.

'Look!' he calls to them from outside. 'I have brought you some new toys to play with — beautiful carts. Come out quickly and choose the one you want!'

Joyfully the children pour out, eager to get first choice for the cart each wants for himself. However, once they are safely outside, the father presents each one with an identical cart, a Great Vehicle far more luxurious than any they could have imagined.

Had the father lied to the children when he promised each one a little cart of his own? No, he had used the carts as expedients to gain his end and save his children. In the same way the Buddha uses different teachings to attract his many children out of the burning house of this world. He offers them rewards which are within the range of their understanding. Most people are attracted to a religion for selfish reasons; they want a private vehicle which will carry them up to heaven. But there is no private vehicle. There is only one Great Vehicle which carries all together.

Where is this Great Vehicle to be found? It is here all the time, within one's self.

Another parable tells the story of a boy who ran away from home and grew up in a hostile world that utterly defeated him. He slipped lower and lower on the social scale until he was reduced to begging for a living. His father, meanwhile, had become wealthy and powerful. He lived in a palace in a different city and commanded a large staff of servants and employees. He had everything he wanted except what he wanted most of all, his lost son.

One day as the white-bearded and richly arrayed father sat in state outside his palace, he spied a miserable beggar cowering by the gate. Could it be . . .? Yes it was! It was his son! He told some retainers to bring the man in.

But the son was not ready for this. When he saw the approaching uniformed attendants, he turned and ran. To him uniforms meant only one thing — police! He could not dream that the wealthy merchant, who commanded such power, was his own father. By now he had almost forgotten that he had ever had a father or any home except the street.

The attendants chased after the son, captured him, and dragged him back, protesting and whimpering with terror. When finally they pushed him roughly into the presence of his father, the miserable son fainted. The father saw that his son had sunk so low that an immediate reconciliation would be impossible, even cruel. A good name cannot be granted; it must be earned. Unless the son has self-respect, his father's love could seem like poison to him.

'Let him go!' he ordered. 'I do not need this man.'

The attendants poured water on the son's head, shook him awake, and told him to leave. He scurried off, much to the amusement of the onlookers.

But the father did not give up so easily. Later he called two of his shabbiest hired men and told them to find the beggar who was there that day. 'Offer him a job clearing trash,' he told them. 'Pay him enough for food but not enough to spend on wine.'

The son accepted the offer. Three meals a day and a place to sleep offered more security than he had known for a long time.

One day the father was looking out the window when he saw his son working outside, 'gaunt, lean, and doleful, filthy and covered with dirt and dust'. The sight broke his heart. He removed his own fine robes and disguised himself as a foreman. In this guise, he was able to get close to the young man and start a conversation with him. 'You're a good worker, boy,' he told him. 'I'll recommend you for a promotion.'

Years passed. The son's self-respect grew gradually as he assumed higher and higher positions. Eventually he became the trusted manager of the entire business; he was known and respected everywhere. Only then was the father ready. He called together all his employees and announced that the manager was none other than his son, the rightful heir to all his fortune.

Thus the son, unlike the prodigal of the Bible, was brought into his inheritance only when he was ready to receive it. This required more than just love from the father; it took patience and a little guile as well. The son had to be led step by step into what was rightfully his since the beginning. So skilful was the father's preparation that the son was not aware that he had done anything to 'earn' his inheritance. 'Without any mind for, or effort on my part,' he says, 'these treasures now come to me of themselves.'

Another parable in the Sutra treats the matter from a different angle. A young man became drunk after an evening of carousing and passed out. A wealthy friend had to leave him there, but decided first to do him a favour. He took a valuable jewel and placed it in the drunken man's topknot. Surely, he reasoned, when his friend woke up, he would notice the jewel, use it to pay any expenses, and still have plenty left over for whatever he wanted.

But this did not happen. When the drunken man got up the next day, it never occurred to him that he was now wealthy. First he was thrown out of the inn for not paying his bill. Then things went from bad to worse. He wandered from place to place, doing odd jobs when he could and living from hand to mouth.

Years later, his wealthy friend ran into him and was shocked by his appearance. 'What happened to you?' he asked. 'How did you lose all your money?'

'What money? I never had any. You know that.'

'The money from the jewel I left in your topknot. I left it for you so that you could pay your expenses, invest the rest, and go into business for yourself.'

The poor man dug into his topknot and, sure enough, there was the priceless jewel! It had been there all along. He had been a rich man, carrying a fortune with him wherever he went, but he had never known it.

So it is, says the Buddha, with everyone. The priceless jewel, the Buddha nature, lies within us untapped. The only difference between the Buddha and us is that he knows this, has unravelled his topknot, and exposed the jewel of the Buddhahood.

Here lies an important difference between the *Dharma Flower* and many other sutras of the Great Vehicle. Mahayana sutras are apt to be critical — sometimes highly critical — of the 'narrow' way of the Hinayana disciples. Common mortals and even sinners can attain Buddhahood, but the arhats, who have attained Nirvana, cannot. Blinded by their own success, they have ceased to look further. The 'Sutra of the Great Assembly' says that they have 'fallen into the pit of Nirvana' from which they can neither free themselves nor be of any use to others. Having destroyed their earthly passions, they have destroyed the seeds of Buddhahood. Greed, anger, and ignorance can kindle the flame of Buddhahood; cold detachment and self-satisfaction cannot.

The *Dharma Flower*, on the other hand, is called the 'Round Teaching'. It completes the circle, gathering in the Hinayana disciples, the solitary sages (*Pratyekabuddhas*), and the Mahayana Bodhisattvas. They all follow their own rules to reach the goal, but the goal is the same and so is the destiny. Like different plants in a tropical jungle during a rain storm, all are nourished by the same cloud, the bountiful rain-cloud of the all-compassionate Buddha. There are not 'three vehicles', the Sutra repeats over and over again; there is only one, the Buddha Vehicle.

> Just as rain falls on all vegetation, so Buddha's compassion
> extends equally to all people. Just as different plants receive
> particular benefits from the same rain, so people of different
> natures and circumstances are blessed in different ways.
> (*Teaching* 23)

Chih-i divided the *Dharma Flower* into two sections of 14 chapters each.[13] The first half, which has been cited thus far, is devoted mostly to the theory of the universal Buddha-nature. Since it consists of the Buddha's teachings, it is called the Imprinted Gate (*Shakumon* in Japanese). In the second half, the Buddha reveals his own inner nature. It is called the Original Gate (*Hommon*). It is this second half, the Original Gate, which gives the Sutra its dynamic punch. Spanning the two halves like a bridge is the Ceremony in Space.

Suddenly there springs up from the ground and stands in the sky a glorious tower, or stupa, '500 yojanas in height and 250 yojanas in length and width', sparkling with jewels and decorated with flowers and banners. A voice rings out from within: 'Excellent, excellent! You, Shakyamuni Buddha, the World-Honored One, have expounded to this great multitude the Wonderful Dharma Flower Sutra, the Teaching of Equality, the Great Wisdom, the Dharma for Bodhisattvas, the Dharma protected by the Buddhas. So it is, so it is! What you have expounded, World-Honored Shakyamuni, is all true' (Chap. 11).

When he is asked about the meaning of this remarkable apparition and the voice, the Buddha explains that within the Treasure Tower is the perfect body of a Tathagata named Many Treasures (*Taho-nyorai*). He lived ages ago in a world 'far to the east' called Treasure-Purity. 'While he was still practising the Way of Bodhisattvas, he made a great vow, "If after I become a Buddha and pass away, anyone in any of the worlds of the ten quarters expounds the Dharma Flower Sutra, I will cause my stupa-mausoleum to spring up before him so that I can prove the truthfulness of the sutra and say 'excellent' in his praise, because I wish to hear that sutra directly from him."'

One of the listeners, a Bodhisattva named Great Eloquence, says that he would like to see that Buddha. Shakyamuni replies that this cannot be done until he has recalled 'all the Buddhas emanated from me who are now expounding the Dharma in the worlds of the ten quarters.' He now does this. This world of ours (the *saha*-world, the 'world of endurance') is purified three times as the emanations of Shakyamuni, 'as innumerable as the sands of the River Ganges', assemble about the Treasure Tower.

Once they have all gathered, Shakyamuni rises up to the sky and with the fingers of his right hand opens the door of the Treasure Tower. 'The opening of the door made a sound as large as that of the removal of the bolt and lock of the gate of a great city. At that instant all the congregation sees Many Treasures Tathagata sitting with his perfect and undestroyed body on the lion-like seat in the stupa of treasures as if he had been sitting in dhyana-concentration.' Many Treasures then invites Shakyamuni to sit beside him.

The scene is so rich in symbolism that any explanation risks spoiling the effect. One interpretation is that we have here a concept which is basic to the Great Vehicle, the 'Three Bodies of the Buddha' (*Tri-kaya* in Sanskrit, *Sanjin* in Japanese). The first 'body' (Dharma-body) is the ultimate truth in itself. It is symbolized by the Treasure Tower, which contains the second 'body', the truth in an intelligible form, in this case the form of Many Treasures Buddha. It is called the Reward-body, but this form is invisible to us until it has been revealed by the Action-body of the Buddha, Shakyamuni. He does this only when he has assembled all partial truths — all his replicas — in one place.

The Three Bodies are seen 'in the sky' (in the mind), but in fact they spring from the earth, this physical–spiritual world of ours. Nichiren says that when the door of the tower is closed, it represents the Imprinted Gate, the theoretical teachings of the Buddha; and when it is open, it represents the Original Gate, the Buddha's self-revelation. Most important of all, he says, is to realize that the Treasure Tower is none other than the human body, the throne of all the Buddhas. 'You are the Treasure Tower, itself, and the Treasure Tower is you. No other knowledge is purposeful' (MW 1:30).

As in all good symbolism, various interpretations are possible. Chih-i says that Many Treasures Buddha represents objective truth, and Shakyamuni is the subjective wisdom which perceives it. In this case Many Treasures is the Dharma-body, Shakyamuni is the Wisdom-body, and the emanated Buddhas are the Manifest-body.

Directions, too, have symbolic significance in the *Dharma Flower*. The East, where the sun rises, is the temporal origin, the past. Many Treasures comes from 'far to the East'. The West is the temporal future; Amida Buddha has his Pure Land in the West. The nadir is death, emptiness, 'the beginning with no beginning'. Many Treasures, having lived in the East, now rises up from beneath the earth. The zenith is transcendent reality, resurrection, 'the end with no ending'. The two Buddhas rise to the sky. Nichiren says that they represent the two inseparable aspects of reality, death and life. Many Treasures symbolizes the past, death; Shakyamuni is life. The two sit side by side within the Treasure Tower, demonstrating their inseparability.

When Shakyamuni preaches his sermons of the Imprinted Gate, he sits facing the East; he is addressing his temporal disciples. However, when he enters the Treasure Tower and joins Many Treasures there, he is now facing West. His teaching of the eight key chapters of the Original Gate is for future generations. This Original Teaching (*Honge*) requires the presence of the original disciples (*Honge no Bosatsu*), who arise from 'beneath the earth'. When he completes this teaching, he dismisses the original disciples, descends to the earth, faces eastward again, and preaches the final chapters (23–8) for his contemporaries.

The teachings of the Imprinted Gate conclude with three chapters on the proper way to disseminate the Sutra in the future. The first of these, Chapter 12, is the famous Devadatta Chapter. It pushes the doctrine of the one Buddha-nature in all beings to logical conclusions, and these conclusions are truly revolutionary.

In Buddhism there is no such thing as chance or coincidence. Everything takes place because of causes, and this includes our human relationships. Our friends are those whom we met under favourable circumstances; our enemies are those whom we encountered under unfavourable circumstances. But neither the circumstances nor the people involved came out of nowhere. All life, as the Flower Garland Sutra so vividly demonstrates, is a network of connections. We come into favourable contacts because of favourable connecting causes. This is especially true of the people with whom we are most intimately associated: our parents, brothers and sisters, spouse. We are drawn to such people because of powerful prior causes. Our relationships in the past may have been entirely different from what they are now, but they existed in one form or another.

The life force (the Buddha-nature) is one, but its forms are endless. These forms are linked to each other in the one Buddha-nature (i.e. they are all alive), and they affect each other for better or worse.

This brings us to the pointed question of Queen Vaidehi: What evil deed in the past did Shakyamuni do that he was born with such a wretched cousin as Devadatta? He ignored her question at the time (there were other more pressing matters at stake), but now he answers it. There was, indeed, a very close relationship in the past between Devadatta and himself.

Devadatta was once his teacher, and he was the faithful disciple who served his master loyally. Today the relationship is reversed: Shakyamuni, the more pure-hearted, is the teacher, and Devadatta is (or should be) the disciple. But Devadatta cannot accept this change in roles; he is unconsciously jealous and resentful. This resentment has ruined his once noble character. There is no fouler villain than a thwarted saint.

Devadatta, like anyone, must pay the price for his evil deeds. But now

Shakyamuni makes a startling announcement: Devadatta, even Devadatta, will someday become a Buddha. The good in his character may now be hidden beneath layers of jealousy, but it is still there. Buddha-nature is universal; it is the same whether in Devadatta or anyone else. He, too, carries the jewel in his topknot.

The second surprising conclusion to the doctrine of the universal Buddha-nature is not so startling to us today. However, it was a real shocker when it was first preached. Not only do evil men carry the Buddha-nature, but so do women!

The ancients generally looked upon women as spiritually inferior to men. Their function was to serve, not to think. Of course, there were lots of priestesses, witches, and mediums, who exercised considerable influence; but they were looked upon as operating at the lower levels of spirituality, more 'earth-bound' than men. They could be possessed by gods or demons, and speak for them as 'channels'. However, because they are 'closer to the earth' (the words *mater*, 'mother' and 'material' are related), they could not ascend to the realm of pure spirit. This was a male prerogative.

Shakyamuni demolishes all these prejudices, not with a sermon (he has already preached enough of these, and the conclusions should be obvious), but by an example. He does this in the story of the eight-year-old *Naga* princess.

It is not at all clear what is meant by the term *naga*. In Pali the word means 'a cobra, an elephant, or a noble person'. It is either a person with powerful animal-like qualities, or an animal with human qualities. Nagas, under the guise of cobras, are worshipped today in parts of India, but there are also people called Nagas residing in Burma and India. They may have been serpent-worshippers in the past, and have given their name to the sacred cobra. The Chinese did not know what a *naga* was, either, so they translated the term as 'dragon', which may give us a clue. But what is a dragon?

The Chinese dragon, unlike its western counterpart, who sits brooding in a cave where it guards its treasures, represents the vitality of life-giving waters. It comes up 'beating its belly and bellowing, "Haw ha ha haw!"' as Joseph Campbell says (*The Power of Myth* 150). 'Metaphorically, water is the unconscious, and the creature of the water is the life or energy of the unconscious' (1968, 146).

The eight-year-old Dragon Princess represents pure spontaneity. She arrives highly recommended by her sponsor, the Bodhisattva Manjusri, but gets a chilly reception from the other disciples. The scholarly Shariputra and another Bodhisattva, who is appropriately named Accumulated Wisdom, look down their noses at her and patiently explain the many reasons why she can never become a Buddha. For one thing, she is not even a man. Then too, Shakyamuni Buddha accumulated merits by practising austerities. 'Even the smallest part, even a part the size of a poppy-seed of this world — this world being composed of one thousand million Sumeru-worlds — is not outside the places where the Bodhisattva made efforts to save all living beings at the cost of his life. It is only after doing all this that he attained Bodhi.' How could this presumptuous girl equal that?

Instead of arguing with them, the Dragon Princess turns to Shakyamuni and offers him a jewel 'worth one thousand million Sumeru-worlds'. The Buddha immediately accepts.

'Did the Buddha accept my gem quickly or not?' she asks them.

'Very quickly,' they answer.

'Now watch me become a Buddha even more quickly.' In a flash, she completes all the Bodhisattva practices and transforms herself into a Buddha.

Obviously, the jewel which she offered to Shakyamuni was her own life, which was worth just as much as his — 'one thousand million Sumeru-worlds'. Whether one accumulates wisdom and virtue slowly over the ages and so destroys ego-centricity, or whether one does it in one spontaneous act makes no difference. The price is the same: one's own life. The reward is the same: Buddhahood.

Here is the only case in the whole of Buddhist literature where any mortal becomes a Buddha. There is much discussion about the theoretical possibility; she is the only example; Needless to say, this unnamed Naga-princess became a heroine to the feminists of China and Japan.

As the Buddha prepares to reveal his own identity in the Original Gate, he is suddenly surrounded by a host of new Bodhisattvas, who (like the Treasure Tower) spring up 'from under the earth'. They are magnificent to behold, but are entirely unknown to the assembled multitude. Who are they?

There are four leaders to the Bodhisattvas from under the earth. All of them have the word 'action' in their names: Superior Action (Jogyo), Limitless Action (Muhengyo), Pure Action (Jyogyo), and Steadily Established Action (Anryugyo). Later commentators pointed out that these names are analogous to the Four Qualities of Nirvana given in the Nirvana Sutra: Superior Action is true self; Limitless Action is eternity; Pure Action is purity; Steadily Established Action is bliss. [14]

All these great Bodhisattvas have been the Buddha's disciples since endless time. How is such a thing possible? Shakyamuni explains it in the famous sixteenth chapter, 'The Duration of the Life of the Tathagata'. A popular manual, *The Teaching of Buddha*, paraphrases it this way (24–6):

> Common people believe that Buddha was born a prince and
> learned the way to Enlightenment as a mendicant; actually,
> Buddha has always existed in the world which is without
> beginning or end.
> As the Eternal Buddha, He has known all people and applied
> all methods of relief.

There is no falsity in the Eternal Dharma which Buddha taught, for He knows all things in the world as they are, and He teaches them to all people.

Indeed, it is very difficult to understand the world as it is, for, although it seems true, it is not, and, although it seems false, it is not. Ignorant people cannot know the truth concerning the world.

Buddha alone truly and fully knows the world as it is and He never says that it is true or false, or good or evil. He simply portrays the world as it is.

What Buddha does teach is this: 'That all people should cultivate roots of virtue according to their natures, their deeds, and their beliefs.' This teaching transcends all affirmation and negation in the world.

Buddha teaches not only through words, but also through His life. Although His life is endless, in order to awaken greedy people, He uses the expedient of death.

While a certain physician was away from home, his children accidentally took some poison. When the physician returned, he noticed their sickness and prepared an antidote. Some of the children who were not seriously poisoned accepted the medicine and were cured, but others were so seriously affected that they refused to take the medicine.

The physician, prompted by paternal love for his children, decided on an extreme method to press the cure upon them. He said to the children: 'I must go off on a long journey. I am old and may pass away any day. If I am with you I can care for you, but if I should pass away, you will become worse and worse. If you hear of my death, I implore you to take the antidote and be cured of this subtle poisoning.' Then he went on the long journey. After a time, he sent a messenger to his children to inform them of his death.

The children, receiving the message, were deeply affected by the thought of their father's death and by the realization that they would no longer have the benefit of his benevolent care. Recalling his parting request, in a feeling of sorrow and helplessness, they took the medicine and recovered.

People must not condemn the deception of this father-physician. Buddha is like that father. He, too, employs the fiction of life and death to save people who are entangled in the bondage of desires.

The chapter closes with the Buddha saying:

> I know who is practising the Way and who is not.
> Therefore, I expound various teachings

To all living beings,
According to their capacities.
I am always thinking:
'How shall I cause all living beings
To enter into the unsurpassed Way
And quickly become Buddhas, themselves?'

No condensation or translation can do justice to the great rolling cadences of the Chinese version. Endless time is equated with endless space. Here the Buddha states explicitly what hitherto he had implied negatively. Between the extremes of existence and non-existence, reality and falsity, eternity and annihilation lies the concrete entity of life itself.

The truth-order exists whether a Buddha announces it or not. However, unless at least one being realizes it and fathoms its meaning, the truth-order is incomplete. Truth is not a series of acts; it has an inside as well as an outside. Truth comprehends itself, otherwise nothing could comprehend anything. In the person of the Buddha, the cosmos fulfils itself in its own inner comprehension.

An individual is neither real nor unreal. On the one hand, he is not a permanent entity; on the other hand, he appears phenomenally. However, the Buddha is a real individual, *the* real individual. The truth-order is represented, embodied, and realized in his person as the Thus-Come-One (Tathagata). He is *the* person in communion with all others. By the same token, any individual is a Thus-Come-One if he realizes the universal truth-order of the cosmos, 'not only in his ideas,' says Anesaki, 'but in his life, and lives the life of the universal self' (1966, 144–5).

Then in answer to his rhetorical question, 'Who will spread this teaching in the future?' the Buddha rejects the proferred offers of his ethereal saints and Bodhisattvas. Instead, he suprises them by raising up 'innumerable Bodhisattvas from under the earth'. It is they, not superhuman beings, who will spread the Dharma. For the Wonderful Dharma cannot be simply 'taught'; it must be lived, it must be embodied. It is embodied already — in living men and women. It is to them that he entrusts the future.

The Lotus Sutra expounds unqualified universalism. It leaves out no one, men or women, saints or sinners, sages or the ignorant, humans or non-humans, believers or non-believers. But the key is not merely to accept this, to believe it, as was the case with the Imprinted Gate. The key with the Original Gate is to live it, to put it into practice. It is no longer just a doctrine; it is now a clarion call to action. This is why the new Bodhisattvas do not descend from the heavens; they rise up from the earth. This is why each has the word 'action' appended to his name.

This action can be summed up in the Four Great Vows of a Bodhisattva:

Sentient beings are innumerable; I vow to save them all.
Our evil desires are inexhaustible; I vow to quench them all.
The Buddha's teachings are immeasurable; I vow to study them all.
The Way of the Buddha is unexcelled; I vow to attain the Path Sublime.[15]

Chapter 5

The Lotus Blossoms _____

The Original Gate closes with instructions on how to put it into practice, just as the Imprinted Gate did. From the second half of Chapter 17 until the final 28th chapter, the *Dharma Flower* is devoted exclusively to practice, not theory. One Bodhisattva after another preaches, not with words but by example.

One of them is named Never-Despise or Never-Despising (*Jo-fukyo*).[16] He respects all people, bows when he meets anyone, and announces, 'you will all become Buddhas.'

The Sutra says, 'Some of the four kinds of devotees had impure minds.[17] They got angry, spoke ill of him, and abused him, saying, "Where did this ignorant bhikshu (monk) come from? He says that he does not despise us, and assures us that we shall be able to become Buddhas. We do not need such a false assurance of our future Buddhahood." Although he was abused like this for many years, he did not get angry. He always said to them, "You will be able to become Buddhas." When he said this, people would strike him with sticks, pieces of wood, tiles or stones. He would run away to a distance, and call out in a loud voice from afar, "I do not despise you. You will be able to become Buddhas"' (*Lotus* XX).

Eventually Never-Despising hears 'in the sky the twenty trillion *gathas* (verses) of the Dharma Flower Sutra', and then he is able to purify his senses and lead many people to Buddhahood. Clearly the *Dharma Flower* is here considered as more than just a book. The written Sutra does not have 20,000,000,000,000 verses or anywhere near that amount. The written Sutra is a symbol or manifestation of the universal Truth, which is everywhere ('in the sky'). It is not just the words of the Original Buddha — it is the Original Buddha himself, in visible form. As later Buddhists were to say, 'We can see him in the letters of this Sutra. The letters are the Buddha, himself, in his manifestation' (*Kaikyoge*, Prelude to sutra reading, verse 3).

Perhaps even better known than Never-Despising is the Bodhisattva Avalokiteshvara (*Kanzeon* in Japanese; *Kuan Yin* in Chinese). The name means, 'World-Voice-Perceiver'. Avalokiteshvara was originally a man who could take the form of a woman — or of anyone, for that matter — to help suffering beings. As the personification of compassion, he/she came to be regarded as female, and was depicted in art as a loving mother. Her graceful form is familiar to many Westerners as the 'Goddess of mercy'. John Blofeld emphasises her feminine attributes in his *Bodhisattva of Compassion* and gives a complete translation of the popular verses in the *Dharma Flower* which describe her powers:

> To hear her name or see her form,
> Or fervently recite her name
> Delivers beings from every woe

So popular did this chapter become that it was printed and recited as a separate sutra, forming the basis for a Kanzeon cult. Even the scholarly Chih-i was devoted to Kuan Yin and considered this chapter to be one of the four most important in the Sutra. He is said to have recited it daily.[18]

However, a shift in location has taken place between these two chapters (20 and 25), and its significance was not lost on Nichiren. Shakyamuni descends from the Treasure Tower in the sky after describing the many merits earned by one who keeps the Sutra in the future, and receiving confirmation from all the assembled Buddhas. He charges the Bodhisattvas from the earth with the task of spreading the Sutra in the future. Then he dismisses Many Treasures Buddha and all the others, who return to their respective worlds.

Logically the Sutra should end here (Chap. 22), and probably it did originally. The final chapters, which extol various Bodhisattvas, bear no apparent connection to what has previously transpired. Each, like the Kanzeon Chapter, is complete in itself. All modern scholars agree that they are late additions to the text. They introduce elements which will develop eventually into separate sects: the popular cult of Kanzeon, who is invoked as the 'goddess of mercy' (Chap. 25); esotericism, with its use of magical *dharanis* (formulas) to invoke protective demons (Chaps. 26 and 28); and the cult of the Buddha Amitayus (Amida), who is invoked for a happy rebirth in a better world than this one (Chap. 24). The only logic to their appearance at this point in the book is that Bodhisattvas use any and all means to save suffering people, and therefore chapters on Bodhisattva-practices could be added indefinitely.

There is a danger here that the *Dharma Flower* is becoming so broad, so all-encompassing, that it is accepting seeds which will grow up to choke it. Those who venerate Kanzeon will look upon her as a goddess and not bother with the deeper meaning of the *Dharma Flower*. Those who go in for magical formulas will become immersed in esoterica. Those who long for a happy afterlife in the paradise of Amitayus (Amida) will forget the affirmation of Chapter 16, that the Buddha-land is right here.

All these aberrations did, indeed, take place. Roughly speaking, the Dharma Flower School has been represented by two branches: the broad branch of Chih-i and his T'ien-t'ai School (Japanese *Tendai*), which seeks to encompass everything, and the narrow branch of Nichiren, which places all religious teachings in an ascending hierarchical order: 1) the religions of Confucius and Lao Tzu (ethical and magical); 2) Indian non-Buddhist religions (philosophical and devotional); 3) Buddhist teachings before the *Dharma Flower*, which expound enlightenment for some; 4) the Imprinted Gate of the *Dharma Flower*, which expounds enlightenment for all; 5) the Original Gate, which gives it life (*Kaimoku Sho*). Each includes its predecessor, and should replace it in practice when its time comes.

If the *Dharma Flower* is important as the manifestation of an idea, it is also significant as a book, as a work of literature. It was not until four or five centuries after the death of Shakyamuni that his words and deeds were put into writing. Of course these words and deeds were known, but they were passed on by oral transmission, not in writing. Buddhist tradition tells how shortly after Shakyamuni's death, 500 of his leading disciples gathered near Rajagriha and recited his words. The sutras, as they exist today, full of repetitions, are obviously written versions of lessons which were originally taught and learned by rote. As these recited sutras were translated into various languages, differences between them became troublesome. This is one reason why there arose the need for a written text: there is a fixed quality to the written word that is lacking in the spoken word.

Beginning around 100 B.C. and continuing for the next three centuries, there was an outpouring of Buddhist literature as the various schools of transmission wrote down their own versions. Each claimed that its tradition was the first and most accurate. Nevertheless, later Buddhists were to say that the appearance of the written word marked the end of the Age of the True Norm (*Shoho*) and the beginning of the Age of the Formal Norm (*Zoho*). Written words and letters are not the truth; they symbolize the truth. The truth itself can be transmitted only from mind to mind.

It may have been not the monks but laymen who first wanted the teachings in writing. The oldest Buddhist inscriptions which have survived were carved on stone pillars by orders of the Emperor Asoka (3rd century B.C.). They were written in the various languages of the

FIRE IN THE LOTUS

countries in which they were meant to be read.[19]

King Vattagamani of Ceylon (29–17 B.C.) ordered that the sutras be recorded in the 'original' tongue, i.e. that by which the Dharma had been transmitted to his country. This was Pali, once a spoken tongue of western India but by then a dead language. The word *Pali* means 'holy scripture', and does not appear in the early sutras (Mizuno 1980, 29). Once put in writing, it became the *lingua franca* of Theravada Buddhism, 'the Way of the Elders' (the only surviving branch of Hinayana, the Lesser Vehicle), and is still read today in Ceylon, Burma, Thailand, and wherever the Theravada is taught.

Theravada has the only complete canon of sacred Buddhist scriptures; it consists of 45 large volumes. This canon is called the Three Baskets (*Tipitaka* in Pali), because it is divided into three sections. One section consists of sutras (sermons), the second of monastic rules, and the third, which is not attributed to the Buddha, of theological and philosophical explanations.

In northern India, King Kanishka (first or second century A.D.) ordered the recension of the canon of the local Sarvastavadins (a Hinayana sect, now extinct) in Sanskrit, a corrupt version of which was still spoken in his kingdom.

Laymen also seem to have been responsible for the appearance of the Mahayana sutras. The *Dharma Flower* is one of the earliest of these, and it has a distinctly anti-clerical tone. 'Evil bhikshus will insult us, drive us far from the monasteries, and make fun of us, saying, "So you think you are buddhas!"' Early Mahayanists expected no help from the religious establishment. Laymen, who formed the bulk of its members, had no time to go to a monastery or sit in silent meditation, but they did have time to read books and chant important passages. They also enjoyed pilgrimages to the sacred towers (*stupas*) containing relics of the Buddha and other saints. Both of these practices are extolled in the *Lotus*, but to read, recite, or copy a sutra is ranked higher than merely bowing before sacred relics.

Gradually new monastic brotherhoods developed to promulgate the expanded teachings. They were still Hinayana in their rules of discipline but Mahayana in their theology. Pure Mahayana monasticism did not appear until it was introduced by Saicho of Japan (767–822). Paul Groner has given us a detailed study of Saicho's struggles to realize his aim.

The early Mahayana sutras were written in the local languages and then translated later into the more elegant Sanskrit. Ancient Sanskrit was the sacred language of the rival Brahmin priesthood; it enjoyed a social prestige which put the 'vulgar' Buddhist tongues at a disadvantage. Regional languages also evolved into social languages. Kogen Mizuno says, 'In plays one could identify a character's occupation and social status through the prescribed language he or she spoke. Kings, ministers, and Brahmans spoke Sanskrit, the most esteemed and highly inflected language; queens, princesses, nuns, and courtesans spoke a graceful language called Shauraseni; the general populace, such as merchants and artisans, spoke Magadhi; and the lower classes spoke Paishachi. Even lyrics had their own pleasant-to-the-ear language, Maharashtri' (26). All of these were originally regional languages, not social. Since the Buddha spoke Magadhi, we can see why no sutras have come down to us in his own tongue, which came later to be associated with the middle class — hardly suitable for the words of the World-Honoured One!

The library of Mahayana works is even larger than the Hinayana canon. However, there is no Mahayana closed canon comparable to the Three Baskets. Instead there is a vast proliferation of sutras and commentaries, many of which are admittedly of late origin. The attempt of most of them is to get back behind the Buddha's words to his mind, to his intentions, to his great compassionate heart. The leading question is not, 'What did the Buddha say?' but 'What did he intend to do, and who was he, in the first place?'

This is why the doctrinal part of the Lotus Sutra, the Imprinted Gate (*Shakumon*), is ranked lower than the Original Gate (*Hommon*). The Imprinted Gate is an 'imprint' of the living Original Gate. It can be studied, learned, and understood; it can also be taught to others. Its subject is life, universal life, called the Buddha-nature. We can understand it and even approve of it while we are sitting by the fire and reading a book.

The second part, the Original Gate, is beyond rational comprehension. It goes beyond life through death and then to eternal life. It can be grasped only by those who 'die', those 'who wish to see me with all their hearts and at the cost of their lives'. It demands a conversion — complete destruction of the ego so that the Eternal Buddha becomes all in all. This cannot be done while sitting by a friendly crackling fire on the hearth, but only by plunging into 'the raging conflagration of destruction' (Chapter 16).

The Imprinted Gate paves the way by destroying the distinction between the self and 'others'. The other is nothing but the self of the one who is called the other. 'That his self and the other self are equal,' says Professor Shoson Miyamoto, 'was the teaching of "selflessness" (*muga, higa*), and the way, which put life into both the self and the other together, was the Middle Way of non-duality of self and other.'[20]

It is not necessary to be a Buddhist or even to read the *Lotus* to be able to attain to the Imprinted Gate. Many who have never read the book have shared its ideology. The American Universalist Clarence R. Skinner proclaims the *Lotus* doctrine in *A Religion for Greatness* (1945, 13):

Beneath all curious customs and beliefs, deeper than
ecclesiastical creeds, more vital than priestly rites, stands out one

impressive fact — namely, man touches infinity; his home is in immensity; he lives, moves, and has his being in an eternity. This magnificent assertion is man's greatest affirmation. Nothing else surpasses it in sweep of the imagination or depth of understanding. It is a truth proclaimed by all that we know of modern science, and it stands the test of experience as the enduring reality.[21]

But all of this is incomplete until it is given life. The great sixteenth chapter of *Hommon*, the Original Gate, sets the Sutra on fire.

By the time Buddhism began to penetrate China (the official date is A.D. 64, when the Emperor Ming dreamed of a golden Buddha), Buddhist scholasticism in India and Central Asia was in full flower. The new religion arrived via the trade routes of Central Asia, and for the first couple of centuries it remained a foreign and somewhat exotic cult. The Chinese had a rich culture of their own, which gave primary importance to family obligations. They were suspicious of monasticism and celibacy, which seemed to threaten these deeply rooted values. It was not until A.D. 333 that native Chinese were given permission to enter the Monastic Brotherhood. From then on Buddhism in China quickly took on its own national characteristics. Many emperors supported Buddhism, and some of them even became Buddhists.

Chinese Buddhism did not always have clear sailing, however, and the old anti-Buddhist complaints kept cropping up, especially among government ministers. Sometimes these resulted in severe persecutions. The persecution which began in 845 was so violent that Chinese Buddhism never fully recovered. Nevertheless, Buddhism had sunk its roots deep into the Chinese soul, and it retained a strong popular following even after it had lost official favour.

No one did more to advance the cause of Buddhism in China than the brilliant scholar and translator Kumarajiva (344–413). Kogen Mizuno in his book, *Buddhist Sutras*, says:

The sutras translated by Kumarajiva have had the greatest influence on Buddhism in China and Japan. It could be said that the essential meaning of Buddhism was introduced to China through the sutra translations of Kumarajiva, even though several hundred sutras had already been translated into Chinese before he began his work. By the latter part of the fourth century the true doctrines of Buddhism still had not been conveyed fully to the Chinese, either because lack of knowledge prevented their understanding completely those sutras that had been translated or because the true concepts of Buddhism had not been transmitted in the translations. The Chinese did not fully understand Buddhism until Kumarajiva had translated sutras, lectured, and written his commentaries. Thus Kumarajiva's work was extraordinarily important to Buddhism in both China and Japan.   (57)

Kumarajiva was born in Kucha, a Central Asian city on the northern trade route between India and China. His father Kumarayana was an Indian Brahmin of high rank, who had abandoned court life for that of an itinerant preacher. His mother Jiva was a sister of the King of Kucha. When Kumarayana's travels took him to Kucha, he caused such a sensation that the princess demanded to have him for a husband. Their child was named after both his distinguished parents, Kumara for his father and Jiva for his mother.

Princess Jiva was a most remarkable woman. Under her husband's influence, she became more and more interested in Buddhism and eventually surpassed him in wisdom and practice. She wanted to become a nun, but her husband objected, at least until a second child was born. When Kumarajiva was seven, his father finally relented. The mother took her son, and both of them entered the Buddhist Order.

When Kumarajiva was nine or ten, he travelled with his mother to India, where they studied under a famous Hinayana teacher. When he was 12, they returned to Central Asia, this time to Kushan, where they continued their studies. Already the boy was known as a precocious scholar and debater. The two spent a year in Kashgar studying Abhidharma (Hinayana philosophy) and other sutras, and then returned to Kucha to study the Hindu Vedas. Finally they were introduced to Mahayana, and Kumarajiva began his career of copying, translating, and lecturing on Mahayana sutras. He became a fully ordained monk, at the age of 20. His mother, who had attained the level of enlightenment called *anagamin* (one who will never be reborn in this world), retired to India.

Kumarajiva's star was still rising. He became the most celebrated teacher in Central Asia, and his fame spread abroad as far as China. King Fu Chien (Fu Jian) of the former Ch'in kingdom resolved to bring him to his capital of Ch'ang-an. Around 382 he sent his general Lu Kuang (Lu Guang) with an army of 70,000 men to capture Kucha and bring back Kumarajiva. It was to be nearly 20 years, however, before Kumarajiva reached China.

General Lu Kuang stormed Kucha, killed the king, and captured the Buddhist sage. However, when he heard bad news from China, that the king had been overthrown and replaced by an inimical monarch, the general decided not to return home. Instead he returned only part of the way, carved out a petty kingdom of his own, and took his prize captive with him.

The general took perverse delight in humiliating his prisoner. He was not a Buddhist, and was not impressed by Kumarajiva, who was then about 40 years old. He insisted that the monk marry a princess of Kucha. When Kumarajiva refused, the general got him drunk and locked him up in the same room with the princess. By dawn Kumarajiva was no longer either a teetotaler or a virgin.

Kumarajiva, always a scholar at heart, did not waste his time during his long sojourn in western China. He became fluent in the Chinese language, attracted many disciples, and even won the grudging admiration of the general. When the new king of Ch'in (called Later Ch'in), who was a Buddhist, begged the general to send Kumarajiva to China the general refused.

It took a second military invasion to get Kumarajiva into China at last. In 401 an army from China overthrew the general and brought his hostage safely to the capital of Ch'ang-an.

Here the famous teacher was treated with great respect. He was given the title of National Preceptor and put in charge of translating the sutras into Chinese. He was given every facility, including a team of linguists to assist him, and splendid quarters in the royal palace. Under such favourable circumstances he was able to turn out one translation after another, all of them unexcelled in their accuracy and elegant style. The Sutra of the Lotus Flower of the Wonderful Dharma (*Myoho Renge-kyo* in Sino-Japanese) was his masterpiece.

As Kumarajiva grew older, the king began to fear that his incomparable talent would be lost to the world after his death. The solution seemed to be for him to have an heir, who would carry on his work. He ordered that the sage be waited upon by ten comely maidens, hoping that at least one of them would become the mother of his child. Kumarajiva relented, but he was not proud of his luxurious life-style. He is said to have told his pupils, 'You must take only the lotus flower that grows out of the mire, and not touch the mire itself'.

Many Buddhist monks resented Kumarajiva's way of life, and a fellow Central Asian, Buddhabhadra, translator of the Flower Garland Sutra, criticized him openly. So popular was Kumarajiva, however, that it was the critic Buddhabhadra who was forced to leave the capital. Kumarajiva continued to live there in splendour until the day he died (Mizuno 57–62).

Kumarajiva was the greatest of the translators, but not the only one. Native Chinese scholars later dominated the field, and some of them undertook hazardous journeys to Central Asia or India in search of new texts.

So numerous did these texts become that the Chinese were bewildered by their different styles and doctrines. This is where Chih-i (Zhi-yi) came in. He was the great systematizer, who organized them into a coherent whole. Chih-i (538–97), called Chigi in Japanese, is also known as the Great Teacher T'ien-t'ai (Japanese *Tendai Daishi*) after the Heavenly Terrace Monastery (*T'ien-t'ai*) where he did most of his teaching.

His work was truly encyclopaedic. He studied all the sutras, both Hinayana and Mahayana, dated them by internal evidence, and classified them by their teaching methods, the time when they were taught, their contents, and their doctrines. 'The Fourfold Methods of Conversion' are Sudden, Gradual, Secret (individual), and Variable (each listener understanding according to his own capacity). 'The Five Periods (or flavours)' are the Flower Garland, the Deer Park, Expanded (Mahayana), Wisdom, and Lotus-Nirvana. The contents are Combined, Sole, Contrasted, Inclusive, and Pure. 'The Fourfold Doctrines' are Tripitaka (Hinayana), Shared (Hinayana plus Mahayana), Distinctive (Mahayana only), and Complete.

The interlocking of these various components is complex but logical.[22] For example, the highly esteemed Flower Garland Sutra is deemed Sudden in that it is taught without any preparation. Its contents are Combined, i.e. it has the Distinctive and the Complete Doctrines, but it is not 'pure' because it does not contain the Deer Park teachings. Purity belongs to the *Lotus*, which alone teaches the Complete One Vehicle. The final Nirvana Sutra completes the *Lotus* by 'gathering up the remnant' and elaborating some of its points (Chappell 1983, 66).

Chih-i then lines up all the Buddhist systems and compares them to show that all roads lead to Buddhahood. We find statements such as this: 'The First Degree of Faith [in the Complete Doctrine] cuts off false views and reveals the Truth. It is equal to the First Attainment in the Tripitaka Doctrine; to the Stage of Those Who Have the Eight Endurances and the Stage of Insight in the Shared Doctrine; and to the First Abode of the Distinctive Doctrine. Having reached this stage, there is no retrogression' (153).

This is certainly dry reading, and helps explain why Chih-i is much praised and little read. Few readers know enough about the vocabulary used in the many systems to understand what he is talking about. Chih-i is a 'scholar's scholar'; he speaks to the specialist. Yet his aim was practical, not merely theoretical. In maintaining that all of Buddhism found its fulfilment in the Lotus Sutra, he wanted to show that by understanding that sutra, one could achieve Buddhahood in this very life. It was not necessary to pass through all the arduous stages of the various systems if one could go immediately to the final goal. This, he said, could be accomplished by means of correct meditation, which he called 'concentration and insight' or 'stopping and realizing' (*shikan* in Japanese): cutting off the extraneous and realizing insight into the world of reality.

When he founded his monastery at Mount Heavenly Terrace in 575, students flocked there from all over China. They saw in him not only the pillar of orthodoxy but also the daring proponent of something new. His was a new kind of Buddhism, a product of the native soil.

'Chih-i, the greatest Buddhist philosopher in China,' says Zen author D.T. Suzuki, 'was fully awake to the significance of *dhyana* (zen) as the means of attaining Enlightenment ... His idea was to carry out intellectual and spiritual exercises in perfect harmony, and not particularly to emphasize either one of the two . . . at the expense of the other' (*Zen Buddhism* 52).

It is to this 'perfect harmony' that we must now turn our attention.

Chapter 6

The Three Thousand Things _____

Chih-i (A.D. 538–97) did not consider himself the founder of a philosophical school but a successor to a long line of orthodox thinkers
stretching back through several Chinese masters to Kumarajiva, on
back to Nagarjuna in India, and finally to Shakyamuni himself. His
direct Chinese lineage came from Hui-wen, a meditation master who
lived earlier in the sixth century. Once when Hui-wen was reading a
work by Nagarjuna (now available in its translation by Kumarajiva) he
was suddenly struck by these lines:

> What is produced by causes,
> That, I say, is identical with Void.
> It is also identical with mere name.
> It is again the purport of the Middle Path. [23]

Shoko Watanabe, in his 'critical approach' to Japanese Buddhism,
claims that Hui-wen misunderstood the meaning of the original
Sanskrit text (*Japanese Buddhism* 148). However, that is beside the
point. Hui-wen was not simply following the Indian masters, but
opening up new vistas according to his own insight. He felt that at last
he had discovered what the Buddha meant by the Middle Path. Eagerly
he turned to the Wisdom Scriptures and their commentaries by
Nagarjuna, and soon found other passages which seemed to confirm
his thesis.

From this quiet beginning was to emerge a great philosophical
system, the pinnacle of all Buddhist thought. It has had its ups and
downs, sometimes gaining the highest approval and sometimes being
eclipsed by its rival, the monistic Flower Garland School of Kegon. This
school maintains that the phenomenal world is derived from the

noumenal world of the One Mind. It tends to be quietistic and individualistic. Tendai thought, as Hui-wen's system came to be called in Japan, rejects this genetic principle, saying that any emanation of the particular from the universal, of the phenomenal from the absolute, is an impossibility. The phenomenal world can only exist as being comprised in the absolute. Thus this system maintains dynamic tensions, insisting on the reality — the absolute value — of both the universal and the phenomenal. This makes it active and social. Today it is on the ascendancy once more.

The system was developed further by Hui-wen's successor, Hui-ssu (Hui-si, 514–77), and especially by the third patriarch of the T'ien-t'ai ('Heavenly Terrace') School, Chih-i. Saicho (Dengyo Daishi) introduced it to Japan in 805, and it soon came to dominate Japanese Buddhist thought. Nichiren accepted it as axiomatic, and it is his application of the system which is being expounded so vigorously around the world today.

The Perfectly Harmonious Threefold Truth, as the completed doctrine is called, means that the particular apart from the universal is unreal. the universal realizes its true nature in the particular, and the particular derives its meaning from the universal. The Middle Path unites these two aspects of reality. The universal apart from the particular is an abstraction. The particular apart from the universal is unreal (Soothill and Hodous, *Dictionary* 397). 'One is all and all is one' (Takakasu 134). The key lies in the middle term, 'is'.

Mystical philosophers, from Plato in the West to Shankara in the East, have tended to begin in dualism and end in monism. They begin by distinguishing between spirit and body, mind and matter, substance and accident, the One (principle) and the many (phenomena), good and evil, Nirvana and Samsara (the world of change), permanence (Law, Dharma) and change (facts, dharmas), God and the world. They usually end with mind-only (or its opposite, matter-only), spirit-only, substance-only, the One, Nirvana-only, or God becoming 'all in all'. (1 Cor. 15:28).

The Buddha neither began with dualism nor ended with monism, but his followers were not always able to resist the temptation to speak in these categories. Constantly reiterated statements that 'the world is neither real nor unreal, thus nor otherwise' (*Dharma Flower* XVI) are difficult to grasp. Mahayana Wisdom teachings tried to oppose the tendency towards monism with the formula 'Emptiness is Form and Form is Emptiness'. The reader, however, is left bewildered (which is exactly what the author intended), his mind swinging between the two apparent opposites. Nagarjuna, Madhyamika philosophy, and Zen stop at this point, insisting that the reader or practitioner cut the knot by himself (Cheng, *Empty Logic* 55 ff). Chih-i goes right ahead and cuts it for us.

It was Chih-i who brought Buddhist thought to its ultimate exposition. Reality, he said, is not two-fold but three-fold. Phenomena (*ke*) are, indeed, constantly changing, precisely because they have no permanent substance. They are empty, void (*ku*), just as the sutras have said. Therefore, the 'true state' (*jisso*) is *both* empty *and* transiently real. It is the Middle (*chu*).

For example, a cherry blossom is a temporary phenomenon; it blooms, filling the world with fragrance, and then is scattered by the winds of time. Nevertheless, by nature it is always a cherry blossom; it is not a horse. Oriental philosophers had been turning away from the cherry blossom, seeing it only as a temporary manifestation of an unchanging absolute. They had divided the world into two parts, one of which was visible but unreal (because it is constantly changing), and the other invisible but real (because it is the eternal principle). Others, reversing the two elements, claimed that only the visible was real; the invisible principle was a figment of human imagination.

Now the Heavenly Terrace thinkers pointed out that without void there could be no temporariness (everything would be permanent, which obviously it is not); and without temporariness, there would be no Principle. Change, itself, is principle. Each reveals the other in the third element: the middle.

Chih-i's philosophy can be visualized in an image which he uses in his major work, 'Great Concentration and Insight' (*Maha Shikan*): two intersecting lines (+). The horizontal line represents ever-changing phenomena arising from prior causes in the past and moving off into the future. The vertical line is emptiness, the ungrounded ground of being. They intersect at the middle.

We can easily understand the transient world of causes and effects. We see it around us and within us all the time. By deep thought or meditation we can understand the Void, too, but it is difficult to grasp the Middle where they intersect. The Middle is both temporariness and emptiness; it is also neither temporariness nor emptiness. It is 'thusness'.

'This conception of the Middle Way,' explains Tendai authority Bruno Petzold, 'like the conception of Emptiness, we meet already in the philosophy of Nagarjuna. But here the Middle Way is merely negatively formulated as neither actual existence nor non-existence. In the Tendai philosophy we have a positive definition of the Middle Way (*chu do*), as something that harmonizes Existence (*ke*) and Non-Existence (*ku*). The *Chu Ron* (Madhyamika Sastra) or "Treatise on the Middle", by Nagarjuna, merely rejects the two extremes of "being" and "non-being". The Tendai philosophy puts them into complete harmony and calls that which neither exists nor non-exists *Shin Nyo* or *Bhuta-tathata*, ie., the highest reality' ('Tendai Buddhism as Modern World View', 296).

'The ultimate truth,' explains Dr Takakusu, '. . . is Thusness (*Tathata*), not thisness (*tattva*). Thusness means the true state of things in themselves, the phenomenal world being the state of things manifested before us. The true state of things cannot be seen directly or immediately. We must see it in the phenomena which are ever changing and becoming. Thus the true state is dynamic. The phenomena themselves *are identical with* the true state of things' (137).

This philosophy of Chih-i is called *Jisso-ron* after the phrase in the Lotus Sutra, *Shoho jisso*, 'all things are the true state'. It is contrasted with the basic teaching of its rival school, the Flower Garland (*Kegon*), which is called *Engi-ron*: 'the doctrine of production by causation'. The latter is totalistic; the former is phenomenological.

Chih-i claimed that if one can fully grasp this dynamic three-fold nature of reality, one has attained enlightenment in this very life. But how is this to be done? How can we hold together in one thought the three truths? How can we avoid going off in one direction or another?

Chih-i thought that this could be done by right meditation. The student can realize void by stopping all discursive thinking while at the same time developing insight into temporariness. If he can keep a perfect balance between the two extremes, he realizes the Middle Path in his own life.

Still, this is easier said than done. It is unfortunate that Chih-i has left no works written in his own hand. All the books attributed to him are really lecture notes compiled by his students. In their present form they make rather dry reading and fail to reveal the vibrant personality of this man who attracted so many disciples. He was a one-to-one teacher. Meditation techniques are strictly personal; no one knew this better than he. The only treatise that may be his own writing is said to have been addressed to his brother, an army officer. It is called 'The Practice of Meditation for Beginners', and is an instruction manual complete with such details as where to live, what to eat, how to sit in meditation, how to prevent illness, how to avoid extraneous thoughts.[24]

Practising two types of meditation at once ('stopping' and 'realizing') is not easy. Edward Conze says in his *Buddhist Meditation* that 'there is even some tension between the two modes of approach, and in a given instant most people are forced to specialize in one' (17). In China most meditators prefer the method of no-thought ('stopping'), and this became the standard practice of the Meditation School of *Chan* (Zen). In India and southern Buddhist countries the way of insight (vipassana) is generally practised. Chih-i's 'three-in-one' method, however excellent in theory, is difficult for the majority of meditators to put into practice. Indeed, this very difficulty was to become the stimulus for new developments in Buddhism.

Nevertheless, Tendai adepts insist that it is the only legitimate way. According to Petzold:

> Meditation in the Tendai Sect is called *Shi kan* or Fixedness and Observation, and not *Zenna* or *Dhyana* as in the Zen Sect, and this difference in name denotes a difference in kind.

In the Zen school meditation is purely intuitive. We simply look into our heart, hoping to find there the Buddha. This intuition excludes all logical operations; it is anti-intellectual and closely related to Yoga, which has caustically been characterized as 'navel-contemplating'. Of course, the navel, on which the Indian ascetic fixes his regard, is not identical with the heart, into which the disciple of the Zen sect is looking, and the cosmic view of the one is different from that of the other. Nevertheless, the meditation of the Zen school, which rejects all sutras and relies entirely on discipline (besides the four holy truths) has certainly a great resemblance to the self-hypnosis of the Yogin in India and seems directly derived from it.

Quite different is the meditation or *Shi Kan* of the Tendai believer. He does not merely rely upon mystical intuition to find the Buddha in himself, but associates with it metaphysical speculation, and with the help of these 'two wheels' he tries to reach enlightenment. So the Tendai believer on the one hand does not pretend that the mind of the vulgar man, simply by intellectual analyzing and logical systematizing, can comprehend the highest truth, and on the other hand he rejects mere self-absorption. He combines both, holding that the one method which we can call the religious one, does not exclude the other which is evidently philosophical . . .. The Tendai school does not consider our momentary mind as an essentially inferior instrument or as a bar to true knowledge, but on the contrary relies upon this actual mind as an indispensable aid in gaining Anuttara Samyak Sambodhi or Unexcelled Perfect Enlightenment (298–99).

The creative reason in the nature of things and the thinking reason in the human mind are one and the same . . .. If any knowledge of the Absolute is possible at all, it must be based on the knowledge of ourselves, i.e., on our consciousness, which reaches from the abyss of the unconscious to the summit of the human mind, and which in self-contemplation, with its searching glance, penetrates the labyrinth of human nature . . .. As the methods of meditation are more developed in Tendai than in Zen, the effect of meditation will accordingly be greater in the former than in the latter. One who practices Tendai meditation considers consequently, that his own cognition of the Absolute is deeper and more comprehensive than that of the Zen sect practitioner of meditation, in other words that the union with the Absolute . . . reached by *Shi Kan* is more intimate than that accomplished by Dharma Daishi's *Dhyana*.

(300–1)

This concept of the ultimate reality in all passing phenomena has had enormous influence on Chinese and Japanese art. Every tree, every blade of grass, has cosmic significance. The phenomenal *is* the absolute. A sparrow perched on a rain pipe is more than a bird that appears momentarily and then flies away forever. It is also *jisso*, the true state. It does not symbolize the true state — it manifests the true state.

Chih-i's doctrine of *santai* (the three kinds of truth) has another corollary, one which was brought out more clearly later on by Nichiren. It comes very close to monotheism. Of course, it is not the same. God (*theos*) is conceived as being outside the cosmic process; he creates it 'out of nothing' and can destroy it at will. The Buddha, on the other hand, is the self-realization and self-expression of the cosmos. Since there is only one cosmic process, one Law (Dharma), so there can be only one self-realization of the one truth — one Eternal Original Buddha (*Hombutsu*). There may be buddhas by the billions, but they are all emanations of the Original Buddha. His unexcelled perfect Enlightenment (*Anuttara samyak sambodhi*) transcends the cosmos.

'Emanations', on the other hand, do not mean identity or the loss of personality. 'In Buddhism,' says Dr Takakusu, 'a Buddha, however remote in age or however great in origin, will be individual, for the perfection of knowledge and wisdom is the perfection of personality, and that is a Buddha' (149).

Petzold calls this 'panentheism' (*pan en theo* — all in God) and distinct from pantheism (*pan theo* — all is God). 'God is immanent in the world, but at the same time transcends it — God not being the sum or totality of actual things (i.e., the Universe). That is the teaching of Tendai properly understood . . . It is represented in modern German philosophy by thinkers like Lotze, Fechner, Wundt, and Eucken, and — in classical philosophy at the beginning of the last century — by Schelling, who held that the Absolute is identical with the universe, but the universe is not identical with the Absolute, the world existing inside the Absolute without however being simply identical with it' (291).

Chih-i found these ideas expressed in the *Dharma Flower*, and from it he drew his terminology. From it, too, he worked out an expression of how all things interpenetrate within the Triple Truth. He called this 'the three thousand things in a single life-thought' (*Ichinen sanzen*). By naming 'three thousand things', he did not mean to enumerate all the possible physical and mental combinations. This, indeed, had been done by other thinkers, particularly those of the several Abhidharma schools, who had drawn up long lists of such categories as the '84 types of consciousness in 4 classes and on 4 planes', or similar arrangements.[25] Chih-i's reckoning of 'three thousand' is symbolic, being deduced mostly from indications in Kumarajiva's translation of the *Dharma Flower*.

Buddhist tradition had long held that there are six basic types of living beings, or 'six worlds of existence'. They are human beings, animals, heavenly beings, furious spirits called *asuras*, hungry spirits, and beings in hell. Since the wheel of life rolls on endlessly, one can be reborn into any of these six worlds depending on one's thoughts and actions in this present life. In Buddhism nothing takes place by chance; everything has a prior cause. A greedy person becomes a hungry spirit; an animal-like being becomes an animal; a cruel person will suffer the cruelties of hell; one-pointed fanaticism leads to rebirth among the *asuras*; the average person is reborn as a human, rich or poor, handsome or ugly, healthy or sickly, depending on prior causes; a kindly or spiritually minded person will be reborn in one of the many heavens. In other words, each being creates his own destiny and manifests the world which he envisions in his innermost self. At the next stage he may rise higher or fall back to a lower realm. All life is in constant flux from moment to moment; there is nothing fixed or permanent about one's world of existence.[26]

Chi-i implicitly and Nichiren explicitly gave this scheme a psychological interpretation (Nichiren, *Kanjin Honzon Sho* 13). Chih-i added four more worlds to the six, making ten in all. These comprise the world of the Buddha's Disciples, of the solitary self-enlightened ones (*pratyekabuddhas*), of the altruistic Bodhisattvas, and of the perfectly enlightened Buddha. Nichiren taught that these worlds exist within all of us.

We can consider this classification in terms of motion. Life begins when the first tiny one-celled creature detaches itself from the primeval ooze and begins to float towards the light. It starts with self-mobility, but mobility of the most limited sort. This is the realm of Hell — minimum mobility. It is like being buried alive, unable to move freely.

The next step in the evolution of life is to the realm of Hunger. Primitive creatures are ruled by their appetites, but they are not entirely helpless like the denizens of Hell.

The realm of animality has even more mobility, sometimes to an extraordinary degree. But here fear plays an equally vital role, for the animal is both hunter and hunted.

A human being has more mobility than the animal. He is the hunter more often than the hunted. He can move about with relative impunity, especially in his mind. The more mobile he can become, the happier he believes himself to be. Early human history is the story of migrations and counter-migrations back and forth across the globe. It is also the story of restless minds attempting to push back the frontiers of ignorance. However, if we chain a man to a dungeon wall, he sinks back to animality, hunger, and hell.

Folk art depicts the *asuras*, denizens of the next world, as horsemen galloping wildly across the heavens. They are also said to reside in the billows which pound against the shore where the sea of the unconscious breaks into the physical world. Their unleashed frenzy can be terrifying; it can also be purifying. Spiritually the *asuras* are the critics and reformers, those who strike out boldly at what they consider wrong. From this they derive their satisfaction and sense of self-esteem.

However, there is an even higher happiness, a state of unlimited mobility. We call this Heaven; here there are no limits imposed by space. Even righteous anger is dissolved in pure well-being and joy. When we think of heaven, we imagine it inhabited by winged beings who can go wherever they like.

However, according to Buddhism, even Heaven has its limits; whatever has a beginning must also have an end. So Chih-i, following the *Dharma Flower*, postulated three even higher worlds, free not only from the limitations of space but to a greater or lesser extent from time as well.

The first of these higher mental worlds is that of the disciple. In a world of learning, time and space melt away in the thrill of discovery. A true student can forget all about poverty or hunger as long as he can penetrate further into the unknown. To him this is a happiness that far outdistances the passive rapture of Heaven. No monk ever feels that he has given up anything of value as long as he is learning something he did not know before. However, even learning has limits, and a monk will want to return to the world of common pleasures if he feels that he is no longer making progress. For this reason Buddhist monastic vows can be broken. Learning cannot be forced; it must spring from an inner drive.

All studies are solitary and therefore celibate. The student can be devoted only to his object of learning. Any student is a temporary monk; a monk is a dedicated student. Celibacy plays an important role in Buddhism, but it is not the only way, at least in Mahayana. If ever a monk feels that his learning has reached its limits, he should abandon monasticism and live like other men.

This was the course taken by Shinran (1173-1262), a Tendai monk who decided that nothing could be gained by studies. The grace of the Buddha, he said, is received by absolute trust in him, and learning only postpones the arising of such faith. According to Shinran, faith is the Buddha-nature, while doubt (necessary in any learning process) arises from the disruptive ego (Bloom, *Shinran* 39, 41). Since there can be no learning without some prior doubt, Shinran abandoned his studies and monasticism, got married, and raised a family. He was the first Japanese Buddhist teacher officially to do so, setting a precedent among his followers that has continued down to modern times. Branches of the sect which he founded have been headed by his descendants ever since.

Martin Luther also gave up monasticism and married once he decided that salvation was received by faith alone. Kumarajiva, on the other hand, was never at ease with women until late in his life, when most of his learning was behind him. Chih-i, an eternal student, remained celibate all his life. Nichiren saw nothing wrong with marriage in itself, but preferred celibacy, being a life-long student. 'The Buddha's thought is unfathomable,' he wrote. 'I, myself, have not yet realized it' (*Kembutsu Mirai Ki*).

Similar to learning is the next highest world, that of the solitary buddhas (*pratyekabuddhas*). This is the realm of self-realization. It might also be called the world of creativity, for it is inhabited especially by painters, dancers, writers, musicians, and other artists, who become completely absorbed in the task at hand. It can be realized by anyone who throws himself into some work and transforms it into a piece of art. At such times the ego is dissolved. Robert Bellah points out that during the Tokugawa Period in Japan (1600–1868), many Buddhists felt they could express Buddhism better by working at their profession than by retiring to a monastery (*Tokugawa Religion*, 119).

Like learning, self-realization involves celibacy. One cannot share one's self-realization with someone else; it is a solitary experience. There have been some who have held that self-realization need not be solitary. There is a 'left-handed path' that maintains that the same state of self-realization can be attained by two lovers in the sexual act. This is a basic idea of Tantrism. 'Without — in the true sense — the lustiness of sex,' says Alan Watts in *Nature, Man and Woman*, 'religion is joyless and abstract; without the self-abandonment of religion, sex is a mechanical masturbation' (204).

Most Buddhists, however, are suspicious of the 'left-handed path', and it never had a large following in China or Japan. Self-realization is normally achieved by oneself, alone.

Next we come to the noble world of the Bodhisattvas. The Bodhisattva seeks only to help others. He has maximum mobility because he is not fettered by cares for his own life. Being without pride, he is also without fear. The *Flower Dharma* praises many Bodhisattvas, but its real heroes are the Bodhisattvas from the Earth — men and women of flesh and blood, not supernatural beings. It is they who are entrusted with the task of disseminating to future generations the liberating Sutra.

The tenth and ultimate world is that of Buddha. It has no limits of any kind, penetrating all time and space. Words cannot describe it; it must be experienced to be known. 'Come and see,' said the Buddha. '*Ehipasiko!*'

The Bodhisattvas save from without; the Buddhas save from within. The Sutra says, 'The Buddhas have appeared in this world to purify all beings by having them open the treasury of the Buddha-wisdom which they are unaware of possessing within themselves. The Buddhas have appeared in this world to show the Buddha-wisdom to them. The Buddhas have appeared in this world to have them understand what the Buddha-wisdom is. The Buddhas have appeared in this world to lead them into the path of the Buddha-wisdom.'[27]

Since Chih-i teaches one-in-all and all-in-one, the ten worlds are not merely future states after death. They exist, all ten of them, in our everyday life. Each exists potentially in the other nine, so any one of them can emerge into being at any moment. I can be at work in an office, completely absorbed in what I am doing (the world of self-realization). An assistant blunders, I am annoyed (*asura* — anger). I scold him (animality). He looks hurt and confused, so I calm down (the normal human state) and try to help him (Bodhisattva). The boss enters. I stand up, wondering what to expect (animality again). He congratulates us for our good work. I am surprised and delighted (Heaven). And so it goes throughout the day. Sometimes I remain in one world for a relatively long time. At other times I pass abruptly from one world to another.

I can do this because none of the ten worlds is pure and whole in itself; they are not mutually exclusive. On the contrary, each of them contains all the others. There is an element of pain (Hell) in even the most ecstatic pleasure (Heaven), and vice versa. There is Heaven in Hunger (anticipating the joys of satisfaction) as well as Hell (the gnawing pains). Even motives may be mixed. A thief may rob a petrol station (animality) in order to feed his children (Bodhisattva). Each of the ten worlds contains all the others, at least potentially. Since Shakyamuni Buddha was a mortal living in all the other nine worlds, Buddhahood must exist in our mortal bodies as well. Therefore Buddhahood, too, is everywhere, even in Hell.

Nichiren reaches an exciting conclusion from this. It is commonly said that Shakyamuni Buddha is our ruler, teacher, and parent. But he could be none of these things if he were not first an ordinary mortal. We are not 'created' by the Buddha. On the contrary, it is we ordinary mortals who create him. Everything necessary to become a Buddha lies within our own selves. The difference between him and us is qualitative: he is enlightened, we are not (M.W. 1:90–91). We become Buddhas not by eradicating our deeply rooted desires but by changing the quality of our lives.

Thus the ten worlds have now multiplied to one hundred. In our predominant state of the moment all the others are included. This is true of all living beings. In addition there are ten factors, which differ from one being to another. These are listed in the *Dharma Flower* as 1) appearance, 2) self-identification or nature, 3) embodiment, 4) potency, 5) function 6) inner cause or motive, 7) environmental cause, 8) effects, 9) rewards or retributions, and 10) the unity of these nine factors, their inseparability. Our 100 states are really 10×10×10, or one thousand.

There are three more categories of basic importance; these are individual, social, and temporal/geographical. Individual differences were explained in the early Buddhist sutras. The ever-changing individual is made up of five 'bundles' (*skandhas*): material form, sense reactions (perception), mental ideas of what has been perceived (conception), volition, and consciousness. The first could be called

THE THREE THOUSAND THINGS

'physical' and the others 'spiritual', but all five depend on each other and interact.

Consciousness is the most complex category, and Buddhist thinkers subjected it to minute scrutiny centuries before the beginnings of modern psychology. Nine levels of consciousness are distinguished. The first six correspond to the six sense organs: sight, hearing, smell, taste, touch, and the conscious mind. The seventh is self-consciousness. Next comes the subconscious or 'store-consciousness' (*alaya-vijnana*). The subconscious stores memories of everything that has ever been perceived since beginningless time, buried in layer after layer. Modern psychotherapy seeks to delve down to this level. Finally, at the very basis, lies the pure consciousness of the Buddha (*amala-vijnana*).

Social differences, which make up the next category, are obvious. For example, it makes a tremendous difference to me whether I am born into a prosperous or a backward society, into a loving or a broken home.

Finally there are the differences of time and place. There is all the difference in the world between being in an automobile accident and observing it from the next car. A few seconds or a few inches can change my destiny.

For convenience, we can classify these differences into three groups, although in reality they are innumerable. Thus we have the symbolic counting of 10 worlds × 10 (their mutual possession) × 10 individual factors × 3 realms of existence, giving us the figure of three thousand. The three thousand simply stand for all possibilities. Since all is one and one is all, the three thousand possibilities exist in a single moment of thought. This is called the 'Three Thousand Things in One Mind' (*Ichinen Sanzen*), and it is the key to the practical side of Chih-i's philosophy. All possibilities for good or evil lie dormant within us. We do not have to train ourselves for aeons and aeons until we reach a higher state; that higher state is available right now. What we have to do is bring it out into the open.

Chih-i did not teach a kind of idealism, 'It's all in the mind'. This was the position of the rival Flower Garland (*Kegon*) and 'Consciousness Only' (*Yogachara*, Japanese *Hosso*) schools. He does not say that outer objects are only actual or potential contents of inner consciousness and have no real existence, but rather that both the individual mind and the surrounding world have objective existence and are involved in each other.

'I do not say: "One mind exists first and all things exist afterwards" — nor do I say: "All things exist first and one mind exists afterwards."' (*Maka Shikan*)

He rejects the subjective idealism of Asanga's *Yogacharya* school, which established the view that the world is only a reflex of the subjective mind. He also rejects the realism of the Sarvastivada school, which acknowledged the existence of matter and mind, but only as a plurality of so many phenomenal dharmas independent of each other. He acknowledges the existence of both the mind and the universe, harmonizing them and attributing to each an absolute reality.

Petzold summed up Chih-i's 'pantheistic realism' or 'panentheism' this way:

1. There is no real antithesis between subject and object.
2. The universe, being identical with the mind, is rational; and the mind, being identical with the universe, is irrational.
3. The essence of the mind is eternal like the universe, as there is nothing that precedes the mind or that has produced the mind.
4. The human mind is not a passive receptacle or a mere reflex of nature but, like nature, is active and creative.

(289)

Before leaving Chih-i, one other teaching should be mentioned, which, though not original to him is important to his system. This is the doctrine of the 'Three Bodies of the Buddha" (*Trikaya/Sanjin*). The term 'body' is not to be understood as body opposed to spirit. Rather it is a manifestation — the three properties of the one Buddha. The first is the manifested body (*Ojin*), the Buddha revealing himself in this world as the historical Shakyamuni. Shakyamuni, however, is the living embodiment of absolute truth, the Dharma-body (*Hosshin*). These two 'bodies' are linked in the Reward-body (*Hoshin*), in which the Buddha enjoys the fruits of perfect enlightenment. From our point of view the Manifest-body is the Buddha visible; the Reward-body is the Buddha intelligible; the Dharma-body is the Buddha as he truly is.

Notice how this corresponds with the Triple Truth, which lies at the heart of Chih-i's system. The Dharma-body is the Absolute, Void — potentially anything. The Reward-body is the Middle. The Manifest-body is the man Shakyamuni, who is born, grows, attains enlightenment, teaches, and passes away. The three are the one Buddha.

Both Chih-i and Nichiren stress that we ourselves are the three bodies of Buddha. Nichiren says that our physical body, consisting of the same elements which make up the cosmos, is the Dharma-body; our mind is the Reward-body; our behaviour is the Manifest-body. The innate Buddha-nature lies within us just as the flower is in the seed. In the same way as the flower needs the warming rays of the sun to bring it forth from potentiality into bloom, so our Buddha-nature requires an outside force to draw it into awakening. That force is the *Dharma Flower*.

The final sutra which Shakyamuni preached is called the Nirvana Sutra. Naturally Shakyamuni's followers were particularly concerned to record his last words and deeds, and there are several versions of his final weeks, both in the Hinayana and in the Manayana traditions. As a general rule, the Hinayana sutras, which closely resemble each other, concentrate on his final acts, while the Mahayana sutras, which introduce a great deal of new material, concentrate on his last teachings. Chih-i feels that these teachings are merely amplifications of what has been taught already in the *Dharma Flower*, clarifying various points.

One of these points is that the Buddha-nature is inherent in *all* beings; there are no such things as 'hopeless sinners' or 'eternal damnation'. This had already been discussed in the *Dharma Flower*. Another point is that Nirvana, which had previously been left undefined as 'beyond words', is now given positive qualities: permanence, bliss, personality, and purity. From being the supreme negation of life as we know it, it becomes the supreme affirmation of life in all its pristine glory.

When Chih-i died in 597 he had every reason to believe that his life's work had been an unqualified success. China was united under one emperor, a devout Buddhist, after nearly three centuries of division and warfare. The future of Chinese Buddhism seemed finally secure. Chih-i had contributed to the peace and stability of his country by uniting the many schools of the dynasty's religion into one coherent whole. He had raised Chinese scholarship to new levels, surpassing even the Indians. In demonstrating that all Buddhism was one, he had put back together what centuries of Indian and Chinese philosophers had fragmented. All that remained to be done by his successors was to copy down his lectures, set up schools around the country, and spread the word. His immediate successor, Chang-an (Zhang-an, 561–632), began to do just that.

However, drastic changes were on their way. A new dynasty, the T'ang swept into power in 618 and remained in power for three centuries (618–907). Since Buddhism in general and T'ien-t'ai Buddhism in particular had been so closely associated with the old regime, they now came under fire. Deprived of state support for its schools, T'ien-t'ai Buddhism went into a rapid decline. It might have died out completely had it not been that future scholars frequently rediscovered it and marvelled at its comprehensive grasp of Buddhist fundamentals. To this day it remains both the most scholarly and the most liberal school of the Great Vehicle.

Scholarly Buddhism, however, was forced by the T'ang Dynasty out of the capital and into isolated monasteries. It ceased to have any influence on public life, being replaced by Confucianism and neo-Confucianism, which firmly propped up the social order and culminated in the despotic emperors.[28] Buddhism became the refuge of the dispossessed, the outsiders. As such, it performed a useful function in Chinese life, but this was a secondary role, not the primary one that Chih-i had hoped for (Wright, *Buddhism in Chinese History* 106–7).

Under these circumstances the forms of Buddhism which survived best were anti-intellectual schools. Ch'an (Japanese, Zen) ridiculed 'dependence on words and letters', meaning any kind of scholarly study of the sutras. Chih-i had taught a two-sided meditation involving both reason and intuition. Ch'an used intuition only. It aimed at an immediate awareness of reality in which subjective and objective are transcended. It could not be taught by books or even by teachers.

Ch'an (meditation, from Sanskrit *dhyana*) was for a small, highly disciplined minority. The masses preferred devotion to Kuan Yin to gain benefits in this life or to the Buddha of Infinite Life (Amitayus) to gain benefits in the next. Neither of these types of Buddhism needed government support or contributed anything to the support of the state. Their function was strictly individual.

Chih-i's great vision of a unified Buddhism never quite died out, however. One of his greatest successors was Miao-lo (Miao-luo, 711–82), who is called the Reviver of T'ien-t'ai Buddhism.[29] He systematized the works of Chih-i. In fact, he identified with them so closely that sometimes it is difficult to determine how much comes from his master and how much from himself. Nichiren frequently quotes from Miao-lo, who was indirectly responsible for introducing Chih-i's teachings to Japan. His pupil Tao-sui taught them to Saicho (Dengyo Daishi), who founded the Tendai School of Japan.

It was in Japan that Chih-i's unified Buddhism came close to becoming a reality, and it is there we must next turn our attention.

Chapter 7

Buddhism in Japan ⸻

Buddhism came to Japan from Korea in the sixth century. It arrived under very different circumstances than it had in China. There it had trickled in under the opprobium of a despised foreign culture; it had to convince a society already ancient and sure of its superiority. In Japan, on the other hand, Buddhism came as the vehicle of that same ancient civilization, now doubly venerable in the traditions of both India and China. The Japanese court was impressed from the start, and in spite of violent opposition from a few feudal families, adopted it enthusiastically.

The arrival of Buddhism in Japan could be compared with the introduction of Christianity into Russia in the tenth century. Both began with the conversion of the reigning monarch and his immediate retainers. Both monarchs hoped that the political, cultural, philosophical, and ethical values of the new religion would have a civilizing effect upon their rude and barbarian people. Neither monarch adopted the new religion out of the blue, but only after the groundwork had been laid down by the previous couple of generations. Both were influenced by older women — Grand Prince Vladimir by his grandmother Olga, and Prince Shotoku by his aunt Suiko. Both princes adopted their new faith with sincerity and understanding.

Each religion arrived already hoary with tradition, complete with sacred scriptures in a mysterious foreign tongue, liturgical art and implements, gorgeously arrayed clergy, and foreign scholars, able to instruct on the fine points. Neither country dared tamper with the received scriptures, merely giving their own pronunciation to the foreign words. (Old Slavonic, of course, was much closer to Russian than Chinese was to Japanese; the latter two do not even belong to the same language family.) In both cases a thorough understanding of the new faith could be obtained only by an educated elite, who were trained by the foreign clergy.

There were differences, too. Grand Prince Vladimir had all the idols of the old faith thrown into the river. Prince Regent Shotoku was not disrespectful of the ancestral deities, but permitted them to go on living side by side with the new foreign gods. Vladimir received his religion direct from Constantinople, the capital of the Byzantine Empire. It was already a rigid orthodoxy that had shed all ancient heresies. Shotoku received his from small kingdoms in Korea, where there were various schools of thought. There was no one orthodox system. Instead, the 'six schools of Nara', as they came to be called, settled down side by side, sometimes in the same temples. Educated scholars were expected to be acquainted with all six of them.

Like Vladimir of Russia, Prince Shotoku is looked back to as the real father of his country, the ideal monarch who brought the land out of the darkness of paganism and into the light of civilization. However, Shotoku was more than just a patron of Buddhism. He became a student and then a teacher, writing commentaries and delivering lectures. Although he was not familiar with the works of Chih-i, he wrote seven commentaries, including four on the *Dharma Flower*. In 594 he proclaimed Buddhism the official state religion. There was bitter resentment from some feudal lords, but in the end the new faith prevailed.

From the very beginning there was a close connection between the shamanistic emperor, whose prayers could bring rain in times of drought and safety in times of storms, and the new faith, which was highly regarded for its magical powers.[30] By the end of the Nara period (794) church and state were thoroughly intertwined. Religion was a department of the state, and its purpose was to protect the state. The government decided who was to be ordained to the clergy and even which school of thought he was to study. The monks, as often as not, were aristocrats with political ambitions of their own.

It was partly to break the power of the Nara clergy that the capital was moved from Nara to Kyoto. The emperor wanted not only a purer form of Buddhism but also a more docile one. He sent two outstanding scholars to China to find out how things were done there. The two men met at the seaport but sailed on separate ships, studied under different masters, and returned with different types of Buddhism.

These were the days of the T'ang Dynasty in China. Buddhism had been dispossessed and was no longer a department of the state. Sometimes its very existence was in peril, but at least it was free, for the most part, to run its own house. Thus, instead of encountering a docile Buddhism in China, the two Japanese scholars found models which had been toughened by the fires of persecutions.

The first of the two visiting scholars was Saicho (767–822), who was later called Dengyo Daishi. He was a devout student of the *Dharma*

Flower and had already been introduced to some works of Chih-i. Instead of staying at the corrupt monasteries in Nara, he had withdrawn to the mountains to practise meditation. Paul Groner in his exhaustive study, *Saicho: The Establishment of the Japanese Tendai School*, points out that this virtually unprecedented step deprived him of any hope of advancement within the clerical bureaucracy. However, Saicho was not interested in such things. In the mountains he made his famous five vows:

1. So long as I have not attained the stage where my six faculties are pure, I will not venture out into the world.
2. So long as I have not realized the absolute, I will not acquire any special skills or arts (such as medicine, divination, and calligraphy).
3. So long as I have not kept all of the precepts purely, I will not participate in any lay donor's Buddhist meeting.
4. So long as I have not attained wisdom, I will not participate in any worldly affairs unless it be to benefit others.
5. May any merit from my practice in the past, present, or future be given not to me, but to all sentient beings so that they may attain supreme enlightenment.

(28-9).

When he arrived in China, he knew just where he wanted to go — to T'ien-t'ai, the Heavenly Terrace. There he diligently copied manuscripts by Chih-i, Miao-lo, and other T'ien-t'ai masters. Other forms of Buddhism had arisen in China since the days of Chih-i: esotericism, Zen, and Pure Land. Saicho wanted to find out all he could about them, too. He studied meditation under a Zen master and was initiated into a branch of esotericism. Finally he collected everything he could about Mahayana monastic rules. After only a year in China (804-5), he returned home laden with books, and then set up a study centre on Mount Hiei, not far from the new capital in Kyoto.

Saicho believed that scholarship must serve the nation, and that learning must be eclectic and open to new ideas or discoveries. The search for truth outweighs the obligations of sectarianism. A teacher must teach what he believes to be true even if such teachings are not found in his own sect. And if he finds his own sect, or even his own personal views, to be in error, he should come right out and say so. Partisanship has no place in real scholarship.

When the second envoy, Kukai, returned from China the following year, Saicho was delighted. He did not hesitate to turn to the younger man to see if there was anything more he could learn. He borrowed books from Kukai, sent pupils to learn from him, and kept a lively correspondence with him. Since Kukai had specialized in esotericism, Saicho even accepted initiation from him — an action which implied that Kukai knew some things which he did not.

Gradually it became apparent, however, that the two men had chosen irreconcilable paths. Saicho had preferred the open way; to him all wisdom was good irrespective of its place of origin. Kukai had learned a secret line of transmission; it could be passed on only from master to pupil in strictest confidence. Sooner or later a pupil would have to choose which method he preferred, and some of Saicho's favourite students were so intrigued by the mysteries of esotericism that they abandoned their master and resorted to Kukai instead. These defections must have hurt Saicho, who was having trouble getting students to say at his chilly mountain temple, where they were subjected to a strenuous course of training lasting 12 years.

Both Saicho and Kukai had to have support from the Emperor in order to continue their work, for the court still controlled Buddhism with an iron hand. The Emperor was tired of the political intrigues coming out of the old Nara sects, and he was glad to welcome these new up-to-date sects, the Tendai of Saicho and the Shingon ('True Word') of Kukai.[31] He gave them a status equal to that of the old sects and refused to permit the Nara sects to build temples in the new capital.

For Kukai this was sufficient; all he needed was a place of his own where he could train his disciples and practise his esoteric rites. He asked for and received permission to build a temple on distant Mt. Koya. Then he was requested to come to the capital and supervise the construction of what was to be one of the two temples 'protecting the nation'. He did so, but only on condition that this temple not be eclectic, like those of Nara, but would teach and practise his esotericism exclusively.

'This was revolutionary,' comments Yoshito Hakeda. 'In the great temples of Nara students belonging to many sects were allowed to stay in the same temple and study together, and on Mt. Hiei [under Saicho], where all the monks belonged to the Tendai sect, there were students of both Exoteric and Esoteric practices. Kukai . . . had now succeeded in establishing his religion on a solid institutional basis by state authorization' (*Kukai* 55).

Kukai (or Kobo Daishi, as he was called posthumously) could accomplish so much partly because the time was ripe and partly because of his extraordinary personality. Saicho may have impressed people with his scholarship, but Kukai fascinated them. He was famed as a saint, miracle-worker, inventor of Japanese script, authority on Sanskrit and Chinese, painter, and master builder. He was believed to know everything and be able to do anything. To this day his followers believe that his body remains uncorrupted on Mt. Koya, awaiting the day when he will return to life.

Kukai's secret system of Buddhism can be traced back to India of the sixth or seventh century. At that time, Hinduism was emerging as the dominant religion of the country, replacing Buddhism. In the ferment of new and old faiths, there emerged a new school — or most likely, re-emerged an old school, the ancient 'Great Mother' cult of the pre-Indo-European natives. Now considerably more sophisticated after centuries of contact with Buddhism and Hinduism, it assumed elements of both and claimed to transcend them both in profundity. Known as Tantra, it proclaimed itself 'too hot to handle' lightly, and suitable only for initiated adepts. Its published works are full of cryptic symbolism understandable to the insider but deliberately confusing to the outsider.[32]

It is believed that during the seventh century Tantra divided into two streams of transmission. One stream moved up to Nepal, Tibet, and Mongolia, and down to Java. The Tibetan forms (there are four major branches) are the best known in the West. Since the Chinese conquest of Tibet in 1950 they have been brought to India, Europe, and America by Tibetan refugees, who are anxious to pass them on to worthy recipients.[33]

The other stream of transmission was carried to China by three Indian teachers during the August T'ang period (637–735). The last of the three, Amoghavajra, enjoyed much prestige at the imperial court, where he tutored three successive emperors. He transmitted his secret doctrines to the Chinese master, Hui-kuo, who in turn initiated Kukai. Hui-kuo had already been initiated into the system of the second Indian master, so he and his pupil Kukai could claim to have received the whole of esotericism.

It is curious that Hui-kuo should have decided to pass the secret transmission on to a foreigner rather than to another Chinese. Kukai says that he just 'happened' to meet the master Hui-kuo. As soon as Hui-kuo saw him, he smiled joyfully and said, 'I knew you would come! I have been waiting for such a long time. What pleasure it gives me to look on you today at last! My life is drawing to an end, and until you came there was no one to whom I could transmit the teachings' (Hakeda, *Kukai* 31–2).

Saicho, too, was anxious to learn the secret teachings, and while he was in China, he received some sort of an initiation. It must have been an elementary introduction, however, for when he got back to Japan, he went to Kukai for two more initiations. However, Kukai would not confer the highest initiation upon him unless he would become his disciple. This Saicho could not do.

After Saicho's death, his pupil Ennin went to China to learn the secret doctrines for himself. By then conditions had changed, and Buddhism was once more being persecuted. Esoteric masters had gone into hiding; Ennin had difficulty finding anyone qualified to initiate him. After many adventures he managed to get the necessary initiations and smuggle esoteric texts and implements out of China to Japan. In this way Saicho's Tendai sect acquired an esoteric transmission of its own to compete with that of the rival Shingon sect of Kukai.[34]

While Kukai was enjoying phenomenal success introducing his colourful new style of Buddhism, Saicho was having a harder time. He, too, received permission to train candidates for the priesthood at his retreat on Mount Hiei, not far from the capital. But he wanted more than that. Basing his position on the *Dharma Flower* and Tendai philosophy, he wanted to unify all of Japanese Buddhism under the umbrella of pure Mahayana and free it from the state bureaucracy. However, he had to tread gently so as not to offend the state which was sponsoring him.

Saicho had to fight his battles on two fronts — three, if we include his unfortunate misunderstanding with Kukai (he gradually dropped out of this debate, however). On the one hand, he had to demonstrate the superiority of the 'pure' Mahayana of Tendai over the 'provisional' Mahayana of the six sects of Nara. At the same time he had to convince the state bureaucracy, which was closely allied to the Nara sects, to release its iron grip on the Buddhist clergy.

Saicho called the Nara sects 'provisional' for two reasons. First, they did not teach the *Dharma Flower* doctrine that all living beings participate in the universal Buddha-nature. Secondly, they ordained monks according to Hinayana, not Mahayana precepts. Since the Hinayana precepts were based on entirely different philosophical suppositions (knowing nothing of the universal Buddha-nature), this ordination, he maintained, was basically wrong.

He had challenged the religious establishment at the seat of its power: its selection and control of the clergy. His challenge was soon taken up by the greatest theologian of the old order, Tokuitsu of the Hosso school. Hosso, which by then had nearly eclipsed the other Nara schools in influence, had a venerable tradition going back to Nalanda University in India, where it had been called Yogacara, and boasted such eminent forefathers as the philosopher Vasubandhu and the translator Paramartha, who was second only to Kumarajiva for the quantity and quality of his works. Holding that reality was caused by mere ideation, it had made monumental contributions to Mahayana thought. In the learned Tokuitsu it had a worthy champion.

At issue was the question of the universal Buddha-nature. Tokuitsu maintained that unless one had the 'seeds' of Buddhahood in one's subconscious mind (the eighth consciousness), one could not possibly become a Buddha. Saicho (and esotericism and the Flower Garland School [*Kegon*] along with him) held that Buddhahood resides not in the subconscious, but in the 'pure consciousness' of the Buddha — the ninth consciousness. It is universal (*Ichishima*, 'Lotus Debates').

The debate, which lasted for years and was carried on by correspondence and documents submitted to the court for arbitration, stirred enormous interest. Paul Groner calls it 'one of the high points in the intellectual history of Japanese Buddhism' (93). At issue was the very nature of man. Both scholars quoted copious sources in defence of their arguments, but Saicho, who knew more about Hosso than Tokuitsu did about Tendai, was able to turn Tokuitsu's sources against him. Although Tokuitsu never admitted defeat (the debate was still going on when Saicho died), it was clear that he had met his match. It was Saicho's Tendai school which would dominate Japanese Buddhism for the next four centuries, while the Hosso school slipped slowly into the background.

By winning his theoretical argument Saicho was able to win his practical argument, too. The Six Sects of Nara were only provisionally Mahayana. Real Mahayana recognized the universal Buddha-nature, and real Mahayana ordinations should be controlled by Mahayana clergy (not court bureaucrats) using Mahayana precepts. Unfortunately, he never knew that he had won his greatest and final victory. When he died on 4 June 822, the issue was still under consideration at court. The decision in his favour came one week later.

The most important consequence of Saicho's work was that in maintaining the universal Buddha-nature, he brought Buddhism out of the narrow aristocratic court circles and made it available to everyone. He wanted his school on Mt. Hiei to train scholars who would serve the nation, and that meant sending graduates out into the provinces. These graduates, according to Saicho's plan, were trained in all the philosophical systems of the Great Vehicle and in practical skills which could be put to good use in remote parts of the country. Tendai became the nation's leading school of Buddhist arts and sciences, while esotericism became the most popular practice.

Most of Saicho's successors on Mount Hiei considered the *Dharma Flower* philosophy and esoteric practice to be two sides of the same coin. They used esotericism to answer the old nagging question, 'How does one put the *Dharma Flower* into actual practice? We agree that it is the highest truth, but what are we supposed to *do* about it?' The answer seemed to be, 'Believe the *Dharma Flower*, but practise the esoteric rites of body (gestures), mouth (sacred mantras), and mind.'

These mystical rites appealed to commoners as much as they did to the court aristocrats, especially now that Saicho and Kukai had cleared the way for anyone to enter into them. There took place no revolution, no sudden democratization of what was still a highly intellectual and hieratic religion. But the theoretical groundwork had been laid, and when the old social order did finally break down around the end of the twelfth century, the stage was set for a new type of truly democratic reforms.

During the next period of Japanese Buddhism, called the Heian Period (794–1185), Tendai almost realized the dream of Chih-i of a unified Buddhism. Its only rival was esoteric Shingon, which continued to remain aloof. But once Tendai had acquired an esoteric transmission of its own, it seemed to have everything. It became the watershed of Japanese Buddhism. Nearly all the founders of the 'new Buddhism' that was to follow began their careers by studying Tendai Buddhism at Mt. Hiei.

But Tendai had its Achilles' heel. It is often said that Tendai became so broad-minded and so all-inclusive that it simply disintegrated under its own weight. It lost its central dynamic. Nichiren, himself a Tendai monk, accused Mt. Hiei of having become so engrossed in esotericism and other extraneous practices that it forgot all about Chih-i and Saicho. This was probably true, but why did it happen?

Tendai was launched by Saicho with the motto, 'Buddhahood in this very body'. It criticized other sects for taking aeons and aeons to achieve Buddhahood. Tendai (and Shingon) taught the direct path, which promised results in this lifetime. Now where were those results? What was the meaning of 'to achieve Buddhahood'?

Tendai monks in Japan wrote letters to their T'ien-t'ai brethren in China, asking for clarification. The Chinese answered with more theories. Impatiently, the Japanese wrote back. They knew the theories; they wanted concrete methods. Failing to get what they wanted, they turned to esotericism.

Another new practice grew in popularity in the monasteries, a practice which could be undertaken by laymen, as well. This consisted of calling on the name of Amida Buddha, *Namu Amida-butsu*. Amida had promised that if mortals were too sinful to achieve enlightenment in this life, he would welcome them into his paradise after death. There enlightenment was assured. With most monks, *Nembutsu* (calling Buddha's name) was one practice among many. The Tendai Patriarch Ennin, the same man who travelled to China in search of initiation into esotericism, used to practise *Nembutsu*, himself. He even set it to music. But this was not his sole practice. He and others used it only to prepare for a happy death and rebirth in the next world. What was new after his times was that some monks began to make it their only practice. Finally the Tendai monk Honen (1133–1212) declared that any other practice but *Nembutsu* was totally useless. 'Discard, close, ignore and abandon' all the sutras, he said. For such a shocking proposition, he was expelled from the Tendai Brotherhood and exiled by the emperor. This just gave him the chance to preach to the common people, and his new Buddhism, called Pure Land (*Jodo*), began to spread rapidly.

The dilemma (or impatience) of Tendai monks at this time can be illustrated by the career of Shinran (1173–1262), who founded the True Pure Land Sect (*Jodo Shinshu*). As a young man he suffered agonies of religious doubt. In a dream, he had been told that he would die at the age of 30. He tried desperately to achieve enlightenment before his thirtieth birthday. By the time he was 29, he felt that he had failed; he was no closer to enlightenment then than he was the day he began. At this point someone advised him to visit Honen.

Honen told Shinran that the sun shines whether we want it to or not.

It is the sun's business to shine; it is for us to be shone upon. It is the Buddha's business to save; it is for us to be saved. When he heard these words, Shinran felt his inner doubts melt away. From that day on he abandoned any kind of self-effort, relying enitrely on the 'Other Power' of the compassionate Buddha. For him life meant not to shine, but to be shone upon (Yamamoto, *The Other Power* 19).

'As for me, Shinran, there is nothing left except to believe under the guidance of the teaching of the Venerable Master (Honen): "We are saved by Amida Buddha merely through reciting the Nembutsu alone." For myself, I do not know whether the Nembutsu be truly the cause of Rebirth in the Pure Land, or whether it be the karma to make us sink into the bottomless pit. Even if I am deceived by the Venerable Honen, I shall never regret reciting the Nembutsu and then falling into the bottomless pit. For if I could attain Buddhahood by any other practice and then fall into the pit, then I might feel regret at having been deceived. But since I am capable of no other practice whatsoever, the pit will surely be my dwelling, anyway . . . .. This is my faith; but it is left entirely to your choice to accept the Nembutsu or reject it' (*Tannisho*, II).

Although Shinran always insisted on his fidelity to his teacher Honen, there were differences between the two that became more apparent in the second generation. Honen advocated one practice: chanting the Name of Amida (*nembutsu*). Shinran advocated no practice. He also chanted the name, but did it, he said, only out of gratitude and not because he expected any benefits from it. Salvation is the work of Buddha, not us. So today there are two main branches of Pure Land or *Nembutsu* Buddhism: The original sect of Honen, which is called 'Pure Land' (*Jodo*) and that of Shinran, which calls itself 'True Pure Land' (*Jodo Shin Shu* or simply *Shin*).

It is a characteristic of Pure Land teaching that it appeals more to people in their middle and late years than to young people. In Christianity religious conversion frequently comes during the emotion-packed years of adolescence, prodded by the first stirrings of a sense of guilt. But 'sin' and 'guilt' are not terms in the normal Buddhist vocabulary. Ignorance, not sin, is regarded as the primeval ill, and most young people feel it is their parents who are ignorant — certainly not themselves! In the East, if young people are attracted to religion at all, they usually prefer an active type, which gives them something to do and promises concrete results. Faith in the Pure Land is awakened by a sense of failure, which so often comes during middle-life.

It is true that Shinran was only 29 at the time of his conversion, but he believed that his life was nearing its end. Most of the famous Pure Land teachers were older men when they converted. Doshaku was 40, Donran was 50, Honen was 52. Even D.T. Suzuki, the famous Zen exponent, became more and more interested in the Pure Land during his later years. The older we get, the more aware we become of the approaching end of our life and how little we have improved spiritually over the years. In despair, we turn to the 'Other Power' to take the load of responsibility off our backs.

Shinran defined his religion as non-practice and non-goodness. 'It is non-practice [for its devotee] because he does not practice it at his own discretion, and it is non-goodness because he does not create it at his own discretion. All is through Amida's power alone, not through our own power, which is vain' (*Tannisho* VIII).

Non-practice means non-practice of anything. Even elementary good deeds are of no avail. In fact, according to Shinran, it is easier for an evil man to enter the Pure Land than it is for one who does good and relies on his goodness. 'If even a good man attains Rebirth in the Pure Land, then how much easier should it be for an evildoer' (*Tannisho* III). All ordinary morality is inverted; all that matters is the unlimited compassion of the Buddha.

Of course, such a radical departure from traditional Buddhism led to unexpected results — sometimes bizarre, sometimes bloody. For a while the Shin Sect was dominated by an infallible clergy, 'reincarnations of Amida', who could decide who would go to the Pure Land and who would not.[35] An opposite tendency took place among some peasant followers, who believed that Amida's Universal Vow had broken down all social barriers. They took up arms against the feudal system, and for over a century held the samurai warriors at bay. They were finally crushed at Osaka in 1580 by the military dictator Oda Nobunaga.

The radical faith of Honen and Shinran had an important consequence which they could not have foreseen: their Buddhism, and eventually nearly all of Japanese Buddhism along with it, became concerned primarily with life after death, and in the popular mind came to be associated with funerals and memorial services.

They (Shinran in particular) had abolished the distinction between clergy and laity, a qualitative distinction which had existed from the beginning. In primitive Buddhism the laity had been expected to conform to the five basic moral precepts; the monks of the Sangha, on the other hand, accepted 250 precepts, including the vow of chastity. This made them qualitatively different from the laity and gave them a certain mystique. To 'accept the precepts' meant more than just agreeing to live an austere life; it implied the ability to do so.

In esotericism, too, even though laymen could participate in some of the mystic rites, there was a qualitative distinction between the initiated and the uninitiated. Now Shinran abolished all precepts. Only one thing mattered — faith. A layman could have the same saving faith as a priest; there was no basic difference between them. Shinran used to refer to himself as neither a monk nor a layman. He was not a monk because he married and raised a family; he was not a layman because he devoted all his life to religion.

Since the clergy no longer had any special status, how were they going to make a living? The solution was to charge for funerals and memorial services. To Shinran's way of thinking, there was no justification for memorial services of any kind. 'I, Shinran, have never even once invoked the Nembutsu in the feeling of filial piety for my parents' (*Tannisho* V). Any self-effort, even praying for one's parents, is useless. All depends on Amida's grace. Nevertheless, his followers developed a lengthy series of memorial services for the deceased — 21 of them extending up to the fiftieth year after death — and these became the primary source of income for the clergy.

Even though there was no longer a spiritual distinction between clergy and laity, there still remained a practical one. The clergy could read and write Chinese; this mean that they could read and recite the sacred texts and inscribe Buddhist names for the deceased. In Shin Buddhism this gave them a power greater than they had enjoyed before. If they named the deceased (or the living) before Amida, that soul would enter Paradise; if they deleted a name, that soul was lost. Such an extreme position was eventually rejected by the majority of Shin Buddhists, but it prevailed long enough to establish the importance of having the priests inscribe Buddhist names for the deceased and recite sutras in their memory.

Other sects began doing the same thing, and even the proud old centres of Tendai and Shingon had to depend on memorial donations once they lost the support of the nobility, who had been their protectors, after the pillage and destruction of their temples during the civil wars after the Heian Period. (Watanabe 1980, 98).

In Shin Buddhism (and in Nichiren, as we shall see), the term Sangha no longer means an exclusive brotherhood of monks, but the community of all believers, men, women, and children. A community, however, requires rules of morality, and Shin Buddhism eventually had to make its own. This was done by distinguishing between absolute truth (sole reliance on the grace of Amida) and Secular Truth ('to obey the laws of morality and to be loyal to one's country').[36] The reorganization of Shin Buddhism into a disciplined organization was largely the work of Shinran's greatest successor, Rennyo (1415–99), who tirelessly went from place to place gathering up the scattered flock and bringing them under the rule of his head temple in Kyoto. Although Shin Buddheism, like all branches of Japanese Buddhism, is divided into many sects, the one which can be traced back to Rennyo and Shinran is today the largest and best organized.

If Shinran's version of Buddhism is really the 'final solution', as its adherents claim, it arrives at its position only by side-stepping one of the most important teachings of the *Dharma Flower*, namely, that all living things contain the Buddha-nature. Shin Buddhism specifically repudiates it. According to Karl Philipp Eidmann, a leading American exponent of Shin Buddhism, 'The ordinary human being has no hope of escape from anxiety, frustration, and suffering. Man's nature is made up of desires. He has no inner nature, no soul destined to attain freedom from suffering. Man has no power within himself to attain to Buddhahood. The only power within man is the power of his passions, his desires, his anxieties. He has no innate nature which will manifest itself as enlightenment at some future time' (*The Unimpeded Single Way*, 3).

It was this pessimistic side of Pure Land teachings which was to arouse Nichiren to his vigorous counter-attack.

A Footnote on Zen

So much has been written on Zen in the past 30 or 40 years that one more book or even one more chapter could not add much that is new. For a sect which insists it is 'not dependent on words or letters', Zen has put quite a few of them into print. In Zen it is said that 'those who know, don't speak; and those who speak, don't know'. This should be warning enough for us to maintain a 'noble silence'.

Zen, like esotericism, must be passed on individually from master to pupil. It is not a mass religion except in its externals. A book can describe what Zen looks like, but it cannot reveal what Zen is.

Zen has so charmed the West by its unique blend of piety and irreverence that we forget that not all Buddhists give it unqualified approval. In his introduction to Suzuki's *On Indian Mahayana Buddhism*, Edward Conze points out some of its dangers, especially for Westerners:

Although Zen as an essentially non-discursive response to reality has never set out to formulate a philosophy of its own, it nevertheless everywhere presupposes and takes for granted the philosophy formulated by the Mahayana sutras . . . If [Suzuki] is to be blamed for anything, it is an insufficient awareness of the aridity of the desert into which he transplanted his lovely azalea tree. For what he unsuspectedly did was to feed an Eastern form of spirituality into a predominantly ex-Protestant environment which, having lost touch with spiritual tradition, gravitated inevitably toward a self-assertive nihilism.

Zen was designed to operate within emptiness (Void). On its journey West it has been transferred into a vacuum. Let us recollect what Zen in the East took for granted as its antecedents, basis, and continuing background: a long and unbroken tradition of spiritual 'know-how'; firm and unquestioned metaphysical beliefs, and not just disbelief in everything; a superabundance of scriptures and images; a definite discipline supervised by authoritative persons; insistence on right livelihood and an austere life for all exponents of the Dharma; and a strong Sangha composed of thousands of mature and experienced monks housed in thousands of temples, who could keep deviations from Buddhist principles within narrow bounds.

What Zen wanted to do, Dr Conze points out, was to cut through the trappings and reveal the core, not replace the core.

It is a fundamental error if these denunciations [of the trappings] are mistaken for a desire to altogether abolish traditional spiritual practices. Suzuki in faraway Japan could not possibly have foreseen it. Likewise, when he condemned the intellect as inhibiting our original spontaneity, Suzuki took it for granted that once the intellect is eliminated the Tao will take over. He was relatively unfamiliar with Western irrationalist philosophy, where the elimination of the intellect makes room for nothing more sublime than the uninhibited assertion of self-willed instincts, and where everything is left where it was before. When he spoke of spontaneity, he meant the spontaneity of sages, and not that of unreformed worldlings.

(8–10)

Conze's criticism of Zen in the West today is similar to Nichiren's criticism of Zen in Japan 700 years ago. He, too, felt that by making fun of the sutras, Zen was opening the door to 'nothing more sublime than the uninhibited assertion of self-willed instincts'. He saw that the spiritual values extolled by Conze had, in fact, broken down and lost their authority. Under such circumstances, Zen was dangerous.

His warning, however, fell on deaf ears. The Kamakura warlords, anxious to assert their independence from the old order at Kyoto, were encouraging the rise of new sects, just as the emperors had done at the beginning of the Heian Period. The Great Buddha of Kamakura, perhaps the most famous piece of art in all Japan, was set up to outshine the Great Buddha of Nara and promote the veneration of Amida in defiance of the ecclesiastical authorities in the capital — the same authorities who had exiled Honen. Hojo Tokiyori of Kamakura, the real ruler of Japan, was fascinated by Zen. Its stern discipline appealed to rough Samurai warriors such as himself, and helped prepare them for death on the battlefield. The Pure Land of Amida had a similar appeal, advocating an easy practice of reciting the Sacred name for rebirth in paradise after death in combat. In 1253 Tokiyori sponsored a Chinese Zen master and built for him the first official Zen temple in Japan.[37] Thereafter Zen temples sprang up rapidly, and many older temples switched their allegiance to the new cult of the Samurais.

Just as the elaborated ceremonies and subtle metaphysics of Shingon and Tendai esotericism had satisfied the courtly aristocrats of the previous age, so the austere directness of Zen or the simple chanting of Nembutsu satisfied the rough warriors and down-trodden peasants during the period of warlords and civil wars. When Nichiren called for a return to the old values, he was shouting against the winds of change. Few people heard him. His problem became, therefore, how to preserve the tried and true while adapting it to the changing times. His solution proved viable, not only for the thirteenth century, but for the even more rapidly changing twentieth century as well.

Chapter 8

The Son of a Fisherman __

Nichiren was born on 16 February 1222 at Kominato, Tojo village, in the province of Awa (now part of Chiba Prefecture, east of modern Tokyo). Unlike the other great teachers we have discussed, he did not come from a wealthy or prominent family. Some say that his parents were from the Samurai class, but having lost everything in the civil wars of the period, had been reduced to poverty. If this is so, Nichiren never mentions it; perhaps some later historian wanted to raise his status a bit by giving him an aristocratic lineage. On the other hand, there are some vague references to rich relatives in Shimosa, who might have paid some of his bills during his student days. [38] Family relationships, however, were more of a hindrance than a help for him, for his family was held in contempt by the local lords of the area.

We know for certain that his father made his living by fishing, and no doubt the young Zen'nichimaro, as the boy was first called, had to work on his father's boat as soon as he was old enough to help. Today the Great Head Temple of Tanjo-ji stands by the seashore along the narrow strip of land between the Pacific Ocean and a row of hills which rises abruptly behind it, and marks the spot where the great prophet was born. But the actual house of his father was long ago washed away by tidal waves and buried beneath the sea. Boatmen point out the site to tourists, who peer through the transparent blue waters down to the rocky bottom, where lotus blossoms are said to have bloomed on the day Nichiren was born.

Nichiren was never ashamed of his humble and even despised origin. He used to refer to himself as a *sudra*, the Indian name for someone from the lowest social class. He called his area 'backward' but strategically located near the geographical centre of Japan. He loved his little village of fishermen's huts, and referred to it with nostalgia during his later wanderings. He once called it 'the original abode of the Sun-goddess', for it was there that the sun first shone when it rose from the sea in the east. 'She is, indeed, the loving mother of the people of this country. There must be some remote and mysterious connection with my life, that I, Nichiren, was born in that province' (Anesaki *Nichiren the Buddhist Prophet* 9).

A fisherman needs the help of hard-working sons. This fisherman, however, saw an unusual talent in his fourth son, Zen'nichimaro, and sent him off to a nearby temple school at the age of 11. The temple was called Seicho-ji, the Temple of Clear Luminosity, or Kiyosumi-dera, after the mountain where it is located. It was small but venerable, dating back to 771. It belonged to the Tendai Sect, and like most Tendai temples of the time, specialized in esotericism and chanting the Nembutsu. The young Nichiren was thoroughly trained in these practices; later he would repudiate them both.

When he was 15 he took the vows of a Tendai monk, cutting his hair as Shakyamuni had done about 2000 years before, and taking a new name, Rencho ('Eternal Lotus'). Although in later years he was to see no special value in celibacy as such, he never broke his vow the way Shinran did. Neither did he abandon his studies in despair, even though at one time they almost ruined his health. He was not willing to cast himself into blind faith in Amida's Original Vow. 'Rely on the Dharma, and not on any person,' he said, quoting the Nirvana Sutra. He insisted on three proofs for anything: it must be logical, it must be scriptural, and above all, it must work (Christensen *St. Nichiren* 23–4).

'My wish has always been,' he said later, 'to sow the seeds for the attainment of Buddhahood, and to escape the fetters of births and deaths. For this purpose, I once practiced, according to the custom of most fellow-Buddhists, the method of repeating the name of Amida Buddha, and putting faith in his redeeming power. But since doubt had begun to arise in my mind as to the truth of that belief, I committed myself to the vow that I would study all the branches of Buddhism known in Japan and learn fully what their diverse teachings were' (Anesaki 13). Nichiren made this solemn vow before an image of Akasagarbha (Kokuzo), the Bodhisattva of Wisdom.

Not long after his ordination the fisherman's son moved from his small provincial temple to the bustling *de facto* capital, Kamakura, the seat of the military dictatorship. He remained there for five or six years, studying the new sects favoured by the dictators, Zen and Pure Land. While he was at Kamakura he must have seen the beginning of the construction of the Great Buddha. A wooden image, probably a mould for the projected copper image, was completed in 1243. Amida, the Buddha of Infinite Life and Light, who welcomed sinners into paradise, and the war-god Hachiman were the incongruous patrons of the new capital. Rencho found himself increasingly sceptical. What kind of Buddhism was this, anyway? Where was true Buddhism to be found?

To get his answers he left Kamakura and travelled to the heart of old Buddhism, the great Tendai monastic centre at Mt. Hiei. There he studied under the best teachers in the country.

Saicho, who had founded the school at Mt. Hiei, had insisted that the search for truth must be non-sectarian. At the apex of his system lay the Heavenly Terrace (Tendai) philosophy of Chih-i. However, centuries of accretions had enveloped it, especially in the forms of esotericism and Pure Land teachings. Rencho, not content with learning these doctrines second-hand, travelled to the great centres where they were taught, to Mii-dera for Tendai esotericism and Mt. Koya for Shingon. For the next ten years, he studied all these teachings, as well as those even earlier doctrines that were still taught at Nara. He is known to have visited these various centres, carrying out his vow 'to study all the branches of Buddhism known in Japan'.

To get back even earlier than the six sects of Nara, he travelled to centres that had been founded by Prince Shotoku, the first sponsor of Buddhism in Japan. He wanted to go back further yet, to China, but gave up this plan after an interview with the naturalized Chinese Zen master, Doryu, who told him that Buddhism in China had sunk to a sorry state. Nevertheless, he made it a point to master Confucianism and the Chinese classics, studying them under Saburo Daigaku of Kyoto. Daigaku became his life-long mentor on the fine points of Chinese grammar and calligraphy.

Rencho did not neglect the culture of his own country. He studied Waka poetry under Tame-ie of the Reizei School and later under the nun Abutsu-ni. A Shinto priest tutored him in the indigenous Japanese religion. When he finally completed his studies and was starting home, Rencho went out of his way to visit the Grand Ise Shrine, the spiritual centre of pre-Buddhist Japan.

Once when he was returning to Mt. Hiei after visiting a distant temple, he passed by the Yodo River, which flows into Osaka Bay. It struck him that Buddhism (and Shintoism, too) consists of many rivers, all of which flow into the one sea of the *Dharma Flower* (Kyoyu Fujii, *Nichiren Shonin Eden* 16–28).

In 1253 Rencho returned to his home temple to announce the results of his years of study and meditation. He had been away for 15 years, 10 of them at Mt. Hiei. He had vowed to become the wisest man in all Japan, and by the time he was 31 his academic accomplishments were truly impressive. He reported to Dozen, his original master, and then retired for a few days of solitude before preaching his first sermon.

On the morning of 28 April 1253, he arose before dawn and climbed a steep hill which overlooked the empty sea. There he waited. Finally, as the first rays of light spread over the horizon of the Pacific Ocean, he joined his hands together and solemnly intoned, 'I devote myself to the Sutra of the Lotus Flower of the Wonderful Dharma — *Namu Myoho Renge Kyo!*'[39]

By noon he was back at the temple, where a small crowd of local clergy and residents had gathered to hear the young student preach his first sermon. His exact words that day have not been recorded, but we do know that they scandalized the audience. He probably proclaimed unswerving devotion to the *Dharma Flower*, a return to the teachings of Saicho and Chih-i, and the rejection of the new cult of Amida.[40] Whatever he said, his audience did not like it. Master Dozen was shocked; Rencho had attacked the basic practice of the temple. Dozen withdrew to his quarters and wrote out a writ of interdiction. Rencho was expelled from the order. Forbidden to remain any longer at the temple, he walked forlornly down the mountain to the home of his parents.

Worse was yet to come. The local lord, Kagenobu, was loyal to the ruling Hojo clan and a fervent believer in Amida. He was outraged when he heard about the sermon, and ordered Rencho's arrest. But Rencho had already left the temple. Master Dozen, who still had affectionate feelings for his former pupil, ordered two monks to go quickly down to the village, warn the impetuous preacher of his danger, and lead him to a place of safety.

It was probably while he was at his parents' home that he changed his name from Rencho, which had been given to him at his home temple, to a name of his own invention, Nichiren. For a monk to reject the name given him by his order was to declare independence. He was now a monk without an order, a preacher without credentials. From now on his only authority would be the truth or falsehood of the Dharma he preached. In this capacity his made his first two converts — his own parents. Although they were upset by the misfortunes that had befallen their son, they still had faith in him. He gave his father the Buddhist name of Myonichi ('Wonderful Sun') and his mother Myoren ('Wonderful Lotus').

According to the Nichiren Order of America, he chose the name Nichiren for himself because it is truly universal. 'The Sun brightens the world while the Lotus blooms in every corner of the world. The Sun (*Nichi*) is the salvation of all mankind, and the Lotus represents the purification (*Ren*) for all mankind.'[41] Specifically, the name refers to two verses in the Lotus Sutra: 'Just as the light of the sun and moon expels all dimness and darkness, so this man, living and working in the world, drives out the darkness of all living beings,' and 'Be not influenced by environment. Lo, the Lotus blossoms, never to be soiled by the muddy waters whence it grows.'[42]

The two monks sent by Dozen led Nichiren to a small country temple beyond the jurisdiction of Lord Tojo Kagenobu. There conditions were more congenial, and Nichiren might have remained there peacefully for the rest of his life had he chosen to do so. But he felt that his duty was to save the country, and that meant moving into the lion's mouth, the capital city of Kamakura.

The political situation during the Kamakura Period (1192–1333) was complex and unsettled. Several emperors had come and gone in rapid succession. Real power belonged to the military Shogun, who made and replaced emperors at will. Then the Shogun's authority was usurped by the Regent (*Shikken*), who ruled from Kamakura. The regency was in the hands of the powerful Hojo clan, whose rule was sometimes interrupted by internecine quarrels among themselves.

The petty nobility in the provinces remained neutral for the most part, biding their time, and watching to see which way the political winds were blowing. As long as Nichiren remained among them, he was comparatively safe. Indeed, it was from their ranks that he began to make a few converts. But once he moved back to Kamakura, he was on his own.

Although he still considered himself a Tendai monk, Nichiren no longer had credentials. He was unable to lodge in any of the many temples in the city. Instead, he built himself a hut in the outskirts and became a street corner evangelist, urging passers-by to return to faith in the *Dharma Flower*. In time he was joined by a few disciples. His first convert from the ranks of the clergy was an older classmate from Mt. Hiei, Joben, who changed his name to Nissho. Nissho brought his brother and young nephew into the little group. The 12-year-old nephew was Nichiro, who was to play an important role in the development of Nichiren Buddhism.

It was a time of both prosperity and natural disasters for the capital of the warlords. Many new temples were being built, and the Great Buddha of Kamakura was finally completed in gilt copper. But from 1257 to 1260 both the city and the country suffered from disastrous earthquakes, droughts, severe rains, floods, and pestilence. Nichiren was deeply grieved by the sufferings of the common people, and wondered about the reasons for such misery.

Like most Buddhists, Nichiren believed that conditions in the outer world are reflections of conditions within the mind. A pure Buddha-mind creates a Pure Land; confused minds create the world we live in. According to the Flower Garland Sutra,

> Both delusion and Enlightenment originate within the mind, and every existence or phenomenon arises from the functions of the mind, just as different things appear from the sleeve of a magician. The activities of the mind have no limit, they form the surroundings of life. An impure mind surrounds itself with impure things and a pure mind surrounds itself with pure things; hence, surroundings have no more limits than the activities of the mind. Just as a picture is drawn by an artist, surroundings are created by the activities of the mind. While surroundings created by Buddha are pure and free from defilement, those created by ordinary men are not so. The mind conjures up

multifarious forms just as a skilful painter creates pictures of various worlds. There is nothing in the world that is not mind-created. A Buddha is like our mind; sentient beings are just like Buddha. Therefore there is no difference among the mind, Buddhas and sentient beings in their capability of creating all things.

(*Teaching* 34–5)

Nichiren believed that the calamities which had befallen the country were natural reflections of the greedy minds of the warlords of Kamakura, who proudly raised gigantic monuments to new deities while oppressing the people and murdering and exiling the rightful emperors. Like a prophet from the Old Testament, he decided to speak out.

In 1259 and 1260 he retired to a quiet temple in the country and composed his famous thesis, *Rissho Ankoku Ron*, 'Establish the Right Law and Save Our Country.' He went to great pains with this work, putting it into classical Chinese, and consulting his old Chinese professor on the fine points. In it he quoted from many sutras, not only the *Dharma Flower*, so as not to appear biased. He prepared two drafts, a long one full of references, and a shorter one in case the intended reader lacked the patience to wade through the first. Although it is by no means the best of Nichiren's writings, it is certainly his best known, for its presentation thrust him instantly from obscurity into the national spotlight.

In the *Rissho Ankoku Ron*, Nichiren blames the country's problems on the fact that people everywhere have abandoned the Original Buddha Shakyamuni in favour of Amida. 'Since Honen's *Senchakushu* ('The Sole Selection of the Nembutsu') was published, our Original Teacher (Shakyamuni) has been forgotten, and the Buddha of the Western World (Amida) has been honored instead . . . Only the four volumes of the three sutras (dealing with the Pure Land) are read and recited, and all the other sutras expounded through the five periods of the teachings (of Shakyamuni) have been abandoned. No one makes offerings to temples other than those enshrining Amida Buddha . . . Therefore, the (other) temples are dilapidated. Grass grows on the roofs, and weeds cover the gardens, but no one wishes to support or rebuild those temples. Therefore, no saintly priests live there; no guardian gods stay there . . . Many people have given up the perfect teachings and prefer the one-sided teaching. Will devils miss the chance to take advantage of their mistake?' (Dialogue IV)

The enervating Nembutsu teaching of Honen has turned people's eyes away from this world to the 'western paradise'. But it is our world which the Buddha came to save and where he eternally resides. 'You should convert yourself to the faith in the Good Law of the True Vehicle at once. Then the triple world will become a Buddha-world. How can a Buddha-world decline? The worlds of the ten quarters will become a treasure-world. How can a treasure-world be destroyed? If our country does not decline, and is not destroyed, we shall be safe and peaceful. Believe my words, treasure them!' (39)

Nichiren presented his thesis to the private secretary of Hojo Tokiyori, the ex-regent. Although Tokiyori had officially retired to study Zen, he was still the most important man in the country. Nichiren hoped that his interest in Buddhism would cause him to at least read the thesis. He went home to await a reply. He waited in vain. No answer came.

Twelve days later, says an old story, Nichiren awoke at night to find a monkey tugging on his sleeve. Curious, he followed the monkey out of his hut and up a wooded path towards a cave in the hill. Suddenly he heard a great commotion behind him. Turning, he saw that a mob had surrounded his hut and set it on fire. He had narrowly escaped with his life.

Once more Nichiren was homeless and in danger of losing his life. Again he fled to the countryside, going to Wakamiya in Shimosa Province. There he was offered protection by a squire of some standing, Toki Jonin, who permitted him to lodge in his family temple.[43] Lord Toki, a devout man of means and education, was already a convinced convert. He was to prove an invaluable supporter, and his home became a place of refuge for the believers in times of persecution.

Nichiren remained with Toki Jonin for about six months. He delivered a 100-day lecture on the *Dharma Flower*, attracting a number of new converts. But he could not remain long in a place of security. He did not want to make converts and establish a new sect; he wanted to save the country. So back he went to Kamakura, where he was immediately arrested.

If Nichiren had criticized the Nembutsu a half-century before, he would have caused no commotion. Back in 1205 the Kofuku-ji temple of Nara had protested to the Emperor about the Nembutsu in stronger language than Nichiren had used, pointing out 'nine faults': 1) They call their group a 'sect' without imperial permission; 2) they slander the other Buddhists; 3) they do not venerate Shakyamuni Buddha; 4) they laugh at practices other than the Nembutsu; 5) they do not venerate the national gods; 6) they practise nothing but the Nembutsu; 7) they give up meditation and only utter the Nembutsu; 8) they do not observe the moral precepts; 9) they are misleading the nation of Japan (Hoshino, *Lotus Sutra and Nichiren* 4).

These strong criticisms had helped provoke the banishment of Honen and Shinran. Nichiren certainly did not think of himself as a radical because of having updated a well known public document. But the times and the place were different now. This was not Kyoto or Nara, a conservative centre of the old order, where scholarly discussions whiled away the idle hours. This was Kamakura, a 'boom town' with no traditions of its own, the champion of a new order based on naked power. The rulers and the people were proud of their new 121-ton statue of Amida Buddha, their new temples, and their vigorous new sects: Zen, Pure Land (Nembutsu), Shingon-Ritsu, and Shingi ('new doctrine') Shingon.[44] Nobody loves the voice of a guilty conscience. Nichiren was calling for a return to traditional values, for the harmony which had existed between Emperor and Buddhism in the days of Saicho. No one wanted to hear about this any more. Such talk was disturbing and perhaps even dangerous for the military dictatorship. Nichiren must go.

He was arrested and condemned to exile on the Izu Peninsula. The peninsula was a handy place to get rid of trouble-makers. It was close enough to Kamakura that prisoners could be taken there in a matter of hours; it was isolated and wild enough that the exiles would soon waste away and die, unless they were helped by the few fishermen who lived along the shore. This was unlikely, because to aid an exiled criminal meant swift and severe punishment. A lord steward and his soldiers were stationed on the peninsula to enforce the law.

Nichiren was taken down to the beach and placed on a ship bound for the peninsula. Some of his disciples followed as far as they could. Young Nichiro (he was then sixteen) tried to hold back the boat, but a sailor beat him on the hands with an oar, breaking his right arm. The arm never healed completely, and Nichiro was partially crippled for the rest of his life. As the boat pulled out to sea, Nichiren called words of encouragement to his grief-stricken followers.

At about four in the afternoon the boat reached a reef called Mana-ita ('Butcher's Block') off the coast of Izu. Afraid to approach closer to shore because of the rising tide, the boatmen dropped off their prisoner on the lonely rock and headed for home. In low tide, a man could walk from the reef to the shore. But it was high tide, and the waters were rising about the rock and would soon submerge it. There Nichiren stood until he was spotted by a fisherman rowing home. With great difficulty, the fisherman manoeuvered his small craft close to the reef and took the exiled monk on board. Then he not only took him ashore, but he and his wife invited him to remain in their home.

Nichiren, however, knew that if he stayed with them, he could bring disaster upon his kindly rescuers. So he soon departed and took refuge in a cave which his hosts pointed out to him. Even there they did not forget him, however, and daily they would come secretly to bring him food.

Nichiren never forgot the kindness of this humble couple. He was not a person to forget a favour. A large portion of his letters which have survived are thank-you letters; he was grateful for any gift, even the smallest. For a gift such as this, his gratitude was boundless.

'On the twelfth of the fifth month,' he wrote to them later, 'I was marooned on a beach, the name of which was unknown to me. I suffered much, but you came to my rescue. What was the relationship between you and me in our previous existence? Did you practice the teachings of the *Dharma Flower* in your previous life? You are a man, and a man can be courageous. But I was surprised that your wife was as brave as you in serving an exile. She gave me food, water, and any other necessities. You and your wife took faith in the *Dharma Flower* and made offerings to me for more than thirty days. The people of the village hated me more than the people of Kamakura. In and around the fifth month, there is less rice; but you served me lots of it. Are you two the reincarnations of my parents? Did my parents reappear at Kawana in the Province of Izu in the forms of you two?' (*Showa-teihon*, 229)

Nichiren's fortunes on the peninsula took a turn for the better when the lord steward became ill. His retainers, knowing that an extraordinary monk was in exile nearby, sent for him. Nichiren was able to cure the lord steward, who in gratitude allowed him to move into more comfortable quarters. He also gave him a small statue of Shakyamuni Buddha. Wherever he went after that, Nichiren took the image with him.

Nichiren was pardoned in early 1263 and allowed to return. While he was in exile, he had begun his practice of writing letters of thanks, admonitions, and instructions to his disciples. Today some 500 letters and other documents written by him are still extant, carefully preserved at various temples in Japan. By their sheer quantity, they make Nichiren the best documented religious founder in history. Many of these documents are written in his own hand. Others are authenticated copies.

The Showa Edition of the Complete Works of Nichiren (published in 1952) consists of 2,737 pages, of which 1,927 pages (72 per cent of the whole) contain authentic writings. The balance consists of fragments, memoranda and notes, a commentary on the *Dharma Flower*, and mandalas which he inscribed. Fifty-five forgeries are included in the collection plus two sets of 'oral teachings', which were widely accepted until recent studies exposed them as forgeries, too. These are the *Onko-kikigaki* and *Ongi-kuden* (Murano, *Nichiren's Writings* 1–2).

One document of dubious authenticity, *Sandai-hiho-sho* ('Treatise on the Three Great Secret Dharmas'), said by some to be Nichiren's 'final statement' and by others to be a blatant forgery, is a source of hot political controversy in contemporary Japan. It clearly advocates the establishment of a state religion.[45] There have also been the inevitable 'transfer documents', supposedly dictated by the saint on his deathbed, transferring sole and complete authority to Nikko, one of his disciples. Sceptics claim that these transfer documents were not 'discovered' until 1488 — two centuries later! (Murano, 'Sokagakkai' 6)

While he was in exile Nichiren had time to think through his position and evaluate himself. He still considered himself a loyal priest of the Tendai Sect, faithful to the tradition in which he had been ordained. He signed his letters, 'Nichiren, Follower of the Dengyo Daishi (Saicho)'. Bruno Petzold says:

Nichiren incorporates into his own system the whole Tendai philosophy. He adopts the classification of the Five Periods and the Eight Teachings; he acknowledges the doctrines of the Perfectly Amalgamated Three Truths (i.e., the Synthesis of vacuity and phenomenal reality in the Middle) and the Identity of the One Mind and the Three Thousand (representing the totality of phenomena), and he upholds the practice of the Three Meditations in One Mind. He teaches the Oneness of the World. He proclaims that the whole universe in its essence is nothing but Buddha's own body, so that even trees and grasses do not only attain Buddhahood, but are direct manifestations of Buddha. Similarly, he maintains that the cosmos or the Tathagata is our own body and soul; that Buddhahood can be attained in our present life and in our present body; that the Buddha, the mind, and the living beings form One Unity. There is not a single important Tendai doctrine which is not a part of Nichiren's system.

(Nichiren 50–1)

Nichiren, however, was transforming the Round Teaching of Tendai ('round' here means 'perfect') into a spearhead. All rivers flow to the *Dharma Flower*, to Tendai — true. But they flow in only one direction, from the less perfect to the perfect; the process cannot be reversed. This dynamic thrust in Nichiren is lacking in the Tendai of Saicho and Chih-i.

While he was in exile Nichiren wrote a brief but important essay that he called, 'The Teaching, the Capacity, the Time, and the Country' (*Kyoki Jikoku Sho*). He signed it 'Nichiren, a Shramana in Japan,' using the ancient Indian term for a wandering mendicant. In the essay he names the five principles of his teaching. 1) Doctrine (*kyo*): the true and final teachings of the Buddha are expounded in the *Dharma Flower*. This is the religious principle. 2) Teachings must be applicable to those it hopes to save. Shakyamuni knew how to vary his teaching according to the capacity (*ki*) of his students. This is the psychological principle. 3) Timing (*ji*) is vital. Shakyamuni did not preach the *Dharma Flower* until after 40 years of preparation. The Little Vehicle teachings were the best in their time (*Shobo*, the Age of the Living Dharma), because generations of Indian ascetics had prepared people for them. The Great Vehicle teachings were the best in their time (*Zobo*, the Age of the Copied Dharma), because the Little Vehicle had paved the way for deeper philosophical speculation. Today (*Mappo*, the Age of the Declining Dharma) only the all-embracing *Dharma Flower* can save. This is the historical principle.

Buddhism has declined in both India and China. 4) Only in Japan have all types of Buddhism been taught. It is from Japan that true Buddhism must be spread. This is the geographic or ethnic principle (*koku*, country). Combining the above four principles, he concludes with the fifth. 5) It is wrong to turn backwards and attempt to revive prior teachings, such as Zen, Pure Land, and even academic Tendai, all of which originated in China during the previous age. Today only the *Dharma Flower* must be taught. This is the correct sequence (*jo*), the correlative principle.

Of course, most people are uneducated and unaware of this progressive development of Buddhism. It would be futile to expect them to begin by first mastering the 'Three Baskets' teachings, then the subtleties of Mahayana, and finally the *Dharma Flower*, which is called 'the most difficult to believe'. The Bodhisattva Never-Despise approached all people, regardless of their academic preparation, bowed before them, and proclaimed the *Dharma Flower*. At first they rejected him, but subsequent bitter experience caused them finally to awaken to the truth of what he was saying. This is the teaching method which must be adopted by Nichiren and his disciples.

It is better for a person to hear the *Dharma Flower* and oppose it than not to hear it at all. A negative relationship to the Sutra is better than no relationship. This is called the 'poison drum'. The 'drum of the Dharma' is nectar to those who receive it and poison to those who do not, causing them to fall into hell for slander. But eventually this negative relationship cannot help but become positiive. The Dharma Blossom is the truth, and the truth will finally prevail. The 'poison drum' is a curative poison.

Drums have become a characteristic feature of Nichiren Buddhism. They pound out the good tidings to the rhythm of *Namu Myoho Renge Kyo*, saving all who hear — directly if they believe, indirectly if they do not. All are welcomed into the One Vehicle.

The matter of timing, which was so vital to Nichiren, requires further explanation. His contemporaries did not always understand what he meant by it, and he had to come back to the subject again and again. Buddhists are accustomed to thinking in terms of Nirvana — the still centre which is unaffected by the swirling eddies of time. It is timeless. There is no cosmic beginning or end, no creation or last judgment. There are endless cycles of solar systems which come into being, flourish for a while, then decay into the void, from where new solar systems arise. The void, it will be recalled, is pure potential. Against such a vast background, linear time is insignificant.

However, the rules of growth, decay, and death apply to everything, including Buddhism. When it is new and fresh, Buddhism flourishes. Later it stagnates, becoming more formal than vital. Finally it declines and perishes. There were different opinions on how long this process takes, but it was widely held that the Former Age of growth lasted 1,000 years, the Middle Age of stability another 1,000 years, and the final Age of Decay dwindles away for 10,000 years.

A more elaborate scheme subdivided the three ages into five periods of 500 years each: 1) the period of enlightenment; 2) the period of meditation; 3) the period of reading, reciting, and listening; 4) the period of building temples and stupas; 5) the period of conflicts among rival sects. (This is the beginning of the final Age of Decline.)

Nearly everyone believed that the final age had already begun. According to Honen and Shinran, this meant that enlightenment was now impossible to attain. The only appropriate practice for a Buddhist was to recite the Nembutsu and hope for enlightenment in some better world to come.

Nichiren, however, gave an optimistic interpretation to the three ages. So vast was Shakyamuni Buddha's compassion that he had left just the right medicine for the right times. During the Former Age people could attain enlightenment by following the Eight-fold Path. During the Middle Age they could attain it by understanding that the three thousand things exist in a single moment's thought, as revealed in the Imprinted Gate and elucidated by Chih-i. And for people of the Latter Age the Buddha left the Three Great Secret Dharmas hidden in the Chapter of Eternal Life in the *Dharma Flower*. The teachings for all three ages can be found in the *Dharma Flower*, which is one more reason why it is the 'round' or complete teaching. However, the final remedy becomes applicable only during the Final Age.[46]

In this way Nichiren's Buddhism is both old and new. It is old in that it maintains what has been taught before. It is new in its application, which is exclusively for us who live in the final Age of the Declining Dharma.

The *Dharma Flower Sutra* predicted that its unqualified universalism would be scorned by religious establishments, all of which believed that they had a monopoly on salvation. Anyone attempting to apply the *Dharma Flower* principles would inevitably incur censorship and even persecution. Nichiren said that he had identified himself so completely with the Sutra that he was living out these prophecies in his own body. As the living embodiment of the Sutra, he was able to discern and reveal its innermost secrets.

Nichiren's criticism of the sects was based on his sense of time. Teachings that had been applicable in prior Ages were useless in this Age of the Decline of the Dharma. It was too late to reintroduce strict monastic rules (the Ritsu Sect), mystic rites (esotericism), or silent meditation (Zen). These all belonged to the past, when the times were right for them. As for the Pure Land schools, which cast aside the teachings of Shakyamuni and hoped for rebirth in the Pure Land of Amida, there was nothing good he could say about them. They had betrayed the very foundations of Buddhism.

Nichiren's condemnation of all the sects has sometimes gained him a 'bad press'. Edward Conze says that 'he suffered from self-assertiveness and bad temper, and he manifested a degree of personal and tribal egotism which disqualify him as a Buddhist teacher' (*Buddhism* 206). Such a blanket condemnation of a very complex personality is much too hasty. Nichiren saw himself as a man with a mission, a mission to save Buddhism and to save his country. This mission would probably cost him his life. He was willing to pay this price himself, but he hated seeing his friends run the same risks. His letters reveal how he worried and fretted over them like a mother hen with her chickens. He had a personal interest in each one of them in a manner quite unusual for a great religious leader. They were not just 'souls to be saved'. They were people, and he loved them in spite of all their shortcomings.

Nichiren's letters to his disciples are so personal that from them we can draw clear pictures of the recipients' personalities. Nichiren may have defied the world, but to his friends he was gentle and solicitous. He thundered against injustice, but wept with those who wept and laughed with those who laughed. He took nothing for granted, and would go out of his way to express gratitude for the smallest favour. He was grateful for everything which existed: for his country even when it persecuted him, for his parents who had nourished him, and for the Three Treasures: the Buddha, the Dharma, and the Sangha. Appreciation lies at the very heart of his system. We are obligated to become Buddhas, each one of us, not for selfish gratification, but because that is the only way we can repay the infinite gifts we have received from all living beings.

Nichiren was aware that many people considered him 'self-assertive and bad-tempered'. 'But what am I supposed to do?' he asked. 'It is not that I am so great; it is the *Dharma Flower* which has all power. If I am proud, people will think me arrogant; if I am humble, they will despise the Sutra. The taller the pine tree, the longer the wisteria that hangs from it. That's the way it is with me. How lucky I am!' (*Shonin Chisanze Ji*)

He compared himself to a fly which can travel a hundred miles because it has hidden itself in a horse's tail. Another time he likened himself to a snake in the grass. Other beasts are more noble, but the lowly snake with its ear to the ground can predict a coming flood (MW 3:247).

Noah Brannen, a Christian missionary in Japan, has compared the Japanese prophet to Amos of the Old Testament. Amos, who has been called the first 'ethical prophet', maintained that social injustices and natural calamities prefigured the coming judgment of God, whose righteousness he symbolized by a plumb line.

> This is what he showed me: The Lord was standing by a wall
> that had been built true to plumb, with a plumb line in his hand.
> And the Lord asked me, 'What do you see, Amos?'
>   'A plumb line,' I replied.
>   Then the Lord said, 'Look, I am setting a plumb line among
> my people Israel. I will spare them no longer.
>
> (Amos 7:7–8)

For Nichiren the plumb line was the *Dharma Flower*. If his nation failed to adhere to this standard of measurement, calamities were inevitable.

Nichiren could also be compared to the Prophet Jeremiah, who found himself in the unenviable position of having to predict the devastation of his own country by foreign invaders. For his integrity, he was treated as a traitor, jailed, and subjected to numerous humiliations. Nichiren, like Jeremiah, saw his persecutions and the subsequent foreign invasion as proofs that he was on the right track.

Just as Amos was the first Hebrew prophet to see his small tribal religion in a world-wide perspective, so did Nichiren see Japanese Buddhism in universal proportions. Both men loved their countries, but both of them saw their countries as subject to cosmic law. Amos spoke of God's plumb line. Nichiren was later to depict cosmic law in a sacred mandala that he designed, in which the Chinese characters, *Namu Myoho Renge Kyo*, descend down the centre of the chart as if suspended in infinite space, not unlike the plumb line of Amos.

When Nichiren returned from exile in 1263 he was more convinced than ever of his life's mission. He was not only a believer in the *Dharma Flower*; he was its personification, the 'doer' of the Sutra. He saw himself as another Bodhisattva Never-Despise (*Lotus* XX). 'None of those in Japan who hold to the sutra have yet manifested what is stated in the sutra (since everyone who really holds to it must encounter peril on that account); one person, Nichiren alone has read (put into practice the words), "We shall not care for bodily life, but only cherish the supreme Way." Then Nichiren is Japan's foremost doer of the *Dharma Flower*' (*Hokekyo no Gyoja*, *Showa-teihon* 327).

He knew it, but that was not good enough — the whole country must know it. Across the Sea of Japan there loomed a dreaded menace, worse than anything the country had ever had to face. The fierce Mongol hordes had conquered China and Korea. It was just a matter of time before they attacked Japan. The Age of Tumult and Strife had arrived, and his country was about to be sucked into the maelstrom. Only the Buddha Dharma could save it, and only he knew the Dharma for the Final Age. He had to make himself heard.

He began submitting more appeals to the government authorities.

Chapter 9

Days of Wrath _____

'The times, they are a-changin', sang Bob Dylan in the 1960s. The men and women of thirteenth century Japan were very much aware of the same thing; they thought that the world had entered into its final age of decay. All traditional standards were collapsing. Along with political changes came radical religious movements that shook Japanese Buddhism to its foundations. There were many saints who raised the banners of hope in the stormy seas of collapsing old values. Honen and Shinran preached reliance on the mercy of Amida Buddha. Eisai introduced the mind-boggling puzzles of Rinzai Zen. Dogen advocated the quiet sitting of Soto Zen. Ninsho Ryokan, who was probably the most celebrated at the time, wanted to return to the values of primitive Buddhism with its emphasis on strict monastic discipline and generous acts of charity.

All these spiritual leaders attracted devoted followers, as did the gurus who sprang up across Europe and America in the days of Bob Dylan. People who were disillusioned with the old ways turned to these new leaders for solutions to new problems. The old courtly aristocracy at Kyoto clung to the esotericism of Tendai and Shingon, but they had been shorn of political power. The new aristocracy came from the rough warrior class, the Samurai, and preferred the vigorous new faiths of Zen and Pure Land. The common people, as usual, followed their leaders, but now there was a distinct difference. The common people were being addressed directly and asked to participate in the new movements. This had never happened before.

The reformers of the Kamakura Era differed in their respective solutions to the problems of the day, but they agreed on much. For one thing, all of them believed that the Age of Decline of the Dharma (*Mappo*) had come, and that the old scholastic methods would not work

_____ 111

any more. What could be done? How could humanity be saved from inevitable decay when men and women were no longer capable of or even interested in spiritual combat? The reformers were realists who knew that it was impossible to roll back the wheel of history and reinstate happy conditions that may have existed in the past. Except for Nichiren, they did not want to change history but to adapt to it. They saw themselves as belonging to their own times and subject to its failings. They felt inferior to the great teachers of the past, but because of their love for the Buddha-Dharma and their compassion for suffering humanity, they were compelled to take action. 'I am far from Tendai (Chih-i) and Dengyo in wisdom,' said Nichiren, 'but I surpass them in compassion and patience.'[47]

The reformers were dissatisfied with the scholarship and theorizing of the previous age. They sought solutions not in the head but in the heart. If modern man was no longer capable of understanding the profundities of Buddhism, he was still capable of believing and acting. Honen was probably the first man in Buddhism to rank faith ahead of wisdom. Shinran said that man is so vile that he is not capable even of faith; if he does have faith, he must have received it as a free gift from the Buddha. Therefore, he concluded, faith is equivalent to enlightenment (Bloom 1965 Chap. IV). While the others did not go to this extreme, all of them looked upon faith, not wisdom, as the foundation.

Nichiren often said that previous generations had been more concerned with the first half of the *Dharma Flower* (the theoretical 'Imprinted Gate') than with the second half, the 'Original Gate'. It was not that previous commentators had not read the whole book — of course they had. But the trick was to read it 'backwards', beginning with the burning compassion of the Original Gate. Some men could understand the imprinted theories. All men could experience the blazing fire of the Original Buddha.

'All men' meant all women, too. The Kamakura reformers agreed on this. Nara Buddhism had been established by the state for the protection of the state. Heian Buddhism was also a department of the state, but had introduced the important teaching that everyone partakes of the Buddha-nature. The Kamakura reformers now took the final step, shifting the emphasis from the state to the individual. They spoke directly to the people.

Up until then a large percentage of the people — 50 per cent, in fact — had been relegated to an inferior position in Buddhism. These were the women. The central Buddhist institution, the Sangha, was monastic; there is no place for a woman in a monastery. They were not permitted to set foot in most of the great religious centres, which were, or course, monasteries.

Even the salient feminine qualities of love for home and family were 'fetters' to a monk, who was expected to free himself from them. The Sangha was an all-male society, and it justified itself with numerous anti-female pronouncements. The sutras (up to the *Dharma Flower*) warned against women who are 'always fawning and perverse' and 'can destroy the seeds of Buddhahood' (Flower Garland Sutra). Vasubandhu, who believed that some people could never attain Buddhahood, numbered women among these. 'Woman is a servant of hell, excluded for all time from any hope of attaining Buddhahood. She may have the gentle outward appearance of a bodhisattva, but her inner heart is that of a demon' (*Yuishiki-ron*).

If monks needed 250 precepts to keep them on the narrow path, nuns needed twice as many — 500. In Southern Buddhism (Theravada, the only surviving school of Hinayana), the female Sangha was so over-loaded with regulations that eventually it collapsed and disappeared. Only in the relatively liberal Mahayana did it survive, and then as an extraordinarily austere and puritanical organization. It is a wonder that any women at all were attracted to such a rugged life.[48]

Nevertheless, thousands were, and over the centuries women have made important contributions to Buddhism. In fact, Buddhism is unique among world religions in having a sacred book in its (Pali) canon, the *Therigatha*, composed entirely by women — 73, to be exact. In the Mahayana tradition there is the important sutra of Queen Shrimala, a book that was especially popular among the laity.

In the early days we hear of Baddha Kundalakesin, who could out-debate any man or woman who dared challenge her. She was finally beaten by the Shariputra, reputedly the wisest of all Shakyamuni's disciples, when he asked her, 'The One — what is it?' (When she could not reply, Shariputra told her, 'All beings subsist on food.'[49] However, there is a delightful Sanskrit story that even Shariputra met his match when he encountered a woman saint in heaven and asked her, 'Now that you have the ability, why don't you change yourself into a man?' Instead of answering him, she turned him into a woman and asked him if he felt any different (*Buddha-Dharma*, 324).

In modern times women have played important roles in the dissemination of Buddhism: Alexandra David-Neel, centenarian expert on Tibet; I.B. Horner, president of the Pali Text Society; Constant Lounsbery, founding-president of 'Les Amis du Bouddhisme'; Charlene Young, one of the first Americans ordained to the Buddhist priesthood (in the Nichiren Order); Kimi Kotani of Reiyukai; Myoko Naganuma of Rissho Kosei-kai; Kimiko Okano of Kodo Kyodan (a Tendai lay organization); other women have also been leaders of twentieth-century Buddhism.

During the golden age of the Heian Period, although women were barred from entry to most holy places, they were often active in studying, reading, reciting, and expounding the sutras. Lectures on the *Dharma Flower* were popular events, socially as well as intellectually, and women of the leisured classes often attended in great numbers. Because they could read, they studied; and because they studied, they learned. It certainly did not escape their attention that the *Dharma Flower* features many women who will attain Buddhahood. In fact, in the entire canon of Buddhist scriptures, the *Dharma Flower* is the only book which gives a concrete example of a mortal actually becoming a Buddha — and that mortal is a woman, the Naga princess!

Thus, when Nichiren began preaching the supremacy of the *Dharma Flower*, he had an important, literate, and interested group of people who could respond instantly to his message — women. In reading his letters to women, one is struck by the fact that these are often his most thoughtful and detailed writings. Obviously these women asked tough questions which demanded — and got — serious answers.

Nichiren was adamant on the equality of the sexes; to him this was elementary. He was indignant that some men considered women 'unclean' because they menstruated.

> Many women in their prime became nuns during Shakyamuni's time and practiced the way of the Buddha, but they were never despised because of their menstrual periods. Menstruation is not a pollution that comes from without. It is simply a feminine characteristic, and a proof of the continuity of the human race. For example, human excrement comes from within the body, but as long as one is sanitary, it is no reason for abhorrence. Isn't the same true of menstruation? I have never heard of any strict taboos against menstruation in either India or China. [50]

Nichiren went beyond equality of the sexes. He did not simply see women as equal to men — he praised them as women. When other men criticized them as inconstant, he praised them for honesty. When men answered that women had no minds of their own, Nichiren retorted that 'women seem to be led; actually they lead.' In his usual manner, he treated them as people first and as representatives of their sex second. He was so impressed by the fortitude of one woman that he gave her the title 'saint' (*shonin*). This was no nun, either, but the abandoned mother of a small child — a 'woman of the world'.

Zen Master Dogen also spoke out sharply against discrimination against women. 'If you say that woman should be despised for religious reasons as man's partner in passion,' he snorted, 'then you must say the same for every man, that he too should be despised as woman's partner in passion.' However, after he retired from public life to a monastery in 1243, Dogen said no more on the subject. There was no room for women in his monastery, either (Oguri 1984, 9).

Honen had arrived on the scene a generation before Nichiren, and women had flocked to his teaching that men and women alike can be saved by chanting the Nembutsu. Nichiren complained that these women were 'counting other men's riches'. They should stick with the *Dharma Flower*. The Amida sutras specify that there are no women in his western paradise; women are transformed into men first, and only then are admitted to the Pure Land.

Nichiren was on thin ice here, for the *Dharma Flower* says the same thing in Chapter 23, where the World of Happiness of Amitayus Buddha (Amida) is mentioned. In the incident of the Naga princess, she transforms herself into a man, but Nichiren insists that this is only an appearance. She is a Buddha already without any transformation. 'According to the *Dharma Flower*, one can become a Buddha immediately. There are two ways of attaining Buddhahood abruptly. In the discourses of the historical Buddha of the *Dharma Flower* (as this one), one can become a Buddha at once by transforming onself into a Buddha. In the discourses of the Eternal Buddha of the sutra, one can become a Buddha at once without any transformation' (*Myoichinyo-gohenji*).

This is a good example of how Nichiren reads the sutra 'between the lines', from the inside out. His starting point is always Chapter 16, which reveals that the Buddha's inner life is eternal and identical with our own inner life. The outer appearance is less important than the inner essence.

Since Kamakura Buddhism meant to benefit everyone and not just specialists, and particularly the weak and immoral people living in the Age of Degeneration, it looked for one basic practice which would somehow gather up all of Buddhist wisdom and power. There should be one touchstone, one key which opens all doors and can save the weak along with the strong, sinners as well as saints.

The idea of one key to the whole was not new. The *Dharma Flower* and other sutras frequently mentioned the importance of *dharani*, meaning literally that by which something is sustained or kept up. It is a word, a string of words, or simply sounds without any obvious meaning but said to contain many meanings. In Japanese, *dharani* is translated as *soji*, 'having all'. To 'obtain *dharani*' is to 'get the point'. To utter dharanis is similar to 'speaking in tongues' — releasing sounds from deep in the subconscious.

Shorter and more concise *dharanis* are called *mantras*. The use of *mantras* is basic to Esotericism. In fact, the name of Kukai's sect, *Shingon*, means *mantra*. Esotericism has a *mantra* for every occasion. The Kamakura reformers, however, sought a single *mantra*, one which would contain all the others.

Most of them found it in the Nembutsu, the name of the Buddha of Infinite Light and Life. To repeat the Buddha's name was the 'easy practice' which anyone could undertake without recourse to the mysterious Sanskrit *dharanis* and *mantras*, many of which could only be learned by secret initiations. Nichiren, however, objected that this practice deviated from the mainstream of Buddhism. Shakyamuni had taught Queen Vaidehi and others that Amida Buddha had created a Pure Land 'in the West', where those who called on his name could receive a happy rebirth after death in this world of sorrows. Nevertheless, the main thrust of his teachings was to renew our life in this world. His teachings culminate, not in the 'western paradise' but on the Vulture Peak, where he manifests his — and our — eternal life.

Just as the *Dharma Flower* is the quintessence of both universal truth and universal life, so its sacred title, *Myoho Renge Kyo*, is the quintessence of the sutra. All that remains is for us to identify ourselves with the Absolute. This is done by adding the first word, Namu, 'I devote myself to'. The *dharani* which contains all *dharanis*, the mantra which contains all mantras, is *Namu Myoho Renge Kyo*.

Shakyamuni obtained enlightenment when he completely identified himself with the Absolute. We obtain enlightenment exactly the same way. *Namu Myoho Renge Kyo* is the enlightenment of the Buddha. *Namu Myoho Renge Kyo* is our own enlightenment, too. In *Namu Myoho Renge Kyo* we identify with the Buddha. In *Namu Myoho Renge Kyo* the Buddha identifies with us.

This identification is complete in every respect. Just as the Buddha is three bodies in one, so are we. 'The person who chants *Namu Myoho Renge Kyo* is a Buddha. His body is the Dharma-body of the Buddha; his mind, the Reward-body of the Buddha; and his behavior, the Manifestation-body of the Buddha' (*Myoho-ama-gozen-gohenji*, *Showa-teihon*, 1535).

The sects, Nichiren says, from the old Nara sects on down to the recent Kamakura sects, seek identity with only part of the three-fold body of the Buddha. For example, to concentrate on the precepts taught by the historical Shakyamuni, as is done in the Little Vehicle, is to worship only the Manifestation-body. To go to the other extreme, worshipping only the eternal Principle (Dharma-body) as is done in esotericism, is to cut oneself off from the historical foundations. To worship only Amida is to concentrate on the Reward-body at the expense of the other two. The only correct object of worship is the three-in-one and one-in-three as expounded by Chih-i and Saicho. This is expressed in the *Dharma Flower* as the Eternal Buddha Shakyamuni.

'All the sects except the Tendai Sect', he wrote in 1272, 'worship wrong objects. The Kusha, Jojitsu, and Ritsu Sects (Hinayana) worship Buddha Shakyamuni, who is regarded as the person who eliminated illusions and attained enlightenment for the first time under the bodhi-tree. They are as wrong as a crown prince who thinks that he is the son of a subject. The Kegon (Flower Garland), Shingon, Sanron, and Hosso ('Consciousness-only') Sects are Mahayana. The Hosso and Sanron Sects worship Buddha Shakyamuni as defined in the provisional Mahayana. They are as wrong as a crown prince who thinks he is the son of a colonel. The Kegon and Shingon Sects despise Buddha Shakyamuni and worship Buddha Vairocana (personifying the Absolute). They are as wrong as a crown prince who deserts his father and follows another king of unknown ancestry. The Pure Land Buddhists hold that Buddha Amitabha is their Buddha, and do not worship Buddha Shakyamuni. They do not know that Buddha Amitabha is one of the manifestations of Buddha Shakyamuni. The Zen Buddhists (who reject all traditions) are like a man of low birth who criticizes his parents when he gets some position in society. They despise the Buddhas and the sutras. All these sects worship wrong objects' (*Kaimoku-sho*, 182–4, slightly altered).

Only in the *Dharma Flower* does Shakyamuni reveal the universal Buddha-seed, which permeates all life, and the fulfilment of that seed. It is the king of sutras just as the Original Buddha Shakyamuni, the fulfilment of the seed, is the origin of all Buddhas.

Such talk coming from an unknown monk without credentials left him virtually without allies. Although he supported the Tendai Sect, it did not return the compliment. His own Tendai temple had disowned him, and Tendai as a whole was too engrossed in Nembutsu and esoteric practices to heed his call for a house cleaning. The captive imperial court at Kyoto might have supported him, too, as a nuisance to the Kamakura regents. But Nichiren was not one to permit his religion to be used for political purposes. It should be the other way around: the state must obey the Dharma. Those few persons who did rally to Nichiren came to him singly as individual converts. They included some Tendai monks, provincial nobles and Samurai, merchants, educated women, and eventually members of the lowest social classes — the dispossessed who had been ignored by the state cults.

Although Nichiren was critical of 'wrong Buddhism', he was tolerant of Shinto deities, ancestral spirits, and other local cults as long as they were regarded as secondary. If such deities existed at all, they did so as manifestations of the Wonderful Dharma. Here he differed from the other Kamakura reformers, each of whom insisted that his own system must be followed exclusively. Nichiren even encouraged his followers to study non-Buddhist authors and secular writers. He admired Confucius and certain Hindu philosophers (*Kaimokusho*). Like Saicho, he believed that the truth is the truth regardless of where it is found.[51] He cited with approval Chih-i's dictum that all worldly knowledge is itself Buddhism (MW 2:75). However, we should keep our eyes on the relationship between facts, and not get identified with any one as if it alone were the whole truth. It is the *Dharma Flower* which manifests this relationship (Anesaki 68).

'We cannot exchange letters without knowledge of books outside Buddhism or the books about other sects,' he advised his disciples. 'So you should study them' (*Sado-gosho*).

To him scientific and religious knowledge were one and the same thing. In one of his major essays, 'Opening the Eyes' (*Kaimokusho*), he pays tribute to the great thinkers of China and India, and then demonstrates how their wisdom is completed by Buddhism, and

Buddhism by the *Dharma Flower*. Thus the whole of enlightenment is contained in the title, *Myoho Renge Kyo*, just as — one might say — the whole of scientific methodology and discovery is contained in one word, 'science', and all the triumphs and tragedies, dreams and realities of the American experience are contained within the single word, 'America'. So the whole of the Buddha's original enlightenment is contained within the Sacred Title of his complete teaching.

Since all the ten worlds including Buddhahood contain each other, the sacred title, *Myoho Renge Kyo*, is more than the sum total of human ingenuity. It manifests all the dynamic creativity of the Buddha. It is both 'self-power' and 'other-power'. The *Dharma Flower* is only a graphic description of this inner-power. The power, itself, is expressed in its name, *Myoho Renge Kyo*. The circuit of self-power and other-power is completed when I identify myself with it personally by *Namu*, 'I devote myself to'.

Kishio Satomi elaborates this in his important work, *Japanese Civilization* (68–70):

> The title is the key to the contents . . . We cannot think of any contents without a title, just as nobody can think of Shakespeare without knowing his name. Nichiren, in this respect, took the Sacred Title as Buddha-Seed, in which all virtues are inherent . . . The Sacred Title is the essence of the Lotus Sutra . . . it means at the same time, the essence of life. Buddha's cosmic life is 'Myohorengekyo,' 'Wonderful, mysterious, perfect and right truth.' It is equivalent to the 'Real Suchness.' Everything of the universe is therein contained. Nichiren says:
>
> 'Therefore the manifestation of the cosmos is equivalent to the five words of Myo ho ren ge kyo.'
>
> The Sacred Title is therefore the principle of our lives or essence of our nature, and further this Sacred Title is the name of life which is analysed into ten worlds, and synthesized into One Buddha-centric Existence under the principle of the Mutual Participation (of the ten worlds). He writes in this respect as follows:
>
> 'Therefore if one can perceive that it is not a mere title of the Book, but our substance, because Buddha named our substance and nature as "Myohorengekyo", then our own selves are equivalent to the Lotus Sutra; and we know that we are the Buddhas whose Three aspects of character ("three bodies") are united into One; because Buddha manifested our true substance in the Lotus Sutra'

Nichiren Buddhists do not worship the Book, but the infinite life which manifests in the Book. If other books or other teachers expound the living truth, they are also the 'Lotus Sutra'. Satomi quotes Nichiren as saying:

'If believers of the other Scriptures would only adore the truth of the Hokekyo (*Dharma Flower* or 'Lotus Sutra'), they would acquire the Principle of the Mutual Participation. Then all other Scriptures would be the Hokekyo, and vice versa. The Hokekyo does not deviate from all Pious-imposition-Scriptures nor vice versa. This is what is called the Mysterious Law (*Myoho*). As soon as this understanding is brought about, reading the Hinayana Scriptures is equivalent to reading the Mahayana Scriptures and the Hokekyo.'

Moreover, Nichiren says: 'You may judge everything in accordance with common sense unless it prevents the Path to Buddhahood' (59).

Willingness to learn from others and the adoption of local religious beliefs within the embrace of the *Dharma Flower* have sometimes led to strange bedfellows, and these have often provoked protests from the more discerning Nichiren believers. However, they have also given Nichiren's followers an ability to adapt to new situations. Nichiren Buddhists have been able to take advantage of changing historical conditions that sometimes paralyzed other groups. After 1868, when Buddhism was disestablished by the restored monarchy and replaced by national Shintoism, the Nichiren sects were the first to adapt and launch vigorous counter-measures. After the disasters of World War II, again it was the Nichiren groups that sprang into life and helped lead the Japanese people out of numbed despair.

Not long after Nichiren returned from exile, he received the alarming news that his mother lay close to death. (His father had died a few years before.) Although he had been forbidden under pain of death to return to his home territory, he immediately departed for Kominato. Since no one expected him to make so dangerous a journey, he was able to arrive undetected. He rushed home to find his mother in a coma, surrounded by weeping relatives. He began to pray fervently for her recovery.

To everyone's surprise, his mother did recover. Nichiren was over-joyed. The villagers, who had once looked upon him as a heretic, now decided that he was a saint and a miracle-worker. Many converted to him, including some Samurai warriors who swore to protect him from his old enemy, Tojo Kagenobu, the lord of the area. As for Kagenobu, he was outraged by such disloyalty, and watched for an opportunity to take his revenge.

Nichiren had taught his followers that they owed eternal gratitude to three groups of people: their parents, who gave them life; their teachers, who taught them the truth; and their rulers, who made their lives secure. He was happy that he had converted his parents and saved his mother's life. His rulers still firmly opposed him. However, since he was now so close, he decided to visit his old teacher Dozen, the abbot

FIRE IN THE LOTUS

of Kiyosumi. Perhaps he could even convince him to abandon esotericism and the Nembutsu for the original teachings of Tendai.

His visit was cordial but unsuccessful. The two men embraced and wept with emotion when they met again after so many years. Dozen was touched that his former pupil had risked his life to see him, but he was an old man set in his ways. It was too late for him to change his religious beliefs. Teacher and pupil parted as friends, but their roles could not be reversed. The pupil could not instruct the master.

Nevertheless, Nichiren always respected his first teacher. He understood why the old man could not change, and he did not press the matter. He felt he owed him too much. 'If a tree is deeply rooted,' he wrote later after Dozen's death, 'its branches and leaves will never wither. If a spring is inexhaustible, the river it feeds will never run dry. Without a supply of fuel, a fire will burn out. Without the right soil, plants can never grow. Thus Nichiren is comparable to a plant and my master to the soil. I, Nichiren, am indebted to my revered teacher Dozen-bo for the fact that I have become the exponent of the *Dharma Flower* and am now widely known, sometimes favourably, sometimes unfavourably' (*Keka Joju Gosho, Gosho* 900).

He promised that whatever good he was able to accomplish in this life he would dedicate to Dozen, who had made it possible. 'Rice plants bear flowers and grain; the seeds return to the soil. Thus the seeds sprout and grow again into flowers and grain. Any benefits which I, Nichiren, may enjoy from propagating the *Dharma Flower* will certainly return to the life of Dozen-bo. If a master has a good disciple, both of them will attain Buddhahood. But if a master has a bad disciple, the two of them will fall into hell, so it is said' (*ibid.*).

After a tearful farewell, Nichiren and a little party of companions left the old abbot for the home of a friendly Samurai, Kudo Yoshitaka. As darkness was falling they walked into a pine forest, and right into an ambush. Suddenly they found themselves surrounded by the soldiers of Lord Kagenobu. 'Shooting arrows flew like rain,' recalls Nichiren, 'and the sparks from clashing swords were like lightning.' Fortunately, Nichiren's host, Kudo Yoshitaka, had got wind of what was about to happen and came galloping full tilt to the rescue.

The three parties collided almost simultaneously, and the battle was brief but deadly. The assassins made straight for the prophet; his companions threw themselves in the way. Kudo Yoshitaka was pierced by arrows. An enemy warrior struck at Nichiren's head; the sword sliced across his forehead, toppling him from his horse. As Nichiren hit the ground, he broke his left hand. Around him, horses reared and plunged as the enemy tried to reach him and apply the final blow. Lord Kagenobu made straight for Nichiren, who had nothing to protect him except his prayer beads. Nichiren raised the beads in front of his face, and this sudden gesture caused Kagenobu's horse to rear. Kagenobu was thrown from the saddle and knocked unconscious. His retainers dragged him away, and the assassins disappeared among the pine trees as suddenly as they had come. The attack had failed.

This totally unexpected assault left Nichiren stunned and disheartened. He had lost some of his dearest friends in a matter of minutes. Among them was a faithful disciple named Kyonin. Lord Kudo Yoshitaka, who was to have been his host that night, now lay dying. Others were wounded and in pain, and he himself was suffering from a bloody head-wound and a broken hand. (He would bear the scar across his forehead for the rest of his life.) The dying Yoshitaka begged Nichiren to look after his unborn child, and if he was a boy, to make him a disciple. Nichiren promised solemnly. He later adopted the boy as his own son, giving him the name Nichiryu (Christensen, 82).

After what had happened, Nichiren felt it would not be safe to return to Kamakura. Once more he went out into the provinces, always moving from place to place so that he would not bring troubles upon those who were kind enough to give him shelter and provisions. For four years he wandered, a homeless outcast. The world gradually forgot about him, but he did not forget the world.

If the thirteenth century was a time of drastic political and social change for Japan, it had been even more terrifying and disastrous for a large portion of the civilized world. The dreaded Mongols burst out of central Asia and swept both eastward and westward. Venerable empires toppled to the ground before them, and whole nations were laid waste. Other nations fled in panic, overrunning weaker neighbours who lay in their path of escape. The whole world shuddered in horror, wondering who would be the next victim.

The invincible Mongols swept on, bent on slaughter and conquest for the mere sport of it. They poured over the Great Wall of China to make a grazing ground for their horses. They reduced Russia to smoking ruins to create a no-man's-land that their enemies could not cross. They turned Persia into a cemetery, and devastated Iraq. They stormed Baghdad and made a mountain of skulls. They crushed the mighty Seljuk Turks and exhibited the Sultan in a cage. No one could stop them. They might have conquered the world had they not ended by squabbling among themselves.

In 1268 a Korean delegate arrived in Kamakura and demanded tribute from Japan for Kublai Khan, the Mongolian ruler of China and Korea. This was the usual Mongolian tactic of sowing seeds of terror in the hearts of potential victims before suddenly appearing across the borders. Hojo Masumara, the Regent, forwarded the letter to the Emperor in Kyoto. Shortly afterwards, the nervous Masumara was replaced as regent by another member of his family, Hojo Tokimune. The Mongolian plan seemed to be working. The Japanese government was in confusion.

Hearing the news, Nichiren immediately returned to Kamakura. He began sending letters to important officials of church and state, pointing out that his prophecy made back in 1260 was now coming true, and requesting that a public debate be held to decide what was the true religion, by which Japan could survive the coming storm. He was sure that if he could gain a public hearing, he could easily prove that he stood for the same values which had sustained Japan for centuries. But he was a politician without a constituency, a commander without divisions. He was ignored.

Before the end of the year the Mongols sent a second delegation. This time it was headed not by a Korean but by a Mongol. His fierce aspect struck terror into the hearts of many (as it was meant to do), but Hoji Tokimune sent him away empty-handed. The story was repeated the next year. In 1270 the Mongols began to build up their forces in Korea, outfitting them for a sea-attack and making sure that the Japanese knew they were there. Early in 1271 a third Mongolian envoy came twice to Japan and warned that the mighty Kublai Khan was running out of patience; there would be no further warnings.

It was obvious that the zero-hour was near. Troops were mobilized and prepared to march to probable points of attack. All priests were ordered to pray for victory. The saintly Ryokan was appointed national high priest for the emergency. The idea of a public debate was never even considered. Ryokan had no use for Nichiren and refused to talk to him. Nichiren, for his part, said that even a good man can become deranged from too much *sake*; Ryokan was deranged from wrong doctrine (*Niike Gosho*).

That did it! The Minister of War, Hei-no-Yoritsuna, wanted the country united in one mind behind the fighting men. As a soldier, he knew how to deal with Nichiren — kill him.

Chapter 10

Death and Resurrection __

The summer of 1271 did not bring foreign invaders to the shores of Japan, but it did bring drought. The spring rains were light, and the summer was dry. By September the farmers were desperate.

Since Ryokan would not meet him in open debate, Nichiren challenged him to pray for rain and demonstrate his spiritual powers. Of course, temples throughout the land had been praying for rain all summer, but Nichiren had pointedly avoided all rain-making ceremonies. Then he announced that he would pray for rain. Within a few days the clouds gathered and showers poured down upon the parched earth. As far as the Minister of War was concerned, the prayers of any of the country's temples might have brought the rains, and it was ridiculous for Nichiren to claim sole credit. But ignorant people had been impressed, and that could weaken the authority of the official high priest, Ryokan. It was time to get rid of Nichiren once and for all.

On 10 September 1271 Nichiren was summoned to the office of Hei no Saemon,[52] Minister of War and second in command to the Regent, to answer charges that he had insulted leaders of church and state. He admitted that he had criticized Ryokan, but denied accusations that he had said that Hojo Tokiyori and Hojo Shigetoki had both fallen into hell. Since he had broken no law, he was released. However, Hei no Saemon and other officials were not about to let the matter drop.

On the afternoon of 12 September Hei no Saemon personally led a large party of fully armoured warriors to arrest Nichiren. To overawe the upstart son of a fisherman he wore his full official regalia. Nichiren, when he saw the soldiers coming, said to his frightened students, 'This is what I have been expecting for a long time. How lucky for me that I have been able to devote my life to the Lotus Sutra! It has been like changing sand for gold or pebbles for gems.'

He gathered up his scrolls of the Lotus Sutra — his most precious possessions — and stepped out onto the veranda. The soldiers hesitated for a moment, but then, urged on by their officer, broke into the house and began smashing anything they could find. A civilian retainer named Shofu-bo, who had once been one of Nichiren's pupils, snatched a scroll which Nichiren had tucked into his belt and began to beat him on the head with it. 'I am only human,' Nichiren wrote later. 'My first instinct was to protect myself and grab back the scroll. Then I realized he was beating me with the fifth volume of the Lotus Sutra, the same one which states that the devotee of the Sutra will be beaten and insulted.' The prophecy had come true!

The warriors took all the scrolls, unwound them, tore them up, stamped on them, or wrapped them around their bodies. Nichiren could contain himself no longer. 'What are you doing? Hei no Saemon must be mad! You are felling the pillar of Japan!' Surprised, the warriors stopped their vandalism long enough for the prophet to begin a lecture on the true faith. They listened for a while, half-amused, half-interested. Then Hei no Saemon grew impatient. He ordered Nichiren marched out and brought to trial. The verdict had already been decided: banishment to the Island of Sado. Meanwhile the prisoner was to be confined in the home of Homma Shigetsura, deputy constable of Sado.

Hei no Saemon was not satisfied. Ordered to escort the prisoner to the home of Homma, he decided to make a detour via the execution grounds. Late in the day he had Nichiren brought out and mounted on a saddleless horse. Hei no Saemon, anxious to get the execution over before the Regent found out about it, ordered the party to move out towards Tatsu-no-kuchi, the execution grounds outside the city.

When Nichiren heard the order, he knew that his last hour had come. He sent a boy to find one of his most faithful followers, a Samurai named Shijo Kingo. Shijo and his two brothers came running, catching up with the procession when it was well on its way. He was a man of rank, and although he could not countermand the orders of Hei no Saemon, he demanded the right to hold the bridle of Nichiren's horse. Shijo had left home in such a hurry that he had not even stopped to put on his shoes. He trotted alongside barefoot, sobbing like a child.

Nichiren never forgot the Samurai's devotion. 'Over and over I recall that you came and followed me when I was going to be beheaded,' he wrote to him later, 'and that you cried and wept, holding the bridle of my horse. How can I forget that as long as I live? If some day you should fall into hell because of your grievous sins, I will not follow the call of the Lord Shakyamuni even if he invites me to Buddhahood, but will surely join you in hell. If you and I are in hell, Shakyamuni and the Lotus Sutra will certainly be there with us.'

When they passed in front of the temple of the war-god Hachiman, Nichiren asked permission to dismount. The guards allowed it, thinking that he wanted to pray. However, instead of praying, Nichiren astonished everyone by loudly berating the god for not coming to his rescue. 'Bodhisattva Hachiman, are you really a god? Did not all of you gods swear to the Lord Shakyamuni that you would protect a devotee of the Lotus Sutra? What are you doing, then? If you don't hurry, I will soon be before the Lord in Paradise, and I will report you and all the other gods who failed to keep your promise. If you feel this will go hard on you, hurry up and do something!'

Some of the soldiers were a bit startled by this astonishing speech from one who was about to die. It is said that this is the only time in the history of Japan that anyone has dared publicly to berate a national god. Nevertheless, the procession mounted up and continued to Tatsu-no-kuchi. For the details of what happened next, we are dependent upon a document which was originally in Nichiren's own hand, but which has been so altered by later scribes that it is no longer entirely reliable. It reads as follows:

'At the place which Nichiren had expected to be the site of his execution, many boisterous warriors surrounded him. Shijo Kingo said in tears, "This is your last moment." Nichiren replied, "You don't understand. You should be delighted at this great good fortune [to be able to give one's life for the Sutra]. Don't break your promise." At that moment, a luminous ball as bright as the moon appeared in the direction of Enoshima, and rapidly crossed the sky from southeast to northwest. It was shortly before dawn on the night of the twelfth. It had been too dark to see anyone's face, but the radiant ball made it as bright as a moonlit night so that Nichiren was able to see all the faces there. The executioner fell on his face, his eyes blinded. Some of the warriors, terrified and panic-stricken, ran off a hundred yards; others crouched down on the backs of their horses. At this Nichiren cried, "Here! Why do you shrink from this vile prisoner? Come nearer! Come closer!" However, no one would approach. "What if it dawns? Hurry up and execute me! It will be shameful to behead me after the sun has risen." Nichiren urged them to fulfill their purpose immediately, but there was no answer at all' (*Shuju Ofurumai Gosho*).

This 'luminous ball' has puzzled historians for centuries. Some have said that there was a bolt of lightning which shattered the executioner's sword (De Bary, 1969, 347). Recently Dr Hideo Hirose, a professor at Tokyo University and director of the Tokyo Astronomical Laboratory, reported in the *Seikyo Times* that it was a meteor caused by the passing of Encke's Comet, appearing at 4: a.m. at an elevation of 34° and positioned at an angle from south to west of 79° (September 1985, 56.).

For a long time the guards did not seem to know what to do next. Finally they sent a messenger back to Kamakura for instructions. On the way he met another messenger hastening out from the Regent, who had finally learned what was happening and wanted his original instructions carried out. Nichiren was to be exiled, not executed. The two messengers exchanged dispatches and returned.

Nichiren was kept under house arrest for nearly a month. He was not abused any more, but treated respectfully by the guards. He enjoyed talking to them, and even succeeded in converting some of them to the *Dharma Flower*. Meanwhile the authorities hesitated. They were not sure any more what to do with him. If he really was a great prophet, it would be dangerous to punish him, but if he was causing dissensions in these perilous times, he should be removed as far away as possible. Reflecting the leaders' lack of decision, the city grew restless. The crime rate went up, and there were cases of arson. Nichiren's followers were blamed. Finally the government acted. Nichiren was removed to the distant island of Sado, and his leading disciples were incarcerated.

To Nichiren his miraculous escape from death at Tatsu-no-kuchi was the turning point in his life; it solidified his connection to the *Dharma Flower*. A week after the event he wrote to his faithful Samurai friend, 'Every place where Nichiren meets persecution is the Buddha land. Of all the places in this world, it is at Tatsu-no-kuchi . . . where Nichiren's life dwells. Because he gave his life there for the sake of the Lotus Sutra, Tatsu-no-kuchi may well be called the Buddha land' (MW 1:14).

Now he knew that he had a special role in life. No longer did he call himself, 'a follower of Dengyo Daishi (Saicho)'. Neither Saicho nor Chih-i had offered up his very life for the *Dharma Flower* — only he had done so. He was their equal, probably their superior (*Myomitsu Shonin Goshosoku*). It was clear that he stood in some very special relationship with the Sutra. 'Since I am a common mortal, it is beyond my power to know my previous existences. Apparently I am now the doer of the *Dharma Flower*, and in the future I will be able to reach the seat of enlightenment. Judging the past from this, I must have been present at the ceremony in space (described in the Sutra). There can be no disconnection between the three existences (of the past, present, and future)' (*Shoho Jisso Sho*).

Who was he, then? Nichiren searched the scriptures for the answer. Already he had noticed the similarity between his life and that of Never-Despising Bodhisattva (*Jofukyo*). The latter had been ridiculed and persecuted, and had responded to his tormentors by bowing to them and saying, 'I do not despise you because you will all be able to become Buddhas.' This only drew more scorn down upon him, but he persisted until finally he was able to convert great multitudes. 'The twenty-four (Chinese) characters of his message and the five of mine (*Myo ho ren ge kyo*), are different in word but the same in spirit' (*Kembutsu Mirai Ki*). He said that he would be the Never-Despising Bodhisattva of this Age of Degeneration (*Dan'notsubo Gohenji*).

The parallel was not exact, however, since Never-Despising had lived during a stagnant Age of Imitation Dharma, which was not the same as the present Age of Degeneration. The gentle method of bowing may have worked in such times; today more vigorous methods were necessary. But the Buddha, Nichiren reasoned, had foreseen such differences. When he was about to reveal the heart of his teaching — the very heart of his being — in the Original Gate, he had summoned forth a vast multitude of bodhisattvas who were completely unknown to his other disciples. They were the bodhisattvas 'from under the Earth'. It was to them that he assigned the mission of spreading the message of eternal life for future ages. These were not men of theory, but men of action. Their leaders were called the Four Great Bodhisattvas of action, and he, Nichiren, must have been one of them — maybe even their leader.

In Nichiren's mind, a vast cosmic plan was unfolding. The Buddha was truly wonderful! He had prepared everything in advance so that all living beings could obtain Buddhahood. Long ago in the distant past, he had appeared as Buddha under different names, such as Never-Despising, and sown the seeds of Buddhahood in people's minds. These people were reborn during the days of Shakyamuni, heard the Dharma from him, and attained enlightenment. The seeds, which had been sown in the distant past, were brought to fruition under the glorious sun of Shakyamuni. Meanwhile others heard him for the first time during his half-century of preaching in India. They then received the seed into their hearts, too. During the second thousand years of Buddhism, they were reborn on earth, and their Buddha-seeds came to fruition under the guidance of great bodhisattvas reincarnated as Chih-i, Dengyo Daishi (Saicho), and others. The Buddha, in his infinite compassion, had always used the right method according to the capacities of the people of each age.

But what about the men and women in the present degenerate age? They had never had the seed sown in their hearts in the past, so there was nothing that could be brought to fruition. Or was there? Indeed, there was! They were the very ones who had been summoned 'from under the earth' — from the infinite past. They had received the Buddha-seed 'from the beginning'. Their seed would be brought to fruition under the guidance of the Four Great Bodhisattvas headed by Jogyo, Superior-Practice. That great bodhisattva was none other than Nichiren himself.

The sun was not setting, like everyone thought. It was the moon that was setting — the reflected light of the moon of the old teachings from India and China, which had completed their role. The sun was now rising in the form of the Original Buddha, *Hombutsu*, who was displaying his light within the lives of his Original Disciples (*Honge*). It was rising in the East over Japan; it would extend its light westward until it brightened the entire world. (*Kangyo Hachiman Sho*).

Nichiren came to these optimistic conclusions at a time when his life should have been at its nadir, not its zenith. He had been sentenced to death, spared at the last minute, and then sent far away into exile, where it seemed he would die forgotten. Yet there he was, talking cheerfully about rising over all the world like the sun in the east.

Japanese society has always been group-centred. The individual is under tremendous pressure to conform to the standards of the group — his family, his class, his village, his guild. To be cut off from the group, to be disinherited and set adrift, is a terrible punishment.[53] Only one thing could be worse yet — to be cut off from *all* groups, to be sent into exile. Nichiren had suffered this fate once before, but then he had been sent not too far away. Now he was exiled to the ends of the country, to a lonely wind-swept isle that had become the tomb of more than one enemy of the Hojos.

Sado is a pleasant enough place in the summer, but during the winter icy blasts roar across the Sea of Japan from Siberia and send temperatures plunging. Nichiren had the misfortune to arrive at the beginning of winter. His only shelter was an abandoned hut. His only food was what he could scrounge — which was not very much. 'During the nearly two months since my arrival on this island of Sado,' he wrote in December 1271, 'icy winds have been blowing constantly, and though the snow sometimes stops for a while, the sunlight is never seen. My body is penetrated by the cold' (Anesaki, 62–3).

One man decided to put Nichiren out of his misery. There was an old Samurai named Abutsu-bo, who was living on the island, himself an exile from some long forgotten political intrigue.[54] He decided that it was his moral duty to put the 'devil priest' to death. Honour required, however, that he face his opponent first. Armed with a sword in its scabbard, he confronted Nichiren, but once he was face to face with the man he wanted to kill, he could find no excuse to draw his sword. The conversation grew less gruff and more friendly. After a while Abutsu became so engrossed in their discussion that he took off his sword and sat down; it was the beginning of a life-long friendship. At the end of the day Abutsu went home and told his wife about the extraordinary man he had met.

The next day husband and wife came together. This time they brought provisions, for Abutsu had noticed that the priest had almost nothing to eat. They visited him almost every day after that, frequently coming by night so as not to be noticed by the islanders. Once more Nichiren had found friends in his exile. Just as the fisherman and his wife had looked after him on the Izu Peninsula, so now Abutsu and his wife Sen'nichi-ama did the same. Nichiren came to consider them among his dearest friends. In later years Abutsu would three times make the long journey to Mt. Minobu to see Nichiren. When he died, his son made the trip for him, bringing his ashes to be buried there near those of the master.

When winter had passed, Nichiren began to receive visitors who came trudging up from Kamakura. Among them was the young mother mentioned earlier, who brought her daughter with her. Some of his disciples came to minister to him. One of them was Niko, who was later called Sado Ajari ('Sado Teacher'). Nichiro also came, having escaped prison by a ruse. But when Nichiren heard of the ruse, he ordered the disciple to return so as not to cause others to suffer in his place.

Nichiren was in exile on Sado from 1271 to 1274. During these years he had much time on his hands, and this gave him the opportunity to systematize the main points of his teachings. First of all, as we have seen, he came to a clear understanding of his own identity: he was the exponent of the Lotus Sutra for the Age of Degeneration.

Nichiren saw himself in the role of the leader of the Bodhisattvas from the Earth, Superior-Practice (*Jogyo*). Was he really the reincarnation of the Great Bodhisattva? Although he long wondered about this, he hesitated to give himself such an august title. Generally he described himself as an envoy of Jogyo. 'Although I am not Jogyo, I think I understand what he should do. I have been propagating the Right Dharma of the Buddha for the past twenty some years. I believe that Jogyo Bodhisattva told me to do this' (*Nii-ama-gozen-gohenji*).

In only one document does he specifically identify himself with Bodhisattva Jogyo (Sanskrit, Vishista-caritra), and that is a late work of disputed authenticity, the *Sandai-hiho-sho*.[55] Nevertheless, the parallels between him and Jogyo are too obvious to overlook. Both Jogyo and Nichiren represent the superior man of action — fire in the lotus.

Shortly after his arrival on Sado, Nichiren began writing what was to be his longest work — a 75-page essay entitled, 'Open Your Eyes' (*Kaimokusho*). Because of the adverse circumstances under which he was living and writing, it took him about three months to complete the work. The composition shows indications of frequent interruptions, but he had to get it down on paper. The main topic was his own identity; he had to explain to his followers (and to himself as well) how it could be that he, the practitioner of the Sutra, should be so despised and rejected. Why had all the powers of heaven and earth deserted him? The Buddha had promised to protect a devotee of the Lotus Sutra. Why had not legions of angels been dispatched to his rescue? Since that dramatic night at the execution grounds there had been no favourable signs from heaven — only icy winds that penetrated his miserable hut day and night.

Nichiren seemed to fear that he would not survive that first terrible winter in exile. The essay bears signs of being a last will and testament. It was addressed to those faithful few who had stood by him, some of whom were then languishing in prisons. He sent it to Shijo Kingo, the brave Samurai who had accompanied him to the execution grounds.

'A man called Nichiren was beheaded at midnight on the 12th of the ninth month last year. This is being written by the soul of that man, who is now in the snow of the Province of Sado. This writing will be sent to my disciples who are still following me. Those who read this may be frightened because this seems dreadful although it is not dreadful at all. This essay is a mirror reflecting the future of Japan prophesied by Shakyamuni Buddha, Many-Treasures Buddha, and the Buddhas of the worlds of the ten directions. It should be regarded as my testament.'

He begins with a long discourse on the history of the development of religious thought, which leads to its culmination in the 'Three Thousand Things in One Moment's Thought', as elucidated by Chih-i. Although other philosophers may have had the same insight, credit must be given where credit is due — to Chih-i, who first explained the theory, and to the Lotus Sutra, where it was revealed.

The fulfilment of the Lotus Sutra in the modern age calls for the appearance of Superior-Practice, Jogyo. Is he here yet? Yes, it seems that he is. There is one man who is realizing in his flesh all the persecutions which the Sutra says its devotee must be prepared to endure. That man is Nichiren.

Nichiren must suffer in the flesh to expiate for sins in past lives. Even in this life, he began his career as a practitioner of the Nembutsu, and for this he must pay the price. The more he is persecuted now, the quicker he will expiate his sins and attain Buddhahood.

In a letter sent the next month to his most prominent disciple, Toki Jonin, he elaborated on this point, saying that he was born under all sorts of handicaps: poverty, a heretical family, a hostile ruler, an unattractive physical appearance, and so forth. Such inherited disadvantages must have been merited because of prior sins. In expiating them for himself, he expiates them for others as well. Anesaki explains:

> An existence of any kind is never an individual matter, but always the result of a common karma, shared by all born in the same realm of existence. Hence the expiation made by any one individual is, in fact, made for the sake of all his fellow-beings. Both the persecutors and the persecuted share the common karma accumulated in the past, and therefore share also in the future destiny, the attainment of Buddhahood. Nichiren's repression of others' malice and vice is at the same time his own expiation and self-subjugation. How, then, should his followers not share his merit in extinguishing the accumulated sins, and preparing for the realization of the primeval Buddha-nature? 'Therefore,' Nichiren exhorts his disciples, 'believe in me, and emulate my spirit and work, in the firm faith that the Master is the savior and leader! Work together, united in the same faith! Then, the expiation of sins will be achieved for ourselves and for all our fellow-beings, because we all share in the common karma.'

(75)

His iron determination and irrepressible optimism carried him through that first freezing winter on Sado. In the spring his fortunes took a turn for the better. The government, still a bit worried that he might be a true prophet after all, sent instructions that he should be well treated and installed in adequate quarters. He was moved to a place called Ichi-no-Sawa, where the local ruler took a great liking to him, even permitting his wife and son to become converts. As a government official, however, he dared not take this step himself.

Under these improved circumstances Nichiren was now able to put his deepest thoughts down on paper. During 1273, the second year of his exile, he produced some of his finest writings including his masterpiece, *Kanjin Honzon Sho*. It is shorter than 'Open Your Eyes', but less rambling and better organized. The former, written under great stress, had been concerned primarily with his own identity. The latter is a reasoned explanation of his principal teachings.

The word *kanjin* is a term used by Chih-i. It means 'observation of the mind', or the ability to see that the 3000 things exist in our minds. The second term, *honzon*, is difficult to translate. In traditional Buddhism, it refers to the principal idol in a temple — that which is worshipped. *Hon* means 'root' or 'origin'; *son* or *zon* is 'honoured' or 'worthy of respect'. (We see it in the common epithet for the Buddha, 'World-honoured One', *Seson*.)

With Nichiren the term *honzon* takes on a very specific meaning; the usual translation as 'object of worship' seems inadequate. Petzold gives a very literal translation, 'fundamental venerable'. Earlier translators such as Satomi and Anesaki call it 'Supreme Being', and that seems close to what Nichiren had in mind. He used the term in its literal sense: sacred (*son*) source (*hon*). It is not just an object — a thing — but that from which all being originates, that which essentially *is* and which alone is worthy of our devotion. Nichiren generally distinguishes between his understanding of *honzon* and the more limited usual view by adding an honorific, *go*: *gohonzon*. Therefore the title of the essay, *Kanjin Honzon Sho*, could be rendered, 'The Sacred Source Revealed by Observation of the Mind'.

Again he begins his essay with a discussion of Chih-i's doctrine of the 'Three Thousand Things in a Moment's Thought'. This time he stresses that since all things involve each other, so too is the Buddha involved in all things. Shakyamuni was born as an ordinary mortal, and then became the Buddha, showing that he already had Buddhahood within. There must be a seed before there can be a flower. We mortals contain the same seed.

Professor Kanko Mochizuki of Rissho University summarizes this portion of Nichiren's argument in an essay, 'The Kanjin Honzon Sho':

Nichiren says that this truth is expressed by the Japanese title of the sutra, *Myoho Renge Kyo*. The word *renge* represents the law of causality. *Ren* has two meanings: a lotus-plant and a lotus-fruit. Nichiren takes the latter meaning of the word to make it a symbol of the effect as the contrast to *ge* or flower, which he regards as symbol of cause. And the fact that some lotus flowers bloom while other lotus flowers already bear fruit is utilized to show that cause and effect involve each other. The Buddha was a man; a man will be a Buddha. This is the law of causality expressed by *renge*. This *renge* or law of causality is excellent; therefore it is called *Myoho* or the Excellent Law. Thus, to Nichiren, *Myoho Renge Kyo* is not only the name of the sutra, but also the name of the truth expounded in the sutra. Because the title of the sutra expresses by itself the truth that the Buddha and men are the same in their essence, we shall be able to attain to Buddhahood by chanting the Sacred Title. Nichiren recommends this chanting as the most important practice, rejecting the complicated ways of meditation of the T'ien-t'ai Sect as unfit for the people living in the Age of Degeneration.

(The Nichiren Sect, 11)

In a later writing Nichiren elaborates on this important principle. '*Myo* ("wonderful") represents death, and *Ho* ("Dharma, Law") life. Life and death are the two phases passed through by the entities of the Ten Worlds, the entities of all sentient beings which embody the law of cause and effect (*renge*) . . . Shakyamuni who attained enlightenment countless aeons ago, the Lotus Sutra which leads all people to Buddhahood, and we ordinary human beings are in no way different or separate from each other. Therefore, to chant Myoho-renge-kyo with this realization is to inherit the ultimate law of life and death' (MW 1:22).

Having explained *kanjin*, the method for attaining Buddhahood, Nichiren moves on to what it is that the correct practice reveals, *honzon*, the Sacred Source. It is to be found, he says, not in some imaginary 'western paradise', but right here in our own world and within our own selves. All those distant pure lands or heavenly realms were conceived in the minds of historical beings. When they died, their mental creations passed away with them. We cannot expect to enter their heavens any more than we can enter into their minds. We must find the Pure Land within our own lives.

'The *Saha*-world (this world) of the Original Buddha is the eternal pure land, free from the three calamities and the four *kalpas* (periods of growth stability, decay, and oblivion). In this eternal world, the Buddha never disappeared in the past, nor is he to appear in the future. All living beings under him are one with him because they have the wisdom of the Buddha in their minds.'

Our world of constant flux is revealed in the *Dharma Flower* to be the eternal world of the Original Buddha. Chih-i explained this with his Three Truths: the reality of phenomena (*ke*), Void (*ku*), and the Middle (*chu*). The world as we experience it is phenomenal (*ke*). It is also non-substantial and negated by emptiness (*ku*). Chapter XVI of the Lotus Sutra reveals that the negation is so complete that it negates itself. This is the Middle — 'true suchness' — the 'Pure Land of the Vulture Peak', or as it is generally called in Nichiren Buddhism, the 'Pure Land of Tranquil Light'.

For us mortals, *honzon* in the sense of an object of worship appears at the moment Shakyamuni transmits his sacred truth to us, the Bodhisattvas from the earth. 'The true object of worship (*honzon*) should be the Buddha at the moment of this transmission. The scene of the transmission is described in the following way: 'In the sky above the Eternal Saha-world is seen the Treasure tower, which is nothing but the representation of the Five Words (*myo ho ren ge kyo*). In this stupa sits the Original Buddha Shakyamuni on the right and Many Treasures on the left. The Four Great Bodhisattvas attend on Shakyamuni; Manjusri, Maitreya, Bhaisajyaraja (Yaku-o, Medicine King), and Samantabhadra (Fugen, Universal Sage) are seen in the lower heaven; all the other major and minor Bodhisattvas, be they disciples of the Buddha Shakyamuni of Manifestation or of the Buddhas of other worlds, are seated in the lowest heaven, just as a multitude of subjects prostrate themselves before their king; and all the Buddhas of the worlds in the ten directions take their positions on the ground, showing that they and their lands are but epiphanies of the Eternal Buddha and His land. The scene as such is mentioned nowhere else, only in the eight chapters [of the *Dharma Flower*, from the 15th to the 22nd inclusive]' (*Kanjin Honzon Sho*, 32–3).

We have here three main points of Nichiren's system: the true cause, the true effect, and the true land. The true cause is the Sacred Title. The true effect is Buddhahood. The true land is here, this *Saha*-world, where we meet the Sacred Source. In a slightly altered form, they are called the Three Great Secret Dharmas: The Sacred Title of the Original Gate (*Hommon no daimoku*), the Sacred Source of the Original Gate (*Hommon no honzon*), and the Precepts platform of the original gate (*Hommon no kaidan*).

In this essay, as well as in others written in the same period, Nichiren spoke mostly about the first two Great Secret Dharmas, and scarcely alluded to the third. Only years later, when it was obvious that his teachings were being rejected not only by heretical sects but by his own Tendai Sect as well, did he narrow the idea of the True Land to a *kaidan*, which would replace the official *kaidan* at Mount Hiei. Saicho had established the latter as a place where monks might receive the precepts of Mahayana. Since Nichiren taught only one precept, the Sacred Title, his *kaidan* would be for everyone who would accept it, be they men or women, clergy or laity. Basically the *Hommon no Kaidan* is any place where a believer keeps the Sutra, as is stated in Chapter XXI. Any such place is sacred, but that does not rule out the possibility of erecting an actual *kaidan* for all humanity at some time in the future.

Nichiren now completed his exposition of the Sacred Source by sketching it in the form of a mandala. He did this on 8 July 1273, after writing *Kanjin Honzon Sho* and some other works on the same subject.

A mandala is a graphic design used to help a meditator focus his attention on the oneness that underlies all existence. There are many different types of mandalas, and they are much used in esotericism. Normally a mandala is a balanced design of circles, squares, and other geometric forms which focus finally on a circular centre. If it is illustrated, it shows Buddhas and Bodhisattvas seated in an orderly arrangement.

José and Miriam Argüelles describe and illustrate numerous mandalas in their book of the same name (12–13).

> The universality of the Mandala is in its one constant, *the principle of the center*. The center is the beginning of the Mandala as it is the beginning and origin of all form and of all processes, including the extensions of form into time . . . [It is] symbolic of the eternal potential. From the same inexhaustible source all seeds grow and develop, all cells realize their function . . . This can be realized because the center principle manifests itself through man in the same way as it does through a flower or a star; in it we may discover our cosmic commonality — or cosmic community'.

They go on to say that a mandala has three basic properties: a centre, symmetry, and cardinal points. 'The first principle is constant; the latter two vary according to the nature of the particular Mandala' (13).

Nichiren was well acquainted with this type of mandala, for he had studied many of them. His own, however, is entirely different. It has the three properties of a centre, symmetry, and cardinal points, but they are not immediately obvious. It contains no circles or squares, only Chinese characters written in his bold hand. His Great Mandala (*Daimandara* or *Omandara*) is not designed to help the meditator focus on the still quiet centre, the Void. Instead it is an embodiment of the principle of the Three Thousand Things in a Single Moment's Thought. It bursts with life.

Nichiren is known to have inscribed over 130 mandalas, most of which are still extant. (One was discovered at Nagoya as recently as 1985.) No two are exactly alike, but all express the same theme. The earliest complete one, drawn in 1273 while he was in exile on Sado, was on a piece of silk, 2 ft 6 in wide and 5 ft 6 in long. Down the centre in large letters are written the Chinese characters, NAMU MYOHO RENGE KYO. At the top to the right and left in smaller characters are inscribed Namu Shakyamuni Buddha, Namu Many-Treasures Buddha, and Namu — each of the Four Great Bodhisattvas from under the Earth. At the four corners are the names of the four guardian deities, marking the four cardinal points mentioned by Argüelles. On the two sides are

Sanskrit letters standing for the temple guardians: Acala, the sound 'a', representing the material, and Raga, the sound 'hum', the mind, at least in their benign aspect (Getty 1988, 170). As demons, Acala is desire and Raga determined aggression (Campbell, *Myths, Dreams and Religion* 156–7). The rest of the mandala consists of names of other beings, divine, human, and sub-human, representing all the 'ten worlds'.

Unlike most mandalas, wherein all beings radiate from a common centre and thus manifest their oneness, Nichiren's arrangement shows an ascending hierarchy of life. The higher beings are at the top; lower beings take their places further down in order of rank like attendants at the court of a king. Through the centre, giving meaning to all, is the Tower of Seven Gems, the Sacred Title in seven characters. It is embodied in the one who chants it and especially in Nichiren himself.

'Reading the letters of Nichiren,' says calligrapher John Carpenter, 'one is captivated by the fiery, indomitable nature of the man who revolutionized Japanese Buddhism by making it a vehicle for social reform. One is struck by the handwriting, which strongly conveys the personality of this impatient genius. Nichiren recommended that the Lotus Sutra be "read with the whole body," and one can suppose, too, that in those tempestuous letters he wrote with his whole body.'[56]

In enlightenment, the knower and reality merge as one. 'The Great Mandala,' says an official handbook of the Nichiren Sect, 'represents the enlightenment of the Eternal Buddha Shakyamuni and the very heart of the Buddha, and therefore it is a graphic representation of Shakyamuni Buddha's spirit, itself' (*Shingyo Hikkei*, 5). It is the Sacred Source of the Original Gate (*Hommon-no-Honzon*).

Most Buddhists venerate the Buddha in the form of a statue. Nichiren himself took with him everywhere a small image of Shakyamuni, which had been given to him by the provincial governor whose health he restored on the Izu Peninsula. A statue which is aesthetically pleasing to one person, however, may be repulsive to another. Japanese Buddhists will make the Buddha look Japanese; an Indian will make him look Indian. The very earliest representations, made under the influence of Greek art, made him appear like a Greek god. One artist will make him fat; another will make him thin. Particularly difficult for the artist to represent are the '32 physical marks' symbolizing the Buddha's superiority. They include a protuberance on the top of the head (signifying wisdom), the 'third eye' (omniscience), elongated earlobes, elongated arms, and other features, which may end up looking grotesque on the figure of an otherwise normal human being.

In the Great Mandala, on the other hand, the devotee identifies himself with what he sees written before him. Even if he cannot read all the Chinese characters, he, too, is *Namu Myoho Renge Kyo*. All the ten worlds exist in him, too.

According to Shimizu Ryozan (1865–1928), a prominent Nichiren theologian, there are three mandalas, each with its own 'secret platform' (*mitsudan*), or place where we meet it. The Ceremony in Space, which is described in the middle portion of the Lotus Sutra, is a mandala (a sacred symbol) of the meeting between the Buddha and all beings. In the presence of the Buddha, they are all transfigured, revealing their true nature. Shimizu calls this, 'The Great Mandala Secret Platform of the Great Meeting in Space of the Original Gate' (*Hommon koku dai-e no daimandara mitsudan*).

For the sake of us sinful and spiritually blind beings of the Age of Degeneration, Nichiren now makes a pen and ink mandala, which reveals the former 'as accurately as the print matches the woodblock' from which it derives (*Nichinyo Gozen Gohenji*). Shimizu calls this pen-and-ink mandala 'The Great Mandala Secret Platform for the Age of Degeneration' (*Mappo oji no daimandara mitsudan*). Nichiren, after many preparatory attempts, drew it for the first time on 8 July 1273. He could depict it only after he had first perfectly conceived it in *Kanjin Honzon Sho*.

These two mandalas, the visible and tangible one created by Nichiren, and the symbolic one of the Ceremony in Space are both manifestations of an even more fundamental reality, 'The Great Mandala Secret Platform of Original Existence of Non-beginning (*Mushi honnu no daimandara mitsudan*), which is originally complete and existing originally by itself. It cannot be seen because its form is "non-form"' (Petzold, *Nichiren* 61–2).

Each mandala has its own *kaidan*, place of reception of the precepts, or *mitsudan*, secret place of reception. The most fundamental is invisible and inconceivable to the mind and visible spiritually; it is 'in space'. 'This manifests the superior and wonderful material forms,' says Petzold citing Shimizu, 'by opening the "form of non-form" of the first Mandala, whereby all complete meetings are made to exist completely. That is, the whole universe and all beings and things contained in it now become manifested' (62). The third, which is visible to the eye, manifests the other two. It is where physical beings meet the one Buddha in his manifestation.

When the assembled multitude at the Ceremony in Space saw the great Treasure Tower, its door was closed. The Buddha then opened the door revealing Many-Treasures Buddha within — that is, the Buddha-nature within ourselves. The Buddha now gives us the key to open our Treasure Tower. It is *Namu Myoho Renge Kyo*, the Sacred Formula (*Odaimoku*). The Sacred Formula is not given in the *Dharma Flower* Sutra. It is the Sutra; it is the Sutra's quintessence.

The Sacred Formula, however, is not merely subjective, applying to oneself alone; it is also objective. It is the content of the enlightenment of the Buddha. It is universal, applying to everyone and everything. It is also the heart of the Sacred Source who reveals himself as the Original Gate (*Hommon no honzon*). The Sacred Formula is the subject; the Great Mandala-Gohonzon is the object.

According to Satomi, Nichiren has solved 'the religious problem' by overcoming the distinction between subjective and objective religions. Buddhism, as a rule, is subjective; it looks inward, to the self. Christianity, Judaism, and Islam are objective; they look outward, to God. Subjective religions, which developed among the Aryan races from ancient Hindu sages to modern German philosophers, lean toward pantheism, finding God everywhere and nowhere. Objective religions, which originated among the Semitic races, are monotheistic, seeing God as the 'absolutely other'. Nichiren, says Satomi, is both; he calls this, 'One Buddha-centric Pantheism' (87).

> Confucius or Christ or Mohammed or any sages are nothing but one of the distributive bodies of this One and Only Buddha. Nichiren recognized the One Buddha as the sole and highest existence, who revealed himself as Eternal Buddha in Chapter XVI of the Lotus Sutra, but at the same time he acknowledged the divine nature as intrinsically inherent in all beings, according to the principle of Mutual Participation of the ten worlds. He holds with monotheism in the former sense and holds with pantheism in the latter sense. But as he says in his letter to a lady, *Nichinyo*, he took up the position of One Buddha–centric Pantheism as his ultimate decision. We can see here one of the reasons for determining what the condition of the future religion will be.

This Great Mandala, say Nichiren's followers today, is the banner under which all the people of the world will unite in the twenty-first century.

Chapter 11

Death and Dismemberment _____

Nichiren was recalled from exile in February 1274. The official document ordering his release was given to Nissho, his oldest disciple. Nissho gave it to his nephew Nichiro, who was eager to make the trip to Sado and bring the good news. Indeed, Nichiro pushed himself so hard to get there quickly that he almost failed to arrive at all. He reached the island safely, but then collapsed on the road, unable to proceed further.

Nichiren had a premonition that his disciple Nichiro was on the island but in some kind of trouble. He sent some men out looking for him, and sure enough, they found him not far away, stretched out on the road. They picked him up and carried him in for a joyful reunion.

The winds of change had been in the air for some time. The governor of Sado had arranged for a public debate between Nichiren and some local clergy. The governor, who listened attentively to the proceedings, was impressed by Nichiren's arguments. At the close of the debate, Nichiren turned to him and asked, 'Why haven't you taken your troops to Kamakura to aid the government?' The governor was puzzled by the question. Only later did he learn that Hojo had turned against Hojo in a bloody palace coup. He was able to align himself with the winning side, and was grateful to Nichiren for tipping him off. He ordered the exile moved into more comfortable quarters (*Shuju Ofurumai-gosho*).

Shortly before news of his pardon reached him, Nichiren was surprised to receive a gift from one of the Hojos. Hojo Yagenta sent him two Samurai swords; this was his way of asking Nichiren to pray for victory over the Mongols. Scholars have debated whether or not Yagenta became a convert, but at the very least he was an important friend in high places. No doubt he contributed to getting Nichiren pardoned.

Nichiren left Sado on 15 March 1274 accompanied by a military escort. They had a comfortable journey, arriving in Kamakura a week later. There he was met by a group of his followers, many of whom had been imprisoned during his exile. When he saw them, Nichiren dismounted and greeted each one personally. 'All of you must have persevered greatly. I am gratefully indebted to you,' he told them softly (Christensen 107).

On 8 April, he was summoned to the headquarters of the military government, where he was greeted by none other than Hei no Saemon, the man who had tried to execute him three years before. This time their interview was formal and polite, although still at cross-purposes. The military rulers were interested in the military situation, but Nichiren, as usual, was concerned with the religious situation.

The officials asked the prophet when they could expect the Mongol invasion. He replied within one hundred days. This, indeed, is exactly what happened.

Having failed to cut Nichiren off from the nation, the rulers now wanted to assimilate him somehow into the status quo. Therefore they offered to construct a temple for him, provided he would stop criticizing the other sects. He could continue to teach his own doctrines and join in the prayers for national deliverance. However, the security of a temple of his own with government sponsorship was not at all what he wanted. He still expected what he had preached from the beginning: the conversion of the nation to the Right Law.

It became obvious to Nichiren that his views and those of the public officials were still a long way apart. The conversion of Japan was not going to take place during his lifetime. No matter. It would happen eventually. The billions of Bodhisattvas from the Earth had only begun to appear; more would come afterwards. The Buddha's master plan for the salvation of all living beings would roll ahead irresistibly; it was just a matter of time.

One month after his appearance at court, Nichiren abruptly retired from Kamakura. His public life was over. Three times he had challenged the government; three times he had been rejected. He could do no more. He asked only for some isolated mountain retreat, where he could spend the rest of his days in meditation and strengthening the faith of his followers.

Hearing of his plans, Nambu Sanenaga (1222–97), the Lord of Hakiri and a devout believer in Nichiren, offered him land on his property on Mount Minobu. There he built for him a small hut (until his health began to fail a few years later, Nichiren refused to accept more adequate quarters), where the prophet was to spend the last nine years of his life. Nichiren was delighted. To him Minobu, far from the amenities of civilization and bitterly cold in winter, was a paradise.

'I received the One Great and Secret Truth from Buddha Shakyamuni on the Vulture Peak. I keep this truth in my heart. Therefore my heart is the place where the Buddhas enter profound meditation. The Buddhas turn the wheel of the Dharma on my tongue, manifest themselves in my throat, and attain enlightenment in my mouth. Can this place (Minobu) possibly be inferior to the Pure Land of the Vulture Peak?' (*Nanjo hyoe shichiro dono gohenji*)

He continued to write letters to his followers and prepare mandalas for them. One of his letters, 'The Record of Minobu', is the most lyrical he ever wrote, describing the serenity he felt in his heart while living in loving harmony with the natural beauty of his surroundings. He received visitors during the summers, and even had the joy of seeing his old friend Abutsu-bo, who came all the way from Sado three times although he was now over 90 years old. Some of his younger disciples stayed with him constantly; the older ones were already setting up Nichiren centres of their own. However, they kept in close correspondence with their master. He advised them like a loving parent, telling Shijo Kingo to stay home and drink *sake* with his wife instead of going out and carousing with friends, and counselling another not to be so zealous in displaying his faith unless he come to tire of his own zeal. 'Leave things as they are. There will certainly come the time when at the discretion of God the Creator (Brahma) and God the Lord (Shakra) the entire nation will come to believe without fail. I am confident that on that day there will also be a great number of people who will say, "I have long believed," or "I, too, have believed."'[57]

There was no need to thunder warnings any more. Nichiren was sure of himself. His main concerns were for his followers and for his country.

The first Mongolian invasion came in the autumn of 1274, just as Nichiren had predicted. Nine hundred warships with 25,600 men sailed from Korea and crossed the straits separating the two countries. The impact of their initial thrust drove back the Japanese defenders. After ravaging the town of Hakozaki as a warning of their invincibility and burning the shrine of the war-god Hachiman, the Mongols re-embarked, probably intending to strike again further up the coast. But that night a violent storm arose and wrecked most of the ships. This was the famous *kamikaze*, the 'divine wind', which came to the rescue of the country in the hour of its greatest peril. The long-dreaded invasion was shattered in one night.

The victory confused Nichiren's followers. On the one hand, their master had successfully predicted the invasion. On the other hand, the gods (*kami*) had come to the rescue even though Nichiren had said they would not. Although the prophet kept insisting that the danger was not yet over, his followers found themselves discredited and subject to ridicule or even persecution.

Some wealthy men, such as Shijo Kingo, had their properties confiscated. Nichiren advised his friend not to be discouraged, but to continue serving his master loyally just as if he were still in favour. Shijo obeyed these instructions and waited faithfully on his lord, who wanted nothing more to do with him. Finally he was able to demonstrate his true worth when the lord fell ill. It was Shijo, who was a physician as well as a warrior, who patiently nursed him back to health. The lord was so grateful that he restored Shijo's properties three-fold.

Less prominent followers were not always so fortunate. In 1279, 20 peasant believers were arrested on trumped-up charges and sent to Kamakura for trial. There they had to face the implacable Hei no Saemon, who ordered them put to the torture. When none would recant, he had three of them executed as a warning to other would-be Nichiren believers.

Nichiren was shocked to learn about this. He himself had suffered many persecutions and had faced death more than once — that he had expected. He had seen some of his followers die for the faith, and that was harder to accept, but they had been either monks or Samurai — men who knew how to give up their lives for a cause. Now simple peasants had taken up his banner, and they, too, were facing dire punishments.

It was clear that his career had turned another decisive corner. He was no longer alone, nor was he just the leader of a small band of close disciples. He had become the champion of potentially vast numbers of faithful followers. There were men and women out there who had never even seen him, but who believed in him because they had heard about him. Their welfare — the welfare of these total strangers — was now his responsibility. His message had caught fire, and people were willing to die for it.

In a brief but poignant epistle he says that just as Shakyamuni prepared the soil for 40 years before revealing his true intention in the Lotus Sutra, so it had been 27 years since he, a solitary monk without a single disciple, had first raised the cry of *Namu Myoho Renge Kyo*. He had predicted then that unknown multitudes would take up his cry; now the prediction had become reality (*Shonin Gonan Ji*).

In 1275 a Mongolian envoy and his party came to Kamakura to once more demand the surrender of Japan, but the Japanese were no longer afraid of the enemy. The Regent had the envoys taken to Tatsu-no-kuchi and put to death. There was an uneasy peace for a few years. Then in 1279 Kublai Khan, the Mongol emperor, finished off the South Sung Dynasty in China and turned his full attention to the conquest of Japan. Using Chinese and Korean technicians, he assembled a vast fleet of 3,500 warships. A second fleet of 900 ships set sail at about the same time, and the two armadas converged on Japan like giant pincers. Then it happened all over again. Once more the *kamikaze*, the 'divine wind', swept down from the north and capsized nearly all of both fleets. Over 112,000 men, about 80 per cent of the invaders, were drowned in what was perhaps the most extraordinary military débâcle of all time.

When the second invasion struck some of Nichiren's followers began to predict a Mongol victory, but Nichiren warned them sternly against such unpatriotic outbursts. He referred to the enemy as 'little Mongolia' which dared to attack 'great Japan'. He found himself in very much the same position as the Prophet Jeremiah: predicting the defeat of his own country while hoping in his heart that this would never happen.

After the second victory he still thought that the danger had not yet passed. 'An autumn windstorm has destroyed the enemy's ships, and now the people boast of a great victory, as if the enemy commander had been captured. At the same time, the priests act as if it were all due to the efficacy of their rituals. Just ask them whether they took the head of the Mongol king. Whatever they may say, make no other reply than this' (Anesaki 127).

This response shows a certain pique; things had not worked out exactly as he expected. In fact, he was more correct than he may have realized: the country was headed for ruin. The government, convinced that it had been saved by the prayers of its loyal priests, began to spend lavishly on new temples and gorgeous public ceremonies. The great army, which had been mobilized for the emergency, had to be paid. The treasury was soon exhausted, and civil wars broke out. By 1333 the Hojos had fallen. Civil wars were to go on devastating the country for three centuries. The lonely prophet had been right, after all, about the terrible fate awaiting his beloved country.

Although Nichiren was spiritually happy on Mount Minobu, the dampness of the forest did not agree with him physically. 'Since I retired to this place,' he wrote near the end of his life, 'I have never been out of these mountains. During these eight years, illness and age have brought me severe suffering, and both body and mind seem to be crumbling into ruin. Especially since last spring, my illness has progressed, and from autumn to winter my weakness has increased day by day. For the past ten days, I have taken no food, and my suffering is aggravated by the severe cold in the midst of a huge snowfall. My body is like a piece of stone, and my chest is as cold as ice' (Anesaki 130).

During the last year of his life the old warrior of the spirit grew increasingly despondent. However, he continued to philosophize, finding the cause of both his misery and his happiness in the universal human state. 'All the sufferings that befall my fellow beings are, after all, my own sufferings' (Anesaki 117). Just as all living beings bear the Buddha-nature within them, so they also bear the seed of decay and death. He was no exception.

He felt that he was not fit for the ascetic life any more. 'I was not successful living in the forest without desiring the good things of life. Because I am human, I cannot bear extreme cold or heat. I don't have enough to eat. I am not equal (to the famous ascetics). Under such circumstances, my voice for reciting the Sutra won't hold out long. I can't even concentrate on faith' (*Hakumai Ippyo Gosho, Gosho*, 1596).

He was dying, 'falling apart like an old cart', as Shakyamuni had once said of himself. He faced his death realistically, pointing out the inseparability of the spiritual and the material. In thanking a follower for a gift of food, he wrote, 'Man lives on food, which is his treasure. But life, itself, is the most valuable of all treasures. All the treasures of the universe cannot equal a single human life ... Yet without food, there is no life' (*ibid.*). Anything which sustains life is sacred. He was grateful for every grain of rice he ever received.

As the end drew near, he recalled how Shakyamuni had left the Vulture Peak to travel to Kusinagara, where he preached his final sermon, the Nirvana Sutra. Now the time had come for him, too, to leave his sacred mountain. He set out for a medicinal hot spring, but at Ikegami, near modern Tokyo, he lodged at the house of a friend. He was too tired to travel further. His last letter was, naturally, a thank-you letter. He addressed it to Lord Hakiri of Minobu, who had offered him the hospitality of his land for the past eight years and had recently built a temple for him there. This was Kuon-ji ('Eternity Temple'), which became the most sacred place in Nichiren Buddhism. Nichiren thanked him especially for the fine horse which he had lent him for his journey. Would it be possible, he asked, for the horse to remain here with its keeper? The two were so fond of each other that it would be cruel to separate them. This was his last request — and it was for the happiness of a horse!

After that he was too weak to write any more. For nearly a month he lay near death as his disciples gathered about him to hear his last words. He named six of them the Senior Disciples and nucleus of his new order. By choosing six, he established the independence of his movement. All these men were properly ordained Tendai monks, as was he himself, but no longer would they resort to Tendai for future ordinations. Six was the traditional number of monks necessary for a proper ordination: three to perform the ceremony with the candidate and three to act as witnesses. The Nichiren Order was now to select and ordain candidates of its own. Needless to say, the Tendai Sect, which had government authority behind it, bitterly resented this schism from its ranks, and did its utmost to have Nichiren's followers treated as outlaws in the years to come.

Nichiren died on 13 October 1282, at the home of Ikegami Munenaka. He was only 60, but worn out after years of hardships. He left no successor, although he did assign a 13-year-old boy, Nichizo, with the responsibility of converting the imperial family in Kyoto. The choice, as we shall see, was a good one (Christensen 116).

The immediate task of 'sowing the seed of Buddhahood' was entrusted to the six Senior Disciples and their followers. These men had served the master faithfully for many years. The oldest of them, Nissho, had known Nichiren since they were students together at Mount Hiei. The second, Nichiro, a nephew of Nissho, had been with him since he was a boy and had shared many of his adventures. All six had proved their worth over the years. Now they solemnly cremated Nichiren's body at Ikegami (where the Grand Head Temple Hommon-ji stands today) and then bore the ashes back to Minobu, as he had requested. 'No matter where I die,' he had said in his last letter, 'please build my grave on Mount Minobu, because that is where I spent nine years reciting the Lotus Sutra to my heart's content. My heart lives forever on Mount Minobu' (*Hakii-dono Gosho, Shingyo Hikkei*, 105).

What should they do next? They had conflicting obligations: to tend the master's grave in the wilds of Minobu, and to go out into the world and sow the seeds of Buddhahood in men's minds. It was impossible to do both at the same time. They decided to return to their respective fields of labour, and rotate between them the job of caring for the master's grave on Mount Minobu. Each would return for one month a year, and six junior disciples would do the job on the odd months. Once a year, in October, they would all meet at Minobu for Nichiren's memorial service.

Needless to say, this complicated plan could not be implemented. As soon as the disciples left the isolation of Mount Minobu for Kamakura and elsewhere, they found themselves embroiled in the same old problems. Nichiren's religion still had no official right to exist, and the government treated its leaders as schismatic Tendai priests. Under such circumstances the disciples found it impossible to abandon their flocks for one month every year and a second month in October. Only one of them, Nikko, the third Senior Disciple, who was a native of the Minobu area, found it convenient to remain in the mountains even when he was not scheduled for duty there. Soon he settled in permanently.

Why had Nichiren left the succession to six disciples rather than to only one of them? He made this appointment on 8 October, less than a week before he died. He must have known the Buddhist traditions whereby lines of succession had supposedly been passed down from master to disciple throughout history, but he also knew that such lines of transmission were of little value. The Tendai transmission, according to him, had been betrayed within a generation of Saicho's death. His real model, however, was not Saicho but Shakyamuni, who had passed on his transmission to the four Great Bodhisattvas and to myriads of Bodhisattvas from under the Earth, not to any single successor. 'I wish to give the wisdom of the Buddha, the wisdom of the Tathagata, the wisdom of the Self-Existing One to all living beings,' Shakyamuni had said in the *Lotus* chapter entitled 'Transmission' (Chap. 22). Nichiren desired the same, and chose six as a working number for future ordinations. The number six also had a mystical connotation for him; it means 'perfect', he had said in *Kaimoku Sho*. The transmission of the Dharma would pass not to any one teacher, but to all who kept the Sacred Title.

He had devoted his life to expounding the truth (Dharma). Since his Dharma was so simple, there should be no question about what it was, nor could there be any distinction between superior and inferior disciples, even between male and female. 'Those who spread the five characters of *Myo Ho Ren Ge Kyo* should not be divided into men and women,' he said. 'Unless they be reincarnations of the Bodhisattvas from under the Earth, they cannot chant the Sacred Title. At first, only I, Nichiren, chanted, 'Namu Myoho Renge Kyo,' but little by little I was followed by two, three, and then hundreds, one after the other. This will continue happening in the future. Isn't this the real meaning of *from under the earth?'* (*Shoho Jisso Sho*, MW 1:93).

Nichiren also had a practical reason for choosing the six: each of them could minister to a specific geographical area where he was already established. The first two Elders, Nissho and his nephew Nichiro, would continue to work in the capital of Kamakura. Nikko, the third Elder, was responsible for the provinces of Suruga, Kai, and Izu, where he already had built up a personal following. Niko had a temple and influential friends in Kazusa. Nitcho was in Shimosa with his stepfather Toki Jonin, the most important of Nichiren's lay disciples. And finally Nichiji, the youngest of the six, was the son of a wealthy landowner in Suruga. Between them, the six were strategically located where they could evangelize north-eastern Japan in the area around modern Tokyo.

Minobu, the founder's temple, fell within the territory alloted to Nikko. But Minobu was holy to all the Disciples, not just Nikko, so they arranged to supervise it jointly in rotation. Some younger disciples were also included in the rotation. But this complicated scheme ran counter to the more natural way of just letting Nikko, who lived nearby, take care of everything.

Missionary efforts further afield would have to be left to younger disciples. Nichiren had already begun their training on Minobu. Among them were Nichizo, who would become the most important missionary in the next generation; Nichimoku, who would be the right-hand man to Nikko; and Nichizon, who would found the sect now known as Nichiren Honshu.

The original geographical distribution of the six did not stand the test of time. Nikko, as we shall see, ran afoul of the landlord at Minobu and had to leave. Niko had to move from his original area in order to replace him. He did so reluctantly and continued to make regular trips back to his old temple in Kazusa. Nitcho could not get along with his stepfather Toki Jonin, so he abandoned the area assigned to him and joined Nikko. Finally Nichiji, although comfortably situated under the sponsorship of his wealthy father, became so restless that he left home and embarked on missionary journeys that would take him to the northernmost island in Japan and finally to foreign shores.

These factors and others made it impossible for the followers of Nichiren to remain one united Sangha. Each of the six and some other original disciples had disciples of their own. Each became the nucleus of a separate school of Nichiren Buddhism. Sometimes disciples from these schools set forth on missionary journeys that ended in the foundation of still more schools. Sometimes these schools were able to merge in due course; at other times the separate lines hardened into distinct denominations.

The Buddhist Sangha is not the same as the Christian church, even though both words mean, 'assembly'. All Christians belong to the church; only monks belong to the Sangha. Conze calls the monks, 'the Buddhist elite. They are the only Buddhists in the proper sense of the word' (*Buddhism* 53). The layman believes in the Sangha as an article of faith as he believes in the Buddha and the Dharma. One becomes a Buddhist (in the broad sense of the word) by 'taking refuge' in the Three Treasures: Buddha, Dharma, and Sangha.

We have seen how Mahayana attempted to break down the qualitative distinction between monks and laity. When the *Dharma Flower* speaks of 'the Buddha and his Great Assembly', it means the Buddha surrounded by all living things, not just monks. Nichiren depicts this in his Great Mandala.

The success of the Mahayana in breaking down the distinction between monks and laity was only partial. Dengyo Daishi and Kobo Daishi introduced sectarian monasticism. Laymen, who supported these monasteries, could then be considered as belonging to the Tendai or Shingon Sect, although many of them were probably not aware of it. Lord Hakiri considered himself a devoted follower of Nichiren, gave him land, and even built a temple for him, but he saw nothing wrong with donating lumber for a Nembutsu temple or worshipping at a Shinto shrine. A layman was expected to support the Sangha, say his prayers, lead a moral life, and leave the fine points of theology to the monks.

With the Kamakura reformation, these old attitudes gradually changed. A layman could practise Buddhism as well as a monk could, and the laity became deeply involved in their respective sects. The role of the monks changed from being 'the only real Buddhists' to teachers and ceremonial leaders. The laity, who learned from them, owed them spiritual as well as material support. An outstanding teacher would accumulate a devoted following, which gave its loyalty to him and to his temple, and not to any other. A host of sub-sects arose, not only in Nichiren Buddhism, but in all Japanese Buddhism.

What is remarkable in Nichiren Buddhism is not that there were so many sub-sects, but that there were not more. There are several reasons for this. First, there is the democratic nature of the faith. Teachers are important, but they are not of cardinal importance as they are in esotericism or Zen; they have no esoteric wisdom to pass on to select disciples. The Nichiren believer who chants the Daimoku is the equal to his teacher, and faces the Gohonzon without any intermediary.

The Nichiren sect insists on this point. 'There is no difference in the

Odaimoku recited by people of different social status, social honor, social wealth, age, or sex. The *Odaimoku* recited by our Founder (Nichiren) is the same as the *Odaimoku* recited by us with our hearts' (*Shingyo Hikkei* 28). The individual practitioner is expected to emulate Nichiren, not bow before him.

Secondly, the very spirit of loyalty which had been directed by the believers to the different disciples of Nichiren led to their subsequent loyalty to the temples which carried on the disciples' teachings. During the medieval period there grew up a system of head temples, which had been founded by great missionaries, and subordinate temples which owed them strict obedience. This way the number of schisms was kept down to a reasonable amount.

Thirdly, among the followers of Nichiren there is common love for the sacred mountain of Minobu, where 'Nichiren's heart resides forever'. The great majority of Nichiren believers have always maintained a special feeling about Minobu and a desire to maintain friendly connections with its clergy. But it was at Minobu that the first and deepest schism took place.

In 1281, a year before Nichiren's death, Lord Nambu Sanenaga of Hakiri had finally prevailed upon the old teacher to permit his humble hermitage to be converted into a more spacious temple. This temple was named Kuon-ji by Nichiren (*Kuon*, a key word in Nichiren's interpretation of the Sutra, means 'eternal', and *ji* means 'temple'.) It is the only temple that was founded by Nichiren himself, and it was here that he asked to be buried. It was natural that most Nichiren Buddhists should look upon it as their spiritual centre, and upon the Chief Abbot of Kuon-ji as the symbolic leader of the sect.

At first there was no Chief Abbot. The six Senior Disciples continued to regard Nichiren as their master and his personal temple as their spiritual centre, which is why they agreed to rotate their duties there. But as things turned out, only one of them, Nikko, could remain there for any length of time, while the others would come whenever they could. As time passed, Nikko began to think of himself as the priest-in-charge at Minobu, which for all practical purposes, he was.

Byakuren Ajari Nikko, the third of the six Senior Disciples, had been devoted to Nichiren since he was 14 years old. He was a Tendai novice when he met the master for the first time at the temple of Jisso-ji. Nichiren had gone there to gather material for his *Rissho Ankoku Ron* ('Establish the Right Law and Save Our Country'), and Nikko was tremendously impressed by his breadth of scholarship. When Nichiren left for Kamakura, young Nikko came running up behind him and begged to be allowed to follow him. From that day on he served the master faithfully.

In time Nikko became a successful teacher and missionary in his own right. He had relatives in the area around Minobu, and he was able to make a number of converts there. In fact, of the 12 minor priests who were also serving at Kuon-ji, nine of them were his direct disciples. Thus Nikko was building up for himself a power base at Minobu, where he was looked on more and more as 'the' disciple of Nichiren, the one who had been most loyal to him in life and continued to be so in death.

In 1285 the government ordered all Buddhist temples to pray publicly for the salvation of the country from the Mongols and for the prosperity of the Hojo regime. Nikko, far away in his mountain retreat, ignored the order, but the other Disciples, most of whom were stationed in Kamakura and the vicinity, decided to comply. When Nikko heard of this, he accused them of disloyalty to the memory of Nichiren. He did, however, express sympathy for their predicament and gratitude that the government had left him in peace.

At about the same time Lord Nambu of Hakiri, the landowner at Minobu, built a home shrine for himself and installed in it a statue of the Buddha Shakyamuni. When Nikko saw the image, he could not suppress his indignation. Where were the accompanying images of the Four Great Bodhisattvas? Did Nambu not realize that unless the figure of Shakyamuni was escorted by the Four Great Bodhisattvas, it was a figure of the historical Buddha rather than the eternal Buddha Shakyamuni? No, Nambu had not realized it, and he was embarrassed (and probably somewhat annoyed) to have his error pointed out to him. He also did not want to go to the expense of paying for four additional statues.

Another of the six Senior Disciples, Sado Ajari Niko, who had recently arrived at Minobu, had a solution: all that was necessary to convert the figure of the historical Buddha into one of the eternal Buddha was to place a copy of the Lotus Sutra in front of it. It was as simple as that. Nambu was delighted with this way out of his dilemma, and promptly had it done. Needless to say, Sado Ajari Niko went up in his estimation while the stubborn Nikko went down.

The friction between Nambu and Nikko was aggravated further when Nambu visited the Mishima Shinto Shrine to pray, just as his ancestors had done for generations. Again Nikko berated him. It was wrong, he said, for a Nichiren Buddhist to pray anywhere except in a Nichiren temple. All the gods had left Japan and would not return until the entire nation was converted to the *Dharma Flower*. To pray at a Shinto shrine was meaningless. Again Sado Ajari Niko disagreed. The gods had sworn to protect any believer in the Lotus of the Wonderful Dharma; he could pray anywhere he liked. After all, Nichiren himself had done so. What mattered was his own faith, not the official designation of the shrine.

The final argument came when Nambu donated some lumber to be used in the construction of a Nembutsu pagoda. When Nikko accused him for the third time, Nambu apologized, saying he thought he was performing an act of charity. He had neglected to ask what the lumber was to be used for.

Nambu still respected Nikko as a priest, but obviously did not like him as a person. He would be happier if Nikko would move out and preach his fiery intolerance elsewhere. As for Nikko, he felt more and more uncomfortable and unwanted at Minobu. Finally, in 1289, he left accompanied by his nine disciples. Sado Ajari Niko remained at Minobu where he was recognized by the other disciples as the first permanent Chief Abbot of Kuon-ji and successor to Nichiren.

'I have left the forest of Mount Minobu,' Nikko wrote to a friend. 'How regretfully and unwillingly I depart defies description. However, I have resolved, wherever I may go, to establish the foundations for the true teachings of the Daishonin (Nichiren), faithfully following his will. Although all the other disciples of the Daishonin have acted against his teachings. I shall never forget his will' (*Seikyo Times*, September 1971, 59).

He travelled first to the home of his mother at Kawai in the neighbouring province of Suruga. Two years later a young nobleman named Nanjo Tokimitsu, who had long been a devout Nichiren Buddhist, offered to build Nikko a temple at Oishi-ga-hara. It was named Taiseki-ji ('Great Rock Temple'). A year later, in 1291, Nikko moved to a new hermitage two miles away at Kitayama, where Nanjo, Ishikawa Yoshitada, and others built him a residence. In 1298 he remodelled it into a temple called Hommon-ji ('Temple of the Original Gate'). He remained there until his death 35 years later at the ripe old age of 87.

Nikko never publicly stated why he left his first temple of Taiseki-ji after only a year, though it was probably because he had already had troubles with one landlord and did not want to be dependent on another. Hommon-ji, his new temple, was under joint sponsorship and not the property of one wealthy landowner; there he could enjoy the measure of independence he had always sought, and there he settled down to propound his own brand of Nichiren Buddhism, spiritually independent from Mount Minobu and financially independent from either Hakiri or Nanjo.

After he had left Minobu, Nikko began to accuse the other Senior Disciples of abandoning Nichiren and reverting to Tendai. There was some truth to the accusation. Nissho, the oldest disciple, was living in Kamakura, where he was under constant harassment from government authorities. To defend himself, he stated publicly that he was a lawful Tendai priest, which, of course, technically he was (as was Nikko). To Nissho, if he had to say this in order to get a licence to preach, it was worth the price. To Nikko, on the other hand, it was a betrayal of Nichiren.

When news of his accusation reached Kamakura, the Disciples were distressed. They sent Nichiro to Kitayama to attempt a reconciliation. Nichiro tried in vain to reach a compromise with his intransigent friend, but his efforts were fruitless. From this time on (1299), the break was complete, and Nikko had nothing more to do with his former colleagues. He and his followers founded a separate branch of Nichiren Buddhism, which came to be called the Fuji Branch (*Fuji Monryu*) after the location of its first temples at the foot of Mount Fuji, the *Komon-ha* after its founder (the *Ko* standing for Nikko), or simply the Nikko Branch.

It would not be accurate, on the other hand, to speak of a Nikko school at this point. Nikko's doctrines seem to have been the same as those being taught by the other Disciples. His quarrel with them was personal. He resented being forced to leave Mount Minobu and replaced there by his junior, Sado Ajari Niko. Also he felt that the others were not strict enough in rejecting non-Nichiren teachings and practices., Beyond that there was little difference, so little that in time some of his spiritual descendants were able to merge peacefully with the main body of Nichiren Buddhism at Mount Minobu. Others set up their own schools of interpretation. One line of transmission, however, (at Taiseki-ji) became radically different from anything else in Nichiren Buddhism.

After Nikko's death his followers split into eight sub-sects. There was no single spiritual centre like Mount Minobu about which they could gather, so the first quarrel among them was whether or not Nikko had intended to set up a new *kaidan* at Mount Fuji — and if so, where? As long as Nikko was alive he had directed his movement from Hommon-ji at Kitayama (Omosu), where he had spent the last 42 years of his life. This temple naturally considered itself the rightful heir to the leadership of the Nikko branch, but its claim was rejected by Taiseki-ji, the first temple he had built, and by the Nanjo family who had paid for it. Most of the branch members were accustomed to looking to Hommon-ji for leadership, however, and continued to do so. The claim of Taiseki-ji was further weakened when Nichigo, one of the most dynamic leaders of the branch but not a member of the Nanjo clan, claimed he had been willed the temple by the second high priest. The Nanjos objected and drove him from the premises. Nichigo went to Awa Province, where he built a temple of his own, naming it Myohon-ji, and founded his own sub-sect. From there he and his successors continued to press their claim.

In the seventeenth century most of the Nikko branch temples were able to come to an agreement among themselves, but Taiseki-ji remained aloof. By then it had developed distinctive doctrinal characteristics which set it apart from the others. Late in the nineteenth century Hommon-ji, Taiseki-ji, and other Nikko branch temples attempted to merge, calling themselves the Hommon Sect. Leadership was rotated among the several head temples. The merger was short-lived, however, and by 1900 Taiseki-ji had withdrawn, naming itself the Fuji branch. In 1913, the Fuji branch renamed itself Nichiren Shoshu ('Orthodox Nichiren Sect'), stressing its distinction from any other branch of Nichiren Buddhism.

Hommon-ji, on the other hand, still saw itself as the true transmitter of Nikko's teachings. Since these teachings were basically the same as those being taught by the majority of Nichiren Buddhists, it merged with the Nichiren sect of Minobu in 1941 after some prodding from the government, which was having problems controlling the independent-minded Nichirenites. In this way, Nikko's long self-imposed exile from Mount Minobu was brought to a happy conclusion, and the most intransigent of Nichiren's six Senior Disciples was symbolically returned to the fold.

Chapter 12

Nichiren Shu:
the Nichiren Order _____

When Nikko departed from Mount Minobu to establish his own branch sect, the other Senior Disciples do not seem to have been too concerned. They probably considered the whole incident nothing more than a personal falling-out between Nikko and Lord Nambu Hakiri. Eleven years passed before they made any effort to patch things up with their dissident brother, and that was only after they learned that Nikko had been criticizing them.

Why the long delay? Because their late master had put so much stress on unity, they were unwilling to believe that a breach had occurred so soon. It was unthinkable! If Nikko had a grievance, he could have come to them and discussed the matter. At a time when the other Disciples were suffering from official abuse at Kamakura or setting off on long missionary journeys, Nikko did not stir from his comfortable quarters at Omosu. He could have made the annual trip to Minobu to pay his respects at the founder's grave, since he lived closer by than any of them except for Sado Ajari Niko, who by then had settled down as the permanent chief abbot of Kuon-ji temple. He did not do that, either. Obviously Nikko did not want to see his old friends any more. According to Buddhist protocol, he should have taken any grievance to the oldest Disciple, Nissho. He made no effort to do so. Instead it was Nissho who sent his nephew Nichiro, the second in seniority, to Nikko in Omosu in a vain attempt to settle the differences.

Ben Ajari Nissho (1236–1323), the oldest of the six Senior Disciples, was a gentle man who would have preferred a life of scholarship to vigorous missionary activity. He had known Nichiren since their student days on Mount Hiei, and he was the first ordained monk to be converted. Although he was senior to Nichiren at Mount Hiei, he became his disciple back in the early days of street preaching in

Kamakura (1253). After Nichiren's death the Hojo Regency regarded Nissho as the leader of the despised Nichiren movement, and subjected him to continual abuse. He responded in the style of Never-Despising Bodhisattva (Fukyo), who used to bow to his persecutors, saying, 'I cannot despise you, for you will all become Buddhas.' For this reason he was nick-named Fukyo-in, 'Never-Despising'.

On the third anniversary of Nichiren's death (1284: third anniversary by Buddhist liturgical reckoning), Nissho presented the Kamakura dictatorship with a revised copy of Nichiren's 'Establish the Right Law and Save Our Country'. In the original version, which had earned Nichiren banishment to the Izu Peninsula, the author had criticized only the Nembutsu sects. Nissho's revised version attacked Tendai and Shingon esotericism as well, and its presentation provoked a storm which almost cost him his life. An angry mob gathered outside his house and threatened to burn it to the ground. He pacified the mob by saying that Nichiren had been a loyal Tendai priest, who only wanted to reform the Tendai sect.

Nissho seems to have clung to the hope that one day Tendai would accept Nichiren as its greatest champion. He personified the conservative wing of Nichiren Buddhism, deeply rooted in the Tendai philosophy taught on Mount Hiei. His school of thought, known as the Hama school after its original location in Hamado, Kamakura, maintained friendly ties with Mount Hiei for a long time, and in future years many of its clergy went there to study and even to receive ordination. His spirit of syncretism is found today in modern movements such as Kodo Kyodan and Rissho Kosei-kai.

Daikoku Ajari Nichiro (1243–1320), the second of the six, was a nephew of Nissho. He is called 'the beloved disciple', and there are many stories of his devotion to Nichiren. When the founder was shipped off on his first exile, the young Nichiro dashed into the water and attempted to hold back the boat. A soldier beat his hands with an oar, breaking one hand, and leaving him semi-crippled for life. At the time of the second exile Nichiro was thrown into a dungeon at Kamakura. Nichiren praised him for his courage, and wrote to encourage him. 'I, Nichiren, am leaving tomorrow for the Province of Sado. It is cold tonight. You, confined to the dungeon, must really be suffering from the cold. I do feel sorry for you. You are reading the Lotus Sutra with both your mind and body. Therefore you will be able to save not only your parents and relatives, but also all other living beings . . . Nothing will happen to you. When you are released, come and see me as soon as you can. I shall be delighted to see you again' (Tsuchiro-gosho, Showa-teihon, 509).

But Nichiro could not wait for a legal release. He became so popular with the jailer that the latter agreed to cover up for him while Nichiro travelled to Sado to see his master. He made the journey, but when Nichiren learned of the circumstances, he ordered his beloved disciple to return to prison rather than risk the life of the good-hearted jailer. Nichiro reluctantly did so. When at last the order came through releasing Nichiren and all his disciples, Nichiro wanted to be the one to carry the good news to Sado. This second journey almost cost him his life. He collapsed just short of his goal and might have frozen to death had he not been found lying in the snow. His trip to Sado was depicted by the artist Ando Hiroshige in one of his masterpieces, 'Nichiro in the snow on Sado'. [58]

In 1260 a poor Samurai named Hiki Yoshimoto donated part of his residence at Hikigayatsu, Kamakura, to the disciples for use as a lecture hall. When Nichiren returned from Sado in 1274 he decided to remodel it into a temple called Myohon-ji, and put Nichiro in charge there. Later he sent Nichiro to Ikegami under similar circumstances, to establish what was eventually to become Hommon-ji, one of the Head Temples (*Reiseki*) of the Nichiren Order and today the administrative head-quarters. Nichiren died there in 1282. [59]

Nichiro was an active missionary, and trained numerous disciples, who spread the faith in every direction. He personally prepared young Nichizo (Ryuge) for the task Nichiren had assigned him: to convert the royal family at Kyoto. Eight of his other disciples became famous in their own right. Some of them founded branches of their own and began to expound the *Shoretsu* theory, which we shall discuss below. He seems to have encouraged his disciples to develop their own personalities, and made no effort to mould them into carbon copies of himself. During the last two years of his long and fruitful life, he retired to Ikegami to die where his master had. Nichiro's school was known originally as the Hikigayatsu School, after its original centre in Kamakura, and later as the Ikegami School. Ikegami is on the outskirts of Tokyo, and when the political power eventually shifted from Kamakura to Tokyo, Hommon-ji at Ikegami became the most important Nichiren temple in the country.

The third disciple in order of seniority was Nikko, already mentioned. Then came his rival at Minobu, Sado Ajari Niko. Like the first two Senior Disciples, he was a native of Nichiren's home area of Chiba. He had been a monk since the age of nine and a disciple of Nichiren since he was 12. He was with Nichiren when their party was attacked by soldiers of Lord Tojo Kagenobu in the pine forest. After fleeing the area, they found shelter with a friendly provincial lord, Saito.

When Nichiren arrived in the vicinity, a retainer of Saito named Sumisa had a dream in which the Bodhisattva Kannon appeared to him and announced the arrival of the saviour of the world. He immediately sought out Nichiren and brought him to the home of his liege lord Saito. Saito, in turn, was impressed by Nichiren, and offered to build him a temple. Nichiren accepted the offer, but as it was his custom in those days to keep moving from one place to another, he soon departed, leaving Niko behind to take charge of it.

The temple was named Sogen-ji, and it became Niko's permanent assignment. So it was that when Nichiren was condemned to death, and Nichiro and others were thrown into prison, Niko was safe in his little country temple. When he learned what had happened, however, he rushed to join his master in exile on Sado Island. This is why he was known later as the Sado Master (Sado Ajari).

When Nichiren went to Minobu, Niko returned to Sogen-ji to continue his work there. He never forgot his first temple, and even after he had become chief abbot at Mount Minobu, he made frequent trips back to Sogen-ji. Today Sogen-ji is called the 'Eastern Mount Minobu', because the services at the two temples, while differing in details from those at other Nichiren temples, are the same in both places. Sogen-ji, which is built in an Indian style and is a short distance from Tokyo, is now a popular tourist attraction. Niko lies buried there, not at Minobu, with which his name is always associated. There is also a permanently sealed cave on the premises, which is said to contain some original writings of Nichiren, but since no one is permitted to break the seal, we will never know. [60] Niko's branch is known as the Minobu school.

Iyo Ajari Nitcho (1252–1317), the fifth Senior Disciple, was the son of Lord Iyo in Shizuoka Prefecture. He was ordained, however, at Guho-ji in Chiba. In 1274 the temple converted to Nichiren, who put Nitcho in charge. There he remained until 1302, when he had a disagreement with his adoptive father, Toki Jonin. He left abruptly, returning home to Iyo to hold memorial services for his natural father. He joined Nikko at Omosu, which was not far away, and stayed with him until his death 16 years later.

Renge Ajari Nichiji (1250–?1305) was the most energetic missionary of the six. For centuries much of his life has been shrouded in mystery, and only in recent times did it begin to come to light. He was born the second son of a Hojo Samurai, the lord of a village named Matsuno. He entered the Tendai noviciate as a boy, studying at Jisso-ji, the same temple where his older schoolmate Nikko had met Nichiren. The chief priest was sympathetic towards Nichiren, and made no objection when Nikko left to become a disciple. A few years later he too converted, taking the name Nichigen and bringing the temple with him. Nichiji and his whole family became Nichiren Buddhists at about this time.

Nichiji began his career the easy way, as priest-in-charge of a temple built for him by his wealthy family. However, he was the son of a Samurai and had the Samurai spirit, constantly setting himself challenges to overcome. He was a skilled calligrapher and artist, and when the founder died, he promised to complete a statue of him within seven years. He did so, and the image can be seen today at Ikegami Hommon-ji in Tokyo.

On the thirteenth anniversary of Nichiren's death he went to Mount Minobu for the memorial service, and made a new vow before the founder's tomb. He would carry the faith to distant lands where it was still unknown. In 1295 he turned over his temple to his leading disciple and set forth on his journeys. He walked all the way to the far north of Honshu, the main island of Japan, and lived for a while at the home of a fisherman. Then he crossed over to the northernmost island of Hokkaido, where Buddhism had hardly penetrated. He preached for a while to the Ainu tribesmen, and then set sail for Siberia in 1298. At this point he disappeared from history.

Only in this century was his trail uncovered. In 1936 a Japanese tourist in Manchuria purchased a silver-coated incense case from a Chinese antique shop. Three poems in Chinese characters were inscribed on the case. All of them spoke of homesickness. To his surprise, the buyer saw that one of them mentioned 'my teacher Nichiren Shonin'. An investigation was begun. The incense case, it was found, had been stolen from a Chinese Buddhist temple in Hsuan-hua near the Sino-Mongolian border about 600 kilometres north-west of Peking. The temple, called Li-hua, had been founded by a Japanese priest, who had toured northern China and Mongolia in the fourteenth century. Li-hua means a mandarin orange — the family crest of Nichiren. The inscription read:

> It is not clear whether awake or asleep, real or
>   imaginary,
> I just dreamed a scene of coming back to my home at
>   Matsuno,
> Joining the retinue of my teacher Nichiren Shonin.
> In the dream I had on my sick bed, I returned to the old
>   days twenty years ago;
> I was bathed in tears as I remembered my parents and
>   my brothers.

Nichiji had been found at last. Many Japanese monks had gone to China to study; he is the first one ever to go abroad as a missionary. 'The sun of Buddhism,' Nichiren had said, 'is rising in the east and will shine over the west.' Nichiji, unique in Japanese Buddhism until the twentieth century, had put this maxim into practice, carrying the word from the East to the West. Today he is revered as the patron saint of Nichiren Buddhist foreign missions.

Before leaving this first generation of Nichiren's immediate disciples, there is one other who should be mentioned. He was not a priest, but a layman — Toki Jonin. Toki had been a rock of refuge for Nichiren almost since the beginning. He had opened his home in Shimosa Province for the protection of persecuted believers, and had converted it into an important Nichiren centre. He was a devout man, a *nyudo* (a layman who had taken religious vows but had not abandoned his family obligations). The Hojo regency distrusted him, and once had him, Shijo Kingo, and Ota Jomyo — the three most prominent lay believers in the area — brought in for questioning.

Because he was exceptionally learned, Toki received some of Nichiren's most important epistles. He treasured these letters, and made it a point to preserve them. Later he made an effort to collect copies of all of the founder's writings, carefully cataloguing them for future generations. In his will he specified that these documents were never to be removed from the archives of his family temple, and there they have remained to this day (*Nichiren Shu News*, No. 30).

Three temples in the area became the nucleus of what was later called the Nakayama school. They were Mama Guho-ji, a former Tendai temple which Nichiren put under the direction of the Senior Disciple Nitcho; Nakayama Hommyo-ji, formerly the residence of Ota Jomyo; and Wakamiya Hokke-ji, the family temple of Toki Jonin. Ota Jomyo's son Nikko (not the same as the Senior Disciple Nikko) served as chief priest of the latter two temples, which eventually merged into one entity called Hokekyo-ji, which has been one of the most important Nichiren centres ever since.

The natural leader of the group was Toki Jonin. After Nichiren's death, Toki decided to ordain himself as a monk, taking the name Nichijo. Few people had enjoyed Nichiren's confidence as much as he, and to none had Nichiren entrusted more important documents. Had he already been a monk prior to Nichiren's death, he certainly would have been appointed one of the six Senior Disciples, perhaps even the leader. Since Nichiren could no longer ordain him personally, Toki Jonin decided to ordain himself.

Such a procedure was not unprecedented, but hitherto had been resorted to only in dire emergencies, when no members of the Sangha were available to perform the ceremony. The appendix to the Lotus Sutra, the 'Sutra of Meditation on the Bodhisattva Universal Virtue', describes how a self-ordination can be performed. After strenuous spiritual preparation the candidate takes the monastic vows before the invisible but omnipresent Buddha. 'Sakyamuni Buddha! Be now pleased to be my preceptor! Manjusri! Be pleased to be my teacher! Maitreya in the world to come! Be pleased to bestow on me the Law! Buddhas in all directions! Be pleased to bear witness to me! Bodhisattvas of great virtue! Be pleased to be my friends! I now, by means of the profound and mysterious meaning of the Great-vehicle sutras, take refuge in the Buddha, take refuge in the Law, and take refuge in the Sangha' (*Threefold Lotus Sutra* 367–8).

Toki's step-son Nitcho, a properly ordained Tendai monk, must have been shocked that Toki would resort to a self-ordination when he, one of the six Senior Disciples, was available to administer the oaths. On the other hand, Toki, raised in the strict Confucian ethic that a father (or stepfather) is always superior to a son, could not possibly lower himself to be ordained by his stepson. Relying on the special relation he had with Nichiren, he turned directly to the Buddha. This is probably the reason for the break between Toki Jonin and Nitcho.

The Nakayama school, which began as a self-consecrated body of well-to-do laymen, turned out to be one of the most aggressive and successful branches of Nichiren Buddhism. During the medieval period it was scorned by the other branches as unauthorized by Nichiren, but it made up in zeal and scholarship for what it lacked in legitimacy. It developed an esoteric tradition of its own, which today continues to cast its spell far beyond the borders of its own school. Nichiren priests, who seek special spiritual insights, resort to Nakayama for special training. There they undergo a strenuous 100-day programme designed to open their inner eye. The successful candidates emerge exhausted but radiant, and are greeted by crowds of well-wishers seeking their blessings. The graduates, who form a special class of iluminati, are authorized to perform rites of healing and spiritual succour. Laymen and laywomen also resort to Nakayama when they seek mystical illumination.

With the passing of the first generation of Nichiren's followers, the movement was flourishing but still small. There were five separate adminstrative bodies:

1. The Minobu school of Niko.
2. The Fuji school of Nikko.
3. The Hama school of Nissho.
4. The Ikegami school of Nichiro.
5. The Nakayama school of Toki Jonin (Nichijo).

There were also some independent temples founded by other direct disciples of Nichiren.

It could still not be called a major religious movement, each of the five centres being dependent on the benevolence of local feudal lords who wanted to dicate policy. The temples tended to be clan temples for the Samurai families who paid for them. Minobu was controlled by Lord Hakiri, who ousted Nikko and replaced him with Niko. The Fuji school was sub-divided between the Nanjo family (Taiseki-ji) and the Ishikawa family (Hommon-ji). The Nakayama School was dominated by the Chiba clan. The Ikegami, Kano, and other families were influential in the Ikegami School. Lacking state support, early Nichiren Buddhism was dependent entirely on the few feudal families who were willing to sponsor it for reasons of their own. All of this was changed dramatically by the efforts of one man, Ryuge-in Nichizo.

Ryuge was six years old when he first met Nichiren, and he served him as a page boy for the next seven years. When he was 13 he was summoned by the dying Nichiren, who took his hands in both of his, looked him straight in the eye, and made him promise that one day he would go to Kyoto and convert the Imperial Family.

Ryuge never forgot that solemn moment. He trained for his assignment like an athlete, spiritually under the tutorage of Nichiro and physically by hours of exercise on the beach. To gain skill of hand and mind he copied the entire Sutra in letters half the size of a grain of rice. This extraordinary book, only 4 cm wide and 158 cm long, is preserved today at Myoken-ji in Kyoto. By the time he was 27 Ryuge felt ready to go, but only after he had retired for 100 days of yet more rigorous self-discipline.

He arrived in Kyoto for the first time in 1294 and began to preach on the street outside the palace walls. Three times he was expelled from the city, and three times he returned. In 1307 he was sentenced to three years of exile in Toda Province on the Island of Shikoku. Always he came back, and gradually he began to make progress. In 1321 he was allowed to settle in Kyoto and build Myoken-ji outside the palace moat.

The political situation was changing. The Hojos were losing their grip, and the Imperial Family was eager to get back into power. Most of the Buddhist clergy still trembled before Hojo authority, but not Ryuge. When the Emperor Godaigo, himself a victim of Hojo power and an exile in the Sea of Japan, requested the clergy to pray for his eventual victory and return from exile, none did so except Ryuge. In 1333 the Hojo Regency fell, the Emperor returned, and Ryuge, the thrice-rejected, found himself a hero. It had taken him 40 years, but he had succeeded. In gratitude, the Emperor ordered Myoken-ji designated an Imperial Temple for the royal family.

In 1340 Ryuge-in Nichizo died in Kyoto at the age of 74, just 58 years after the death of Nichiren. He was succeeded by Daikaku Myojitsu, an aristocratic scion of a prominent family at court. Daikaku had been converted by Ryuge at the age of 17, had shared in his trials, and now shared in his triumph. Partly because of his high social position and partly because of his own missionary zeal, he was able to carry the cause further yet.

In 1358 after a prolonged period of drought, he was asked to pray for rain. Daikaku did so, and Kyoto was deluged with rain for the next 24 hours. In gratitude, the Emperor Gokogen officially gave Nichiro and Ryuge Nichizo the title of Bodhisattva, and named Nichiren, Great Bodhisattva. Daikaku also did not go without honours. He was designated Chief Abbot of the Nichiren sect. He was the first Nichiren priest given a high rank by Imperial command.

Once Ryuge Nichizo had paved the way, other Nichiren preachers began to arrive in the capital, where they generally found a warm welcome. Since they came from no single centre, they set up a number of head temples to form new branches under their temples at the capital. No sooner had the Hojos fallen than the Nikko branch sent a delegation of three evangelists. One died *en route*, one returned home, but the third, Nichizon, stayed to found his own branch under its own head temple. Toki Jonin's group was also soon well represented in town, where it established its own head temple, Honkoku-ji.

By 1400 Nichiren temples had sprung up all over Kyoto, outnumbering all other sects except Zen, which was favoured by the military shoguns. The head temples established subordinate temples, which owed them strict obedience. Sometimes doctrinal differences within a group caused a break-away and the establishment of a new head temple. The various sub-sects were administratively independent, but met together in council to solve common problems (Itohisa, *Osaki Gakuho*, No. 140).

During the fourteenth and fifteenth centuries Nichiren Buddhism spread not only in the capital but throughout the country. It ceased to be the religion of a few big landowners, and extended its membership among all classes of society: court aristocrats, Samurai, merchants, and peasants. It was propagated by zealous missionaries, who were frequently willing to risk their lives for the cause: to establish the Pure Land of the Buddha on this earth. As its influence in the capital increased, that of the Tendai sect declined. And as the Tendai sect declined, it began to resort to force to hang on to its ancient privileges.

Nichiren Buddhism might have eventually dominated the capital and the surrounding country were it not that the political situation was still inimical. The Hojo regents were gone, and once more the Emperor ruled from his ancient capital of Kyoto. The Imperial House and Nichiren Buddhism were natural allies, sharing a dream for a united Japan. But, alas! it remained a dream. Real power belonged not to the Emperor, but to new shoguns, the Ashikaga (1333–1568), who established their residence in the Muromachi district of Kyoto. For this reason the troubled period which followed the Kamakura period is called the Ashikaga or Muromachi period.

It was a time of near anarchy. The Shoguns were strong enough to control the Emperor, but not strong enough to dominate the country or, at times, even to defend the capital city. Like most Samurai, the Ashikagas preferred the austere Zen imported from China. Indeed, Zen monks with connections in China played an important role in international trade, and the Ashikagas were quick to benefit from it. Nichiren Buddhism, on the other hand, had nothing to offer them except possible national union under the Emperor, which they certainly did not want. They preferred to control the Emperor, themselves.

Dale Saunders writes in *Buddhism in Japan* (238):

> The Ashikaga period was one of great disturbance and at the same time of remarkable artistic production. In a period when war and rebellion were the order of the day, land and wealth were for those who could hold them. Hence it is from this time that the rise of masculine prerogative dates and, in contrast to Fujiwara times, the subordination of women.

Public order and morality sank to such a low point that even some of the great Buddhist monasteries, traditional centres of pacificism, became fortresses complete with soldier-monks. Mount Hiei, so close to the capital, became especially powerful and troublesome. The armed Tendai monks at Mount Hiei grew increasingly jealous and resentful of Nichiren Buddhism, which they regarded as a schism from their own authority. They did not hesitate to come storming into town and burn down any Nichiren temple which dared to defy them. In 1536 Tendai soldier-monks, with reinforcements from Shin Shu, Shingon, and other armed temples, burned all 21 Nichiren head temples in the city. This rampage was accompanied by great slaughter, for by then the majority of the citizens of the capital were Nichiren Buddhists, who had been looking forward to the end of the old social order and the establishment of the Buddha-land in this *Saha*-world.

The Shoguns, who permitted such outrages, used the Tendai soldier-monks to their own purposes — to help keep the Nichiren Buddhists in line. The result is that while Nichiren Buddhism came to enjoy great prestige, it never knew safety. This is illustrated by the careers of two men of the times.

Gatsumyo (1386–1440) was the son of a prime minister, which made him just the kind of Nichiren leader whom the Tendai monks did not want to have around. He was a successor to Ryuge Nichizo at Myoken-ji. The Tendai soldier-monks had already destroyed this temple once, in 1387; it was rebuilt in 1398. With the election of Gatsumyo as chief abbot in 1413, the Tendai solider-monks stormed into town again and burned the great temple to the ground. Gatsumyo had to flee for his life. He went out into the country and became a wandering missionary for eight years until influential friends in Kyoto could assure him that it was safe to return. Some wealthy merchants in Kyoto and Osaka promised to pay for a new temple. In 1421 Gatsumyo came back and supervised the erection of a new temple, where he spent the rest of his life under the ever-watchful eye of Mount Hiei.

Even more extraordinary is the story of Nisshin Nabekamuri, the 'pot-wearer' (1407–88). A representative of Toki Jonin's Nakayama School, he arrived in Kyoto at the age of 22, and promptly set to work writing a thesis in imitation of Nichiren's, which he called, 'Establish the Right Law and Rule the Country'. When he finished it he presented it to Shogun Ashikaga Yoshinori, which was a mistake. The Shogun had once been an ordained monk on Mount Hiei, and had inherited a bitter hatred for Nichiren Buddhism. He decided to break Nisshin for his impertinence. The young priest was arrested and tortured. Nisshin was not tortured only once, but daily for two years. The Shogun took a perverse delight in watching the sufferings of the priest; he supervised the daily tortures by fire, rack, sword, and whatever else he could think of. Nothing would make Nisshin stop chanting, *Nam-myoho-renge-kyo*. Finally the Shogun ordered that a metal pot be jammed over his head to keep him quiet, but from underneath the pot could still be heard, *Nam-myoho-renge-kyo! Nam-myoho-renge-kyo!*

Nisshin's ordeal might have continued indefinitely had not the cruel Shogun been assassinated one day while watching a theatrical performance. Nisshin was released, and the pot was removed from his head. He rebuilt his temple, which had been destroyed, took up his drum, and went back to the street corners to chant, *Nam-myoho-renge-kyo! Nam-myoho-renge-kyo!* Never one to avoid a challenge, he is said to have triumphed in 60 religious debates in the course of his 65-year career.

Debates took place among the Nichiren believers, too. There were two tendencies constantly at odds. One was conservative, seeking alliances with the court or Samurai nobility; the other was aggressive, pressing for a pure form of Nichiren Buddhism at any cost. This sometimes set juniors against their seniors and resulted in the formation of new sects. During the fourteenth and fifteenth centuries a number of them appeared, and most of them exist to this day. All of them emphasized the uniqueness of Nichiren Buddhism and the necessity for aggressive propagation. They include the Manifest Dharma-Flower sect (*Kempon Hokke-shu*), founded by Nichiju in 1384; Dharma-Flower sect, Jin branch (*Hokke-shu Jin Monryu*), founded by Nichijin in 1406; Dharma-Flower sect, Original branch (*Hokke-shu Hon Monryu*), founded by Nichiryu in 1423; and Dharma-Flower sect, Shin branch (*Hokke-shu Shin Monryu*), founded by Nisshin in 1488.

Of course, all of these bodies consider themselves orthodox, and none called itself a 'sect' until modern times. Previously they were known as 'branches' of the same faith. However, after the Meiji Restoration, the Imperial Japanese government found it easier to deal with centrally organized religious bodies than with independent 'branches'. They were ordered to unite for administrative purposes. The great majority gathered around Minobu to form the 'Nichiren sect' (*Nichiren-shu*). The former Nikko branch became the Hommon Shu, while the other branches took on various new names. In 1940 the government decreed that all religious organizations with less than 50 established places of worship must either shut up shop or join a larger body. Hommon Shu merged with the Nichiren Sect the following year. Taiseki-ji was excepted, however, for it had already withdrawn from Hommon Shu (1900) and named itself Nichiren Shoshu (1912). At the end of World War II and the promulgation of religious freedom, the various sub-sects reorganized once more and gave themselves new names. [61]

Nichiren laity as well as clergy sometimes had to put their lives on the line. In 1435, after a noisy public debate between two Nichiren priests and a Tendai priest, the military governor of Kamakura ordered all 16 Nichiren temples in the city to be destroyed, all Samurai members to have their properties confiscated, and all commoners to cease chanting the Sacred Title under pain of death. When dozens and then hundreds of chanting people began to present themselves at the palace for voluntary execution, he was so impressed by their courage that he rescinded his order, promising to build them a new hall instead. They were the kind of people he wanted on his side.

Nichiren priests were constantly demanding public debates, but the results were not always what they might have desired. In 1579 over a hundred representatives of Nichiren Buddhism gathered at the castle of the powerful feudal lord Oda Nobunaga to debate with proponents of the Pure Land (*Jodo*) sect. The cards were stacked against them, however, for Nobunaga was himself a member of the *Jodo* sect, which until his time had enjoyed no social prestige. Presiding at the debate was the chief abbot of an important Zen temple. When the presiding judge ruled in favour of the Pure Land disputants, Nobunaga had the three leading Nichiren priests taken out and executed.

Oda Nobunaga, the warlord who finally began to bring the divided country under one iron fist, took even worse vengeance on the warrior monks of Mount Hiei. He utterly destroyed the venerable monastic centre and killed every monk, whether he bore arms or not. To counter the political power of the large Buddhist sects he encouraged the expansion of the newly introduced Christianity as well as his own hitherto insignificant sect of *Jodo*. Tendai, Jodo Shinshu, and Nichiren Buddhism all felt his wrath. Esotericism fell victim to his successor, Hideyoshi. By 1600 the independent power of the great Buddhist establishments was broken. Tokugawa Ieyasu, the successor to Hideyoshi, completed bringing them all into line and making them departments of the state.

The Nichiren Buddhists were the last to give up. In 1608 a large group of them under Jorakuin Nikkyo, chief priest of Myoman-ji in Kyoto, gathered at the Tokugawa castle in Edo (Tokyo) for a debate with Jodo Shinshu leaders. The night before the scheduled event Nikkyo and his party were attacked and beaten by unknown assailants. The next day they did poorly in the debate. Tokugawa Ieyasu ordered their noses and ears cut off, and all dissemination of Nichiren Buddhism to cease at once. Nichion, chief priest at Kuon-ji, Mount Minobu, resolutely refused to obey the order. Ieyasu, who was not a man to be trifled with, ordered him to be arrested and put to death by crucifixion.

At this point a remarkable woman entered the story and saved the day. She was Lady Oman-no-Kata, one of Ieyasu's concubines and the mother of two of his sons. She came from a large family of Nichiren Buddhists; in fact, her father, an aristocrat who found himself on the losing side in the civil wars, had retired from the world to become a Nichiren priest. Lady Oman had had to live by her wits since she was 14.

When she heard what was about to happen to Nichion, she prepared to commit suicide. She allowed her two little boys, aged six and seven, to watch her preparations, and then sent them to their father with a message: at the moment Nichion was crucified, she would take her own life. Ieyasu was so moved by the tears of his two sons and the determination of his mistress that he countermanded his order, and Nichion was spared.

Although Nichion was freed from prison, he did not want to return to Mount Minobu, where he might still be prevented from spreading the gospel of Nichiren. Instead he built himself a small hut by the Fuji River, and took up his preaching from there. When Lady Oman heard of this she began what was to become a lifelong career of Nichiren philanthropy. She built Nichion a fine temple to replace his hut, and continued building temples and endowing Nichiren causes until the day she died 44 years later. She was Nichiren Buddhism's greatest benefactor.

She is remembered today primarily as the lady who broke the sexual barrier. Nichiren had said that the liberation of women was the primary doctrine of the *Dharma Flower*, which Lady Oman knew perfectly well, but the status of women had changed for the worse since Nichiren's days. Once when she was visiting Mount Minobu, she expressed the desire to climb the neighbouring Mount Shichimen, but was told that no woman was permitted to climb the sacred mountain. Lady Oman was not to be put off so easily, and asked permission to visit the waterfall at the foot of the mountain. This was granted, but once she arrived at the waterfall, she bathed herself there according to the traditional purification ritual. Then up the mountain she went — the first woman ever to do so. This was the first of her three ascents. She climbed the mountain the last time when she was 74 years old.

Today the climb up Mount Shichimen is a popular expedition for plilgrims of both sexes, who wind up and down the footpaths as they chant the Sacred Title to the beat of hand-drums. They are dressed in sandals, white trousers, and white kimono-like shirts inscribed, 'Namu Myoho Renge Kyo'. Those not beating drums carry staffs. At the foot of the ascent by the waterfall is a statue of Lady Oman dressed in the same costume (*Minobusan Kuon-ji*, 23).

Nichiren Buddhism no longer faced persecution, but instead had to deal with just the opposite danger: a life of ease and acceptance. This was exactly the offer which had been made to the founder when he was recalled from his exile on Sado, but now it came from wealthy patrons closely tied to the all-powerful Tokugawa regime. Every Nichiren Buddhist knew how the founder had responded when tempted with the same sort of compromise: he had withdrawn to Mount Minobu, and had neither received support from nor given support to non-believers, no matter how exalted their rank. This came to be called the principle of *Fujufuse*, 'not-receive-not-give'. What it really involved was freedom from government control.

Most Nichiren Buddhists believed in this principle. Troubles came, however, when the government commanded interdenominational prayer services. Nichiren priests would beg to be excused on the grounds that such services were forbidden by their religion. The relatively weak Ashikaga Shogunate had always acceded to the request. The oldest extant document of the government's approving such an appeal is dated 1492, and it mentions that the Nichiren Buddhists were excused 'according to precedents'. In other words, this had been going on a long time by then. The same appeal was granted in 1571, 1572, 1577, and 1589.

In 1595, however, the victorious Hideyoshi made it plain that he would make no exceptions; he expected to bring the great religious orders to heel, and that meant all of them. The Nichiren clergy of Kyoto met to discuss the situation, and decided to obey the government order. Only one chief priest, objected — Kyoei Nichio. On the day of the ceremony he arose before dawn, retired to the country, and went into seclusion.

Hideyoshi died in 1598, and was succeeded by the even more powerful Tokugawa Ieyasu. In 1600 he sentenced Kyoei Nichio to exile on Tsushima Island. Nichiren Buddhists, who were well aware of the harsh measures being taken against them everywhere (mutilations and executions were not uncommon), tended to sympathize with Kyoei Nichio. In 1612, thanks to the influence of important people at the Shogunate, they were able to get him pardoned. Nichio returned to Kyoto and engaged in spirited debates with his brethren who had given in. He was the man of the hour, and the *Fujufuse* movement spread rapidly, much to the embarrassment of the accommodating head temples.

In 1623 the government legalized *Fujufuse*, and it seemed that the battle had been won. By the middle of the seventeenth century at least half the Nichiren temples supported the principle.

However, by then there were many important personages, such as Lady Oman and her relatives, sponsoring the bigger and wealthier temples. It was people like them, not outsiders, who brought the movement down. In 1665 the government, as part of its plan to control all religious properties, declared that temples which possessed government-granted land must report it to the Shogunate. Accommodating clergy saw this as an opportunity to get rid of the troublesome *Fujufuse* members. They convinced the government to word the decree so that it specified that the government had granted these lands 'for worship'. In other words, the *Fujufuse* priests would have to admit that they had accepted what they could not accept: government support.

Christianity had been forbidden in 1638, and Buddhism was now the state religion. Every citizen had to be able to prove that he belonged to some Buddhist temple. The priests, on their part, were authorized to grant certificates of membership, which meant in effect certificates of citizenship. *Fujufuse* priests were now forbidden to grant certificates. This meant that their parishioners became outlaws; they were beyond the protection of the law and had no rights to either property or life.

The *Fujufuse* believers were treated with the same severity as the Christians had been a few years earlier: they were hunted down and wiped out. They survived, however, just as Christians did, by going 'underground'. They would register at a government-approved temple, but secretly maintain their cherished faith from generation to generation, generally being careful to marry within their own group.

The last great hero of the movement was Nichiko, who was hounded from place to place until he was hidden by a sympathetic baron. There he wrote volumes of commentaries on Nichiren and the Sutra. When he had completed them, he went out into the world again to face his opponents in open debates. He died in 1698 at the age of 73, and his body was exposed to the elements as if he were a common criminal. *Fujufuse* seemed to be over. It was not dead, however, and in 1876, nearly two centuries after the death of Nichiko and the fall of the Tokugawa Shogunate in 1868, the 'Nichiren Shu: Fujufuse Branch' came out of hiding and was formally granted the right to exist.

The *Fujufuse* controversy of the seventeenth century was a great tragedy for Nichiren Buddhism; it pit brother against brother, and resulted in victory for those who would support the status quo. Nichiren Buddhism settled down into the same dull complacency which gripped the whole of Japanese Buddhism during the two and a half centuries of Tokugawa rule. It was jolted awake only by the opening of Japan by Commodore Perry, the collapse of the Tokugawa Shogunate, and the Meiji Restoration, all of which took place in rapid succession. In 1868 Buddhism was rudely disestablished and replaced by State Shinto. Buddhism, which had dozed for two and a half centuries under the shade of the Shogunate, was suddenly the symbol of everything that was old-fashioned and backward. It was the object of scorn and even violence. Japan rushed to catch up with the West. Buddhism had to adapt to the new world or perish.

Shinto became the state religion in 1870, and anti-Buddhist violence peaked around 1871. Then Japanese Buddhism caught its breath and began to get back on its feet. In 1889 a new constitution was promulgated guaranteeing a limited freedom of religion. 'Japanese subjects shall, within limits not prejudicial to peace and order, and not antagonistic to their duties as subjects, enjoy freedom of religious beliefs' (Article 28). State Shinto remained the officially established religion, however, and all others had to say prayers for its divine head, the Emperor. However, the worst crisis had passed, although the challenges of accommodation to a totalitarian state and adaption to the modern world were barely beginning.

Today the term *Nichiren-shu* (Nichiren Sect or Order) means the federation of four of the original five schools and parts of the fifth — one major branch of the Fuji School of Nikko being excluded. The reform movements from the medieval period, generally calling themselves, 'Hokke' ('Dharma Flower'), are also excluded, as are some smaller groups, most of which arose after the Second World War. Nichiren Shu makes the greatly exaggerated claim of 'over five million members' (*The Nichiren Shu* 9), maintains all the historic temples associated with the life of the founder, has over 5,300 temples and churches (about 70 per cent of all Nichiren temples), including 15 in America, and over 8,000 clergy. Its spiritual centre is Kuon-ji on Mount Minobu; the administrative centre is at Ikegami Hommon-ji, Tokyo. It also manages Rissho University in Tokyo, the world centre for Nichiren Buddhist scholarship. Its branch in the United States and Canada is called the Nichiren Buddhist Order of America.

Nichiren Shu could be said to represent a centrist position in Nichiren Buddhism. It accepts the whole of the *Dharma Flower* and all the teachings of Nichiren. It is a consensus of the various schools developed by Nissho, Nichiro, Toki Jonin, Nichizo, and even some of the disciples of Nikko. It is liberal in that it gives its various branches considerable autonomy, and encourages open scholarship. Not until 1972 did it attempt to create any kind of liturgical uniformity (*Shingyo Hikkei*, iii).

To its left are some syncretistic groups who look upon Nichiren as an exemplar of the spirit of the *Dharma Flower* rather than as their founder and teacher. To its right are purist sects who maintain that they alone have correctly understood the master. Of these, by far the most important is the 'Orthodox Nichiren Sect' founded by Nikko at Taiseki-ji: Nichiren Shoshu.

Chapter 13

Nichiren Shoshu _____

Nichiren Shoshu can trace its origins back to the first split among Nichiren's Disciples, the departure of Nikko from Mount Minobu in 1289, and the beginning of his temple at Taiseki-ji two years later. Money and land for the temple were donated by Nanjo Tokimitsu, who had been a supporter of Nichiren since youth. Nikko remained there only about a year, however, and then moved two miles away to the village of Omosu. In 1298 he remodelled his hermitage into a temple, which he called (Kitayama) Hommon-ji. [62] This second temple was paid for by several wealthy laymen, but the principal donors, the Ishikawa family, eventually became dominant there and made it their clan temple. Nikko made the Kitayama Hommon-ji the centre of his teaching activities, and there he remained until his death 35 years later.

   In 1302 he was joined by Nitcho, the fifth Senior Disciple, who had had a falling-out with his stepfather, Toki Jonin, and had left the temple to which Nichiren had assigned him. Nitcho was the only one of the six who had no success as a missionary. His presence at Omosu, however, meant that two of the six were now together, giving additional ammunition to the Nikko Branch's claim to orthodoxy.

   When Nikko died in 1333 at the age of 88, he left six main disciples at Taiseki-ji and six at Hommon-ji, following the example of his master Nichiren. But if Nichiren's transmission to six disciples had caused problems. Nikko's transmission to two sets of six caused even more. Both groups claimed that their temple was the head temple of the Nikko Branch — Taiseki-ji because it had been founded first and Hommon-ji because it had been Nikko's own headquarters. The rivalry degenerated into dynastic squabbles when the landowners began to exercise their authority as chiefs of their respective clans. It was they who chose the chief abbots and dictated temple policies.

Nikko left Nichimoku (1260–1333) in charge at Taiseki-ji when he moved to Hommon-ji. Nichimoku was a nephew of Nanjo Tokimitsu; he survived Nikko by only a few months. The Nanjos then installed another member of their family, Nichido (1283–1341), as chief abbot.

When he learned of the fall of the Hojos in 1333, Nichimoku decided to go to Kyoto to remonstrate with the Emperor. He departed accompanied by two more of Nikko's disciples, Nichigo (1272–1353) and Nichizon (1265–1345). However, he died on the way, and the two disciples completed his mission for him. Nichizon remained in Kyoto, building a temple called Jogyo-in. Nichigo returned to Taiseki-ji with the ashes of Nichimoku, but soon found himself in conflict with the Nanjos. They forced him to leave, but for 70 years his followers continued to press their claim for Taiseki-ji. Nichigo founded a temple of his own in opposition to Taiseki-ji. Nichizon in Kyoto sympathized with him, with the result that the disciples at Taiseki-ji were split three ways. Today the succession at Taiseki-ji is called Nichiren Shoshu, the 'Orthodox Sect of Nichiren'.

The same sort of thing happened at Hommon-ji, where Nikko had left his disciple Nichidai in charge. The influential Ishikawa family preferred Nichimyo, however, and had Nichidai expelled. Nichidai (1294–1394) founded his own temple in Nishiyama, not far away, and gave it the same name, Hommon-ji. The Nikko branch was now split five ways, and these divisions weakened the school as an effective missionary force.

These sub-sects, cut off from the sacred Mount Minobu, from the principal temples in Kyoto, and from each other, were hard-pressed to establish their titles to orthodoxy. The distinctive feature of the Fuji school is its claim that the only true line of descent from Nichiren is via Nikko, the chosen heir. In 1488, two centuries after the death of Nichiren, Nikkyo, a priest at Taiseki-ji, claimed to have discovered two documents written by Nichiren, passing on full authority to Nikko alone (Murano, 'Sokagakkai'). The original documents have disappeared, but 'true copies' are preserved at Taiseki-ji. Other Nichiren bodies ignore them as forgeries.

The first of these documents, called the 'Document for Entrusting the Dharma which Nichiren Propagated throughout His Life', is said to have been written by Nichiren on Mount Minobu in September 1282, a month before his death. It reads, 'I transfer all my Buddhism to Byakuren Ajari Nikko. He should therefore be the great leader for the propagation of true Buddhism. When the sovereign establishes this religion, he should erect the Kaidan of Hommon-ji at the foot of Mount Fuji. All we have to do is await the time. This will be the Ordination Platform of the Original Gate (*Hommon no Kaidan*).'

Needless to say, this document played especially into the hands of the Hommon-ji party since that temple is specifically named, but it says nothing about Taiseki-ji. Since it was written in Chinese, the key phrase could also be interpreted as, 'At Hommon-ji of Mount Fuji the Kaidan ought to be established,' thus making it more specific yet. In any case, its propagation did nothing to settle the dispute between the two temples.

The second document, called 'Document for Entrusting Mount Minobu', is supposed to have been written by Nichiren on the day he died. It reads, 'I transfer the fifty-year teachings of Shakyamuni to Byakuren Ajari Nikko. He is to be the Chief Abbot of Kuon-ji on Mount Minobu. If anyone, clergy or layman, opposes this, he is no disciple of mine.'

The two documents are contradictory. The second says that all authority is to go to Nikko, who is appointed High Priest at Kuon-ji, Mount Minobu, whereas the first says that the official High Sanctuary (*Kaidan*) is not Mount Minobu, but Hommon-ji at the foot of Mount Fuji. In any case these documents convinced few people, and Nichiren Shoshu, which published them, remained a minor sect right up to the end of World War II, when it had less than 3 per cent of the Nichiren faithful. Its sudden rise to prominence since then has been owing to other causes.

Besides claiming the legitimate succession, Nichiren Shoshu puts forth a claim unique to itself. In 1273 Nichiren had created the Great Mandala (*Omandara*) after describing it in his essay, *Kanjin Honzon Sho*. The Great Mandala, the *Gohonzon*, is one of the Three Great Secret Dharmas and is vital to Nichiren's system. He had sent copies of this mandala to various disciples, and is thought to have inscribed about 130 of them, 125 of which are still extant. His disciples continued the tradition of copying Nichiren's mandalas and giving them to the faithful. Today few Nichiren homes are without one.

Nichiren Shoshu, however, claims that it alone possesses a super-*Gohonzon*, called *Dai-Gohonzon*, which is the one true *Gohonzon*. Furthermore, it is said to be the very embodiment of the life of Nichiren himself — his physical presence, 'the entity of the Person and the Law' (Nichiren Shoshu *Dictionary* 141). It is said that although Nichiren inscribed many *Gohonzons* for different individuals, he inscribed only one 'for all mankind'. He is said to have done this on 12 October 1279, although there is no mention of it in any of Nichiren's extant letters. [63] The Dai-Gohonzon was inscribed on a wooden plank and presented to Nikko, who took it with him from Minobu to Taiseki-ji and then left it behind when he moved to Kitayama Hommon-ji a year later.

This Dai-Gohonzon is the heart of the Nichiren Shoshu religion; it is described as the 'reality' of the god worshipped by Christians, Jews, and Moslems. 'Atheists as well as Christians and Mohammedans can neither hear nor see what they believe to exist,' says Nichiren Shoshu apologist Einosuke Akiya. 'This very "reality" is the *Gohonzon* we, Nichiren Shoshu believers, worship. God is, so to speak, a faint shadow on the frosted glass. I think Christians are anxious to grasp the concrete image of God, but actually they cannot. Their God is embodied in the

Gohonzon. If they believe in the *Gohonzon*, they will find in the *Gohonzon* what they call God. Likewise, Mohammedans can find Allah in the *Gohonzon*' (*Guide to Buddhism* 72–3).

Thus Taiseki-ji has become a very special place. Not only is it the first temple founded by Nikko, the only legitimate successor to Nichiren, but it contains the very 'embodiment' of Nichiren himself. And Nichiren, as we shall see below, is none other than the Eternal Buddha.

Herein lies the basic difference between Nichiren Shoshu and other Nichiren sects. Nichiren Shu, for example, uses the term *Gohonzon* (most sacred source) to mean the transmission of the Dharma from the Original Buddha Shakyamuni to ourselves as Original Disciples, as this is described in the Ceremony in Space and depicted in the Great Mandala.[64] To Nichiren Shoshu, on the other hand, *Gohonzon* means the Mandala itself — not just any mandala, but the one which is inscribed on a plank and enshrined at Taiseki-ji: the Dai-Gonhonzon.[65]

In none of Nichiren's writings does he mention this. Scriptural proof for this doctrine is said to be found in his words, 'I, Nichiren, have inscribed my life in *sumi* (ink), so that you may believe with your whole heart' (*Kyo'o-dono Gohenji*). Therefore the ink of the Dai-Gohonzon is the life of Nichiren; and since Nichiren is the Original Buddha, so the Dai-Gonhonzon is the life of the Eternal Original Buddha.

The words, 'I have inscribed my life in *sumi*,' were written in 1273, six years before the supposed inscription of the Dai-Gohonzon. They are taken from a letter to an anxious parent, explaining the meaning of a mandala which Nichiren had sent for her sick child. It was a very personal letter expressing Nichiren's anxiety for the child, and it said nothing about a super-mandala 'for all mankind'.

Non-believers say that first historical reference to the existence of a Dai-Gohonzon was made by Nichiu (1409–82), the ninth High Priest of Taiseki-ji.[66] Nichiu devoted his life to forwarding the claim that his temple was the true mother temple of the Nikko branch. He was a member of the Nanjo family, as were most of the early high priests. All of them were proud of the fact that it had been their ancestor, Nanjo Tokimitsu, who had welcomed Nikko after his departure from Mount Minobu, and at his own expense had built him a temple. But the line of transmission from Nikko was not clear; there were conflicting claimants at Kitayama Hommon-ji, Kyoto Jogyo-in, Nishiyama Hommon-ji, and even at Taiseki-ji. The Nanjo family had managed to keep control of its temple, but not of the others. Taiseki-ji was only one of the head temples of the Fuji branch, which represented a minority in the Nichiren movement as a whole.

Nichiu strove to alter this situation. Before his time the most celebrated relic at Taiseki-ji had been the Ozagawari Gohonzon, which had been inscribed by Nikko on the day the temple was completed, and presented personally by him to his disciple Nichimoku. Nichiu, however, proclaimed that the temple possessed an even greater treasure, one that could be rivalled by no other. It had the Dai-Gohonzon, which Nichiren himself had inscribed, not for Nichimoku or any other individual, but 'for all mankind'.

Nichiu travelled about the countryside spreading the word and collecting funds for his little country temple. By the time of his death in 1482 he had firmly established Taiseki-ji as the centre of the small but prosperous organization which eventually became Nichiren Shoshu. Today, on the grounds of the temple which he saved from obscurity, there stands the largest temple in all Japan — indeed, one of the largest in the world.

The doctrinal exclusiveness of Nichiren Shoshu was codified by the twenty-sixth High Priest, Nichikan (1665–1726). He maintained that Nichiren, not Shakyamuni, is the Eternal Buddha. Every time Nichiren had mentioned the Eternal Buddha Shakyamuni, he really meant himself, and he alone is to be worshipped in the Age of Degeneracy. The *Dharma Flower* of Shakyamuni is 'repudiated' and replaced by the writings of Nichiren, although the Sutra may be 'borrowed from' to illustrate his teachings (Toda, *Lecture on the Sutra* 18).

'The Gohonzon we worship,' says Josei Toda, the outstanding modern exponent of Nichiren Shoshu, 'is the entity of the Law of Nam-myoho-renge-kyo and the Person of Nichiren Daishonin ... Shakyamuni Buddha is not the entity of the Nam-myoho-renge-kyo, but the one who attained enlightenment by practicing the law of Nam-myoho-renge-kyo, itself, and therefore is the original Buddha who leads all other Buddhas to enlightenment. Hence we call Nichiren Diashonin the True Buddha and Shakyamuni and all the other Buddhas simply the buddha' (*Lecture*, 57).

Nichiren Shoshu theologians say that when others speak of 'the Eternal Buddha Shakyamuni', they are really using poetic licence. A literal translation of the title of the *Dharma Flower*, Chapter 16, is not, 'The Eternal Life of the Tathagata', but, 'The Duration of the Tathagata's Life'. The word, 'eternal' does not appear. And in the course of the chapter the Buddha never places his enlightenment beyond the boundaries of time and space. It took place, he says, an unimaginably long time ago, but it had a beginning. Before his enlightenment he practised the Bodhisattva Way.

Shakyamuni, they say, attained enlightenment ages ago (*kuon jitsujo*) but not in 'time without beginning' (*kuon ganjo*). There is a difference between immortality and eternity: immortality has a beginning but no end, whereas eternity has neither a beginning nor an end; it is beyond time and space. The *Dharma Flower* speaks of vast stretches of time. It may imply eternity, but it does not state it in so many words.

To Nichiren Shu, on the other hand, the Original Buddha Shakyamuni and Original Enlightenment are one and the same. There can be no Enlightenment without the One who is enlightened, and vice versa. To Nichiren Shoshu, there is a difference. True Enlightenment is beyond time and space; it exists prior to the historical or even the prehistorical Shakyamuni. Shakyamuni attained enlightenment because it already exists, and his enlightened life is the *result* of this preexistent transcendence. He is 'the Buddha of True Effect'. The true cause, 'the Law of Namu Myoho Renge Kyo', is revealed by Nichiren, 'the Buddha of the True Cause'.[67]

The Nichiren Shoshu argument is reinforced by Nichiren's Great Mandala, the Gohonzon. There Shakyamuni Buddha is given the place of honour at the right hand of the Dharma, which is written in large letters: NAMU MYOHO RENGE KYO. It is the Dharma that dominates the chart, not Shakyamuni.

Shakyamuni is enlightened by this Dharma; Nichiren is identified with it. This identity of Nichiren with the absolute can best be seen in the 'Mandala on the Plank' (*Ita-mandara*), the Dai-Gohonzon venerated by Nichiren Shoshu. Like other Nichiren mandalas, it has the words, *Namu Myoho Renge Kyo* hanging suspended down the centre. Other details are similar to or identical with those found on other mandalas. At the bottom is Nichiren's signature. Normally he would leave some space between the last letter of the *Odaimoku* (*kyo*) and his name, but if there was no room at the bottom, the two might be squeezed together. In the Dai-Gohonzon at Taiseki-ji, the two are so close that they look like one continuous set of nine Chinese characters: *Na-mu-myo-ho-ren-ge-kyo-nichi-ren*. Here Nichiren (the Person) and the *Odaimoku* (the Law) are one.

Nichiren had insisted on the primacy of the Dharma, the truth. Quoting the Mahaparinirvana Sutra, he says, 'The Dharma is the teacher of the Buddhas. Therefore the Buddhas honor the Dharma and make offerings to it. Because the Dharma is eternal, the Buddhas are eternal.' And in his own words, 'The Title of the *Dharma Flower* is the Sacred Source of Buddha Shakyamuni, Many Treasures Buddha, and all the Buddhas of the worlds of the ten directions. As did the Buddha and Tendai Daishi (Chih-i), so do I also worship the *Dharma Flower*. The *Dharma Flower* is the parents of Buddha Shakyamuni and the eyes of all the Buddhas. All the Buddhas, including Shakyamuni and Maha-Vairocana, were born from the *Dharma Flower*' (*Honzon Mondo Sho, Showa-teihon*, 1573).

Nikkyo Niwano, founder of Rissho Kosei-kai, feels that Nichiren's Great Mandala does not adequately represent the union of the Person (the Eternal Buddha Shakyamuni) and the Law, and so he has replaced it with a statue containing a copy of the Sutra. This may or may not be in accord with Nichiren's true intention. Traditional Nichiren Buddhists continue to prefer the Mandala to statues. In Nichiren Shoshu, the Mandala is obligatory.

However, the Great Mandala has one serious disadvantage: the humid Japanese climate. Mandalas are drawn on perishable paper. If a temple was fortunate enough to have one of the original ones drawn by Nichiren, or by one of his famous disciples, it was more likely put away for safe keeping than exposed to the elements. On display was a copy or a statue of Nichiren, Shakyamuni, or some guardian deity. The fact that the Dai-Gohonzon was not displayed until the time of Nichiu does not necessarily mean that it had not existed previously; it may have been preserved in some safe place. (Critics of the Dai-Gohonzon's authenticity usually point instead to the fact that the plank on which it was written was planed by a planer, not an adze; the planer did not exist in Nichiren's time.)

In modern Japan various arrangements of the Gohonzon can be seen among the various Nichiren sects. One popular version shows statues of Shakyamuni Buddha and Many-Treasures Buddha seated side by side as described in the Lotus Sutra; between them are the words, *Namu Myoho Renge Kyo* written on a small pagoda ('This tower,' Nichiren told Abutsu-bo, 'is yourself.'). Sometimes the Mandala is shown with a statue of Shakyamuni seated in front of it and perhaps a figure of Nichiren before them both, signifying the Dharma, the embodiment of the Dharma, and the expounder of the Dharma in this Age of Degeneration. A popular arrangement places a statue of Nichiren before a copy of the Mandala. It is easy for the believers to feel that they are worshipping Nichiren, whom they can see before them, rather than the Dharma, which is depicted only as the background. Nichiren believers, like many other Japanese Buddhists, often ended up worshipping the founder of their sect rather than his teachings. Even in Nichiren Shoshu temples there were varieties of honzons until fairly recently. Only modern photographic techniques and the zeal of Sokagakkai members caused statues to be replaced by copies of the Dai-Gohonzon of Taiseki-ji, which alone is considered proper today.

Nichiren Shoshu has taken the Three Great Secret Dharmas and given them special meanings. *Hommon-no-Honzon* refers not only to the Ground of Being, but especially to its manifestation in the Dai-Gohonzon at Taiseki-ji. *Hommon-no-Daimoku* does not mean what the words say; it is the primary 'vibration' of the Cosmos.[68] *Hommon-no-Kaidan* means not only the place where the devotee practises, but especially the temple of Taiseki-ji. Nichiren is identified with all three. He is physically present in the *Daimoku* written on the *Gohonzon* at the *Kaidan* at Taiseki-ji.

We have here the seeds of a dynamic religion in which the absolute penetrates the physical. It bears some striking similarities to Roman Catholicism. Just as Christ is 'True God of True God . . . through whom all things were made' (Nicene Creed), so Nichiren Daishonin is the True Buddha who manifests the transcendent. And just as Christ is physically present in the bread and the wine, so Nichiren is physically present in the Dai-Gohonzon. Catholicism has its earthly centre at the Vatican; Nichiren Shoshu has its own at Taiseki-ji. (The High Priest at Taiseki-ji is not graced with infallibility, however, although the words of the Patriarch Nichikan are beyond dispute.) Catholicism has its one successor to Christ, St Peter and his successors at Rome; Nichiren Shoshu has its one successor to Nichiren, Nikko and his successors at Taiseki-ji. Catholicism had its spurious 'Donation of Constantine'; Nichiren Shoshu had its 'Transfer Documents'.

Christianity gives much more importance to the words of Christ (the New Testament) than to the Holy Scripture which he so often quoted (the Old Testament). Likewise, Nichiren Shoshu considers the *Dharma Flower* as preliminary to the writings of Nichiren (*Gosho*). Just as Christians borrow from the Psalms, reading into them references to Christ, so Nichiren Shoshu devotees borrow from the Sutra, claiming that its words are cryptic allusions to Nichiren. Christianity fulfils and then rejects Judaism; Nichiren Shoshu fulfils and then rejects Buddhism.

However, Nichiren Shoshu did not develop in a vacuum. Like other Nichiren bodies, it was also a product of its times. During the Muromachi period and beyond there were intellectual cross-currents within Buddhism. There was an ardent dispute about the relationship between the Imprinted Gate and the Original Gate. This was an internal debate among Nichiren Buddhists, but its outcome was important; it would determine the relationship of Nichiren Buddhism to other sects, especially Tendai. A second controversy concerned the very essence of the religious life. What is it? Can it actually accomplish anything? Is it worth all the trouble? These questions concerned everyone.

The first dispute began among certain students of Nikko and Nichiro, and eventually became a bone of contention among all Nichiren philosophers. Nichiren had taught that the Original Gate, the second half of the Sutra, is more important than the Imprinted Gate, the first half. That much was obvious, and the six Senior Disciples accepted it. But the next generation of students wanted to know more: what did this mean, exactly? Did it mean that the Imprinted Gate should now be discarded entirely? If so, why had Nichiren read and quoted from the whole Sutra, and not just the second half? How could you teach the Three Thousand Categories of Existence if you eliminated Chapter II, where the mutual possession of the Ten Worlds is taught? Or perhaps the whole of Tendai philosophy should be discarded? There were many related questions, which called forth many responses.

The answers soon broke down into two general positions. The majority supported a view known as *Itchi*, which means 'unity' or 'harmony'. This maintains that although the second half is more important than the first half, they still form one Sutra. The first half is an imprint of the second half, as its name implies. There is harmony between the two halves as, indeed, there is harmony between all the teachings of Shakyamuni, which find their fulfilment in the *Dharma Flower*. This is the position taken by Nichiren Shu and even its outlawed minority, the *Fujufuse* Branch.

Others, however, disagree. They take a position called *Shoretsu*, which is a contraction of two words meaning, 'superior/inferior'. To them the Original Gate displaces not only the Imprinted Gate but all historical Buddhism in the modern age. This, they believe, was the teaching of Nichiren, but they do not always agree with each other on the definition of the term 'Original Gate'. Is it the second half of the Sutra as taught by Chih-i? Does it consist only of the Eight Key Chapters, as Nichiren seemed to imply sometimes? Is it found in Chapter 16 alone, 'The Duration of the Life of the Tathagata'? Or does it have some deeper esoteric meaning?

However, all the *Shoretsu* exponents agree on one general principle. With the teachings of Nichiren, we have stepped out of historical Buddhism into something completely new. The Buddha expounded the Original Gate not for his famous disciples or even for the gods who had gathered on the Vulture Peak. This Original Teaching (*Honge*) was entrusted to the Bodhisattvas from 'under the earth'. These Bodhisattvas were not 'Buddhists'; they were entirely unknown to anyone in the assembly, even to Maitreya, the future Buddha. Who were they then? They were Everyman.

Nichiren had taught that there is a proper time for planting and a time for reaping. Buddhism was the soil into which the Dharma seed had been planted, and now the seed had flowered. The promised Dharma Flower (*Hokke*) had bloomed. It is not the culmination of Buddhism; it appears in Buddhist soil but transcends it. It is the fundamental reality, antecedent to any philosophy or religion. It is the timeless, universal, innermost reality now opening for all to see.

Because *Shoretsu* has no Buddhist orthodoxy on which it can build, it is more individualist than the 'unity' branch. With the exception of Nichiren Shoshu, *Shoretsu* sects are not built around a sacred temple. Introspection and doctrinal correctness are more important than ecclesiastical authority. Often calling themselves the Dharma Flower sect (*Hokke-shu*), the same name by which Nichiren identified himself, they see nothing wrong with being divided into various independent branches. What matters is the individual who emulates the dynamic spirit of Nichiren, not submission to an outside ecclesiastical authority. Each *Shoretsu* branch was founded by a colourful non-conformist.

The *Itchi-shoretsu* controversy was of no interest to outsiders, but it kept Nichiren theologians on their toes and forced them to define their positions with more clarity. It did result in the formation of new subsects, but these gave impetus to missionary enterprises which expanded Nichiren Buddhism and helped spread it throughout the country.

A far more serious threat to Nichiren Buddhism — to the whole of Japanese Buddhism, in fact — came in a teaching called Original Enlightenment (*Hongaku*). The idea originated in China, and the term was taken from a translation in 550 of a book written in India, *The Awakening of Faith in Mahayana*. Both Saicho (Tendai) and Kukai (esotericism) are credited with bringing the doctrine to Japan. Speaking for Kukai, Yoshito Hakeda writes (6–7):

> Kukai was the first in Japan to hold that man is originally enlightened (*hongaku*). His insistence that one can attain enlightenment here and now was grounded on this belief, a belief derived from the simple insight that unless a man is enlightened from the very beginning he has no way to reach enlightenment. Kukai could not have been innocent enough to hold such an optimistic view without being aware of the darker aspect of man's mind. He was not a born optimist; in fact, it was only in his forties that he started to advocate this idea. He exhorted his followers to be aware of the bondage of evil karma but encouraged them to perceive the originally enlightened nature of man through the veils of evil karma. He believed that evil karma could be wiped away but not man's originally enlightened nature. 'If one has faith and practices, then, whether one is male or female, or of high or low birth, one will qualify as having a great capacity.' The thought of original enlightenment appealed to the basically optimistic Shinto mentality of the Japanese. The Esoteric Buddhism of Kukai, though incomparably more complex and sophisticated than Shinto, had many elements compatible with the latter. A few of these were the idea of the oneness of man and nature, a belief in the magical efficacy of the word (mantra in the former, *Kotodama* in the latter), and the concept of a ritually consecrated realm. It was only natural that as time went by Esoteric Buddhism should come into close association with Shinto.

There is a difference between Original Enlightenment as taught in India and China, and as it developed in Japan, where it encountered 'the basically optimistic Shinto mentality of the Japanese'. In its pure form Original Enlightenment may be the highest reaches of Buddhist thought. The idea is that all the contradictions and conflicts of the world as we know it are transcended by Emptiness. Subject and object, male and female, mind and body, life and death, good and evil, and other polarities are not opposed to each other, but mutually dependent. Take away one, and you lose the other. In the Vimalakirti Sutra this idea of interdependence is expressed as non-duality (Japanese, *funi*). Non-duality refers to the absolute, not to the everyday world, which is clearly full of dualities and contradictions.

In Japan, however, Tendai thinkers pushed the idea further. They affirmed the *absolute nature of the contradictions*. The everyday world *is* the absolute; it is not-two.

Yoshiro Tamura, in his study entitled 'Interaction between Japanese Culture and Buddhism: the Thought of Original Enlightenment', points out that a very thin dividing line has been crossed here. From maintaining the tension between the absolute and the relative as not-two, we have crossed over to the affirmation of the relative itself as the not-two (*Osaki Gakuho*, No. 138 (1985) 2).

This is the Japanese version of Original Enlightenment. It spread gradually, almost as if its proponents were not fully aware of what they were implying. The idea of Original Enlightenment was already developing at the time of the Kamakura reformers, and it became pervasive after them. It is found everywhere, especially in Tendai, Shingon, Nichiren, Kegon and Zen. It is forcefully repudiated only by the Pure Land schools, who reject this world entirely, putting all their hope in the world to come. But even there, it sometimes sneaked in by the back door, for we are saved naturally by Amida without any contrivance on our part.

The logic of Original Enlightenment is that since we are already enlightened, we do not have to do anything about it. We are already Buddhas just as we are. It follows that any religious practice — any morality, for that matter — will only confuse the matter. We must 'do our own thing' because 'our own thing' is the Buddha nature operating within us.

The vocabulary of Original Enlightenment produced grandiose slogans: 'I am Buddha'; 'illusions are enlightenment'; 'this world is the Buddha-land'; 'the three bodies of Buddha are one'; 'one is three'; 'earthly desires are enlightenment'; 'body and mind are one'; 'the sufferings of life and death are nirvana'. In his authenticated writings Nichiren rarely used such terms, and when he did, he carefully explained their meaning.

> Earthly desires are enlightenment and . . . the sufferings of life and death are nirvana. When one chants Namu Myoho Renge Kyo even during sexual union of man and woman, then earthly desires are enlightenment and the sufferings of life and death are nirvana. *Sufferings are nirvana only when one realizes that the entity of human life throughout its cycle of birth and death is neither born nor destroyed.*
>
> (MW 2:229)

Nichiren's explanation is orthodox Mahayana. Reality viewed from wisdom is nirvana and enlightenment (*bodai*); reality viewed from illusion is passion and suffering. In either case, reality is reality. Many Tendai, Shingon, and Pure Land teachers of the times crossed a subtle line here with their careless use of dramatic slogans, but Nichiren held to that line. A highly moral man, he objected to the amorality latent in Original Enlightenment. He saw it clearly in the iconoclasm of Zen, which he described as 'inspired by devils'.

After his death, however, there appeared collections of his unauthenticated 'oral teachings', which were loaded with the vocabulary of Original Enlightenment. A well-meaning author compiled a book to bring Nichiren up-to-date by recasting his teachings in the then-popular slogans of Original Enlightenment. He called it *Ongi Kuden* ('Record of the Orally Transmitted Teachings [attributed to Nichiren]'). Appearing at the height of the Original Enlightenment craze, it is saturated with its phraseology. Here is its exegesis of a line from Chapter 16 of the Lotus Sutra:

'Since I truly became Buddha (there have passed) infinite, boundless . . .' (*Ga jitsu jobutsu irai muryo muhen*): *Ga jitsu* ('I truly') means Buddha's attaining enlightenment in *kuon*, the infinite past. However, the true meaning is that *Ga* ('I') is indicative of all living things in the universe or each of the Ten Worlds, and that *Jitsu* ('truly') is defined as Buddha of *Musa Sanjin* (natural Three Bodies) . . . The person who realizes this is named Buddha. *I* (literally, 'already') means the past and *rai* (literally, 'to come') the future. *Irai* includes the present in it. Buddha has attained the enlightenment of *Ga jitsu*, and His past and future are of uncountable and unfathomable length . . . *Kuon* means having neither beginning nor end, being just as man is, and being natural. It has neither beginning nor end because *Musa Sanjin* is not created in its original form. It is just as man is because it is not adorned by the 32 wonderful physical features and 80 favorable characters [of a Buddha]. It is natural because the Buddha of *Honnu Joju* ('unchanging inherently existing') is natural. *Kuon* is Namu Myoho Renge Kyo. *Kuon Jitsujo* — really enlightened, enlightened as *Musa* ('not being produced by conditions').

(*Ongi Kuden*, quoted by Ikeda,
Science and Religion 200)

All the main ideas of Original Enlightenment are here: 'just as man is'; 'not produced by conditions'; 'not adorned with any special characteristics'; 'inherently existing'; 'all living things are originally enlightened'. The only important idea which is missing is 'earthly desires are enlightenment', but that appears elsewhere in the same text: 'Burn the firewood of earthly desires and reveal the fire of enlightened wisdom' (*Ongi Kuden*, quoted by Kirimura, *Outline of Buddhism* 172).

Ongi Kuden, which may have been written at Taiseki-ji in the first place, became prominent in the theology of Nichiren Shoshu. It was widely believed to contain the authentic verbal teachings of Nichiren as recorded by Nikko. Ironically, one forgery provoked another one. The rival 'Unity' branch produced its own 'oral transmission' called

Onko-kikigaki, and claimed that it had been put into writing by Niko of Mount Minobu. Its real purpose seems to have been to counteract the influence of *Ongi Kuden*. Only in recent times have both works come to be regarded as pious forgeries (Murano 1982).

The Nichiren Shoshu doctrine that Nichiren himself is the Original Buddha follows logically from Original Enlightenment. Nichiren is originally enlightened to the true Dharma. 'Original' here does not mean first at a point in time, but eternal — timeless. We are all originally enlightened, and Nichiren reveals what this means. When we practise what he practised (as when Shakyamuni practises what he practised) we uncover our originally enlightened nature.

Nichiren is said to have realized his own Original Enlightenment at the moment the executioner raised the sword above his head on the beach at Tatsunokuchi. From that moment on Nichiren's teachings are the infallible words of the Originally Enlightened Buddha.

In Original Enlightenment thought, any study of scriptures is a waste of time. We can see how it influenced *Shoretsu* thinkers, who sliced the scriptural bases thinner and thinner. Its most insidious influence, however, was on Japanese society as a whole. Once it left the quiet halls of academia for the anarchic world outside, it led quickly to hedonism, to the justification of self-indulgence. If everyone is originally enlightened just as he is, then religion and morality go out the window. In Tendai and Shingon, where it had begun, it turned monks into soldiers; other religious establishments soon followed suit. In the outside world it justified sensuality, vulgarity, and cruelty. It helped to remove Buddhism from its traditional role of moral arbiter, and allowed neo-Confucianism to pour into the vacuum. Society had to have moral rules in order to survive, and if Buddhism could no longer supply them, Confucianism would have to do the job.

It took a while for Buddhist leaders to realize that they had created a 'Frankenstein's monster'. For a long time any document written in the vocabulary of Original Enlightenment was sure to get a hearing. The end justified the means, and as a result, forgeries abounded. Today that same vocabulary gives the forgeries away as period pieces. The fascination for the slogans of Original Enlightenment eventually passed, and Japanese Buddhism returned to its proper bases, but by then the damage had been done.

The slogans of Original Enlightenment can still be discerned in the terminologies of Nichiren liturgies of many schools, Nichiren Shoshu among them. Scholars can spot them and put them into context, but the uninitiated can as easily fall under their spell today as they did five centuries ago.

Chapter 14

Sokagakkai: the Creation of Values ___

It is only since the Second World War that Nichiren Shoshu has been transformed from a minor sect into the largest religious body in Japan. This remarkable achievement was initiated by two school teachers. The first of them, Tsunesaburo Makiguchi[69] (1871–1944), was a grammar school principal who came to Tokyo from Hokkaido. He wrote some books, one on geography and four volumes on pedagogy, which sold well enough to encourage him to try becoming a full-time author and publisher. But Imperial Japan of the 1930s wanted only conformity in education, not individual 'value creation', which Makiguchi advocated. Value was to be determined by the state, not created from within the individual. The educational bureaucracy obstructed Makiguchi's career at every step.

In 1928 Makiguchi converted to Nichiren Shoshu at the instigation of a fellow principal. Two years later he published the first volume of his theories on education and named as publisher *Soka Kyoiku Gakkai* (Value-Creating Educational Society). Although this book says nothing about religion and the actual society of that name was not begun until 1937, Sokagakkai today formally dates its inception from this first appearance of its title in 1930.

At the time Makiguchi joined Nichiren Shoshu the sect had 75 temples as compared with 4,962 in the other Nichiren groups (mostly Nichiren Shu), and 85,541 adherents as compared with 3,393,051 among the others (Murata, *Japan's New Buddhism* 71). Makiguchi was able to do little to change the situation. The first general meeting of his society consisted of about 60 people, many of them fellow-educators. By November 1941, just before the attack on Pearl Harbor, there were 400. Total readership may have reached a thousand. However, once the country was engaged in a desperate war, all such independent little societies were expected to contribute to the war effort or disappear. By 1943 Soka Kyoiku Gakkai was snuffed out of existence.

Part of the governments's plan for national unity was religious unity. Small sects were ordered to merge with larger ones, which could be controlled more easily. The writings of Nichiren had already fallen foul of the censors, and 'offensive passages' had been deleted (Ienaga, *The Pacific War*, 105). Now the independent-minded Nichiren groups had to be brought into line. They were instructed to affiliate either with the 'Unity' branch (*Itchi-ha*) headed by Mount Minobu or with the loosely federated 'Superior/Inferior' branch (*Shoretsu-ha*). The tiny Nichiren Shoshu, with less than 2 per cent of the temples, stood proudly aloof from either branch. It now had to find some justification for its continued separate existence or face possible closure.

A leading priest of the sect, Jimon Ogasawara, published a journal in which he advocated a solution. The Original Buddha was not Shakyamuni but Myoho Renge Kyo, 'a manifestation of the god Ame-no-minakanushi-no-kami', mythical ancestor of the Emperor. Thus Nichiren Shoshu did not worship the foreign deity, Shakyamuni Buddha, but the Emperor of Japan. What could be more patriotic? There was certainly no harm in obeying the government's decree to enshrine tablets of the Grand Shrine of Ise, the symbol of Japanese national unity. Nichiren himself had worshipped there after completing his studies (Fujii, *Nichiren Shonin Eden*, 28).

The High Priest at Taseki-ji and his assembled clergy were willing to accept this stratagem, but Makiguchi resolutely refused. He was summoned to Taiseki-ji and ordered to obey; still he refused. A few weeks later he and 20 leaders of his organization were arrested. Within a few days all recanted except two: Makiguchi and his faithful friend Josei Toda. They were incarcerated for the duration of the war. Makiguchi died in prison in 1944.

Toda had also been a school teacher on Hokkaido. One day he opened his classroom door, stared silently at his students for a moment, then turned and walked away, never to return. He arrived penniless in Tokyo in 1920 and presented himself to his fellow-countryman, Makiguchi, seeking employment. Makiguchi hired him, and Toda remained grateful and loyal to his dying day. When Makiguchi converted to Nichiren Shoshu, Toda followed him.

Toda was a good businessman, able to make education profitable, and within a few years he could leave the classroom and devote himself to different ventures. By 1943 he controlled 17 enterprises, which included publishing, tutoring, life-insurance, stockbroking, and money-lending. He is said to have been worth about a million and a half dollars (Murata, 87, 90). He was the main financial support for Makiguchi's educational society.

Until his imprisonment Toda had been more of a follower than a leader in matters of religion. Once he had suffered a number of personal tragedies which had set him looking for metaphysical consolation. Between 1923 and 1925 his infant daughter died, then his wife. Finally he himself fell ill with tuberculosis from which he never fully recovered. For consolation he turned to Christianity and then to Pure Land Buddhism only to give them up later as 'not logically convincing' (Murata 87–8). He followed Makiguchi into Nichiren Shoshu, but devoted most of his energies to business, letting Makiguchi handle the deeper philosophical questions.

In prison, however, Toda was thrown back upon his own inner resources. There was nothing left for him to do but practise the religion Makiguchi had taught him. He began to read the *Dharma Flower* and the writings of Nichiren in earnest, and also to chant the Sacred Title, hour after hour, day after day. To him religion was like business: you made investments and reaped profits. Therefore he kept a careful count of the number of his recitations. 'When my chanting of the Daimoku (Sacred Title) was about to reach the two million point,' he explained later, 'I happened to have a very mysterious experience, and there emerged a world in front of me, which I had never imagined before' (Ikeda, *The Human Revolution*, IV.22).

As described by Daisaku Ikeda, who later succeeded him as president of Sokagakkai, Toda 'suddenly . . . found himself in the midst of the air, before he knew it, in the huge crowd of people (at the Ceremony in Space), as many as the sands of sixty thousand Ganges, worshipping the brilliant golden statue of the Dai-Gohonzon. It was neither a dream nor an illusion, and seemed as if it lasted only a few seconds, or a few minutes, or again as long as several hours. It was a reality which he experienced for the first time. As this supreme jubilation filled his body, he cried to himself that the testimonial had no falsity and that he actually existed there. At that moment, he suddenly came to himself, seated in the narrow prison cell in the morning sunshine' (14).

Toda's unexpected discovery of himself participating in the Ceremony in Space has been shared by others.[70] It is, indeed, an overwhelming experience, difficult to put into words, and the laconic description given above hardly does it justice. We suspect that Toda, like others who have experienced this, was as much humbled as exalted by what had transpired, and was reluctant to speak about it to anyone. Details may have been added by Ikeda's imagination. Part of the description rings true (as the huge crowd of people — we would say, beings), but it is not clear what he means by the 'brilliant golden statue of the Dai-Gohonzon'. Golden, yes; but statue . . .? The assembly in space does not venerate a statue.

A complete description of the Ceremony in Space is given in the *Flower Dharma*, Chapters 11–22. A more laconic description is found in the Closing Sutra, *Meditation on the Bodhisattva Universal Virtue*:

'At what place may I practice the law of repentance?' 'Thereupon the voice in the sky will speak thus, saying: "Shakyamuni Buddha is called Vairocana Who Pervades All Places, and his dwelling place is called Eternally Tranquil Light, the place which is composed of permanency-paramita, and stabilized by self-paramita, the place where purity-paramita extinguishes the aspect of existence, where bliss-paramita does not abide in the aspect of one's body and mind, and where the aspects of all the laws cannot be seen as either existing or nonexisting, the place of tranquil emancipation or prajna-paramita . . . these forms are based on permanent law"'.

(*The Threefold Lotus Sutra* 362–3).

A theological explanation is given by Shimizu, who names it 'The Great Mandala-Secret Platform of the Great Meeting in the Air of the Original Gate' (*Hommon koku dai-e no daimandara mitsudan*) (see Chapter Ten). Neither of these accounts mentions a 'golden statue'.

When Toda was released from prison at the end of the war, he reorganized Makiguchi's shattered organization, dropped the word 'Educational' from its title (making it *Soka Gakkai*), and named himself its president. His primary aim, however, was to pick up his life where he had left it two years before and reconstruct his commercial empire. Religion was left to the evening hours, when he would deliver lectures to small groups of people. Again he opened a correspondence school, but this time without success. Ventures in publishing and money-lending also failed, and by 1950 he was bankrupt.

It was only then that he decided that he had had his priorities wrong, putting business before faith. He made a pilgrimage to Taiseki-ji, which he found virtually deserted and in a deplorably run-down condition. He apologized to the Dai-Gohonzon, and vowed to devote all his efforts to propagating the teachings of Nichiren Shoshu, and to emphasize the *Ongi Kuden* instead of Chih-i's philosophy (Ikeda, *Human Revolution*, IV, 249–56).

Toda now turned his practical money-making sense to his religion. 'If one measures the power of the Gohonzon in terms of money,' he told his listeners, 'the Gohonzon has the mystic power to present you with billions of dollars . . . Suppose you are poor. The cause of your poverty was laid in some past existence. You have not the cause for becoming rich. If you think you are destined to be poor and cannot change this, you are influenced by ideas of the pre-*Lotus* teachings. There is a prevailing idea that one's destiny is uncontrollable and one should (wait and) ascend to heaven after death.

'This is no joking matter. How can you ascend to heaven when you are afflicted with various sufferings in this world?

'However, the secret of the Buddha is so wonderful that without having the cause for becoming rich, you can realize your desire for obtaining wealth by worshipping the Gohonzon. The power of the

Daimoku enables you to have the cause of becoming a millionaire even though you had not made such a cause in your past existence . . . Then you will gain enough money even if you do not seek money greedily. This is the mystic power of the Gohonzon' (Toda, *Lecture on the Sutra*, 93).

Toda's gospel of health, wealth, and happiness struck a responsive audience in drab post-war Tokyo. The whole purpose of life, he said, is to be happy. Happiness, like the flavouring in soup, consists in the right mixtures of sweet and sour. Too much sour makes the soup inedible; it is time to pour in the sweet (137).

Toda would drive his point home with passionate sincerity. 'If you do as I tell you, and if things don't work out as you want by the time I come to (this town) next (year), then you may come up here and beat me and kick me as much as you want. This is a promise' (Murata 110, slightly altered).

It was easy for his dispirited audience, discouraged by defeat in war, grinding poverty, and the collapse of traditional values, to respond hopefully to such a message. Although he had a stock answer for all problems ('Chant Daimoku and convert others'), Toda liked to treat his audience as individuals. After an animated speech or lecture, he would open the floor to questions and answers. He would reason with the philosophically inclined, encourage the down-hearted, sympathize with the bereaved, but sternly rebuke the scoffers or recalcitrant.

Toda was not only a good teacher but a skilled businessman who knew how to organize his subordinates so that they would work as a team. His Sokagakkai became a tightly knit society in which everyone had his place on the table of organization. Each member was expected to bring in new members by *shakubuku*, aggressive proselytizing. This, was one of his two basic obligations, the other being to chant morning and evening services (*Gongyo*) with lots of Daimoku. The more converts he brought in, the more material and spiritual benefits he could expect, and the higher he would rise on the table of organization.

In May 1951 Toda was officially inaugurated president of Sokagakkai, which then had about 1,500 members. As he took his oath of office, he promised to convert 750,000 families. 'If I do not achieve this by the time of my death, don't hold funeral services for me, but throw my ashes into the sea off Shinagawa' (Murata 94).

The inspired members eagerly set out to do *shakubuku*. This often meant virtual intimidation of the prospective convert and gained for Sokagakkai as many enemies as friends. Many Japanese objected to being accosted on the streets, at their places of business, or in their homes by zealous missionaries who refused to relent until they had achieved their aim.

Although all critics of Sokagakkai express aversion for *shakubuku*, the method is not very different from that used in the West by Mormons, Jehovah's Witnesses, 'Born-again' Christians, 'Moonies', and others. Most modern Japanese sects practise aggressive proselytizing, but not as successfully as Sokagakkai. Reiyukai and Rissho Kosei-kai do *michibiki*, 'guiding others along the way'; P.L. Kyodan has *shinge*, 'sharing our blessings'; Tenrikyo 'pours perfume' (*nioigake*). But none of these has the fiery intensity of *shakubuku*.

Shakubuku is aggressive, but it is not 'forced conversion', as some have said. When Charlemagne told the Saxons to be baptized or die, that was forced conversion. Sokagakkai members are said to warn potential converts of dire consequences if they fail to join up, but they do not have the power of life or death. They leave that up to the Gohonzon, who apparently can be as vengeful as Jehovah when spurned.[71]

The Sokagakkai tactics may have offended many, but they did not fail to get results. From 1951 to 1957 the organization doubled or tripled its membership every year. When Toda died in 1958 there was no need to cast his ashes into the sea. He had gone beyond his goal of converting 750,000 families.

Only a year after Toda's inauguration, however, the society's zeal almost brought it to an ignominious end. In April 1952 Taiseki-ji and other Nichiren temples throughout the land were celebrating the 700th anniversary of the founder's first proclamation of the Daimoku, *Namu Myoho Renge Kyo*. Believers from around the country came to their head temples for special festivities. At Taiseki-ji four gala days were planned. The first two were to be managed by the sect's official laymen's association, called Hokkeko, the last two days were for Sokagakkai. Toda planned a show of force. The Hokkeko was bringing 2,500 members, and he would muster 4,000 from his one-year-old society. He also saw an opportunity to avenge his two years of imprisonment during the war: he had learned that the leader of the compromising party, the priest Jimon Ogasawara, was going to be present.[72] There could be no better time for a showdown.

Before leaving for the head temple Toda organized his younger members like shock troops. He instructed them to search discreetly for the offending priest, and then be ready for action once they found him. They were to challenge him to debate his views right then and there. Forty-seven leaders of the Youth Division, one of whom was Daisaku Ikeda, worked out a systematic plan to locate Ogasawara and bring him to judgement. On arriving at Taiseki-ji, they fanned out and carefully combed the temple grounds. Nevertheless, they might have missed him entirely had not a young lady from Hokkeko inadvertently tipped them off by innocently remarking that she had seen the famous Reverend Ogasawara at one of the priests' lodging houses. Instantly, the Youth Division members sent one of their number to advise Toda while the rest of them converged on the house. They barged straight in, and found the 69-year-old theologian clad in his priestly garments and talking cheerfully to several other clergymen.

The young men immediately challenged him to debate his views.

The old priest tried to put them off, saying that the hour was late, and he was tired after his long journey to the temple, but Sokagakkai members kept pouring into the room and demanding that Ogasawara retract his views and take the blame for the imprisonment and death of Makiguchi. The old man, now thoroughly annoyed, told them to go away and leave him alone. The lady from Hokkeko, embarrassed by the results of her innocent introduction, slipped away without a word. Three other priests, who had been chatting with Ogasawara, sat in shocked silence, unable to believe they were hearing such abuse heaped on so venerable a divine.

'Take off his robe!' someone shouted. 'Take off his robe and take him to the grave of Makiguchi!'

Four men picked up the squirming priest. They were just about to carry him out when Toda appeared in the doorway.

'Stop!'

What happened next is not clear. According to Ikeda, Toda reasoned calmly with Ogasawara, demanding an apology, while the old man 'drooled at the mouth' and 'howled like a rabid dog'. But Murata claims that Toda told him in an interview that he struck the priest 'twice' (96). In any case, Ogasawara would not be intimidated, and would admit to nothing.

Seeing that he was getting nowhere, Toda finally strode out, leaving the old priest to the mercies of his tormentors. 'If you so stubbornly refuse to apologize, whatever may happen to you is no longer my concern. Whatever the Youth Division members may do to you, I will not take the responsibility.'

As soon as their leader had left, the young men once more hoisted the priest up onto their shoulders. By then they had torn off his priestly robe and stripped him down to his underclothes. They carried him out into the temple grounds, shouting through megaphones, 'This is Jimon Ogasawara, a parasite in the lion's body, gnawing at Nichiren Shoshu . . . This is the villanous monk, the actual murderer of Mr. Makiguchi!' They tagged him with a placard reading, 'Racoon Monk', and bore him to the grave of Makiguchi. There the thoroughly shaken old man was forced to sign a prepared apology and repudiation of his theological opinions.

By then a large crowd had gathered at the scene. Chief Director Izumida of Sokagakkai took charge. The scene in the cemetery was lit eerily by lights from exploding fireworks celebrating the festival. Ogasawara tried to joke about the incongruity of it all, but this only enraged his captors all the more.

Some local firemen serving as temple guards, thinking that the priest was about to be lynched, finally managed to break through the mob. However, when it turned out that the firechief was Izumida's brother-in-law, the matter was settled amicably. Ogasawara was released, and the crowd dispersed.

Toda's victory almost proved his undoing. Nearly all the clergy and laity of Nichiren Shoshu were shocked by this violence, and the press picked up the story and reported it sensationally. The High Priest sent a stern reprimand to Toda, demanding that he apologize.

The great strength of Sokagakkai lies in its affiliation with Nichiren Shoshu. Of all the new Japanese religions that came into prominence after the war, Sokagakkai is the only one associated with a historical Japanese sect. It alone is both ancient and modern; it can appeal both to Japanese pride in a heroic past and to hopes for a better future. If this affiliation had been broken at this early stage, neither Sokagakkai nor Nichiren Shoshu would have grown into the powerful force they were soon to become.

When Toda realized that nearly all of Nichiren Shoshu was arrayed against him, he backed down, humbly apologized to the High Priest, and vowed to atone by converting the entire nation. Meanwhile he offered to raise funds for repairs on the pagoda at the Head Temple. His offer was accepted. Nevertheless, it was six months before the crisis finally passed, and smoulde
ing resentments remained for years. Members of Sokagakkai went from temple to temple trying to convince their priests of the justice of their cause, but they often received a cool reception. Ogasawara, realizing that he had the support of the majority, brought legal charges against the leaders of Sokagakkai. Both Toda and Izumida had to appear before the civil authorities and were detained overnight.

High Priest Nissho saw that his sect was risking not only very bad publicity but a serious schism within its ranks. Toda, after all, had shown repentence while Ogasawara had acted on his own. He therefore ordered Ogasawara, as a priest under his jurisdiction, to withdraw his civil suit. At this point, Ogasawara overstepped his bounds. He filed suit against the High Priest.

Opinion within the sect now swung quickly to Toda's favour, and Ogasawara's supporters melted away. Eventually it was he who had to beg forgiveness for his 'indiscretion in having had the unfortunate conflict with Sokagakkai'. Toda had won. For the next two decades there was to be no real challenge to the dominant position of Sokagakkai within Nichiren Shoshu.

One of Toda's most important contributions to his sect was the publication of its version of Nichiren's collected writings. Throughout all these centuries Nichiren Shoshu, while insisting that it was the only orthodox transmitter of Nichiren's Buddhism, had not had a sacred scripture of its own. All the major editions of Nichiren's writings had been produced outside the sect. Collections of Nichiren's writings had been made since a year after his death, but they were often incomplete or not scholarly enough to separate the genuine from the spurious. In the early 1950s Rissho University was hard at work producing a definitive collection. Now known as the Showa Standard Edition, it was published by Mount Minobu in 1952 in four volumes with a detailed topical index. It is a scholarly work, which carefully distinguishes between the entries on the basis of their authenticity.

Nichiren Shoshu was displeased with this project, which would classify some of its own documents, such as the 'Transfer Documents' and the 'Record of Orally Transmitted Teachings' (*Ongi Kuden*), as spurious. Toda came to the rescue and offered to pay for the publication of an official Nichiren Shoshu version. The work was done by members of the Study Department of Sokagakkai under the supervision of an 84-year-old retired High Priest, Nichiko Hori. Under Toda's prodding, a 2,000 page volume, entitled 'New Edition of the Complete Writings of Nichiren the Great Saint' (*Shimpen Nichiren Daishonin Gosho Zenshu*), was compiled and printed in only one year (1951), beating the Showa Edition to the press (Ikeda, *The Human Revolution*, V, 499–500). Since its appearance, the *Gosho*, as it is generally called for short, has become the sacred scripture of Nichiren Shoshu, replacing the *Dharma Flower* in importance.

Armed with their new bible and well drilled in the art of *shakubuku*, Toda's bodhisattvas marched forth to convert the nation. Their methods won them as many enemies as converts. 'In practice, *shakubuku* often amounted to violent, forceful harassment of individuals by Soka Gakkai members,' says Jerrold Schecter in *The New Face of Buddha*. 'Relays of the Soka Gakkai members would maintain a schedule of chanting the *Daimoku* for a full week, twenty-four hours a day, in a prospective recruit's home and literally wear him out. Membership requires that the new members discard all other objects of religious worship, and often the Soka Gakkai members would destroy the family altars of prospective converts ... Those who have been exposed to *shakubuku* or to the intolerance of the Soka Gakkai members who have already found the true religion, find that they are often the object of verbal abuse, threats and dire warnings of disaster if they resist conversion' (261–2).

But shock tactics are not the only reason for Toda's success. He was an experienced businessman who once before had amassed a considerable fortune; he was now marketing a sure-fire product. He knew that what people want most in the world is not 'truth', but health, wealth, and happiness. This is what he offered them, and at a very nominal cost; he called it the 'happiness machine'.

How can we live happily in this world and enjoy life? If anyone says he enjoys life without being rich and even when he is sick, he is a liar. We've got to have money and physical vigor, and underneath all we need life force. This we cannot get by theorizing or mere efforts as such. You can't get it until you worship the Gohonzon. It may be irreverent to use this figure of speech, but a Gohonzon is a machine that makes you happy.

How to use this machine? You conduct five sittings of prayer in the morning and three sittings in the evening and *shakubuku* ten people. Let's make money and build health and enjoy life to our hearts' content before we die!

(Murata 108)

If a company were to manufacture a 'happiness machine', he said, it could merchandize it for at least one hundred thousand yen, and make a fortune. If a hospital could give happiness injections, people would be lined up for blocks every morning waiting their shot. Well, the 'happiness machine' does, indeed, exist. It was made by Nichiren Daishonin here in Japan 700 years ago. And instead of standing in line for hours outside a hospital every morning, waiting in the rain or the hot sun, anyone can get his daily injection of health and happiness in the privacy and comfort of his own home by chanting the Sacred Formula before his copy of the Gohonzon.

However, the disciple is not to expect 'pennies from heaven'. The Gohonzon — the 'happiness machine' — will supply the energy. It is up to each individual to put this energy to work.

Some believers may say, 'As I believe in the Gohonzon, my business will prosper even without my effort.' Nothing is as unreasonable as this! . . . They are so idle as to try to earn money without working for it. 'Then it is not absolute benefit, is it?' Some may say this, but it is far from true. To earn money without working is like roasting a chicken without adjusting the oven's temperature. Even if you put the chicken in the oven, it cannot be cooked without lighting the fire however hard you may chant Daimoku to the Gohonzon. However earnestly you practice *Shakubuku*, you will suffer punishment if you neglect your work. A passage from the *Gosho* reads, 'Make your best service in your occupation; that is the practice of the *Hokekyo*.' Working even equals belief in the Gohonzon.

(Toda, 110)

Happiness is sure to come to the sincere believer, but he should not expect it immediately.

Some people often say, 'Why can't I enter into the supreme state of happiness?' when they have been believers in the Gohonzon for only a year or two. They need not be so hasty. If one is destined to die at the age of 60, I think he can feel satisfied if he can fully enjoy a happy life for five years after the age of fifty-five. Is it not satisfactory to live happily day after day for five full years without any anxiety? However, I hear some people say, 'Although I have been practicing this religion for years, I am still

SOKAGAKKAI: THE CREATION OF VALUES

unable to reach the destination of happiness.' Unless they experience the sorrows of life, they cannot realize its joys. I do not mean that they should endure a poor life, but they must fight against their evil destiny until they can see the evidence of happiness . . . I know very well that there is no believer who is assiduous in this faith but who failed to build a happy life.

(Toda, 147–8)

Toda died suddenly at the age of 58. If success was his criterion for happiness, then his 'last five years' were certainly good years. He attained his goal of a membership of 750,000 families by 1957; the following year he completed the construction of a one-million-dollar Grand Lecture Hall at Taiseki-ji. Two hundred thousand members gathered for the celebration. Toda invited the Prime Minister, whose presence would have signified that Sokagakkai had finally been recognized as an important factor in Japanese national life. The Prime Minister declined the first invitation but accepted a second one two weeks later. However, although six thousand young people were lined up to welcome him, he failed to appear. Instead he sent a former cabinet member, his wife, daughter, and son-in-law to represent him.

Toda became ill during the festivities that he was supervising and had to be rushed to the hospital in Tokyo. He died the next day of causes which have never been made public. A year before he had complained of liver trouble, but later announced that he was 'completely cured'. Diabetes plagued him all his life, and he also suffered from troubles with his pancreas and his left eye. His 'happiness machine' had not relieved him from chronic ill health. However, like Nichiren, he was never overcome by despondency, believing that the next life would be better. 'Are you tired of life? . . . I recommend that you accumulate good fortune in this life so that in the next existence of life, you can be born into a family possessing five Cadillacs. For that purpose, you should believe in the Gohonzon. All human life is eternal. This is the secret of the Buddha. Whether or not you may believe it, it is the truth of the universe. You cannot help it. Let us devote ourselves to the practice of Buddhism and enjoy good fortune in the next life!' (Toda, 100).

Two hundred and fifty thousand people came to his funeral. Among them was the Prime Minister.

Chapter 15

From Backwater Sect to World Religion _____

At Toda's death, he was succeeded by his closest disciple, Daisaku Ikeda, who had been chief of staff of the Youth Division. Ikeda, who was only 32, was made General Director in June 1958 and installed as president two years later. At the time, Nichiren Shoshu-Sokagakkai claimed a membership of around one million families. Ten years later this figure had shot up to nearly seven million. Sokagakkai had become the most powerful religious force in the country and the largest lay religious organization in the world.

Who is this man Ikeda who has accomplished such wonders? To his millions of followers he is the perfect man: generous, upright, patient, vigorous, contemplative, and wise. Sokagakkai publications always feature several pages of photographs of the great leader in a variety of situations: Ikeda addressing a huge assembly; Ikeda wading in the sea, trousers rolled up to his knees; Ikeda slicing a water melon; Ikeda comforting an American teenager, who sobs with emotion at being in his presence. The people around him in the photograph are rarely identified; he is the only one who matters, unless the other person happens to be the High Priest or a celebrity. Directors of Sokagakkai, smiling cheerfully behind their leader, remain anonymous.

When he speaks in public, often addressing a huge but orderly audience of thousands, the local, national, or international leaders sit in rows beside and behind him, carefully placed in order of seniority. They sit poised on the edges of their chairs, leaning forward as if about to spring into action, eyes riveted on the President throughout the entire hour or hour-and-a-half speech. If the President is wearing a jacket, they wear jackets; if the President is in shirt-sleeves, they are in shirt-sleeves. Often the entire audience will sit leaning forward in the same uncomfortable posture, all dressed identically.

President Ikeda likes his followers to participate in his decisions 'democratically'. He will frequently pause after announcing some new course of action, and ask, 'Do you agree?' Thunderous applause indicates consent; not to agree would be unthinkable.

Like Makiguchi and Toda, President Ikeda was born in a poor family and knew poverty throughout his early life. He did manage to complete high school, but it was not until after he became president of Sokagakkai that he submitted a thesis and was awarded a diploma from Fuji Junior College. He is an avid reader, and is largely self-taught. At the age of 19 he attended a lecture by Josei Toda. One week later he converted to Nichiren Shoshu, and soon became Toda's devoted assistant, both in business and in the fledgling Sokagakkai.

His first years with Toda were hard ones, for Toda's business ventures were failing, and the employees never knew when they might be laid off. Ikeda's health was poor and his life threadbare, but he served Toda faithfully, and had explicit faith in the power of the Gohonzon to improve their lot. By the time Toda's fortunes finally emerged into the sunlight, Ikeda had been moulded into his most capable and dedicated disciple.

Ikeda is every inch the child and product of Sokagakkai. Reporters, who may not really grasp the religious significance of Nichiren Shoshu, sometimes wonder how this man, who seems so ordinary, can merit such blind devotion from so many millions of people. Jerrold Schecter, observing him through the eyes of an American reporter, said that 'Ikeda is best in small groups, advocating the happiness that joining Sokagakkai can bring. He is a fiery debater, and is a great spellbinder for the crowd. He is a short man with a large nose and cold eyes. He remains aloof and rather superior in personal contact, and it is difficult to speak with him in anything but his own terms of Nichiren Buddhism . . . His writings, as translated into English, are rambling — long on theory and short on specifics' (*The New Face of Buddha* 263).

In a slashing attack called *I Denounce Sokagakkai*, Dr Hirotatsu Fujiwara expresses alarm at the 'deification' of Ikeda, which he compares to the deification of the Japanese Emperor before World War II.

From the standpoint of appearance, Ikeda seems to have developed a career of an unimaginably audacious man. But his writings, inspite of a wordy style, lack content. There are doubts as to whether he has superior intelligence, and his statements are very abstract and vague. When compared with other fascist leaders, he is not nearly as charming as was Hitler or Mussolini. About the best that can be said for him is that he is the type who would make good as a television personality. Ordinarily speaking, he would be estimated as a man of the bank branch manager capacity, but the problem is, that as he has these ordinary abilities, he is the head of a group of fanatics.

(141)

The charge of fascism is especially repugnant to Ikeda. Speaking to the general meeting of the Students Division in 1965, he said:

> One of the oft-repeated criticisms is that the Sokagakkai is a fascist organization. They fear the well disciplined and united Sokagakkai — a discipline which no other organization has ever achieved. . . .
>
> Fascism has four main characteristics. First, it is a dictatorship built on violence; second, it supports exclusive capitalism; third, it denies both parliamentarian democracy and man's basic rights; and fourth, it does not admit the equality of men. However, none of these characteristics are applicable to Sokagakkai. . . .
>
> First, as to dictatorship through violence, how could violence save more than five million families? There is no other organization like the Sokagakkai in which members enjoy peace and harmony, while creating value in society. . . .
>
> As for dictatorship, again the Sokagakkai does not qualify, because we have the definite law of Nam-myoho-renge-kyo, whereas dictatorship has no basic law, philosophy, or ideology. . . .
>
> Second, fascism supports capitalism exclusively. When has the Sokagakkai stood by the capitalists? On the contrary, capitalists have ridiculed the Sokagakkai, saying that it is an organization of the poor. However, they are now surprised to find that many Sokagakkai members work actively in almost every company in the nation. It is unreasonable to say that the Sokagakkai, which has never received any contribution from non-believers in its past 700 years, conspires with the covetous capitalists interested only in collecting money.
>
> Third, as to the denial of parliamentary democracy and men's rights, the truth is just the opposite. Enlightenment in Buddhism can be translated as establishment of a truly independent self, since the purpose of faith lies in obtaining absolutely free circumstances. Nichiren Daishonin's philosophy fully expounds the basic rights of man, which you as believers acquire in your daily lives.
>
> In reference to the denial of parliamentarianism by dictatorship, I want to say this: Why then did the Sokagakkai send in earnest twenty representatives to the House of Councillors unless the Sokagakkai abided by parliamentarianism? I wish to declare that the Sokagakkai is the best example of law-abiding democracy in parliament.
>
> The fourth is no exception. Buddhism respects the equality of man in the exact sense of the term. All are equal before the Daishonin, be they company presidents, ex-nobles, maid-servants, students or statesmen. . . .

It is true that the Sokagakkai is well organized, but if as such our society is branded as fascist, the Nichibo volley-ball team . . . may be called fascist, and the Yomiuri Giants, one of Japan's leading professional baseball teams, may also be called fascist. This is too foolish even to consider. (*Lectures on Buddhism*, 4:322–5)

In spite of the vicious attacks sometimes launched upon him by outsiders, President Ikeda never replies in kind, but retains his composure and tries to reason with his detractors. He has little formal education but is widely read. Occasionally his writings contain factual errors, but he is sincerely dedicated to the ideals of Nichiren Shoshu. If idolization has been heaped upon him by his devoted followers, it seems to affect him no more than criticism.

'Enlightenment in Buddhism,' he says, 'can be translated as establishment of a truly independent self, since the purpose of faith lies in obtaining absolutely free circumstances.' No Nichiren Buddhist will dispute that. Nichiren lived under a military dictatorship, and he had no use for it, believing that it would impose exterior criteria preventing people from living according to natural law. The *Dharma Flower* is the ultimate teaching of the Buddha because it opens the individual to his own inner potential. This is the essence of *Namu Myoho Renge Kyo*.

Nichiren Shoshu sees itself as the vanguard of a new world view encompassing both man and nature. 'What most concerns me here,' said Ikeda in this respect, 'is the European-led conception of human being as against nature, and its headlong direction in placing humanity above nature. It is the stalemate arrived at by this notion that I simply must point out. For the human is but a part of nature' (*Seikyo Times*, March 1970, 39). Ikeda is convinced that modern science, modern political aspirations, and the age-old religious questions of mankind all find their solution only in Nichiren Shoshu. In his book *Science and Religion*, which is surprisingly erudite for an author who never got past a junior college education, he develops the theme that Buddhism in general and Nichiren Shoshu in particular stand in complete harmony with the discoveries of modern science (vii).

The argument between religion and science has been repeated over and over, but in such cases, 'religion' meant mainly Christianity. Therefore, the contradiction between science and religion was merely that between science and Christianity, thus proving the inferiority of Christian theology . . . Science and religion are fittingly compatible. As a matter of fact, science is learning which takes natural phenomena as the subject of study, and pursues the law of causality. On the other hand, Buddhism is the philosophy which makes life the object of study and clarifies the inner law of cause and effect. In methodological terms, the former is analytical and inductive, and the latter is synthetic and deductive. However, the two cannot be incompatible in the final analysis.

In politics, Ikeda came to feel the same way. If it could convert one-third of the nation and win the good will of a second third, then Nichiren Shoshu would dominate Japan. With 15,000,000 members, Sokagakkai was well on its way towards this goal. 'Government aims at realizing the happiness of the individual through rectification of the order and systems of society, while Buddhism attempts to bring true happiness to the individual by removing the causes of unhappiness found in his own life. Therefore it is possible to build a supreme cultural state and an ideal society by merging government and Buddhist philosophy' (Murata 169).

In 1961 Ikeda stated firmly that 'we are not a political party. Therefore we will not get into the House of Representatives.' Three years later, however, he had changed his mind. Sokagakkai officially launched the *Komeito*, 'The Clean Government Party'. In 1965 it ran 14 candidates for the House, and all of them won. With every election thereafter, *Komeito* grew in strength. In the 1975 elections it was the third largest party, winning 95 seats in the House, more than the Communist or the once-powerful Democratic Socialist Party. But it was still a long way from the one-third that Ikeda had been aiming for; that would require over 156 seats. However, it was enough to cause its votes to be courted by the two larger parties in the House.

As Sokagakkai gained in political punch, opposition grew proportionately. Many citizens, who might once have looked on Sokagakkai as just an off-beat religious sect, now began to be alarmed. Most Japanese are nominal Buddhists, belonging to many different sects and head temples. These sects may differ on many details, but on one thing they are agreed: Nichiren Shoshu is heretical — even 'non-Buddhist', in that it replaces the Buddha with Nichiren. Japanese, like Americans, are accustomed to religious pluralism, and the exclusiveness of Nichiren Shoshu rubbed them the wrong way. A socialist writer, Hirotatsu Fujiwara, managed to bring the issue to a boil in 1969 with the publication of his book, *I Denounce Sokagakkai*.

There had been many hostile press reports on Sokagakkai, and one more book would not have had such an impact had not word got around that the Clean Government Party and Sokagakkai were trying to prevent its publication. Einosuke Akiya, a General Director of Sokagakkai, and Yukimasa Fujiwara, a Komeito Metropolitan Assemblyman, visited the author in his home and tried to persuade him not to publish his book. They claimed later that their visit was 'friendly', but Fujiwara cried, 'Foul!' According to him, book distributors, advertisers, and he himself were threatened with reprisals if they so much as mentioned the existence of such a book. Soon the story was in all the papers, and the book, needless to say, became a best-seller.

The book was a broadside against Ikeda, Sokagakkai, and Komeito, all of which the author labelled as 'fascist'. He showed little understanding of Buddhism and considered that the merits or demerits of a religious sect were of minor importance. What did matter, according to him, was the fanaticism of the Sokagakkai adherents, the absolute power of Ikeda over the organization, and the potential danger of such a man and such a group gaining control of the nation. The 'suppression' issue, with its threat to freedom of speech, played right into his hands. The final edition of his book contained an appendix with a day-by-day account of all the events surrounding its publication.

Newspapers gave the 'suppression' story a lot of coverage. When the Diet (Japanese Congress) reconvened in February 1970, members of opposition parties — Socialists, Communists, and Social Democrats — brought the matter onto the floor of the House, demanding a full investigation. They claimed that the constitutional provision of separation of church and state was in jeopardy, and demanded that Ikeda be brought before an investigating committee. Prime Minister Sato who, according to Fujiwara, had once expressed admiration for 'such a brave book', was now non-committal. Perhaps he felt that opposition parties were trying to involve his administration in the affair (Fujiwara, 258, 282, 283).

Nevertheless, Sokagakkai was increasingly embarrassed by the vehemence of these attacks. Ikeda found himself forced to make a choice between politics and religion. He opted for the latter.

In May 1970, at the annual general meeting of Sokagakkai, Ikeda made an open apology: 'I wish to apologize frankly to all concerned and to the people. There was no intent to interfere with freedom of speech, but nonetheless (some) activities were interpreted as interference. It made the persons concerned feel they were being pressured.'

He went on to state that from now on the administration of Sokagakkai and Komeito would be clearly separated; Sokagakkai would continue to give its support to Komeito, but individual members could vote for the party of their choice. Emma Layman points out that in the next elections they did just that, and Komeito lost a number of seats to the Socialists (*Buddhism in America*, 124). Nevertheless, it has continued to be the nation's third largest political party.

Ikeda also backed off on two other controversial issues. The Sokagakkai methods of violent conversion (*shakubuku*) had been much criticized. Such methods, he said, would no longer be used. Finally, he denied that Nichiren Shoshu wished to build a National Kaidan by government decree. Nichiren Shoshu would build its own Kaidan, and Sokagakkai would pay for it. (Fujiwara, 287).

The head temple of Nichiren Shoshu, Taiseki-ji, is 700 years old, founded by Nikko in 1290 after he left Mount Minobu. However, he did not stay there very long. By 1298 he had established a new temple two miles away called Hommon-ji, from which he directed his branch sect for the next 35 years until his death at the age of 87. The two temples have disputed the title of Head Temple ever since, and also disagreed on theology. Taiseki-ji came to maintain that the Three Treasures of Buddhism — Buddha, Dharma, and Sangha — mean that Nichiren is the Original Buddha, Daimoku is the Dharma, and Nikko the Sangha. Hommon-ji maintained that Shakyamuni is the Original Buddha, Daimoku is the Dharma, and Nichiren heads the Sangha. As this is the same position as that held by Nichiren Shu at Mount Minobu, it was able to amalgamate peacefully with the latter in 1941. Taiseki-ji resisted amalgamation and remained independent.

For seven centuries Taiseki-ji was not a great centre for pilgrimages like Mount Minobu, Ikegami Hommon-ji, and other places associated with the life of Nichiren. Nichiren himself had never been there, and even Nikko had lived there for only a year or two. His tomb is at Hommon-ji, where he died. Taiseki-ji did not have any impressive buildings or works of art other than the massive main gate built by Nikkan in 1717. Before the war it had 259 acres of arable land; after the war its holdings were reduced to 42 acres. When Toda visited there after his release from prison, he found the Head Temple neglected and run-down, and vowed to do something about it.

Taiseki-ji had one thing possessed by nobody else: the very 'embodiment' of Nichiren himself, in the Mandala on the Plank (*Ita-mandara*), the Dai-Gohonzon. This is the heart, soul, and 'embodiment' of the Nichiren Shoshu faith.

'The cardinal point of faith,' said Toda, 'lies first and foremost in pilgrimage (to Taiseki-ji). No one can develop true faith unless and until he faces and worships the Dai-Gohonzon directly' (*Seikyo Times*, August 1971, 37). Both he and Ikeda made the embellishment of the Head Temple a matter of high priority.

Sokagakkai has transformed Taiseki-ji from a sleepy country temple complex into one of the biggest and busiest religious centres in the world. By the 1970s it was welcoming over 3,500,000 pilgrims a year — more than Lourdes in France (*Seikyo Times*, March 1972, 20). To accommodate these ever-increasing crowds, Sokagakkai launched an ambitious building programme. It raised a larger sanctuary for the Dai-Gohonzon (1955), a Grand Lecture Hall (1958), lodgings for pilgrims, and various other buildings, but the greatest of all was yet to come. In 1972 President Ikeda officially inaugurated a mammoth new Grand Main Temple, the Sho-Hondo. This, he boasted, is 'the paramount of religious architecture in the world . . . In size, the Sho-Hondo surpasses even the renowned St. Peter's in the Vatican' (*Seikyo Times*, December 1972, 11, 12).

This huge edifice was paid for by eight million contributors with money raised during a four-day drive in 1965. They are said to have donated 35,500 million yen in those four days — a truly remarkable

fund-raising achievement. In a long speech at the completion ceremony, Ikeda sounded like the Emperor Justinian who 'surpassed
Solomon' in creating the greatest religious edifice in the world.

> Thus completed, the great building lies in all its splendor,
> immaculately white and brilliant in the brightness of the sun, a
> magnificent sight in central Japan. It soars towards the sky which
> is permeated with the immortal life of the universe, and rivals
> the sacred peak of Fuji in dignity. To the south, it commands the
> cobalt blue of the pacific, the unbounded expanse of water
> which reminds one of the infinite wisdom of Buddha. Its figure is
> graceful, its appearance spectacular, perfectly blending with the
> perpetuity of the surrounding landscape. Where can a match be
> found for this edifice, either in solemnity or in grandeur?
> (*Seikyo Times*, December 1972, 11)

According to High Priest Nittatsu Hosoi, 'Now that the supreme object
of worship (Dai-Gohonzon) in true Buddhism is placed in its rightful
seat, everlasting peace and prosperity will undoubtedly prevail. This
place is none other than the Pure Land and the land of eternal
enlightenment.'

> When once one comes and visits this sanctuary for worship, he
> will immediately be able to expiate his sins from the infinite past
> and transform his earthly desires into enlightenment, his karma-
> bound life into an unrestricted one, and his sufferings into
> happiness. In so doing, he discovers the true law of the lotus
> within himself and becomes the Buddha of the 'Infinite Life'
> Chapter of the true teachings, the Enlightened One endowed
> with unrestricted freedom and the three noble attributes. At that
> moment, his action and influence, his life and environment, his
> body and mind, his entity and functions — all of these become
> those of the Buddha. All this is attributed solely to the limitless
> mystic power of the Dai-Gohonzon.
> (*ibid.* 7)

Peace and prosperity over all the earth was Nichiren's dream. Now at
last, says Nichiren Shoshu, this dream is being fulfilled. The third of the
Founder's Three Great Secret Dharmas, the sacred ground where the
benefits of the *Dharma Flower* are to be realized, the *Hommon-no-
kaidan*, is a reality. Everlasting peace and universal enlightenment are
now assured because this building has been erected in Fujinomiya,
Japan.
    It is clear from the above statements that in Nichiren Shoshu the
Hommon-no-kaidan is viewed as the physical structure which houses
the physical Gohonzon. Now that this structure has been immensely

enlarged, so the benefits of the Gohonzon are proportionately increased. This again is the reverse of the teachings in Nichiren Shu. According to the official handbook of the latter, *Shingyo Hikkei*. 'To uphold the Lotus Sutra is to observe the commandments (*kai*), and the place where we uphold the Lotus Sutra will become the Sacred Platform (*kaidan*). When all people uphold the Lotus Sutra, however, there will be a Sacred Platform where qualified discipline masters may give Buddhist commandments in order to perpetuate the true Dharma. Aiming at such a goal, for us to firmly uphold the Lotus Sutra, which is difficult to do, is a step towards the establishment of the true Sacred Platform of Hommon. In other words, we reach the state in which all people live in peace. Therefore it could be said that the ultimate Sacred Platform of Hommon is for all people to uphold the Lotus Sutra' (112).

The Nichiren Shu interpretation is spiritual: each of us builds his own *kaidan*; as the faith expands, *kaidan* expands until finally it will embrace all people. Then a building may be constructed to symbolize its reality. In Nichiren Shoshu, the interpretation is physical: the ultimate *kaidan* is already built, and all mankind will now resort to it.

Unfortunately, the euphoria at the completion of the Sho-Hondo gradually subsided as a more mundane consideration began to assert itself: who was the real owner of the Sho-Hondo? Originally, Soka-gakkai had been a laymen's auxiliary of Nichiren Shoshu and its Head Temple of Taiseki-ji. When Toda had overstepped his authority by allowing a venerable clergyman to be man-handled by Sokagakkai members, he atoned by apologizing and making generous contri-butions. But Ikeda did not consider the glorious Sho-Hondo to be a donation, as it had been paid for entirely by Sokagakkai members. It belonged to them, not to the clergy of Nichiren Shoshu.

During the 1970s the alliance between High Priest Nittatsu Hosoi with his hierarchical clerical organization and President Ikeda with his hierarchical secular society began to show signs of strain. The largest religious edifice in the world was not big enough for both of them. By the end of the decade the High Priest and the President were no longer on speaking terms, and the question of legal ownership had gone into the courts. In an effort to defuse the situation, Ikeda resigned as president of Sokagakkai in 1979, naming himself president of a new organization, Soka Gakkai International.

He need not have bothered. The courts ruled that Sokagakkai, which had paid all the bills, was the legal owner of its own property, the Sho-Hondo. High Priest Nittatsu Hosoi would have exclusive rights to the temple only on one day every month. He was forced to resign his position at Nichiren Shoshu, and Sokagakkai was able to hand-pick his successor. In defiance, Nittatsu founded a new organization claiming to represent traditional Nichiren Shoshu. It was called Nichiren Shoshu Yoshinkai, and it appealed to those temples, priests, and laymen who had never felt at ease with the flamboyant leadership of Sokagakkai, but its following was small. Although some members of Sokagakkai joined the new organization, and others dropped out altogether, most preferred Ikeda to the dour High Priest.

In spite of the crises at the beginning and end of the decade, Sokagakkai continued to advance during the 1970s and on into the 1980s. It built the biggest temple that Japan had ever seen, and consolidated its position of leadership within Nichiren Shoshu. While Nichiren Shu suffered the pangs of student unrest at its Rissho University, Sokagakkai retained the loyalty of its youth and built them a new ultra-modern institution named Soka University. The Nichiren Shu monopoly on higher education had been broken. Sokagakkai expanded abroad as well; its foreign missions became so prosperous that they had to be reconstituted into a new society, Sokagakkai International. It published a number of scholarly books in English, including four volumes of *The Major Works of Nichiren Daishonin* and an excellent *Dictionary of Buddhist Terms and Concepts*. Its political party, Komeito, while not yet able to win a national election, continued to do well. By the end of the 1980s Sokagakkai, having overcome one obstacle after another, and having attained the status of the largest sect in Japan and largest lay organization in the world, was confidently rolling along towards the happy day of *Kosen-rufu*: worldwide peace and happiness.

Chapter 16

Have a Gohonzon: Nichiren Shoshu in America

'Would you like to attend a Buddhist meeting?'

The speakers are two young women in their early twenties. One of them is Japanese, the other Caucasian. They are standing on a street not far from the campus of an American university, stopping any pedestrian who seems to have no place to go in particular.

'A Buddhist meeting? Where?'

'Right inside. It starts in ten minutes.'

'Well, why not?' It might be interesting. Buddhist meeting? It sounds exotic, something you don't run into every day.

The prospective convert is ushered into a small room nearly empty of furniture. There are 10 or 20 people seated on the floor, mostly as young as himself. Before entering, he is asked to take off his shoes and leave them by the door. He does so, wondering if he will ever see them again. Then he takes his place somewhat uncomfortably in the back of the room along with others who have wandered in to find out what this is all about. Those in front, however, are different. They are neatly if casually dressed, and chatter with each other in a friendly manner. They wave for him to sit up closer, but he prefers to remain in the rear where he can make a discreet exit if necessary. At the front of the room he sees a large black and gold, box-like structure with artificial metallic flowers on either side. The smell of incense hangs in the air.

In a little while another man enters quietly; he is a little older than the rest and is apparently the local leader. He kneels down in front of the black box and opens the door, revealing a scroll with Chinese letters. All conversation stops. The leader sits back on his feet in the Japanese style. Most of his followers do the same, although a few, who find this method of sitting uncomfortable, sit sprawled. The leader strikes a bell three times and leads the others in chanting something in a foreign language (*Nam' Myoho Renge Kyo*). Then suddenly all are busily reciting from little blue books in rapid and rhythmic Sino-Japanese: *Myo ho ren ge kyo ho ben pon dai ni ni ji se son ju san mai an jo ni ki* . . . It goes on and on. One of the young women who met him outside on the street has sat down beside him and is showing him the English transliteration of the words, urging him to join in. He mutters a few sounds, but soon loses his place. The rest go charging ahead: *Sho i sha ga Butsu zo shin gon hyaku sen man noku mu shu sho butsu* . . .

Finally they reach the end. The bell rings; all chant slowly, *Nam' Myoho Renge Kyo*, three times, and then fall silent. Next, to the horror of the visitor, they turn back to page one of their little books and begin all over again. Soon he is wondering why he came and whether he should get up and leave. Just when he thinks that he cannot take one more minute of this nonsense, they all put down their books and begin to chant repeatedly, *Nam' Myoho Renge Kyo*. The chanting drones on and on, gradually getting faster. Some people rub beads together as they chant, making an eerie rattling sound. The whole performance has a rather hypnotic effect, and our visitor finds that he is joining in the chant in spite of himself. But when he is beginning to think that the chanting will continue all night, it stops abruptly at the sound of the ringing of the bell.

So far, everything has seemed like some curious Oriental rite — interesting, but hardly worth writing home about. Now the mood changes. The leader gets to his feet with a big smile.

'Good evening!' The words are English and the face is American, but the intonation is distinctly Japanese.

'Good evening!' answer back his happy disciples.

'Welcome to the Main Street Group of Nichiren Shoshu! We have a lot to talk about tonight. But first, how about warming up with a song led by the YMD?'

There are cheers and applause as a young man leaps to his feet. Waving his arms vigorously, he leads a song to the tune of, 'I've been working on the railroad'.

> I've been doing Shakubuku,
> All the live long day.
> I've been chanting Daimoku
> To get me on my way.
> The eyes of the world are upon me,
> And I shall never stray.
> Can't you hear the members calling,
> And happiness on your way.

There are more cheers and applause. Then a young woman jumps up, a representative of the 'YWD'. Eyes sparkling with excitement, she directs with arms waving and hips snapping. This time the song is set to a well known Jewish melody:

Have a Go-hon-zon,
Have a Go-hon-zon,
Have a Go-hon-zon,
Chant for a while.

When day is dawning,
Gon-gyo each morning
Keeps you from yawning
And makes you smile.

You'll find that you will be
Full of vitality
Watching your benefits
Grow in a pile.

And do Sha-ku-bu-ku!

You will find your days run smoother,
Even if you've been a loser
Your surroundings may be loony;
Just remember Esho Funi.

Turn it on! Karma's gone!
And be happy evermore!

Is this Buddhism? Next, various members get to their feet to give testimonies about the many good things they have received because of chanting to the Gohonzon. Each testimony is greeted with enthusiastic applause. Here is one example:

'I was out on the West Coast and I had to get back East, but I had no car. I had $600.00. I decided to chant for a $600 car, a Chevrolet, ten years old, and coloured blue. I went to this meeting out in L.A., and, man, we really chanted up a storm!

'There was this guy chanting next to me. When we stopped to rest, I asked him what he was chanting for. "I want someone to buy my car," he said. "How much are you asking for it?" "Six hundred." "What kind of car is it?" "It's a Chevvy, ten years old." "What colour is it?" "Blue." "Sold!"'

The meeting erupts in wild cheers. 'I'm telling you, man, this Gohonzon is fantastic! Ask for anything — anything — and if you chant hard enough, you get it!'

By now the visitor is either incredulous or beginning to get interested. Questions are invited from the floor. Most of them are obvious:

'What is Gohonzon? . . . Kosen rufu . . . Why does the chant work? . . . Are there any rules to be followed? (None. Just chant.) . . . Will it work even if I don't believe in it?' (Yes.)

The answers are friendly but brief. There is no getting side-tracked into any kind of deep philosophical discussion — that can come later. 'Buddhism is not theory, but practice. It will work for anybody, whether you believe in it or not. Just try it! Try chanting for 30 days, and if your life has not changed for the better in that time, I'll let you beat me over the head right here in front of everybody!'

Some of the guests are non-committal, but others are willing to give it a try. They are greeted with a warm hand-shake from the leader and happy applause from all the members. When it is clear that all have joined who are going to for that evening, the leader calls for a final round of chanting *Daimoku*. The newcomer is shown how to hold the prayer beads and how to pronounce the wonderful words.

The meeting finally breaks up into little groups of happy conversationalists. The newcomer asks more questions, but the members are eager to encourage him to start practising. The chances are that at least one of them comes from a background similar to his, or once had similar problems. Now, thanks to the Gohonzon, things have changed.

The leader will probably not join in these informal chats; he has more serious matters to take care of. Taking aside two or three of his more faithful members, he begins to go over with them plans for the next District or General Chapter meeting. Being a *hancho* (Group Chief) takes up all his free time. He has been doing a good job, however, and may soon be promoted to *shikibucho*, District Chief.

Of course there will be a follow-up on our convert. He will be visited in his home and helped to set up his own 'little black box' for enshrining his personal copy of the Gohonzon. At first he may be satisfied with a simple shrine (*butsudan*) for his Gohonzon, or even none at all. But eventually, if he stays in the movement, he will want a more elaborate one, imported from Japan complete with incense burner, bell, candlesticks, artificial metallic flowers, and other paraphernalia. This is his *kaidan*, the centre of his life. He will be taught how to recite *Gongyo* (portions of the Lotus Sutra in Chinese), which he will be expected to do every morning and evening. At first this will be a painful process for him, and he may struggle with the strange Chinese words for as long as an hour and a half at each sitting. But if he tries hard and comes to meetings often enough, he will be able to practise with the others, gradually improving until he is able to zip through it in 30 minutes.

During the 1960s and 1970s Nichiren Shoshu made joining and receiving a Gohonzon as simple as merely asking for it. We will never know how many 'converts' entered just out of curiosity, received a Gohonzon, and then forgot all about it. Japanese members, who look on the Gohonzon as the symbol of their own life (so that should it be torn or damaged, the same fate would befall the owner), were shocked to enter homes of supposed members in America and find Gohonzons used as wall decorations or lying forgotten in a drawer. New regulations came into effect requiring converts to attend at least three meetings before receiving a Gohonzon, have the consent of their families, and be approved by a senior leader (Layman, *Buddhism in America* 133–4).

A particular obstacle to conversion was (and still is) the opposition of a young convert's parents and family. There were tales of youngsters hiding in closets to chant softly. Of course, no Gohonzon could be enshrined under such circumstances. Nichiren Shoshu, therefore, tried to get young converts to bring their parents to the meetings, confident that the parents would be impressed by the cheerful atmosphere and the change in their child's behaviour.

The following, from a young convert in Malibu, California, is a typical testimonial:

> I attended my first discussion meeting in November, 1967. At that time, I was really unhappy. I was a very confused young man of 18. From the time I was fifteen years old, I had been taking drugs to escape from my problems. My 17th and 18th years were the worst. I began to inject drugs and became dependent on them. I became very skinny and turned yellow all over. My mind was really confused and paranoid.
>
> I had a persecution complex and thought people were conspiring against me and making jokes about me. I did many things to cover up for my insecurities. I became known among my friends as the boy who took the most drugs. This I really bragged of.
>
> Just prior to attending a discussion meeting, I was seeing two doctors, one a psychiatrist and the other a drug specialist. I was going to a clinic for drug addicts, struggling to find happiness.
>
> When I attended my first discussion meeting, the person who brought me to the meeting encouraged me from every angle to chant *Daimoku*. After chanting *Daimoku* for half an hour, I felt really good. I was extremely impressed by the testimonials and I really felt I belonged there. I raised my hand to receive a Gohonzon at the end of the meeting.
>
> I started to practice very sincerely from that night. My life began changing immediately. I overcame all my physical problems and this really surprised me. Within the next few weeks, I overcame many of my weak natures, and my life changed greatly. I cut my long hair, got a job, and re-enrolled in school. I started to love and understand my family.
>
> It has now been over two years since I joined, and the change has been great. I am happy at home, on my job, and in school. I never run from them like I used to. I am determined to reach

these goals. In only a year, I completely changed my life. Each day I go through more changes. I know that by chanting many *Daimoku* I can become closer to President Ikeda and really become a leader in the society of the future.

(*Seikyo Times*, June 1970, 72).

The most striking feature of converts to Nichiren Shoshu is not that they become more 'religious' or even that they are happier than before; this is characteristic of converts to any faith. What is special about them is that they become more energetic; a new vitality permeates their activities. They chant vigorously, sing vigorously, walk vigorously (or even run instead of walk), and work vigorously. They expect to be successful at whatever they do, and generally they are. Words like *life-force, determination* and *attack*! lace their vocabularies. People who once drifted aimlessly through life now feel the need to go somewhere and be somebody. By making a positive contribution to society, they believe they are hastening the day of *Kosen-rufu*, world peace and happiness.

Once he has been practising for a while, the newcomer will be expected to begin regular study of Nichiren Shoshu doctrines and philosophy. He has an ample collection of books and magazines to help him. Written examinations are held at regular intervals. Candidates can move up the academic ladder to Assistant Lecturer, Lecturer, Associate Assistant Professor, Assistant Professor, and Associate Professor. Except in the highest degrees, no originality or special research is required to pass these examinations. All the answers are given in the publications of the society, and every effort is made to get the candidate to learn them and pass to the next level. The more advanced degrees require essays on some phase of Nichiren Shoshu. Candidates are expected to be well versed on the life and writings of Nichiren, though study of the *Dharma Flower* is not stressed.

Beginning in 1968, the Nichiren Shoshu Academy (as Nichiren Shoshu of America called itself), extended its academic outreach to outsiders by inaugurating a series of highly successful seminars at major campuses across the country. 'Professor' George Williams (who had changed his name from Masayasu Sadanaga), director of NSA, gave a series of entertaining and thought-provoking lectures at such far-flung colleges as the University of California, UCLA, Boston University, Memphis State, U.S. Air Force Academy, University of Nebraska, Pennsylvania, Princeton, Cornell, Rice, Harvard, Maryland, Amhurst, York University of Toronto, and many more. By 1971 he had given 70 seminars on 40 college campuses (*NSA Seminary Report, 1968, 1971* 71–3).

According to the report.

In an informal way, Professor Williams explains the Philosophy of

Happiness, relating Buddhist terms directly to (the student's) own daily life. 'Hell is how you feel when you get all D's, and heaven is when you get all A's,' he tells them. 'Heaven and hell are not waiting for you when you die, but rather are conditions in your life right now. So why don't you work hard to change your life of hell into heaven?' Then he gives them the key to this happy life — Nam' Myoho Renge Kyo — and all the students have the experience of chanting, themselves. Accustomed to large impersonal lectures, the students are at first startled by this new type of learning experience.

(i–ii)

The report contains interesting statistics of NSA. It claimed 200,000 members in 1970, with individuals in every state in the Union. Membership more than doubled in the years 1968–70. Thirty-five per cent of the members were between 21 and 30 years of age, with only 9 per cent over 51. Fifty-nine per cent were female, and most members were single. Twenty-seven per cent listed their occupation as housewife, 19 per cent as student, 10 per cent professional, and 4 per cent executive. Religious family backgrounds were equally divided between Catholic and Protestant (30 per cent each); minorities gave their backgrounds as Jewish (6 per cent) and atheist (5 per cent). Of the former Protestants, 40 per cent were Baptists and 19 per cent Methodists. In 1960, 96 per cent of the members were Orientals. Ten years later the Orientals were in the minority: 30 per cent; 41 per cent were Caucasian, 13 per cent Latin American, 12 per cent Afro-American, and 4 per cent 'other' (95–106).

By the end of the 1970s, however, there had been some changes. First of all, the total number of members had declined after reaching a peak of 237,500 claimed in 1976. There were many reasons for the decline, not the least of which was the changing mood of the times. The college students of 1980 differed from those of 1970; they were more interested in careers than in 'cults'. The Vietnam war was over, and students were less eager to drop out of society. The Jonestown massacre in South America had given a bad name to all religious cults. NSA discovered that easy converts were not dependable; too many Gohonzons were ending up in desk drawers.

According to Yoko Parks in an article appearing in 1980 entitled, 'Nichiren Shoshu Academy in America: Changes during the 1970s', the hard-core members were probably about 20 per cent of the total; it was considered more important to build on them than on the fringe members. They were now older, better educated, and of a higher income level than when they had first joined 10 or 15 years before. They were less interested in group activities and more concerned with personal development. They were disillusioned with easy-come-easy-go converts. Obeying orders from Japan, they toned down efforts to *shakubuku* everyone in sight. Finally, the schism in Japan between the Sokagakkai and the High Priest had wide repercussions (*Journal of Nichiren Buddhism*, Winter 1980, 25 ff). Nevertheless, it is evident that by the mid-1980s NSA had recovered from its setbacks of the previous decade and was expanding once more. Recent NSA conventions have been more spectacular than ever.

An important part of NSA activities is song and dance. Musical productions come under the supervision of a special department called *Minon*. It is not necessary to be a member of NSA to participate in *Minon* productions, but the performance is always tied in with some NSA activity. There are many professional entertainers in NSA as well as talented amateurs. Add all this natural talent to the special Nichiren Shoshu ingredient of enthusiasm, and the public is guaranteed first-rate entertainment, be it a rock concert, a parade, or an opera.

After observing the NSA general meeting in Akron, Ohio, in 1973, the manager of the Akron Civic Center reported:

> The first thing I was impressed with was the detail of the organization. They came in almost every day — not just one guy or two guys, but every day it was different people. Each had their own area of responsibility. After a while, I said, 'This thing is going to be the most fantastically organized thing I ever saw,' because everybody was taking care of all those little details down to the last inch. You know, measuring the place, taking photographs, getting drawings of the building, which they reproduced. That impressed me. I thought, 'The organization is really on the ball as far as attention to detail.' Today when I arrived . . . people were all over the place, here, there, everywhere, just hussling and bustling. But the thing that caught my eye right away was that they knew what they were doing.
>
> So that impressed me, and, of course, I think there is no one who couldn't help but be impressed by the show. Like Bill the engineer and Mike and I were laughing, saying we were glad it was dark because we were standing there with tears coming out of our eyes, and we weren't even members of the group! But you just got to be impressed by one thing — with the performances the people put on and the band. I mean, a thousand people strong filled the balcony; I mean, it's just an experience; you have to see it to believe it. It's like you can't describe it to someone. I could never describe to my board what happened today because they just wouldn't be able to conceive of anything like it. You just have to see it to believe it . . . Another very impressive thing was the end. They sang one of the songs of the organization, I guess, and they linked arms and then swayed back and forth, and every other row was leaning a different way . . . Golly, I wish I had a movie of the thing! [73]

A number of entertainers have been attracted to Nichiren Shoshu. Among them are jazz saxaphonist Wayne Shorter, jazz pianist Herbie Hancock, actor Sal Mineo, actor John Astin, actor Beau Bridges, popular TV comedienne Roseanne Barr, and rock superstar Tina Turner. In her autobiography, *I, Tina*, she attributes the happy turn in her fortunes to the day she first chanted, *Nam' Myoho Renge Kyo* (173–4). She has been an enthusiastic member of Nichiren Shoshu ever since.

The innovative jazz musician Robin Eubanks, leading proponent of M-BASE (computer and electronic music), had stopped composing altogether to listen to sounds like waves at the seashore. From there he moved to the sound of *Nam' Myoho Renge Kyo*, and it soon became the main source of inspiration for his 'hyperspace' jazz (*Smithsonian* August 1989, 194).

Nichiren Shoshu also appeals to professional athletes. 'This religion is simply a must for sportsmen,' said Los Angeles outfielder Willie Davis to *Time* magazine. 'I was never a great home-run hitter. I hit only ten home-runs in the 1971 season. Last year I suddenly ended up hitting 19 because I chanted my prayers every morning and every night before every game.' When asked why his batting average had dropped from .309 to .289, he replied, 'I didn't pray hard enough' (II/5/73).

If *Nam' Myoho Renge Kyo* is not yet a household word in America, it is not entirely unknown. It has been heard in movie and TV productions. In a TV crime thriller we saw recently, a young woman expecting to be murdered began to chant fervently. Sure enough, she was rescued at the last minute.

Another prominent feature of Nichiren Shoshu International (of which NSA is a part) is pilgrimages to Taiseki-ji. Every member hopes to participate in at least one *tozan* to Japan and pray directly to the Dai-Gohonzon. Flights of eager pilgrims wing their way to Japan from around the world throughout the year, and up to a thousand will attend the Summer Training Courses. They return home even more imbued with 'the Gakkai spirit'.

President Ikeda first came to America on 2 October 1960. He announced 'modestly' that his arrival would become more important in American history than the landing of Columbus. At that time the membership in America consisted of a few hundred Japanese and a handful of American ex-servicemen married to Japanese brides, but organization got under way immediately. Leaders were assigned and mission territories were staked out. One year later 61 American members made the first group pilgrimage to Taiseki-ji. After two years membership had grown to 3,500 families.

In 1963 Ikeda returned to America and revamped the organization. He appointed 32-year-old Masayasu Sadanaga as General Chapter Chief, which proved to be a good choice, although by no means a blind one. He had known the young man and his family back in Japan.

Sadanaga had come to America in 1957 to study at UCLA. Within five days of his arrival, he was shocked to learn of the death of his father. The first letter of condolence (and encouragement) he received was from Daisaku Ikeda.

The first year was not easy. He struggled to learn English so as to improve his low grades, and worked from midnight until 8.00 a.m. as a janitor and dishwasher. 'He screamed *Daimoku* to the Gohonzon, saying, "I've got to win!"' reports the *Seikyo Times*. Eventually his grades improved enough to earn him a scholarship. He completed his studies at the University of Maryland, where he earned an M.A. in Political Science, and then returned to California to greet Ikeda.

At first he was unhappy when President Ikeda assigned him permanently to the United States, since he had hoped to return home to Japan, but he adapted quickly. 'I decided to become a good communicator,' he said. 'I even changed my name to an American name (George Williams). I feel like an American. This is my home. The U.S. has a great heritage which has been forgotten by many. I want to help Americans remember that heritage and make it even greater in the future' (*Seikyo Times*, March 1972, 30–31).

Mr Sadanaga/Williams is a very good 'communicator' indeed. The *Princeton Notice* commented that 'he has the ability to drop a pipe line to people listening and turn them right on to his level' (29 October 1969). His talks are flavoured with humour and sparkle with vitality. He is at his best with small groups where his personal magnetism fills the room.

Nichiren Shoshu of America, like its counterparts in over a hundred countries around the world, is a part of Soka Gakkai International and directly under President Ikeda.[74] It is organized along lines similar to Sokagakkai in Japan, although it is no longer a part of it. The General Director has his headquarters in Santa Monica, California, where he is assisted by executive directors, each of whom is responsible for a 'territory'. Territories are divided into 'areas', each with its own office and director. Further subdivisions are called communities, chapters, districts, and groups or cells (*han*). As the organization expands or as turnovers occur, there are plenty of opportunities for potential leaders to rise up the ladder. There are also peer structures for men (Men's Division and Young Men's Division) and women (WD and YWD), each of which has its own table of organization.

While the Japanese Sokagakkai is very nationalistic, Soka Gakkai International is truly what its name implies. Every subordinate foreign group is encouraged to develop along local patriotic lines. In America patriotism was forced down the throats of members from the 'hippie generation', many of whom had been attracted to NSA precisely because of its foreign flavour. The 1960s, says one NSA leader, was 'a time when we could get many young people to join just because we were non-Americans, unorthodox, and very different.' Nevertheless, orders came from Japan to display the Stars and Stripes, use patriotic slogans, and revitalize the 'spirit of '76'. Members were urged to participate in uniformed parades and cultural festivities. In 1976 NSA celebrated the bicentennial with three elaborate conventions, one in Boston, one in Philadelphia, and one in New York. The focus was on the American flag and all that it stands for.

Charles Prebish points out in *American Buddhism* that alone among Buddhist groups in America, NSA has acquired an indigenous flavour (81).

> Nichiren Shoshu offers a sacred center that is overwhelmingly American. I say this not only because the American flag flies over all Nichiren Shoshu buildings in the country, but rather because the leaders and members of the organization seem to offer this not *merely* as a perfunctory gesture of respect, but with a real understanding of what the American flag symbolizes. In understanding the advantages of having established a sacred center that is in America and of America, Nichiren Shoshu is able to tap into the creative power inherent in that center.

Since 1976 NSA has turned its attention from quantity to quality. Ten years later the average member was older, better educated, more affluent, and less anxious to dress up in a Revolutionary War uniform and march on a hot fourth of July. The patriotic undertones were not abandoned — if anything, they increased. But there were fewer group activities (once a week instead of several times a week), less street corner evangelism, and more emphasis on individual practice and study. The split between Ikeda and the High Priest had a sobering effect for a while, but the crisis passed. Some members dropped out, others began to explore other Nichiren sects as alternatives. Those who remained demanded more say in how their organization was run (it was, after all, now supposed to epitomize American democracy, and not be directed solely from the top), and they were less willing to be spoon-fed doctrines from Japan. They wanted to be able to think for themselves. In 1979 the annual examinations based on rote learning were abolished (Parks 29–34).

Nevertheless, there is still one aspect of NSA life where democracy does not apply: no opposition is tolerated. Nichiren Shoshu has been more successful censuring criticism in the United States than in Japan. When it tried to prevent the publication in Japan of Fujiwara's book, *I Denounce Sokagakkai*, it was firmly rebuffed. In the United States, on the other hand, it has been able to silence voices speaking from a non-Shoshu perspective. In 1980 the University of Hawaii Press published *Nichiren: Selected Writings* by Laurel R. Rodd, with a cover illustration of a copy of the Dai-Gohonzon. To Nichiren Shoshu, the Dai-Gohonzon is sacred and does not belong on a book cover, so NSA threatened legal action for 'violation of copyright'. Rather than enter costly litigation, the University withdrew the book from circulation, destroyed the offending book jacket, and kept the work available only in costly photocopies.

NSA may not be as vociferous as it was a decade or two ago, but it is more democratic and more solidly entrenched. An increasingly large proportion of the members are the grown-up children of the original converts. The old fire has not gone, but it has been redirected from overseas to the USA. Emphasis is placed on the work ethic, and members are urged to 'become leaders in society'.

'This country,' says General Director Williams, 'is of the people, by the people, and for the people. But if it is of lousy people, by lousy people, and for lousy people, it is a lousy country.' It is the mission of the 'human revolution' to transform it into a country of happy people, by happy people, and for happy people. Then America will be what it was meant to be: the land of the free and the home of the brave.

Chapter 17

Reiyukai: the Spiritual Friendship Society ⸺

'Looking for the spirit of Buddha? Find it in beautiful Japan . . . Your cost: only $400.00.'

With these words printed on an attractive, full-colour brochure, Reiyukai introduced itself to America in 1972. Tickets sold out quickly, and a few weeks later, 140 Americans flew across the Pacific for a first-class tour of central Japan. When they returned home, a handful of them had signed up as charter members of Reiyukai America. Most were uncommitted, but none were unimpressed by the quality of their accommodation and the hospitality of their hosts. As a travel bargain the 'First Inner Trip' had few equals, but as a religion Reiyukai remained a puzzle to most of the tourists. Few had any prior knowledge of Buddhism and even fewer could grasp what Reiyukai was trying to communicate.

Other 'Inner Trips' followed annually for several years. The price went up and the quality of accommodations went down, but the warm hospitality of the Japanese hosts remained constant. It was probably this, more than the lectures, which accounted for the slow but steady increase in foreign members. Reiyukai, they were told, meant 'Spiritual Friendship Society', and the spirit of friendship was obvious.

Reiyukai was formally incorporated in 1930, the same year that Makiguchi began what was to become Sokagakkai. Reiyukai is the older of the two, for it grew out of teachings which had been propounded by its founder since 1919. After 1930 it grew rapidly until World War II, when its centre of operations at Tokyo suffered severely from the bombings. By the mid-1950s its rate of growth had levelled off. Membership stood at between two and three million, and has remained fairly constant ever since. Sokagakkai, on the other hand, kept climbing, and now claims over 16,000,000 members.

The differences are more than just numerical. Sokagakkai is built on the philosophy of Nichiren Shoshu, whereas Reiyukai has its roots in not one but several subsoils. It is not affiliated with any Nichiren sect, calling itself '*Dharma Flower* Oriented' (*Hoke-kyo Kei*) rather than 'Nichiren Oriented'. Nichiren is only one of its sources.

The founder, Kakutaro Kubo (1892–1944), was the orphaned son of a fish merchant from Kominato, the birthplace of Nichiren. Helen Hardacre points out that Kubo saw an esoteric significance in this. He was the Nichiren of the Taisho Era (1912–26) (1984, 10). While only a boy of 13, he moved to Tokyo to work as a carpenter and attend technical schools. He did well at his craft, and by 1914 he was supervising construction projects for the Imperial Household Agency. It was there that he caught the eye of Count Sengoku (1872–1935), a prominent bureaucrat who in 1920 was elected to the House of Peers. The count took a liking to the young man and arranged for him to marry the only daughter of the widow of one of his retainers and to adopt her family name of Kubo. Thus the orphaned son of a village fishmonger found himself installed in a respectable family of ancient lineage. The marriage seems to have brought no material benefits, however, for Reiyukai publications stress the poverty of the founders. Nor did Kubo's wife play any part in the organization; even the raising of her child was taken over by her sister-in-law, Kimi Kotani.

Both Count Sengoku and the widowed Mrs Kubo were devout Nichiren Buddhists, and they arranged for Kubo to be trained by a teacher from *Nichirenshugi* ('Nichirenism'), a nationalist movement led by Chigaku Tanaka. Kubo had no interest in the political aspects of Nichirenism, but he liked its appeal to traditional values of loyalty and filial piety. As the adopted son of the Kubo family, it became his duty to supervise the memorial services for the family's ancestors, and this he did diligently.

Around 1919, Kubo's brother introduced him to the writings of one Mugaku Nishida, and Kubo immediately found them congenial. Nishida said:

> The living individual is the body left behind by the ancestors in this world, so we should treat our ancestors as if they were our own bodies . . . In our hearts we have the seed of buddhahood, which also remains in the ancestors' souls, so we must protect it for our own salvation. The salvation of the ancestors is our own salvation, and our salvation is the ancestors' salvation.
>
> (Hardacre, 14)

Our own life is intimately related to those of our ancestors; to care for one is to care for the other. The important point is that we must do this ourselves, and not expect some priest to do it for us. Nishida worked out specific methods for doing this, and Kubo adopted them *in toto*.

They include chanting the sutra oneself instead of paying a priest to do it, keeping the family death register in the home rather than in a temple, and giving posthumous names not only to one's direct ancestors, but also to relatives, friends, aborted or deceased children, and even pets. This also could be done without recourse to the clergy (T. Kubo, *Development of Japanese Lay Buddhism* 17).

The *Dharma Flower* mentions 'repaying debts of gratitude', although this is not one of its principal themes. Nichiren, however, considered it important and often said so. One of his major writings is entitled 'Repaying Debts of Gratitude' (*Ho-on Jo*). In his introduction to this work, editor Taikyo Yajima says that 'Nichiren believed that attainment of Buddhahood was not a step in which individuals reached an ideal state, but was the only way to perform the recompense of indebtedness to all living beings. The Saint came to believe this as he saw that worldly and spiritual ideas are ultimately one and the same. In other words, the Saint realized that complete attainment of Buddhahood meant complete recompense of indebtedness to all living beings, and that they are merely two sides of a coin. This is clearly stated in the closing part of this essay' (xi–xiii).

Buddhahood is not individual but universal. Since all living beings are interconnected, if one person attains Buddhahood, he enables others to do the same. Nichiren 'vowed to . . . attain Buddhahood so that I could save the people from whom I had received favors' (*Sado Gokanki Sho, Showa-teihon*, 570).

Nichiren praised Toki Jonin for bringing his mother's ashes to Minobu for burial. 'All of your body — your head, hands, legs, and mouth — are all inherited from your parents. This kinship between your parents and you is like the relationship between seed and fruit. Therefore, as your mother is saved, you also are saved by the teachings of the *Dharma Flower*' (*Bo Jikyo Ji*). And to Nichiro in prison, he wrote, 'You have read and practiced the *Dharma Flower* with your heart and action, which will save your parents, brothers, sisters, relatives, ancestors, and everyone around you' (*Tsuchi-ro Gosho, Showa-teihon*, 509).

In the *Kaimoku Sho* he wrote: 'To be filial (*ko*) means to be high (*ko*); heaven is high but not at all higher than being filial. To be filial (*ko*) also means to be deep (*ko*); the earth is deep but is not any deeper than being filial . . . Disciples of the Buddha should not fail to feel grateful for the four favors received from parents, all people, the ruler, and Buddhism. Show gratitude to them.'

Kubo accepted Nichiren's reasoning but, following Nishida, he narrowed the focus from gratitude to all living things to gratitude to one's own parents and ancestors. This, he felt, would give people a personal motivation to achieve Buddhahood.

Kubo went on a spiritual retreat to Nakayama Hokekyo-ji, a temple which had been founded by Nichiren's lay disciple Toki Jonin and which had always emphasized direct spiritual insights. There he met a spiritualist named Chise Wakatsuki (1884–1971), and in 1919 the two of them decided to found a lay group 'Friends of the Spirits' (*Rei no Tomo Kai*). The organization failed to prosper and was dissolved a few years later. Nevertheless, Reiyukai officially dates itself from this time (*Reiyukai Today*).

In 1924 they tried again, changing the name to Reiyukai (which is written with the same Chinese characters). This time the organization caught on, although a split developed between the two leaders. The original group headed by Wakatsuki retained the name Reiyukai until 1936, then changed it to Reihokai, and in 1939 to Hochikai, by which designation it is known today. Meanwhile, Kubo, his brother, and his sister-in-law founded a second branch in the Akasaka Ward of Tokyo around 1927, which the Reiyukai of today descends from. Finally, a third branch was founded the same year in Fukushima City by Kubo's friend Sadao Bekki (1897–1965). It soon broke away and is known today as Nihon Keishin Suso Jishudan (T. Kubo, *Development*, 18).

Since the collapse of the Tokugawa Shogunate and the restoration of the monarchy in 1868, Buddhism had been rudely shunted aside as a relic from the past. The nation rushed to catch up with the West philosophically, industrially, and militarily. While learning everything they could from the West, the national leaders tried to rally the people around the 'Japanese National Principles' (*Nippon Kokutai*), a 'catch-all' term for whatever was considered unique in Japanese spirituality. Buddhism, which had been imported from China and Korea, was excluded as a degenerate foreign interloper, and for a few years in the 1870s it was proscribed by law. Many Buddhist temples were closed and sacred images smashed. The persecution peaked in 1871, but the Buddhist sects never regained their former prestige.

Nichiren Buddhism survived the onslaught better than most other sects. One reason for this was the identification of Nichiren as a national hero, the epitome of a brave and patriotic Japanese. Also Nichirenism was the only form of Buddhism exclusively Japanese in origin. It could be made to fit in harmoniously with the new nationalism being sponsored by the government, and some Nichiren Buddhists did their utmost to exploit this possibility.

Chigaku Tanaka (1861–1939), a brilliant writer and lecturer, had left the priesthood of Nichiren Shu to found a lay organization advocating vigorous *shakubuku*, not only in Japan but throughout the world. It was Japan's 'manifest destiny' to 'embody' the *Dharma Flower* and spread it everywhere — by force if necessary. The one all-embracing truth is embodied in the *Dharma Flower*, which in turn is embodied in the nation of Japan under its one Emperor. In the words of Tanaka's son, Kishio Satomi, 'The *Hokekyo* must have a state like Japan in order to validate its pregnant value, and Japan should have the *Hokekyo* for the sake of the realization of her national ideal' (*Japanese Civilization*, 27).

To distinguish his nationalistic philosophical interpretation of Nichiren from traditional Nichiren Buddhism, Tanaka invented a new term, *Nichirenshugi*, which could be translated as 'Nichirenism'. It includes traditional sectarian Nichiren Buddhism but claims to transcend sectarian differences and to be applicable universally (Satomi, 11).

> Religion should redeem the body as well (as the soul) . . . Actual life is religion and religion is actual. The depravity of all religions from olden times to the present day has its root in the fallacy of a vague dualism of actual life and religion . . . Religion must be woven into actual life, otherwise it would appear to be of no avail . . . Religion has the State and the world at large as well as the individual as objects of its salvation. But the unit of salvation is the State.
>
> (8)

Nichirenism, however, did not deify the State as such, although the State can be the 'unit of salvation' when it is moral.

> We must bring about in the near future an international constitution so that the State and the world may be judged. It is illogical that a State should punish an individual man or woman for a theft or other crime of which the State, itself, is guilty on a much larger scale. It is out of all reason to ascribe equity to national greediness. Therefore the State must undergo a moral reconstruction. So we must strive to bring about a reconstruction of the world, its countries, and individuals. We offer Nichirenism and the Japanese National Principles (*Nippon kokutai*) as the means to be considered by the nations.
>
> (10)

Yukichi Masuko, a qualified teacher of Nichirenism, was Kubo's teacher until the latter joined up with the spiritualist Wakatsuki and began to practise spiritual healing. Such practices had nothing to do with patriotic Nichirenism, so Masuko renounced his former pupil (Hardacre, 17).

Thus the philosophical foundations of Reiyukai, rarely articulated but always implicit, include Nichirenism as taught to Kubo by Masuko, Count Sengoku, and Madam Kubo. Among its features are the pre-eminence of the *Dharma Flower*, the unity of self and society and the importance of teaching others, the unity of the generations and the significance of chanting the Sutra and the Sacred Title for one's parents, facing the Absolute directly without any intermediary, the imperative to convert our world into the Pure Land of the Buddha, and the vision of Japan as the *kaidan* for the world. Even though Reiyukai rarely quotes Nichiren, the official prayer book, *The Blue Sutra*, rightfully calls him 'the Eminent Founder' (*Hokekyoguzo-daidoshi-shinnokoso-Nichiren-Daibosatsu*). The central practices of ancestor worship, however, are lifted bodily from Nishida. Finally, the strong shamanistic element of spiritual healing comes from Wakatsuki and indirectly from Hokekyo-ji, Nakayama, the temple where she and Kubo were studying when they met.

While Kubo did not espouse a 'Lotus imperialism', his patriotism was no less intense than Tanaka's. 'Loyalty and filial piety are the basis of a truly Japanese humanity; they are the Japanese way . . . Japanese Buddhism is actually Buddhism for the protection of the state. Buddhism in our country exists for the purpose of promoting loyalty and filial piety, and for protecting the nation.'[75] These words, written in a Reiyukai publication, faithfully reflect the thoughts of Tanaka.

Kubo became a soapbox orator in Hibaya Park, calling for a return to traditional family values. The abstract 'Japanese National Principles' basic to *Nichirenshugi* became concrete to Kubo. These principles could be maintained by propping up the family and revering one's ancestors. To do this it was necessary to take Buddhism out of the temples and into the home. Nominal Buddhists must become practising Bodhisattvas, leading others long the same way which they themselves were going. In other words, they must convince others to undertake these same practices.

For the first few years Kubo made few converts. He, his older brother Yasukichi Kotani, and a few other friends seem to have been the only practitioners. When Yasukichi fell ill, Kubo insisted that his wife Kimi practise according to his instructions. Kimi did so, Yasukichi recovered, and Kimi became a true believer. With the conversion of this humble housemaid with a fifth-grade education, Reiyukai began to expand rapidly. Kimi was burning to tell others about her new faith. Night and day she wandered about the slums of the Arakawa Ward, Tokyo, making converts among itinerant labourers and ragpickers — the poorest of the poor (Hardacre, 26).

She not only preached to these people but ministered to them in every sense of the word. She would collect cabbages and greens that had fallen from produce trucks and bring them to her miserable flock. She brought them clothes to wear and soap to wash with. She gave them self-respect and a sense of purpose. She taught them elementary sanitation, cured them of their diseases, and earned for herself the reputation of a faith healer. In three months she converted an entire neighbourhood of ragpickers (*ibid.*).

This was the real beginning of Reiyukai. It soon moved up the social ladder to include small shopkeepers and tradesmen. Kimi's husband died in 1929, allowing her to give all her time to proselytizing. Reiyukai was officially incorporated the next year. Baron Taketoshi Nagayama (1871–1938), a member of the House of Peers, was named President —

a titular post which gave the organization both respectability and protection from interference from the police. Kubo was Chairman of the Board of Directors, and Kimi Kotani was named Honorary President (Kubo, *Development of Japanese Lay Buddhism*, 20).

Kakutaro Kubo died in 1944 at the age of 52. Kimi Kotani took over the leadership of the movement and the upbringing of his young son, Tsugunari, whom she was determined to mould into a worthy leader for the future.

Kimi Kotani (1901–71) was a very different type of leader from the friendly Kakutaro Kubo. What she lacked in tact (and she seems to have had very little of it) she made up for in energy and single-minded dedication to her cause. She wanted her followers to be as self-reliant as she was, but at the same time she would tolerate no contradiction. People either worshipped her or hated her; she offered no middle road. 'The severity of her scoldings,' says her nephew and step-son Tsugunari Kubo, 'was surpassed by few. It was by such harsh scoldings that I was trained.'

> Once when I was in the fifth grade of elementary school, I happened to be late returning home from school. I arrived five minutes late. My aunt would never overlook my tardiness. On this occasion, I was made to sit on the ground before her to be reprimanded. The words came in rapid succession as if fired by a machine gun.
>
> This kind of thing happened repeatedly. I cannot begin to remember how often. My aunt never failed to focus her remarks on my daily *konjo* (character). Whenever I was due punishment, I was made acutely aware of the *konjo*, that is to say, what attitude I should take toward my life and how it should appear in my daily conduct.
>
> As usual, the scolding did not stop with this. Her final words were, 'Even though I forgive you, the Spiritual World will not.' With these words she withdrew and climbed the stairs to the room where our family altar was kept, and recited the Sutra. All of a sudden, I was alone without the comfort of being able to apologize. The only sound was the voice of my aunt upstairs reciting the Sutra. The attention that had been paid to my aunt came undone after that usual parting thrust: 'Even if I forgive you, the Spiritual World will not.' These words echoed over and over in my mind.
>
> Whenever I was scolded by her in this way, it was the Spiritual World that I had to face instead of my aunt, who was a real living being. In other words, she required me to face a moral code which only I, myself, could interpret and practice in my life.
>
> (*BW* February 1975, 4–5)

This was the kind of strict standard which Kimi Kotani set down for herself, her nephew and ward, the leaders of Reiyukai, and all the members. We may fool others or even fool ourselves, but we cannot deceive the spiritual world. Like the Buddha, she taught, 'Make yourself a light. Rely upon yourself; do not depend upon anyone else' (*Mahaparinibbana Sutta*).

She herself had had to rely upon her own inner resources since childhood. Born into the family of a poverty-stricken farmer, she lost her father when she was four. Her mother remarried, but was widowed again in 1914. One of Kimi's most vivid childhood memories was of being turned away from a party at the home of a relative; she was so shabby that it was believed she would bring the house bad luck. At the age of 17 she went to Tokyo to work as a housemaid. She married, but was soon widowed. In 1925 she married again, this time to Yasukichi Kotani, an older brother of Kakutaro Kubo.

Her husband's chronic illness sapped their resources. They spent every penny on medicines, and even sold the household furniture. Finally, with her husband hovering on the verge of death, her brother-in-law laid all the blame on her. She had been neglecting their ancestors. He instructed her to recite the Sutra, chant *Namu Myoho Renge Kyo*, and go to her home town to collect the names of her ancestors. In desperation, she did as he said. Within a few days, her husband was up and around again. This remarkable recovery astonished her and won her over completely to the teachings of Kubo. From that time on she devoted all of her life to the propagation of Reiyukai.

The imperious leadership of Kimi Kotani was a mixed blessing. New members kept coming in, but old members, especially leaders, often clashed with her and broke away to found splinter groups. Kubo's son Tsugunari says (20–1):

> In the sixty-seven years of Reiyukai history, nearly thirty groups have split off and become independent organizations. As of December 31, 1984, the total membership of the Reiyukai and Reiyukai-derived groups numbered over twelve million; the Reiyukai itself had 3,000,000. Over the years, the teachings of the Reiyukai-derived organizations have not changed fundamentally from those of the Reiyukai. Some of the larger groups include Kodo Kyodan, Shishinkai and Rissho Koseikai (which, with a membership of around 6,013,401, has become twice the size of the Reiyukai), all three of which split off in the late thirties, and Bussho Gonenkai and Myochikai, which separated from the Reiyukai in 1950 and 1951 respectively.
> (*Development*).[76]

These splits were due at least in part to the peculiar Reiyukai system of organization, in which a member is more obligated to the 'parent' who converts him than to the central headquarters. However, a considerable portion of the blame must go to Kimi Kotani's short temper. The present leader, Tsugunari Kubo, readily admits this in an article appearing in the Reiyukai International magazine, *Circle* (Spring 1979, 5):

> No other society has formed as many separate sects as Reiyukai. Some people put the reason for this on my aunt's personality. Looking at the situation from the inside, I think this may be true. My aunt didn't care about appearances, so when she got angry she showed it. She never compromised. Therefore, no matter who they were, people couldn't help but feel naked in my aunt's presence.

However, he accepts this philosophically.

> The Reiyukai teaches us not to rely on any one thing in particular, but to pray to our ancestors who are in the Spiritual World. Because of this, anyone can split from the Reiyukai at any time ... Those who meet must eventually part; human bonds are impermanent. Not only do we separate from each other physically, but our hearts also part.
>
> (*ibid.*)

Kimi Kotani came to be known far beyond the circle of her immediate disciples. For her, the principal task of a Buddhist was to perform acts of mercy and compassion. Every member of Reiyukai was expected to help the poor, the sick, the orphans, the elderly, and the homeless. Groups of volunteers would arrive suddenly at a hospital or an old people's home and busily set to work sweeping, scrubbing, replacing old bed clothes with new ones, and distributing sweets, pocket money, and good cheer. Reiyukai ran no charitable institutions of its own, but contributed liberally wherever it saw a need.

> It has donated to the inmates of the national rehabilitation centers pianos, musical instruments, athletic goods, TV sets, records, motion picture cameras and projectors, flower hothouses, special promenades, cages of small birds, small workshop equipment ... small cottages to hold tea ceremonies or cooking classes for blind female trainees, poultry farming equipment for blind male trainees, etc.
>
> (*Reiyukai and Social Services*, 24)

As Reiyukai became more widely known, it began to receive criticism as well as praise. The post-war Japanese press loved to dig up scandals about the 'new religions'. In 1950 an original work in Nichiren's own hand disappeared from Kuon-ji on Mount Minobu and reappeared mysteriously at Reiyukai headquarters. Reiyukai 'in-fighting' seems to have been the cause. In 1953 Reiyukai was accused of embezzling funds destined for the Red Cross, and Kotani and two leaders were arrested. The other two confessed, and Mrs Kotani was released. Both incidents were bad publicity for Reiyukai, and caused many leaders and members to withdraw from the society. The years of steady growth came to an end. Those leaders who remained in the organization were the most devotedly loyal to Mrs Kotani. She emerged from the crises as absolute ruler.[77]

By the late 1950s Kimi Kotani felt that she was ready to fulfil the dream of Nichiren and build 'the *kaidan* of this century'. Years before, Kakutaro Kubo had spoken of the importance of establishing 'a single holy Buddhist temple in this land'. Unlike other temples, which were run by professional priests, this one would be run by and for the people. It would be dedicated to Maitreya (Japanese, *Miroku*), the Buddha of the future, whose name means 'friendliness'.[78]

Mrs Kotani chose an isolated site on Mount Togasayama on the Izu Peninsula, a difficult spot on which to raise the 'Kaidan for the twentieth century'. Roads had to be built up the mountain, wells had to be sunk for water, and 2.5 million square metres of land had to be cleared. The construction was begun in 1960 and completed in 1964 — not, it was said, without a little miraculous help from the Bodhisattva Maitreya. First he arranged for much needed water to come pouring forth from the site where his statue was to be placed. Later, when workers could not fit the huge statue into its base, he shook the earth, and the image slid neatly into its designated place (DW special edition 1975, 10–19).

Mirokusan, as it is called, is certainly one of the most spectacular religious structures in Japan. Although not as large or as innovative as the Sho-Hondo of Sokagakkai, it fits harmoniously into the mountainside and commands a magnificent view of the sea and the islands beyond. The main building is in the classical style of the Asuka era (552–645), similar to the oldest Japanese Buddhist temples. It is crowned by a graceful, three-storied pagoda, which houses the image of Maitreya Bodhisattva (*Miroku* in Japanese), the future Buddha. The image is flanked by two angels suspended from the ceiling as if in flight. When seen at night lit by spotlights, they seem to be descending to earth to bring humanity new life and hope. Below the Prayer Hall, down a wide staircase flanked by Japanese lanterns, is a retreat house capable of holding 1,200 visitors. Here also are the refectories and recreational facilities. This is the spiritual heart of Reiyukai. Here some 50,000 young people come each year for spiritual guidance and a chance to make new friends and enjoy some dancing and singing. Reiyukai, like other derivatives of Nichiren, is basically a happy religion that encourages youthful enthusiasm and high spirits.

Kimi Kotani died in 1971 at the age of 71. Shortly before her death she instructed that another great building project should take place, in the heart of Tokyo. Instead of a place of retreat like Mirokusan, it would be where the Buddha could come into direct contact with the public. It was to be called the *Shakaden*, the House of Shakyamuni. Perhaps unwittingly, she was placing a heavy financial burden on the shoulders of her followers. Reiyukai does not accept donations, so every penny for the *Shakaden* would have to be paid by membership dues alone. This great structure, with a seating capacity of 8,000, plus a nursery, television studio, library, and art gallery, was completed in 1975 under the direction of Mrs Kotani's successor, Tsugunari Kubo. Three hundred thousand members, including representatives from 30 countries, attended the opening ceremonies over a 62-day period. The exact cost was not made public, but it must have put considerable strain on the resources of the organization, tied in as it is by the rule against accepting donations (BW VIII, 1975, No. 9; IX, 1976, No. 1).

Mrs Kotani was succeeded by her nephew and ward, Tsugunari Kubo, son of the founder. She had trained him for the post since his childhood. She had also ensured that he got a good academic training, especially in Buddhism. He majored in Indian Philosophy at Tokyo University, Japan's most prestigious university, and earned a Ph.D. in Buddhism from the Nichiren Buddhist Rissho University. One of his professors, Senchu Murano, recalls him with affection: 'Unlike so many people associated with the "new religions",' he says, 'Kubo is a real scholar — more, he is a profound thinker.'

Tsugunari Kubo is married to Katsuko, who is the author of several best-selling books. Her books are devoted mainly to the application of Buddhism in the home, a major concern of Reiyukai. They have four children. Kubo has travelled widely promoting Reiyukai, and speaks good English.

Assisting Dr Kubo in the direction of Reiyukai are directors and about 400 salaried staff members. The individual members belong to semi-independent branches, of which there are about 2,500, each with 500 or more members. At the head of each branch is a *shibucho* (branch director), who is respected by the members as their 'parent (*oya*) in the Dharma'. Frequently the branch directors are a husband-and-wife team. Each member becomes the 'parent' of anyone he or she converts; this parent–child relationship is basic in Reiyukai. A member automatically belongs to the branch of his 'parent', and not necessarily to the one which meets down the street. Sometimes American members are puzzled to discover that they belong, not to the Los Angeles headquarters, but to some branch in distant Japan. 'If you are not sure which branch you are part of,' says a Reiyukai publication, 'please call the office and we will help you' (BW IX, 1979, No. 4, 18).

Converting another to Reiyukai is called *michibiki*; it is explained by Tsugunari Kubo as person-to-person contact, 'like one alcoholic curing himself by helping another alcoholic' (BW VIII No. 5, 3, 4). Unlike

Nichiren Shoshu-Sokagakkai, Reiyukai does not require a member to give up his ancestral religion. By the same token, members can feel free to visit and pray in any temple, church or synagogue. Japanese members enjoy making pilgrimages to famous Nichiren temples, and if they enter a non-Buddhist place of worship, they behave decorously, praying fervently for the ancestors of all who are gathered there.

Each member sets up a small altar in his own home. Instead of an object of worship (*honzon*), it has a tablet with Chinese characters giving a posthumous name for his family and that of his spouse or, if he is single, for the families of both his parents. This is called the *Sokaimyo*. It is described as 'not an object of worhsip, but rather a focusing point for your personal Buddhist practice.' The enshrining of a *kaimyo* is an ancient Japanese custom. On a scroll or board is written the posthumous name of a parent or relative. The *Sokaimyo* differs in that it gives a name to the entire family.

The following Chinese characters are inscribed on the *Sokaimyo*: *truth, birth, house, Dharma, way, compassion, goodness, transfer,* [names] *families, virtue,* and *enlightenment*. This is interpreted to mean: 'May the *truth live* in this *house* in accordance with the *Law* so that we may follow the *way* of mercy, *compassion*, and *goodness*. Let our *virtue* be *transferred* to our *ancestors* of the [named] *families*. Please inspire our *hearts*, minds, and souls to *enlightenment*' (*Reiyukai: People Promoting Friendship and Awareness*, 14).

In front of the *Sokaimyo*, the member places an open book called *Kakocho* (death register), which has a page for every day of the month. On each page is written the name and posthumous name of the ancestor, relative, or friend, who died on that particular day. The altar is usually decorated with glasses of fresh water, flowers, a small bell on a cushion, an incense burner, and a candle. The devotee may sit on the floor or on a chair, whichever he prefers. He holds beads (*juzu*), and wears a special sash over one shoulder inscribed with *Namu Myoho Renge Kyo* on the outside and his own name on the inside.

As his minimal practice the member is expected to treat his home altar with respect, change the water daily, and fold his hands and recite *Daimoku* three times every morning and again every evening. But more likely, he will do the complete service, which consists of an invocation to the Buddhas and Bodhisattvas (including Nichiren), prayers for the enlightenment of his ancestors, and a recitation of passages from the Threefold Lotus Sutra. His prayer book is called *The Blue Sutra*, and its recitation takes about 30 minutes; it is written in the vernacular. For foreign members there are translations in English, Spanish, French, Italian, and other languages. A 'culturally adapted' version was published in 1988 for English speakers.

Through this daily practice the member is brought into communion with the 'spiritual world'. Some members claim that sometimes when they are reciting, the water in the glass begins to bubble; this is viewed as a sign that the 'spiritual world' is responding. For the more advanced practitioner there is *O-kuji* (mystic power). *O-kuji* is considered too dangerous for the average member, however, and it is never described in print. It may be taught only by a 'parent' to his spiritual child on a one-to-one basis.

Exactly what the 'spiritual world' consists of is never spelled out. The individual is taught only how to contact it; the rest is up to him. Reiyukai leans over backwards not to be doctrinaire. 'Reiyukai has no doctrine,' says Tsugunari Kubo. 'It is not something intellectual, but such as you should feel with your body . . . It should be fresh at all times' (BW IV, No. 7, 11).

This lack of doctrines is an obstacle to proselytizing, and a prospective convert may find that he knows almost nothing about Reiyukai even after a weekend of intense activities at Mirokusan. He learns that it has something to do with veneration of ancestors, which is done by reading passages from the *Dharma Flower* — passages which say nothing about ancestors, and the meaning of which is not explained to him. He is expected to join on the basis of 'friendship' alone — friendship with the spirits and friendship with his peers. An English member writes:

> My initial experience of the Sutra and its recitation was one of total incomprehension — I could see no point in it. What kept me going to the meetings was the discussions which followed the Sutra. I still don't get any more from the Sutra than I do from other texts of various philosophical/religious origins, but what remains is the contact with the people within Reiyukai.
> (*The Reiyukai Movement* 35)

According to Reiyukai our self-development begins when we see ourselves as the centre of a cross. Horizontally we interrelate with our peers; vertically we interrelate with our ancestors in the past and our descendants in the future. We accomplish the former by forming friendships and particularly by introducing others to Reiyukai by the 'Bodhisattva practice' of *michibiki*, guiding others along the way. We accomplish the latter by praying for our ancestors and changing inherited evil karma to good karma for the future.

Shintaro Ishihara — author of *The Japan that Can Say No*, member of the Japanese House of Representatives, and one of Reiyukai's most distinguished members — explains:

> It is necessary to feel ourselves not merely as isolated individuals, but as part of the stream of life flowing on from the first germ to the unknown future. It is also necessary that we should care not only for our parents and grandparents, but for our ancestors who died before we were born, and by doing so,

we can easily feel some mysterious power with regard to our existence, and we are sure to have a deep emotion stimulating our religious mind.

(*BW* August 1971, 8.)

'Those who do not look upon themselves as a link connecting the past with the future,' said Daniel Webster, 'do not perform their duty in the world.' This is Reiyukai's sentiment, exactly. If everyone acquired a sense of reverence at being in this world at all, this world would become Buddha's World, 'the place where every personality, keeping in harmonious relations and being required to show a certain delicacy and reverence for another personality, ought to shine reciprocally in sympathizing with other good personalities, as Plato suggests in his dialogue' (*Ishihara, BW* IV, No. 7, 11).

Reiyukai has no *Honzon* or Object of Worship. Like primitive Buddhism, it neither affirms nor denies the existence of God, and thus claims to be not a religion, but 'interreligious'. The 'spiritual world', which is mentioned so often, is left undefined. Dr Kubo says that it is the 'sum of all invisible or super-human factors, such as one's own unconscious self, our ancestors which we are a part of, the eternal Buddha, etc.' (*BW* IX, No. 2, 4). Nor is it clear to whom or to what we are to direct our prayer. According to Joe Walters, Manager of Reiyukai America Association,

Our prayer, which in reality is a sincere wish from the bottom of our heart, is not directed towards any particular deity, but is given freely for the ears of whomever or whatever is in the unseen world, the spiritual world, and may have the power to help us fulfill that wish. In this way, we can all harmoniously wish for and strive for world peace together.

(*BW* IX, No. 3, 14)

Thus Reiyukai remains intentionally undogmatic. The Japanese, who generally look upon religion more as an attitude of reverence than as specific beliefs, can appreciate this. Kimi Kotani's book, *Sounds of Heaven*, sold over a million copies. But Westerners, who expect their religious practices to be based on logical theories, often find such a lack of concrete doctrine an obstacle to appreciating Reiyukai. Missionary progress in the Western world has been slow despite large expenditures of money and effort. Americans and Europeans have joined the dogmatic Nichiren Shoshu in far greater numbers than they have Reiyukai, the Spiritual Friendship Society. If Reiyukai really believes what it says, that 'all the people of the world will become members of Reiyukai' (BW October 1970, 15), then there is still a long way to go.

It was the younger Kubo who decided to extend Reiyukai internationally. In 1972 he sponsored the first 'Inner Trip' for foreigners to come to Japan and see Reiyukai for themselves. The number of American converts did not match the efforts and expense of the Japanese members, but it was a beginning, and gradually Reiyukai extended its outreach further afield. By the mid-1980s it had opened missions in Taiwan, the Philippines, Nepal, Thailand, India, England (Liverpool and Norwich), France, Italy, Spain, Brazil, Peru, Paraguay, Canada, Mexico, and the USA.

Reiyukai's open-mindedness combined with a focus on self-expression and heart-to-heart contact appeal to many young people throughout the world. Its present leader, Tsugunari Kubo, personifies these qualities. He assumed his office at the age of 34, and has enjoyed the unqualified backing of the younger members. According to statistics compiled by Helen Hardacre, however, young members under the age of 30 are a vocal minority of only 11 per cent. Most senior directors and branch directors, as well as over 50 per cent of the total membership, are over 50 years old. Foreign visitors on 'Inner Trips' did not see much of them because few speak English. However, whenever Dr Kubo presided at a meeting, the senior leaders lined up behind him in orderly rows, adding solemnity to the occasion by their silent presence. Foreign guests were not aware of the generation gap between younger members, who are enthusiastic followers of Dr Kubo, and the older members, who revere their branch leaders and the memory of Mrs Kotani (T. Kubo, *Development*, 25).

Self-expression is encouraged in Reiyukai, but only within certain limits; it must not rock the boat. Over the years numerous talented potential leaders have resigned after clashing with the well entrenched hierarchy at the top. Spiritual children are expected to be obedient to their spiritual parents. Loyalty is more highly prized than originality, and the senior directors of today are those who remained loyal to Kimi Kotani during her sometimes stormy career. The vertical relationship of all members to their 'parents' and the branch leader gives the latter considerable autonomous authority. Dr Kubo does not enjoy the control over his organization which Ikeda does over Sokagakkai or Niwano over Rissho Kosei-kai. Reiyukai is a fertile breeding ground for new cults. If it had been able to hold on to all the good minds and enthusiastic workers who have passed through its ranks, it would be four times the size that it is today.

Reiyukai attempts to tread a narrow path. On the one hand, it encourages self-discovery and self-expression; on the other hand, it insists that all members are equal. The only seniority is the 'parent-child' relationship between the proselytizer and his convert, not that of teacher and student or rich and poor. This is why it encourages few study classes and will accept no donations. Each member pays identical dues regardless of his ability to pay more. Once he enters Reiyukai, his wealth or education make no difference. If he converts somebody else, he too becomes an *oya*, a spiritual parent. If he and his spiritual offspring make enough additional members, he may become a branch leader; otherwise, he remains at the bottom of the pyramid, no matter who he is.

Reiyukai objects to the term 'conversion', pointing out that new members are not required to give up their old religion. But whether we call it 'conversion' or 'guidance', *michibiki* establishes a permanent bond between the one who leads another into the fold and the one who is led. This strict parent–child relationship has weakened Reiyukai's overseas missionary efforts. Offices have been opened in many countries, but the branch leaders and their co-workers owe their allegiance to mother branches back in Japan, not necessarily to the mission.

Reiyukai America opened its first office in Los Angeles in 1973. In 1977 it bought its own building on Sunset Boulevard, and two years later raised another building, which it named 'Friendship House'. Other offices were opened in Canada and Mexico. All directors have been appointed in Japan, and there has been a fast turnover. Reiyukai America, in accordance with the parent–child relationship, remains dependent on Tokyo. Unlike Nichiren Shoshu, it has not succeeded in forming an 'American sacred centre' (to use the expression of Charles Prebish), nor is it likely to do so without altering its vertical system of membership.

The real 'spark plug' of Reiyukai America was not so much the official leadership as Mrs Gloria Crable of San Diego, who describes herself as a 'Presbyterian Buddhist'. The daughter of a Japanese diplomat and married to a retired American businessman, she is well travelled, a skilled concert pianist, and a survivor of the Hiroshima atomic bomb explosion. She is also an energetic speaker and proponent of Reiyukai, to which she credits her recovery from atomic radiation. Mrs Crable possesses unusual spiritual talents, and she sometimes makes predictions which astonish her many friends. Her optimism and enthusiasm are infectious. She more than anyone has been the 'Kimi Kotani of America'. However, these very abilities brought her into conflict with the bureaucracy of the head office, and in 1980 she resigned. Reiyukai America had lost its most dynamic and popular exponent.

The breach was eventually healed, but not before drastic measures had been taken. The director in America was returned to Japan and replaced by young Kenichi Negishi, who was chosen not because of his seniority but because of his friendship with many American members. For once the seniority system was successfully bypassed (*Inner Trip Friends*, July 1983). This was only a temporary expedient, however, for a few years later he was replaced by a senior officer.

Reiyukai has made a major effort to expand globally. Each of its foreign missions is staffed by a salaried director and assistants; most expenses are paid from Japan. In 1987 the foreign membership was estimated at 60,000 scattered across the globe (T. Kubo, *The Reiyukai Movement*, 33). Although this is not a large number, it probably means more foreign members than any Buddhist group in the world except Sokagakkai.

Reiyukai's central practice of ancestor veneration remains puzzling to most Europeans and Americans, especially when this is accomplished by reading passages from the *Dharma Flower*, which never mention ancestors. In recent years the new leader, Dr Tsugunari Kubo, has placed much more emphasis on 'self-development' than on traditional ancestor worship. The logo now has a more pragmatic ring to it. In the 1970s it was, 'Inner Trip: A Journey into your Heart'. For the success-oriented 1980s it had become 'Reiyukai: the Business of Dynamic Tranquility . . . A Non-profit Enterprise Paying Dividends in Personal Growth'.

Reiyukai, which boasts that it is more open than similar organizations, has changed with the times. But changes always cause tensions, and the danger of another major schism still lurks beneath the surface. Nevertheless, although the younger Kubo has instituted more changes than his aunt ever did, he has managed so far to retain the loyalty of his co-believers and avoid serious break-offs. As Reiyukai pursues its new course, it may yet experience a new period of growth.

Chapter 18

Rissho Kosei-kai: Buddhism Applied

'It was because of the guidance of my teacher, Sukenobu Arai, that I became fond of the Sutra, threw myself into it, and made it a part of me. Until then I had gone from one religion to another; each had the power to save, but they were like coarse nets through which many fish could slip. The more I read the Lotus Sutra, the more I realized that its truth was infinite in scope, infinite in precision, infinite in power to save. The Lotus Sutra, I saw, is a finely woven net through which no captive can slip. The ecstacy of discovering this made me want to shout and sing and dance for joy' (*Dharma World*, December 1980, 4).

These are the words of Nikkyo Niwano, founder and president of Rissho Kosei-kai. No Buddhist leader in the world has become more widely known or showered with more honours than him. Although he possesses only a primary school education from a village school in northern Japan, he has been invited to chair international conferences in Asia, Europe, and America. He has met numerous world leaders and heads of state, accepted honorary degrees from Japanese and foreign institutions of higher learning, and was invited to Windsor Castle by the Duke of Edinburgh to receive the Templeton Foundation Prize for Progress in Religion. He was the only official Buddhist representative at the Vatican Council, and was invited to Iran to hear the Ayatollah Khomeini's interpretation of the American hostage crisis. Whether standing on a podium before a crowd of thousands or seated and chatting informally over a cup of tea with a single guest, he is always the same — smiling, friendly, and intently interested in every word that is spoken.

Nikkyo Niwano was born in 1906, the second son of a large family in a mountain village of Niigata. The village then consisted of 42 families, but has since shrunk to 26. His family were farmers, who managed to eke out an adequate living from the rugged terrain. Life was not easy, and there were endless chores which had to be done around the farm, but there was always enough to eat. The house was warm during the snow-bound winters, and there was enough money for small luxuries at festival times. It was a happy household where three generations lived under the same roof, and every member of the family contributed to the common good.

Because of his physical height and genial disposition, he was looked up to by his peers as a natural leader. He accepted this role with the same equanimity with which he has always accepted everything in life. He never felt pressured to prove himself in a fight unless it was to protect some smaller boy from being bullied. Later he said that he had had only two fights in his entire life, and they were after reaching young adulthood. He dispatched both opponents by means of judo, and looked back on these encounters with some relish. He was a peace-maker, but he knew that he could take care of himself if he ever had to (*DW* February 1978). The reasons he was a man of peace, he said later, were firstly because he was raised in the country, secondly because he came from a happy family, and thirdly because the Lotus Sutra saves everybody. (*DW* May 1975, 30)

During his childhood, however, he knew nothing about the Lotus Sutra. His family belonged to the Soto Zen sect, and religious observations meant simply being helpful to neighbours and bowing respectfully to wayside shrines. In the first of his two autobiographies, *Travel to Infinity*, he claims that he never failed to do either. (20)

Although his formal education stopped after primary school (farm boys were expected to work after that), he was an avid reader, especially of European novels and Chinese classics. He worked for a while as a road labourer, and then received permission from his father to go out into the world to seek his fortune. He set out determined to work harder than anyone else, to do any job no matter how distasteful, and never to compete with his fellow-workers for favours from the boss. He arrived in Tokyo on 23 August 1923, full of hopes. It was just four days before the terrible Kanto Earthquake.

Before ten days had passed he was home again, having survived one of the most terrible earthquakes of modern times. Around 143,000 people were dead, and all of Yokohama and half of Tokyo were in ruins. Niwano escaped unscathed, but his place of employment was gutted. So, too, it seemed, were all his youthful dreams.

Before long he was back, however, working at seasonal jobs in Tokyo and then home on the farm.

> Friends of mine who were working in Tokyo visited me sometimes. They were paid 30 yen to 40 yen a month, while I received only 15 yen. But those who got a higher salary only exchanged their labor for pay. Therefore, they remained

employees forever. I was paid only 15 yen, but as the master treated me as an intimate consultant, I could learn in a short time the secrets of management even though it was only a small business. This was really useful when I became independent later. The value was incomparable to the difference between 15 yen and 40 yen.

(54)

In 1926 he was drafted, and for the next three years he served as a gunner's mate in the navy. As usual, he adapted easily to his new environment. To qualify as a gunner he had to improve his skills in mathematics, a subject for which he always had a special fondness. All his life he valued precision and order, and the navy also taught him stage presence. He became leader of the ship's entertainment committee and would amuse the crews with performances of folk songs and dances.

On the imperial flagship *Haruna*, one of his officers was young Prince Takamatsu. Thirty years later, when they met under very different circumstances, the Prince immediately recognized 'Niwano, Seaman First-class'. Even as an ordinary seaman he was not the kind of person whom one forgets easily.

After his discharge in 1929 he went into business for himself, first as a pickles vendor and later as a milkman. He married a girl from his home district and seemed to have settled down to the life of a small entrepreneur, when the sudden illness of his infant daughter drove him to religion. Someone told him about a type of esoteric Buddhism called *Tengu-fudo*, which could cure sicknesses, and soon he was deeply involved in it. When his daughter recovered mysteriously, he wanted to know why. The cult required rigorous self-discipline and the learning of secret formulas (mantras). He threw himself into the practices with such zeal that he became the assistant master, and found that he could cure people of their diseases and problems.

> I did not know the reason why. I had no confidence at all that I had such an ability. I had no abnormal experiences like the others who in trances saw divine figures or heard divine voices. When I considered myself from every angle, I was quite an ordinary man. I was nothing but an ordinary pickles dealer. Nevertheless, I could cause mysterious things to happen, one after the other.

(86–8)

Mysterious apparitions and heavenly voices were too unreliable for his taste. He wanted something more exact, something which would work under any circumstances, so he turned from *Tengu-fudo* to onomancy: a type of fortune-telling based on a person's name. This too seemed to work in many cases, but not all the time.

When his second daughter became seriously ill and was diagnosed as having Japanese sleeping sickness, he turned to Reiyukai. As soon as he enshrined his ancestors and began to chant the Sutra as instructed in Reiyukai, his daughter quickly recovered. Again he wanted to know why, and this led him to study the book he had been reciting from, the Lotus Sutra. Fortunately for him, his branch leader was one of the few real scholars in Reiyukai, Sukenobu Arai. He was someone whom even Kimi Kotani respected and called *sensei* (teacher). In Niwano's second autobiography, *Lifetime Beginner*, he says:

> The *rokuyo* system and name interpretation were interesting but not entirely effective in relieving suffering. At best they were effective — though not always completely — in eighty-five percent of all instances. In other words, fifteen percent of the suffering people remained unaided by them. Nor had the Shugen-do system proved perfectly effective. Some people were not cured by it. Some were cured physically while their deep suffering and spiritual wounds went unattended. Furthermore, I was never convinced about spiritual powers that could not be understood by the person exerting them. In my own vague way, I constantly sought a rule that would save everyone, a rule that was not mysterious, but was convincingly based on reason and was clearly regulated and systematic.
>
> Listening to the lectures on the Lotus Sutra, I realized that I had found what I had been looking for. The Lotus Sutra was the perfect net in which to save everyone in the world. Physically and spiritually it could help both the individual and all of society. I was profoundly shaken by what I had learned. The impression made on me was of astonishing, vibrant freshness. It has remained fresh for over forty years. During that time, I have not missed reading the Lotus Sutra a single day. And the text has lost none of its subtlety, none of its ability to reverberate in my heart and sink deeply into my spirit. On the contrary, the more I read the sutra, the more impressive and profound it seems. Is there another teaching with this power? Is there another book that can be read with amazement and growing emotional impact every day for forty years?
>
> (76–7)

He gave up his pickles business and opened a milk shop in order to have more time to evangelize for Reiyukai. After completing his milk deliveries (or even while making them), he would make his rounds as a missionary. One of his early converts was a sickly housewife, Mrs Myoko Naganuma, who was 17 years older than he. Under the inspiration of her new faith, Mrs Myoko, as she was affectionately called, rose from her sickbed to become a zealous missionary, some-times converting as many as 50 people in one day. She became Niwano's closest collaborator, and the two could often be seen as he carried her on his bicycle through the streets of Tokyo to visit a prospect. They made an excellent team. He was the enthusiastic organizer and theoretician, while she was the charismatic mystic who could empathize with others, especially with women.

Niwano and Mrs Myoko remained ardent members of Reiyukai for about three years; all their spare time was devoted to their new religion. When they were not evangelizing from house to house, they were sitting with rapt attention at the feet of their teacher Arai, studying the Lotus Sutra. After the other students had gone home for the night, Niwano would remain alone with his teacher engaged in animated conversation. 'He was burningly eager to teach the Sutra,' says Niwano. 'I was burningly eager to be taught. We agreed with each other like lovers; we attracted each other like the north and south poles of two magnets.' (79)

Meanwhile Niwano's business began to suffer from neglect. Worse, his domestic relations underwent a severe strain, which was to last for 20 years. His wife did not accept his total dedication to outside interests and his lack of attention to their everyday needs. Her disapproval was so obvious that some of Niwano's flock suggested that he separate from her or divorce her. Once his wife even swore out a warrant for his arrest. Finally, 'in response to a divine revelation', Niwano separated from his family for 10 years to devote himself exclusively to religion. Gradually, and only after much talk of divorce, his wife came to accept her subordinate role. The marriage survived. (139–45) His partner Mrs Myoko had similar domestic problems. Her husband finally tired of her full-time religious interest, and divorced her. He remarried, but he and his new wife remained active members of Rissho Kosei-kai. (90)

It was inevitable that Niwano should finally break with Reiyukai. He was not the type to knuckle under to the imperious leadership of Kimi Kotani. Moreover, the more he studied the Lotus Sutra, the more he distanced himself from the primary interest of Reiyukai, the veneration of ancestors. To Reiyukai the Sutra was a tool, a means to make 'heart-to-heart contact' with the spiritual world. To Niwano the Sutra was the end, the container of all wisdom and spiritual power. The two approaches could not be reconciled, and the break came after a stormy meeting at Reiyukai headquarters in 1938.

Reiyukai had experienced a number of schisms. Two branch leaders had recently been fired, and Mrs Kotani was anxious to get everything back on track. A meeting of all leaders was called, and everyone was invited to speak his mind, but the meeting did not go as planned. The discussion grew more animated. Mrs Kotani listened with growing impatience, and suddenly stood up.

'What the hell is all this about?' she shouted. 'You are supposed to be believers, but you act as if you were big shots. If anyone has a gripe, speak up!'

Silence fell on the hall. Mrs Kotani went on, giving vent to her pent-up feelings. Study groups, she said, were a waste of time. All that was necessary was discipline and unity of purpose. 'Lectures on the Lotus Sutra are out of date. Anyone who tries anything like that around here must be inspired by the devil.'

Professor Arai, deeply offended, stood up and walked out. Niwano remained to the end, but was engulfed in gloom. By the time the meeting was over, he knew that he and Reiyukai had come to a parting of the ways. It was time to gather his friends into a new organization of their own (87).

Niwano and Mrs Myoko at first tried to enlist the aid of their teacher, Sukenobu Arai. The teacher listened sympathetically, but said that he was too old to help found a new organization and was unwilling to break his personal friendship with Kakutaro Kubo. Disappointed but not discouraged, the two zealots gathered about 30 followers to set up a new society, which they named *Rissho Kosei-kai* (usually called *Kosei-kai* for short). They had few resources, and they used a small room over Niwano's milk shop as their headquarters. They had only some books, scrolls, beads, and other paraphernalia that they had been using in Reiyukai. Who could have imagined that within 35 years, the membership would have grown from 30 to four million, outstripping the parent organization and attaining world-wide status?

The name Rissho Kosei-kai defies a simple translation. *Rissho* is part of the title of a well known treatise by Nichiren, *Rissho ankoku-ron*, meaning 'Establish the Right Dharma'. Nichiren himself bears the honorary title *Rissho Daishi*, 'Great Teacher Establishing the Right Dharma'. *Ko*, according to an explanation for English-speaking members, 'means the pious intercourse of many people and the harmony of believers, that is, "many in body but one in mind" (another expression of Nichiren's). *Sei* expresses the idea of the completion of personality and the attainment of buddhahood . . . The last character, *Kai*, means "society", and when at the end of the name, the preceding characters give the purpose of the society' (*For Our New Members*, 14).

The society has evolved through many stages reflecting the spiritual growth of its co-founder, Nikkyo Niwano. During its early years it was dominated by the charismatic personality of Mrs Myoko, especially her 'revelations' and powers of faith healing. According to Niwano:

> The overwhelming majority of our new members were people who were seriously ill, who had mentally retarded relatives, or who for economic reasons could not call on the services of doctors. In the eyes of the general public, we were no more than a milkman and a vendor of sweet potatoes (Mrs. Myoko) conducting some mysterious religious rites in an upstairs room

over a milk shop. Obviously, only desperate people at their wits' end came to us.

(*Lifetime Beginner*, 95)

Some of Mrs Myoko's 'revelations' imposed severe discipline on members and leaders alike. There were group pilgrimages to the Nichiren Head Temple at Mount Minobu, which were undertaken only after rigorous fasting and spiritual preparations. One revelation instructed Niwano to send his wife and children to the country for a ten-year separation. This happened during wartime, when it seemed sensible to get them away from Tokyo air raids, but the separation continued many years after the danger had passed. Niwano found it especially difficult to go home for special occasions such as funerals, see his family there, but not be permitted to speak to any of them. He wore the robes and followed the discipline of a Buddhist monk, although he belonged to no order. After ten years the family was reunited, 'but not as husband and wife or father and children'. He lived on one floor, his family on another, and they rarely spoke to each other. This went on for three more years until finally the gods and Mrs Myoko decided that he had become spiritually mature and his wife sufficiently submissive.

Niwano was an avid reader. A special revelation, however, decreed that for seven years he should read only the Lotus Sutra, so he thoroughly immersed himself in the book. Finally, shortly after the end of the war, he was given permission to include in his reading the writings of Nichiren. He devoured them with the eagerness of a hungry man who opens a door to see a table richly laden.

This led to the second stage in Kosei-kai's evolution, an attempt to link it to Nichiren Shu. Niwano visited the Head Temple at Mount Minobu in 1948, but no one paid any attention to him. He was, after all, no more than a 'faith-healing milkman'. The following year, however, he was able to meet with the secretary general and propose a merger: Kosei-kai would be a missionary arm of Nichiren Shu just as Sokagakkai was to Nichiren Shoshu. An agreement was reached whereby Nichiren Shu, on its part would set up the principles of 'unification of doctrine, the main object of worship, and the dissemination policy' (*Travel to Infinity*, 124).

For about a year (1949–50) Rissho Kosei-kai was a lay auxiliary of Nichiren Shu. Niwano, however, did not approach the ancient sect with the humility of Josei Toda at Nichiren Shoshu, but with the zeal of a new convert, 'more Catholic than the Pope'. He considered himself an equal partner able to make his own terms, and had no patience with the liberal policies of the Head Temple, which permitted considerable latitude in faith and practice among subordinate temples and organizations. Although it was to take him 30 years to decide on his own 'object of worship', he laid down terms that the ancient denomination must unify those of its 5,000 temples within one year. When this did not happen, he broke off the relationship. He and Mrs Myoko met again with the secretary general of the 'sleeping religious organization' and agreed to a separation. [79]

Since that time, Kosei-kai has moved steadily away from Nichiren Buddhism to become a denomination of its own, complete with its own object of worship, special teachings, and ordained ministry. In the official prayer book published in 1968, and again in the revised editions of 1974 and 1979, Nichiren was still named 'Patriarch' (*Koso*, the title used in Tendai for Saicho and in Shingon for Kukai) and 'Great Bodhisattva' (*Kyoden*, 1979). But in the 1987 English edition his name does not appear.

In *Honzon* (1968) Niwano explains his frequent changes in the society's Object of Veneration as a gradual fulfilment of the true intention of Nichiren. The Great Mandala was replaced by a statue of the Eternal Buddha Shakyamuni because that, he says, was what Nichiren really wanted but could not realize during his lifetime (61–7).

As Rissho Kosei-kai loosened its ties with Nichiren Shu it established new ones with Tendai, with which it has much in common (DW December 1975, 3). It reads the Lotus Sutra in the spirit of Tendai, as a book of rules for life, rather than in the way of Nichiren, as a 'means of grace'. Nichiren used to say that Tendai put the emphasis on the Imprinted Gate (practices), while he put it on the Original Gate (faith). Rissho Kosei-kai does the same. By 1987 Tendai was speaking of having 'ties' with Kosei-kai, although these ties were more spiritual than formal (*DW* September/October 1987, 4).

However, the roots in Nichiren Buddhism are too deep to be eradicated easily. Parts of the daily service are taken from Nichiren Shu. *O-eshiki*, the festival commemorating the death of Nichiren on 23 October, is still Kosei-kai's largest public event. Members still climb Mount Shichimen on pilgrimages. Even the logo of the society is the mandarin orange, the crest of Nichiren.

Kosei-kai grew slowly but steadily during the war. Niwano was called up again for military service, but was soon released. The organization bought a house of its own, which it quickly outgrew, and then put up its own building. The work was done almost entirely by voluntary labour. The building was not bombed during the war, which was regarded as proof of divine protection. (The Nichiren Shu Head Temple at Ikegami, on the other hand, was almost totally destroyed during an air raid and had to be rebuilt after the war.) Considered even more miraculous was the safe return of all of the members who went into military service. The last to return was Motoyuki Naganuma, a nephew of Mrs Myoko. He reappeared in 1946, almost a year after the war ended, thus making the count complete. (*Lifetime*, 136 ff)

After the war and after the break from Nichiren Shu, Kosei-kai grew rapidly like the other Nichiren movements, Sokagakkai and Reiyukai.

The three shared much in common: they chanted selected portions of the Lotus Sutra, used the Sacred Title (*Daimoku*), venerated the memory of Nichiren, proselytized vigorously, and promised quick relief from the most widespread problems in post-war Japan: illness and poverty. All were directed by charismatic leaders. Outsiders often confused them, and a cynical press sometimes tarred them all with the same brush.

However, there were basic differences between them. Sokagakkai was an auxiliary of Nichiren Shoshu, the most dogmatic of all Nichiren sects. It was a unique blend of the old and the new, coming complete with venerable temples and gorgeously arrayed priests combined with modern marching bands and baton-twirling drum majorettes. Reiyukai was independent of any particular sect, and combined traditional ancestor veneration with modern pep rallies. Rissho Kosei-kai much resembled it at first, but gradually developed specific doctrines of its own. It, too, was skilled at organizing mass meetings and parades, although not on as large a scale as Sokagakkai.

At first Kosei-kai, like its parent Reiyukai, had no Object of Worship (*Honzon*), but by its third year of independence it had adopted one. This was simply the Sacred Title, *Namu Myoho Renge Kyo*, inscribed on a flag. In its eighth year this was changed to the Great Mandala of Nichiren. It was changed again in the eleventh year, twenty-first year, twenty-seventh year, and finally in the thirty-first year. By this time it had become a statue of the Original Buddha Shakyamuni, who was called 'Great Beneficient Teacher and Lord Shakyamuni, the Eternal Buddha' (*Kuon-jitsujo Daion Kyoshu Shakamuni-seson*). Photographic copies of this statue, which shows a standing figure of the Buddha surrounded by a flaming halo containing the Four Great Bodhisattvas and the Stupa of Many Treasures Buddha (*Taho-to*), were then ordered installed in the homes of all members (*Honzon*, 77 ff).

The main focus of Rissho Kosei-kai is not on its frequently altered version of the Supreme Being, but on what it calls *hoza*, which has been rendered into English as 'Dharma Circle'. The term is taken from Reiyukai, but in practice it is very different. In Reiyukai a *hoza* is a meeting of a group of members to chant the Sutra and put on some sort of programme, including personal testimonies designed to encourage newcomers to join the group (DW IX, No. 3, 15).

In Kosei-kai a *hoza* is much more specific. Members and guests sit in a circle of 10 or 20 people, and are encouraged to open up and discuss their deepest personal problems. The *hoza* leader, who must have some skills as an amateur psychologist as well as a good understanding of fundamental Buddhism, then attempts to apply Buddhist principles to solve these problems. Other persons present in the circle can contribute their own opinions. 'It is necessary to confess errors and repent shortcomings, for only by doing so can members receive proper guidance and be freed from self-incrimination' (DW March 1979, 21).

The advice given by the *hoza* leader is not a generalization such as might be heard in Sokagakkai ('You must chant more Daimoku'), but is geared to the specific individual and his problem. Buddhism teaches that every phenomenon results from prior causes. The leader tries to discern 'what errors of thought, words, or deeds this person has committed to have fallen into such a state'. He does this by applying the principles of what Kosei-kai calls fundamental Buddhism, which are found in the first half of the Lotus Sutra: the Four Noble Truths, the Eightfold Path, the Six Perfections (*Paramitas*), the Twelve-fold Chain of Dependent Origination, and the Ten Factors of Existence. If sickness, accidents, or bad relationships at home can be seen as opportunities instead of curses, they become *O-satori*, an awakening to instructions from the Buddha.

By participating in *hoza* a member learns to apply Buddhism to every aspect of his life. He is encouraged to 'walk the Bodhisattva way' of helpfulness to others. *Hoza* takes him 'from the mundane to the sublime'. It is 'a way for ordinary people to see the Dharma in ordinary events' (*Kosei Times* March 1975, 2).

The Great Central Hall of Rissho Kosei-kai, which at the time of its completion was the largest religious structure in Asia, is always bustling with people. Ten thousand a day attend worship services, and 25,000 participate in *hoza*, instruction classes, and other activities.

Like other Japanese 'new religions', Rissho Kosei-kai excels in organizing mass meetings and festivals. At the annual *O-eshiki* festival commemorating the death of Nichiren as many as 4,000 colourfully attired members will parade before an audience of up to 180,000 (DW December 1978, 8). Total membership had passed the six million mark by the mid-1980s, and new branch churches, called 'training halls', were rising at the rate of ten a year.

The individual member has to perform private as well as social devotional practices. Every morning and evening he is expected to sit before his family altar and recite the daily service. His altar features a *Sokaimyo* for commemorating his ancestors, just like in Reiyukai. In addition it will have a picture or statue of the Original Buddha Shakyamuni. The *Sokaimyo* is identical to that of Reiyukai, from whom it was taken, although the interpretation of the Chinese characters is slightly different. It refers to 'the Dharma as taught by President Nikkyo Niwano and Vice-President Mrs Myoko Naganuma' (*Rissho Kosei-kai: For Our New Members*, 22–3).

Another feature borrowed directly from Reiyukai is the *Kakocho*, the Death Register, which is kept open on the altar. Except that it is smaller in size, it is identical to the *Kakocho* of Reiyukai.

The daily devotional service is borrowed from Reiyukai and remains about 75 per cent identical. Both have prayers for one's ancestors at the beginning and end, though there are some new elements in Kosei-kai. These include Taking Refuge in the Three Treasures (Buddha, Dharma, and Sangha), which is common to most Buddhists, and the Verses on Opening the Sutra (*Kaikyoge*), which were composed by Udana Nichiki (1800–59) for use in Nichiren Shu. Some of the Reiyukai invocations to the Buddhas and Bodhisattvas are missing, showing the different emphasis. Reiyukai seeks contact with the 'spiritual world', and so names a long list of its denizens, whereas Kosei-kai seeks harmony with the Law (Dharma) and so concentrates on the meaning of the words being recited. The service is chanted in the vernacular, although the traditional Sino-Japanese reading (*Shindoku*) may be used optionally. The members also chant the Sacred Title, *Namu Myoho Renge Kyo*. Niwano insists that this must be done only with sincerity and understanding.

> When we recite the Title of the Lotus Sutra, it seems well enough in theory to recite it only once if we do so with complete sincerity. But in reality, if we do not repeat the Title from three to ten times, the idea of taking refuge in the Buddha does not penetrate completely. Nevertheless, although repetition is very important, if we recite it a thousand or ten thousand times, unless we are superhuman we will become bored or our minds will wander, and we will find ourselves merely mouthing the Title without understanding it. This results in the defect of formalism, the lazy belief that merely by reciting the Title we can be saved. We must realize that real Buddhist practice has three requisites: (1) a good practice, (2) wholehearted conduct, and (3) constant repetition.
>
> (*Buddhism for Today*, 91)

Chanting the Sutra or the Sacred Title is used to achieve concentration:

> How does the ordinary person achieve concentration? My answer is, through action. Instead of sitting and saying nothing, chant the Lotus Sutra or invoke its name (*Daimoku*), or do anything, but put everything you have into the action. Presently you will find that you have reached the state of concentration and selflessness.
>
> (*DW* March 1979, 6)

Thus chanting with total concentration is equivalent to sitting in silent Zen meditation. In a conversation with Niwano, the Zen abbot of Eihei-ji confirms this:

> There is Zen in all religions. To sit in meditation, to recite invocations to the Buddha, to recite invocations to the Lotus Sutra — all are Zen. Zen is concentration. It involves becoming totally absorbed. If one does anything with an attitude of detachment from the self, one can find peace of mind.
>
> (*DW* March 1979, 6)

According to an official Kosei-kai guidebook:

> There are many people in Rissho Kosei-kai who have become
> happy after joining it. This is because while they are chanting
> the Sutra for only 30 minutes in the morning and evening, their
> mind is calm and their way of thinking approaches the words of
> the Sutra. The words of the Sutra are all benevolent. Therefore,
> when the mind is calmed and in a stage free from worldly
> thoughts, each passage in the Sutra impresses them with a very
> grateful sentiment.
>
> (*Rissho Kosei-kai*, 62)

This emphasis on what Nichiren would call *kanjin* (observation of the
mind) reflects the philosophy of President Niwano. Before the death of
Mrs Myoko in 1957 more importance was given to 'getting in touch with'
(*musubi*) spiritual powers, not unlike what we have seen in Reiyukai.
Mrs Myoko herself was a charismatic spiritual leader believed to
possess uncanny psychic powers, and Kosei-kai came close to becoming her 'personality cult'. For many years even Niwano was guided
by her 'revelations', although he later played this down.

> Although I abided by some of the divine revelations, I paid no
> attention to any that deviated from the teachings of the Lotus
> Sutra. I would not countenance those sudden flashes of
> enlightenment that founders of religious organizations are
> sometimes said to experience. The Lotus Sutra was always the
> central element (for me). Spiritual powers were recognized only
> when they assisted in the understanding of the Sutra or served to
> enhance its importance. The Buddha's Law came first; I would
> not accept divine revelations that departed from the Law.
>
> For this reason, I had several disputes with the deities.
> Sometimes at meetings of the senior leaders of Kosei-kai, Myoko
> Sensei would experience visitations. If I was convinced that they
> were in keeping with the Sutra, I explained them to others. But if
> they were unreasonable and unconvincing, I refused to
> comment. The deities were often enraged and scolded me:
> 'Niwano, if you do not do as I say, I will bring physical harm to
> you.' Still I would not give in, but replied, 'Do as you like. Take
> my life. I have devoted it to my task already.'
>
> Judging from my continued good health to this day, I must
> have been right. No, it was the Law that was absolutely right.
>
> (*Lifetime Beginner*, 134–5)[80]

A few years before Mrs Myoko's death Niwano was demoted to a
secondary position. Mrs Myoko, 11 general directors, and 125 chapter
heads prepared a document for Niwano's signature. It stipulated that

henceforth he should do nothing without the agreement of Mrs Myoko; Niwano's wife would not interfere in Kosei-kai affairs; and no non-member could participate in Kosei-kai business without the unanimous approval of all the chapter heads. Niwano signed, but the matter did not end there. It was then proposed that Mrs Myoko should be officially recognized as the founder of the society. This Niwano refused to do. He had converted her (to Reiyukai), and not vice versa. Seeing that they could not convince him to step down to the number two spot, his opponents decided to set up a new organization under the direction of Mrs Myoko. They bought a villa to house the new society.

At this juncture Mrs Myoko's health began to deteriorate, and the schism lost its impetus. During her protracted final illness, Niwano waited on her like a son. All their differences were patched up, and by the time she died they were once more the closest of friends.

The death of Mrs Myoko left Niwano in indisputable control of the society. He promptly launched it on a new course, away from dependence on spiritual voices and towards reliance on the Dharma alone. The society entered a period of spectacular growth, spreading out from Tokyo to the rest of the country and finally even abroad. It began publishing literature in English and other foreign languages. These included general books on the teachings of Rissho Kosei-kai, three translations of the Lotus Sutra,[81] three commentaries on the Sutra by Niwano,[82] two autobiographies of Niwano,[83] and other shorter works by him. Scholarly works by other authors have also been published in English.[84] The monthly magazine *Dharma World* has a worldwide circulation, and features articles by representatives of all the major religions.[85]

Internationalism and inter-religious cooperation have become salient features of Rissho Kosei-kai. Niwano has travelled widely and participated in or headed various organizations promoting world peace. Speaking at St Patrick's Cathedral in New York in 1979 he said, 'If one pursues one's own religion to its depths, one is led, not to self-righteousness, but to an understanding that enables one to grasp the fundamental truth of other religions' (*DW* October 1979, 4).

> Buddhism is not opposed to Christianity, Islam, and other teachings of great sages such as Confucius, Mencius, and Lao-tzu. We understand that such saints and sages are the appearances of the Buddha in other forms and that their teachings are the manifestations of the Buddha's teachings in other forms . . . So long as the Buddha is the great truth and the great life of the universe, there can be no truth that is not included in the Buddha, and no Law other than that of the Buddha. Accordingly, a narrow-minded Buddhist who indiscriminately criticizes other religions and thinks, for example, that Buddhism is the true religion while Christianity is not, cannot claim to be a true

Buddhist . . . A right teaching is right regardless of who preaches it. Truth is truth regardless of who proclaims it.

(*Buddhism for Today*, 228–9)

Because Rissho Kosei-kai purports not to be a new religion but a reformation and updating of a very old one, it has enjoyed spectacular success among nominal Buddhists who are no longer inspired by 'temple religion' with its incomprehensible rituals. It has made Buddhism come alive for millions of Japanese both at home and abroad. On the other hand, because it is so tolerant and even supportive of other faiths, its foreign missions to non-Buddhists have not made similar progress. Successful missionaries, whether Christian or Buddhist, show no mercy on rival faiths and do not hesitate to smash 'heathen' idols and hack down sacred oak trees. Kosei-kai prefers persuasion by example (*shoju*) to that by direct confrontation (*shakubuku*). As a result it has made many friends abroad, especially among Unitarian-Universalists and other religious liberals, but few converts. There are branch churches in America, but their membership consists mostly of ethnic Japanese.[86] Kosei-kai publications give more attention to international inter-religious conferences than to foreign missions.

As early as 1960 President Niwano's oldest son, Nichiko, was named President-designate, thus ensuring that the leadership would remain in the family. However, as the founding president remained active throughout the 1960s, 1970s and into the 1980s, Nichiko has remained in a subordinate position. Although he resembles his father physically, Nichiko is in many ways his father's opposite. His father is an extrovert — outgoing, warm, innovative, curious, and at ease in front of large crowds or total strangers. Nichiko is an introvert — private, cautious, and modest. He used to dread public speaking so much that he would become ill before going on stage.

As a child, Nichiko hardly knew his father. In his autobiography, *My Father, My Teacher*, he describes how he and the other children were raised by their mother in the country. To them their father was distant and awe-inspiring. The older children were aware of their mother's loneliness and resented their father's preoccupations away from home. When finally all of them moved in with him in Tokyo, they were instructed never to call him 'Father', but 'President-teacher' (*Kaicho Sensei*).

The boy took no interest in school, and often skipped classes. Even a reprimand from his father would have been welcome, but when he misbehaved, his father scolded his mother instead of him. If he fought with his younger brother, it was the brother who got spanked, not he. Such neglect made him resentful (55, 63, 66).

College was a disaster. He missed classes and spent days wandering around the streets of Tokyo looking into shop windows. He had no interest in religion, but when his father suggested that he transfer to

Rissho University (the Nichiren Shu univeristy), he readily agreed, happy to see that his father was interested in him at all. However, he made few friends there, and was soon cutting classes again. He enjoyed the lectures of one professor, and attended his classes 'with fair faithfulness', but it took him nine years to get through college and another three years to earn a Master's degree, all because of poor attendance (66, 71–4).

On the day his father informed him he had been named President-designate of Rissho Kosei-kai, he reacted by buying a train ticket to the most distant point in Japan, hoping to vanish off the map. But as he sat brooding and gazing out the train window, he began to realize that he could not escape his destiny. When he arrived at the end of the line, he bought a return ticket and boarded the next train for home. There, to his disappointment, he was greeted as if nothing had happened. No one had missed him.

But his father had missed him, and a few days later, he had a serious talk with his son — perhaps the first such talk they had ever had.

> A while after my flight to Kyushu, Father said to me in a very serious voice, 'People's real capabilities, which lie deeply concealed, are all more or less the same. Success in work depends more on effort than on innate ability.' . . . Then he said something else that touched me: 'I didn't choose to become president. It was just the natural flow of things. I went along with the flow and accepted the decision of the others. I am able to work hard and do my best because of the tremendous support the leaders and other members give me.'
>
> Then I saw what I had to do. I must not try to run counter to the natural current of things. The time had come for me to open my eyes to the great harmony of the world and to my own part in it.
>
> (77–8)

Although this event marked a turning point in the life of Nichiko, it was still many years before he felt at ease in his new position. He dreaded public speaking, and would often become ill before a scheduled speech (92). But by facing his fears, he gradually overcame them. He also developed a more scholarly interest in Buddhism, and by the mid-1980s he could comment that he preferred 'to read the Buddhist scriptures in their original Chinese versions instead of in the annotated, modern-language translations . . . because a careful reading of the old text enables me to plumb the deep meanings that can be contained in only one or two [Chinese] characters' (DW June 1984, 37–8).

Nichiko has gained experience by heading various departments within the society, including the seminary and the missionary department. He has travelled a great deal, sometimes in the company of his father and sometimes as the head of a delegation. His itinerary has included China, India, Ceylon, the Vatican, and the United States, although travel does not interest him particularly. In Washington he met President and Mrs Carter, but 'was not especially thrilled at the meeting . . . I was happy to be back in Japan' (*My Father, My teacher*, 136).

He idolizes his father, but from a distance. The two have never been close.

> The ten years of separation, the years of living like strangers though under the same roof, and then the decision that I must inherit his position in the organization, still exert an influence on relations between Father and me. I have never entrusted my whole naked self to him, and he has always maintained reserve in connection with me. Even when we are watching the same television program, he looks at a set in one room and I a set in another. Mother and my wife ask why we do not use the same TV; but I object, and Father never suggests that we watch together. He believes in letting things take their natural course and never imposes his own will. I, too, believe in letting things go their natural ways. But whereas he is positive in his approach, I am negative.
>
> (127)

Nichiko's wife describes him as cautious, so cautious that 'he will not cross a stone bridge without tapping it beforehand to find out whether it is solid' (8). It seems logical that under his future leadership Rissho Kosei-kai will tap bridges before crossing them. The foundations have been laid and the course has been set; what has worked in the past should continue to work in the future.

President Niwano sometimes laments that the old fire which animated the early members seems to have died down. Rissho Kosei-kai is no longer a movement, but an institution. The milkman who once carried Mrs Myoko on his bicycle through the back streets of Tokyo to visit a prospective convert now rides in a limousine to greet foreign churchmen and statesmen. Rissho Kosei-kai has shifted its aim from the homes of its members, where lives are transformed, to international conference rooms, where resolutions are passed.

It may yet happen that Nichiko, who so hates ostentation and diplomacy, will quietly bring Rissho-Kosei-kai back where it started, and allow the burning embers to flare up from within. Kosei-kai has millions of well informed and enthusiastic members to draw on; it must find ways to let them be heard. It has already started in the right direction by abandoning the parent–child structure inherited from Reiyukai and replacing it with geographical branches. It has laid down solid foundations for future growth, and attained respectability. Now it must rejuvenate.

Chapter 19

Other Nichiren Groups Abroad

When a religion is alive and growing, it spawns sects and spin-off movements. Small doctrinal differences are vigorously debated among capable leaders and a concerned laity. Because the religion is seen as a source of power, that power must be correctly harnessed and directed. Doctrinal accuracy is vital, and misunderstandings are dangerous. On the other hand, when a religion is decaying, sectarianism loses its impetus and is replaced by yearnings for harmony, conformity, and strength in numbers. Burning issues from the past become orthodox traditions in the present — 'acceptable differences of opinion', which can be overlooked for the sake of peace. The white-hot volcanic eruptions of yesterday are the lifeless subsoil of today.

Nichiren Buddhism was conceived in the furnace of controversy. For three centuries it expanded vigorously, spawning new sub-sects as it did so. It replaced Tendai and Shingon esotericism as the favoured religion of the aristocracy at Kyoto and established new centres in the provinces. Tendai and Shingon, which had depended on the aristocracy for financial support, were reduced to the futile counter-measures of sending armed monks into the capital from time to time to burn Nichiren temples.

Nichiren Buddhism was not the only growing faith at the time; the other Kamakura sects of Zen and Pure Land were formidable rivals. Unlike the complex older sects, the new ones were simple enough to appeal to the masses and uncouth feudal barons. It was no longer sufficient, as the early missionaries had thought, just to win over the court at Kyoto. Real political power was divided among various warlords, and there was no way to predict which of them — if any — would finally emerge victorious.

Nichiren Buddhism found strong support among the rising middle class of merchants and craftsmen, who longed for peace and stability in the Buddha's earthly kingdom. They formed a literate class that could appreciate theological debates and support dissident priests founding new sub-sects. Such debates, however, were of little interest to the down-trodden peasants, who hoped for rebirth in Amida's Pure Land after death, or to warriors, who could identify better with wordless Zen and the 'honour' code of Bushido. In the late sixteenth century three warlords, Nobunaga, Hideyoshi, and Tokugawa Ieyasu, tightened their grip on the country and broke the political power of all religious sects.

Nobunaga openly encouraged the spread of Christianity to check the secular power of Buddhism; he almost destroyed Tendai, and massacred 3,000 monks on Mount Hiei. Hideyoshi continued his policy and broke the power of Shingon and Jodo Shinshu. Once he had beaten the Buddhists, he turned on the Christians. Ieyasu finished off the Christians and locked in the beaten Buddhists. Nichiren Buddhists were the last to hold out, but gradually they too succumbed to the lure of patronage instead of persecution.

During the long Tokugawa dictatorship (1600–1868) Buddhism was the official state religion. Every citizen was registered at some Buddhist temple, but was forbiden to change his religion. Proselytizing, so basic to Nichiren, was now forbidden by law. Buddhism basked comfortably under official patronage, and innovations came to a halt. Nonconformists such as the *Fujufuse* zealots were treated as non-persons and forced underground.

After the Meiji Restoration and the disestablishment of Buddhism, some Nichiren Buddhists, instead of despairing, saw new opportunities to convert the nation. For the first time in centuries proselytizing was again legal. However, the military imperialists, who were now the real powers behind the throne, wanted conformity and national unity. New religious movements (and suddenly there were many) were watched warily by the police, and if they were too independent were closed down. This pressure reached its climax during World War II. All Nichiren sects were ordered to unite under the nominal leadership of Mount Minobu. Doctrinal differences were overlooked by the conforming majority, but still vigorously maintained by dissidents.

At the end of the war total freedom of religion was instituted for the first time in Japanese history. Many of the old temple religions, deprived of their vast landholdings, suffered from the change, but new religions exploded into life. Nichiren sectarian movements, which already had a head-start from before the war, took the lead. Today some of the old temple sects are prospering, though others are not. But Nichiren Buddhism as a whole lends itself to lay participation, and it was laymen who took up the cry for building Buddha's world of peace and prosperity.

Hommon Butsuryu-shu

Hommon Butsuryu-shu takes sectarian differences seriously. Although it was founded as recently as the nineteenth century, it considers itself 'the sect that perfectly and thoroughly observes the teachings of Buddha and those of Nichiren Shonin (Sashida, *Guide to a New Believer*, 3). It has now opened a branch of 'the genuine Buddhist faith' in Honolulu. The name could be translated as 'The Fundamental Buddha Sect of the Original Gate'. Its origins go back to Nichiren via Keirin-bo Nichiryu (1384–1464), who was one of the greatest exponents of Nichiren Buddhism during its heroic age.

Nichiryu founded many temples, especially in western Japan, and is said to have written about 300 books. He was the son of a feudal lord from a province facing the Sea of Japan, and he inherited his father's militant spirit. As the oldest son and heir, he was destined to succeed to his father's fief, but at the impressionable age of 12 he was so inspired by the spirit of Nichiren that he asked and received his father's permission to enter the religious life.

His scholarly abilities impressed his teachers, and after only two years they encouraged him to leave the provinces and continue his studies in Kyoto. There he took up residence in the famous temple of Myohon-ji, which had been founded by the indomitable Ryuge-in Nichizo. But by then, life at the temple was very different. Nichiren Buddhism had become popular among the royal aristocracy of Kyoto, and Nichiryu found the temple full of idle courtiers, whose primary concerns were glamorous rituals and generous support from the imperial treasury.

Nichiryu saw that the chief abbot Nissai was under considerable pressure to conform to the status quo. Nissai resisted, winning the approval of his young student and others who believed that the Dharma must rule the state, not vice versa. When Nissai died in 1405 the conflict came to a head. He was succeeded by Gatsumyo, a scion of one of the best families in the capital and leader of the reactionary party. Nichiryu was outspoken in his opposition to this appointment and challenged Gatsumyo to a public debate. The debate aroused much interest in the capital. Gatsumyo, of course, was supported by the Court, which had appointed him, while Nichiryu was considered an upstart from the provinces. However, in spite of pressure on the judges from the Crown, the debate ended in a resounding victory for Nichiryu. But his triumph was short-lived. Nichiryu and his supporters were ordered out of the temple. They moved to another Nichiren temple, Myoren-ji, where they continued their agitation for an independent Nichiren Buddhism.

Six nobles, friends of Gatsumyo, decided to kill the rustic troublemaker. With drawn swords, they burst into the room where Nichiryu was chanting the Sutra before the Gohonzon. There they froze, each waiting for another to strike the first blow.

Nichiryu turned and faced them. 'Who are you?' he shouted. 'Who gave you permission to defile this sacred place?' The six Samurai, astonished at such courage, quickly lost their resolve. One by one they dropped to their knees, begged forgiveness, and asked to become Nichiryu's followers. This famous incident marked the beginning of Nichiryu's branch of Nichiren Buddhism.

Nichiryu, like most Nichiren dissidents, emphasized the *Shoretsu* teaching of the superiority of the Original Gate over the Imprinted Gate. *Shoretsu* proponents did not totally reject the first half of the Sutra, the Imprinted Gate, as Nichiren had sternly forbidden such extremes (MW 3:297). However, they insisted that the Original Gate is radically distinct from all previous Buddhist teachings, including the Tendai theoretical teachings. Their opponents from the majority Harmonious School (*Itchi*) claimed that the Imprinted Gate is indispensable for understanding the Original Gate, and therefore it cannot be said which of the two is superior or inferior. Nichiren may have taken the *Shoretsu* position — at any rate, many of his disciples thought he had — but he had not fully clarified this point, and so left the door open for future debates.

Nichiryu believed in the superiority of the Original Gate, which he defined as not the whole of the second half of the Sutra, but only what Nichiren had called 'the eight core chapters' (15–22). Therefore his branch is called the Eight Chapters Branch (*Happon-ha*).

Even from a purely literary point of view it is obvious that the Eight Chapters form a unit distinct from the chapters which follow, each of which reads like an independent composition. The Eight Chapters begin with the appearance of the Bodhisattvas from the Earth and end with their dismissal with instructions to propagate the Buddha's teachings. Nichiren described his Great Mandala as a graphic depiction of 'the eight vital chapters' (*MW*, 1:67, 1:211). Thus Nichiryu's followers venerate the Great Mandala-Gohonzon and reject all other Buddhist images. (An image of Nichiren, however, is placed in front of the Gohonzon.) They also stress vigorous *shakubuku* (missionary activity).

Hommon Butsuryu-shu began in the nineteenth century as a lay society within the Eight Chapters branch. It was really the first important modern Nichiren movement, antedating Tanaka's Kokuchukai and the more recent Reiyukai, Sokagakkai, and Rissho Kosei-kai. It was founded in 1857 by an Eight Chapters priest, Nagamatsu Nissen, and before its separation into an independent sect was called Hommon Butsuryu-ko.

The founder had been converted as an adult. He entered seminary full of enthusiasm, but was disappointed to find that his younger classmates had little interest in the distinctive teachings of the Eight Chapters Branch. They ignored the needs of the laity and were concerned mostly with carving out lucrative careers for themselves at wealthy temples. Nissen dropped out of the 'temple race', and together with some fellow-believers, both clerical and lay, he organized a lay society. He felt that the clergy were stuffy, mercenary, and over-scholarly, whereas true religion should be joyful and lively. He introduced songs, poetry, and group activities. His society was so successful that eventually the sect's leaders reluctantly had to instal him as chief priest of one of their largest temples.

He could not be lured back completely into the fold, however, and continued to follow an increasingly independent course. He translated the scriptures into the vernacular, organized study groups, and invited the direct participation of the laity in activities which had previously been reserved for the clergy. At the age of 55 he married, further distancing himself from the celibate clergy. He insisted that there are no qualitative differences between clergy and laity or between men and women. In his society the only distinctions between members were based on superior understanding of doctrine, and those who excelled were given honorary titles. This policy did not always go down well with 'male-chauvinist' members, but Nissen insisted, even threatening to resign if women were not treated as equals to men.

After Nissen's death the society carried on into the twentieth century. It was still nominally a part of the Eight Chapters Branch but completely self-governing. It assumed control of Nissen's temple of Yusei-ji and built other centres of its own, and the growth was steady although not spectacular. After World War II it finally declared total independence, changing its name from *ko* (society) to *shu* (sect). Its rate of growth increased, and it now has over half a million members and about 300 temples and study centres.

Hommon Butsuryu-shu now trains clergy of its own, but it still emphasises lay participation, doctrinal understanding, vigorous chanting of the Sacred Title, *shakubuku*, and the worldly benefits which can be gained by practising its teachings. Members follow the 'Bodhisattva way' (*Bosatsugyo*), 'helping others at the cost of our own life', and emphasize an attitude of grateful thanks for all benefits received from heaven and earth. It is still new in America, operating exclusively within the Japanese–American community, but we can expect to hear much more from it in the future.

Buddhist School of America

Nichijo Shaka is the most colourful and controversial Nichiren leader in America. In spite of his Japanese name, he is a Caucasian American from San Francisco. Born John D. Provoo in 1917, he was introduced to Oriental philosophy by his mother, who was an early Montessori advocate. She later converted to Buddhism under the guidance of her son. Provoo was so impressed by Buddhism that in 1940 he accepted the Precepts (formally converted) under the Rev. Shobo Aoyagi of the Sacramento Nichiren Buddhist Church. Never one to do things by halves, he went to Japan to study for the priesthood at Mount Minobu. He had been there seven months when his studies were cut short by a call from his draft board back in California (*Young East*, Autumn 1965, 13).

The draft board ignored his claim to be a theological student and assigned him to the army, which soon shipped him back to the Orient, this time to the Philippines. When the Japanese invaded the Philippines in 1941, Provoo suddenly found himself in the thick of desperate fighting. However, with the fall of the American fortress of Corregidor, he was taken prisoner.

Provoo was one of the few American prisoners who could speak Japanese. Moreover, he had a lively interest in Buddhism and Japanese culture. The Japanese found him a willing spokesman for the prisoners — perhaps too willing. Within two days of his capture, he was thought to have made accusations against an American lieutenant which led to the latter's execution. As the weary years passed, many American prisoners, who were living under appalling conditions, came to resent Provoo's behaviour and favoured treatment from their Japanese captors. They believed that his cooperation with the enemy had passed over to collaboration. 'The consensus among the men on Corregidor,' says Lt. Gen. John Wright, a former fellow-prisoner, 'was that Provoo was a traitor, a turncoat, a self-centered individual not to be trusted.'

When the war ended, Provoo was at first overlooked in the flush of victory, but his fellow-prisoners of war had not forgotten him. Eventually some of them managed to get him charged with collaboration with the enemy — treason — and brought to trial. Throughout the trial Provoo steadfastly maintained his innocence, but former prisoners lined up against him. Among them was no less a personage than General Wainwright, the highest ranking American prisoner of war. Provoo was found guilty and condemned to a federal prison. His lawyers, however, had not yet given up, and carried his case to the Supreme Court of the United States. There he was declared innocent on a technicality: the statute of limitations had expired. Provoo's conviction was reversed, and he was set free.

In 1965 a large Japanese delegation came to the United States to participate in the 12th Congress of the World Association of World Federalists. The delegation was headed by Archbishop Nichijo Fujii, the highest ranking abbot of Nichiren Shu. After the close of the congress some of the delegates, including Archbishop Fujii and Professor Senchu Murano, made a tour of the United States to meet American Buddhists. In New York City Professor Murano was approached by John Provoo, who asked to be introduced to the Archbishop. The two got on well. Provoo became the personal disciple of the Archbishop, who took him back to Japan to continue his studies at Mount Minobu.

Provoo concluded his studies satisfactorily. He was ordained a priest, and in 1968 the Archbishop gave him the right to train and ordain future American aspirants. Provoo changed his name to Nichijo Shaka — Nichijo in honour of the Archbishop and Shaka for Shakyamuni Buddha. By 1981, when he came to the 'Big Island' of Hawaii, he had trained and ordained 17 priests, of whom many were women. (*The Honolulu Advertiser*, 30 August 1981)

Nichijo Shaka never attempted to start a mass movement. His aim was to establish an American training centre for serious students who would then bring orthodox Nichiren Buddhism back to their home towns. Because he wanted his centre to be purely American, he refused to accept official support for it as a Nichiren Shu foreign mission. He lived simply as a Buddhist monk, and it was not until Dr Richard E. Peterson of the University of Hawaii gave him the use of three acres on the 'Big Island' that he was able to build a permanent centre.

Like Nichiren, who was finally granted land on Minobu only to find his health deteriorating, Nichijo Shaka found himself in the same predicament. He founded the 'Buddhist School of America: Perfect Law of the Lotus Teaching' when he was too ill to supervise it properly. Therefore he ordained the Rev. Nichizo Finney as his successor, and took him to Minobu to complete his training. (*History of Nichiren Buddhism in Hawaii*, 34, in Japanese)

Nichjo Shaka's career is drawing to its close. The success or failure of his efforts now rests with those he trained, and their impact remains to be seen.

Great Sangha of Nichihonzan Myohoji _____

The most extraordinary of the modern Nichiren missionaries was the late Nichidatsu Fujii, also known as Guruji. He died in 1985, just short of his 100th birthday, after a lifetime of 'beating the drum for the Dharma'. He, too, made no attempt to found a mass movement, but today his devoted followers, few in numbers but valiant in spirit, can be found on every continent.

In the course of his long and colourful career, Guruji's position underwent a 180-degree turn from ardent nationalist and collaborator with Japanese military expansion to radical pacifist and anti-war activist. He was ordained a priest in 1903 at a temple that traced its lineage back to Toki Jonin. Wishing to get a thorough understanding of all types of Japanese Buddhism, he spent the next 10 years studying the teachings of one sect after another: Nichiren, Tendai, Jodo, Hosso, Shingon, and Zen. Although he never deserted his own sect and always considered it the culmination of the whole of Buddhism, he also developed a deep appreciation for other forms of spirituality. When he was 25 he volunteered for one-year military service in the army, after which he returned to his studies. At the age of 28 he had a dream which told him that after his thirty-third birthday he was to practise not only for himself but for others (*Shujo-kyoke*). When he approached that age he began to undertake severe ascetic training. Finally, in the tradition of Toki Jonin, he ordained himself to his great task to spread the gospel of Nichiren and save the world.

In those days many Nichiren Buddhists were inspired by the fiery teachings of Tanaka, who maintained not only the supremacy of Nichiren Buddhism but also the obligation of the Emperor to sponsor its propagation: 'Japan has the mission to propagate the law of the Lotus Sutra and thereby redeem the world' (Satomi, 1923, 111). When Nichidatsu reached the destined age of 33 he decided to awaken the Emperor to his heaven-given mandate. He sat down before the Royal Palace, picked up his drum, and began to beat it to the chant *Namu Myoho Renge Kyo*. Of course, the police soon removed him, but Tanaka's philosophy was not without sympathizers in the imperial government. They had noticed that Western imperialism generally sent in the missionaries first, the merchants second, and finally the army. Why should Japan not do the same thing? Instead of throwing Nichidatsu into jail, it might be better to harness his zeal and use it for their own purposes.

The Japanese authorities had been setting up National Shinto shrines in China and Korea to mark their conquests in those countries, but the locals resented them and refused to worship there. On the other hand, many Chinese and Koreans were devout Buddhists, and Japanese Buddhism might just be the missing link to join their hearts to those of their new masters.

Nichidatsu was easily persuaded that he could serve both his Emperor and the Dharma if he carried the Dharma westward to Manchuria in the footsteps of the first great Nichiren foreign missionary, Renge Ajari Nichiji. This would seem to fulfil the prophecy of Nichiren in *Kangyo-Hachiman-sho*: 'The moon rises in the west and travels eastward, signifying the spread of the Dharma of the Buddha of *Gasshi* (the country of the moon: India) to the east. The sun rises in the east and travels westward, signifying the spread of the Buddhism of Japan to the west.'

Accordingly Nichidatsu organized a group of fellow-zealots to carry the Dharma to foreign shores. They donned yellow robes like the monks of southern Buddhism rather than the traditional robes of Japanese monks, thus emphasizing their pan-Buddhist internationalism, and departed for Manchuria. There they gave themselves the name of Nippon-zan Myohoji Dai-sanga ('Japan-Mountain Wonderful Dharma-Temple Great Sangha'). The name was a curious mixture of internationalism ('Great Sangha'), Nichiren Buddhism ('Myohoji') and Japanese nationalism ('Nippon-zan'). Later, when the organization had become pacifist, the pronunciation was generally given a more Nichiren-like flavour: 'Nichihonzan'.

The Japanese Imperial Government adopted the new organization, transported the monks to China, and gave them military ranks after the model of Imperial Russia. In the 1920s they were considered important participants in Japan's expansion into China. In fact, when one of the monks was assassinated by a Chinese nationalist in 1931, the Japanese government used the incident as an excuse to punish China. The assassin's shot was really an opening gun of World War II. Nichidatsu, who had the innocent heart of a child, was probably unaware that he was being used as a pawn in international politics. His only desire was to spread the Dharma and, like most Japanese, especially those influenced by Tanaka, he had implicit faith in the noble intentions of the Emperor. What was good for Japan was good for the Dharma, and what was good for the Dharma was good for the world.

His first monastery was built at Tai Lien, Manchuria, in 1918, and it was there that the missionary society was formally inaugurated. The monasteries, which were always quite small, were called simply *dojos* ('places where Buddhism is practised and enlightenment is attained').

Life for the monks was rigorous. They may have held the ranks of military officers, but they considered themselves soldiers of the spirit, locked in deadly combat with the forces of evil. They lived in poverty, suffering from the cold winters, sparse provisions, and silent hostility from the natives. Nichidatsu's father died in northern Korea in 1919, so his mother joined him in Manchuria, where she took monastic vows and shared the hardships (Fujii, *Buddhism for World Peace* 102). Fujii deeply venerated his mother, and after her death in 1930 usually launched important projects on her death-day, 25 February.

The great Kanto earthquake of 1923, which had such impact on Kubo of Reiyukai and Niwano of Rissho Kosei-kai, marked a turning-point in the career of Nichidatsu Fujii as well. He had been planning to carry his mission into Soviet Russia, and had taken the Siberian Railway as far as Harbin, when he heard the dreadful news. Immediately he changed his plans and hurried home (103). As a good Nichiren Buddhist, he was convinced that this terrible catastrophe was the result of the sins of Japan. To the consternation of the government which had been sponsoring him, he began to call for national repentance: Japan was guilty of exchanging Eastern spirituality for Western materialism. He now established his mission in his native country, and soon found himself harrassed by the secret police (103).

The death of his beloved mother in 1930 also marked another turning-point. It freed him to undertake what had always been his supreme ambition: to fulfil the prophecy of Nichiren and carry the Dharma from East to West, further than China — to India itself. The government no longer supported him or wanted him back in China, but it would not object — in fact, it would be pleased — if he went to India as a private citizen. He took the ashes of his mother to Minobu for interment, and there made a solemn vow:

May the Buddha have pity and let my vow be accomplished, the

great vow which is far beyond my capacity. I desire to take the
initiative in realizing the auspicious omen of the Buddhism of
Japan returning to the Western Heaven, India, as it is
prophesied. I desire to regenerated the spiritual civilization of
Asia, the Orient, and subdue the sixty-two kinds of people with
false views. I desire to deliver equally all humanity from the
murderous civilization of the European and United States *asuras*
(fighting spirits), the inferno of confusion consolidated with strife.
Follow me, one after another, to beat the *dokku* (drum) at the
Himalayas, and let the rain of the Dharma pour into the stream
of the Ganga!

If this Dharma does not return to the Western Heaven, the
prophecy of our great master (Nichiren) shall become a
falsehood.

If this Dharma does not return to the Western Heaven, our
bodhisattva-way will not be completed.

If this Dharma does not return to the Western Heaven, sentient
beings of this world of ours will eternally be unable to escape
from the prison of fire, strife, and bloodshed.

(38–9)

Although the Imperial Japanese government was already casting
covetous eyes towards India, it no longer trusted Nichidatsu to further
its purposes, and this time offered him no assistance. He arrived in
Calcutta in 1931 with little more than his drum and a few Japanese
trinkets, and set off at once to visit Indian Buddhist holy places. The
sight of their ruined and abandoned condition filled him with sorrow,
and he resolved to do something about it. Meanwhile he settled on the
premises of a crematory at Bombay, where he practised rigid asceticism, surviving on scraps of food which were tossed his way. Day and
night he beat his drum to the chant *Namu Myoho Renge Kyo*. People
regarded him as some sort of foreign fakir.

Then he met Gandhi, and once more his life turned a corner. Their
first meeting lasted only 15 minutes, but Nichidatsu was so overcome
with emotion at being in the presence of Gandhi that he could only
stand with his hands pressed reverently together while tears of joy
poured down his face. His translator, one of his monks, had to do all the
talking. At first, Gandhi was somewhat suspicious of these two representatives of 'Japanese imperialism', but soon Nichidatsu's sincerity
began to impress him. He invited him to stay on at the ashram so that
they could speak further. Nichidatsu accepted gladly.

It is thanks to Gandhi that Nichidatsu became completely dedicated
to the cause of non-violence, or as he put it, the Buddhist precept of
non-killing. In Gandhi he saw the personification of his idea: the
spirituality of the East overcoming the materialism of the West. Gandhi
saw in Nichidatsu a kindred soul, and it was he who gave him the Indian

name of Guruji. When one day Gandhi picked up Guruji's drum and began to beat it in time to the chant, Nichidatsu was overjoyed.

> When Gandhi-ji beat the Dharma-drum of *Na mu Myo Ho Ren Ge Kyo*, and when the Japanese disciples of the Buddha lived with him in his ashram, the independence of India was assured in the near future. Ah! Indeed, today we were able to fulfill the momentous mission of Japan borne by our great master and founder Nichiren at the Age of *Mappo* (Decline of the Dharma) in the Western Heaven! Whatever slander and calumny I must bear, who can negate the fact that I have been able to fulfill (my) mission? ... I have beaten the drum ... seeking for this single man. He was the person I had long been looking for. He, who had considered even the sweets, beautiful fan, and cotton goods from Japan [which Nichidatsu had brought as gifts] as enemies of India, needless to mention the policies of the Japanese government, has today immediately accepted without doubt, the traditional Japanese instrument handed down from the ages of the gods, the sound of the Dharma-drum of *Na mu Myo Ho Ren Ge Kyo*, which is the prayer for *Rissho-ankoku*, as a peerless friend to his religious life ... The profound sound of a single Japanese round drum beaten by Gandhi-ji, who is bursting into laughter, was the war drum of India's independence movement ... We were drawn into the laughter of Gandhi-ji and laughed rejoicingly together. It was like a dream.
>
> (62–3)

When Gandhi departed on his mission to the Untouchables, he took the drum with him. Is it only coincidental that the Untouchables later began to convert by the millions to Buddhism?

Guruji spent many years wandering about India and Ceylon (Sri Lanka) beating his drum. He began to attract attention as a friend of Gandhi and a holy man in his own right. In 1935 he opened a *dojo* in Calcutta, and the following year he started the restoration of Rajgir, the Vulture Peak where the Buddha had preached the *Dharma Flower*. The project was not to be completed, however, until 1969, after World War II and the independence of India. His movement continued without him in China and Japan, but the outbreak of the war brought further expansion to a halt. During the war Guruji devoted himself to fasting and praying for peace.

He was 60 years old when the atomic bombs were dropped on Hiroshima and Nagasaki. By the following year he was launched on the final and most active period of his life, the quest for world peace. The invention and use of the atomic bomb convinced him that Western civilization, which he equated with materialism, could bring the world to destruction. He would resist it everywhere by erecting 'peace pagodas', which would stand like beacons reminding people of the primacy of the spiritual over the material. These peace pagodas, generally built in the traditional bell-shaped style of Indian stupas, were to be strictly non-sectarian; they were for all mankind.

Nichihonzan Myohoji has become famous for its construction of peace pagodas. As of this writing, more than 50 of them have been built, mostly in Japan, but also in Sri Lanka, India, and even London. All were built free of charge by the monks and volunteers from various world peace movements. Whenever possible, Guruji would supervise each one personally. The dedication of a peace pagoda was often accompanied by much ceremony and publicity, sometimes involving heads of state. The inauguration of one at the model village of Milton Keynes, UK, was attended by Her Majesty the Queen.

During the last 20 years of his life Guruji was loaded with honours, especially from India and Sri Lanka. In 1979, when he was 95 years old, he was given the Jawaharlal Nehru Award for International Understanding. Crowds turned out to see him wherever he went. He made no effort to convert them, particularly if they were already Buddhists as in Sri Lanka, but would beam with happiness if anyone would pick up a drum and begin to chant *Namu Myoho Renge Kyo*.

He was not always well received. In Nepal, where he planned to erect a peace pagoda at Lumbini (Shakyamuni's birthplace), he attracted large crowds of eager volunteers and well-wishers. But the project ran foul of local politics, and the construction was destroyed by government order (*Rissho Ankoku*, 45). It took the efforts of the United Nations to get a monument finally raised there.

Guruji made it easy for people to become one of his monks or nuns. Celibacy was not required (*World Peace*, 227), and there were few rules. He believed that once the Dharma seed is planted in someone's heart, it will bring forth fruit by itself; sincerity is the one requisite. However, when 'hippies' began to be attracted to his order, he forbade the use of drugs (243).

The monks and nuns were also forbidden to solicit funds even for good causes. 'The propagation of the truth of the Lotus Sutra is incompatible with the collection of donations. We should carefully keep ourselves from collecting wealth under the pretext of the construction of Peace Pagodas or Monasteries. The realization of Buddhahood and world peace can be obtained only through our strenuous work based on persistent faith, and never through receiving donations' (*Ju Ryo Hon*).

His theology, built firmly on the teachings of Nichiren, was simple. 'To actually carry out religious teachings is called *shugyo* (religious practice). It must be one which is the simplest and can be the most easily performed. That is, to place one's hands together, worshipping through the body, chanting *Na mu Myo Ho Ren Ge Kyo* through the mouth, and cherishing respect [for all living beings] in the mind and heart (like the Bodhisattva Never-Despise). Spiritual salvation, the fervent desire of the World Honored One, Shakyamuni Buddha, will be fulfilled by such minute actions by us. When religious and spiritual teachings towards the heaven and earth, the universe, are applied to the social life of man, and when everyone respects and venerates each other, how can there be room for war to break out? The fundamental cause of war, nuclear warfare, is nothing more than a calamity incurred by the non-religious faithless civilization of science, which neither respects nor pays veneration towards others' (*World Peace*, 262).

He was an outspoken critic of American foreign policy. In 1968 he came to New York to participate in the anti-Vietnam War movement. Ten years later, when he was 94, he returned to deliver to Kurt Waldheim, Secretary General of the United Nations, 20 million signatures calling for the liquidation of atomic weapons. He supported the 'Longest Walk' of the American Indian Movement, although by then he was too old to participate in the walk personally. Many of his monks did, however, and he met them in Washington, D.C., where he founded a *dojo*. Other American *dojos* were established on the West Coast.

Nichidatsu Fujii Guruji never intended his Nipponzan Myohoji to be a sect. He considered that Nichiren Buddhism transcends all sectarianism, and he always remained spiritually if not administratively loyal to Mount Minobu. Not long before his death he said:

It appears that what I have been devoting my life to, the Righteous Dharma, is now going to be spread throughout the world. I am fully confident about it.

There is no other way out today if humanity wishes to survive. And this is the only reason for which Nichiren Bodhisattva appeared on this earth at the beginning of the Era of Decay.

Seven hundred years after his demise, I repeated his action, coming into the world for the sole purpose of saving humanity from the danger of total annihilation by propagating ODAIMOKU (NAMU MYOHO RENGE KYO) throughout the world.

This single word, the RIGHTEOUS AND ALL EMBRACING DHARMA, can alone be the last refuge for all humanity in the future.

The Saddharma Pundarika (Lotus) Sutra says, 'I leave this powerful medicine for you at this place.' and this is the wholesome means of salvation of the compassionate Tathagata.

Then, 'Take it! Do not be afraid that you will not be cured.'

You shall be cured!

You shall be cured without fail!

NA MU MYO HO REN GE KYO.

(*Ju-Ryoh-Hon*)

Chapter 20

'To Save All the People of the World'

'All that we are,' says an early Buddhist sutra, 'is the result of what we have thought; it is founded on our thoughts; it is made up of our thoughts. If a man speaks or acts with an evil thought, pain follows him, as the wheel follows the foot of the ox that draws the carriage' (*Dhammapada*).

This basic idea is found in all schools of Buddhism: we are responsible for our own destiny. Nichiren, however, extends it further: destiny is not only individual, it is collective. We suffer as individuals because suffering is universal. The remedy is not escape from this world; this is impossible, as we are part and parcel of the world. The remedy is to remove *collective* suffering: 'Establish the Right Law and save the country.'

It is for the purpose of attaining Buddhahood by the teaching of the Buddha that one renounces his family and becomes a monk. I also became a monk for the same purpose. Now I see that no Shinto or Buddhist god can do anything to avert these calamities. Judging from this, I cannot believe that I shall be able to be reborn in a Buddha-world and attain Buddhahood in my future life. This may come from my ignorance. Looking up to heaven, I lamented bitterly, and lying with my face to the ground, I pondered the reasons for such calamities.

I racked my poor brain and read sutras to find out why these things happened. At last I have reached the following conclusion. The government and people of this country are standing against the Right Law. They believe wrong teachings. Therefore, the gods have deserted this country and the saints have left us. *Maras* and devils have come instead. That is why the calamities have taken place. I should say this. The cause of [dreadful] calamities is [itself] dreadful.

(*Rissho Ankoku Ron*)

The cause of so many calamities is wrong thinking, but especially the most prevalent wrong thinking. He identified this as the Pure Land Buddhism advocated by Honen. It was sweeping the country at the same time that the country was sinking into misery, and this could not be a coincidence. 'If a man speaks or acts with an evil thought, pain follows him as the wheel follows the foot of the ox that draws the carriage.' To eradicate the pain, one must eliminate the cause — wrong thought.

Nichiren attacked Honen's doctrine from every angle. It is basically selfish because it seeks individual escape, and selfishness is the root cause of all sufferings. It is one-sided, closing the door on all other teachings of the Buddha. It is novel and unorthodox. It is other-worldly, turning people's attention from this world to a paradise beyond the grave. It is inconsistent, claiming that it can save even evil men, while its own sutra, *Muryoju-kyo*, bars from Amida's paradise 'those beings who have committed the five deadly sins, and who have spoken evil of the good Law'. And finally, it fails to acknowledge the supremacy of the *Dharma Flower*. At its best the Pure Land doctrine is a temporary teaching capable of helping ignorant and uneducated people along the way; at its worst, by becoming exclusive and shutting out all other teaching (as advocated by Honen), it is a source of infinite miseries.

Later Nichiren extended his criticisms to include any system short of the all-inclusive *Dharma Flower*. Religions distinguish between insiders and outsiders, the saved and the damned. According to the *Dharma Flower* there are no outsiders. Sectarianism, the attempt to separate 'us' from 'them', is wrong from the outset.

Since all beings exist within the one Buddha-nature, there would seem to be no reason to evangelize or propagate the right Dharma. Everyone is enlightened already, no matter who or what he is, but 'Original Enlightenment' is a perversion of what the *Dharma Flower* teaches. *There is no individual enlightenment*; enlightenment is universal.[87] The Sacred Source is itself enlightenment and 'the parent of all the Buddhas'. The Mahayana Sutras constantly tell us that we cannot 'grasp' enlightenment. We can receive it, we can participate in it, but we cannot possess it.

This is the significance of the Sacred Formula, *Odaimoku*. Nichidatsu Fujii says, 'It is the power of the Lord Buddha given to us by him. It took the form of a word and was bestowed on us. All the Dharma, all the unrestricted transcendental powers, and all the inconceivable spheres of the Buddha were encompassed by the word of *Odaimoku* and given to us' (*World Peace*, 188–9).

It will do me no good to go off to a mountaintop and there awaken to enlightenment. Unless you are enlightened, too, my enlightenment is only partial — an expedient, to use the term of the *Dharma Flower*. Even Shakyamuni Buddha's enlightenment under the Bodhi Tree was just an expedient. Perfect enlightenment (*Anuttara-samyak-sambodhi*) is universal and timeless by its very nature; either it involves everyone or it does not take place at all. Meanwhile, the only advantage held by a believer over a non-believer lies in 'benefits'; his life will run smoother, and he will be happier than the non-believer. Firmly centred in the Buddha's infinite compassion, he can face obstacles in his path and overcome them one by one, but until he can spread that security to others his own happiness is partial, not total. He must proclaim *Odaimoku* for others as well as for himself. This is the built-in missionary imperative of Nichiren Buddhism.

In the twentieth century Nichiren Buddhism has burst forth from its Japanese boundaries and become global. Sometimes its missionary effort is institutional, well financed, and well organized; at other times it is personal, without any visible means of support, and strongly individualistic. Nichiren Shoshu/Sokagakkai is the best example of the former; Nichidatsu Fujii Guruji and Nichijo Shaka are exemplars of the latter. They did not seek to make converts, their only desire being to let people hear the drumbeat of the Wonderful Dharma and become aware of its existence. They wanted to 'sow the seed of Buddhahood' far and wide. The Lord Buddha would bring the seeds to fruition in good time, just as the warming rays of the sun cause plants to shoot up once the seed has been sown. This is why so many Nichiren Buddhists pound a drum as they chant. It is not necessary that people believe; belief and understanding will come eventually. The truth is irresistible, but it is necessary that everyone should hear it.

Guruji sought to make the all-saving Dharma visible as well as audible. He built Peace Pagodas from Nepal to London as beacons to hasten the day of world harmony. Other Nichiren groups have raised the banner of world peace in their own ways. Reiyukai seeks to realize it through friendship, Rissho Kosei-kai through mutual understanding. Under the leadership of Archbishop Nichijo Fujii, Nichiren Shu espoused the cause of World Federalism. However, none are as active as Sokagakkai in sponsoring huge rallies for world peace and friendship.

Nichiren Shu, too, after basking for centuries under official patronage, is now reaching out to the laity. In 1966 it launched the 'Protect the Dharma Movement' to organize its followers locally and regionally along lines not unlike those of the new religions. A uniform service for all members was put into effect, which is exactly what Niwano of Kosei-kai had wanted Nichiren Shu to do 20 years before.

Nichiren's missionary imperative divides the world into two classes of people: those who are consciously saving the world and those who are unconsciously causing its misery. No one is neutral. The only way to save the world from its sorrows is to 'beat the drum of the Dharma' as far afield as possible. Now that centuries of government-imposed restrictions have been lifted, Nichiren Buddhists have once more sprung into action. Since the Second World War, Nichiren Buddhism has grown more rapidly than any other Japanese religion and has now moved into the number one slot long enjoyed by Pure Land (Shin) Buddhism, as well as branching out to foreign shores. Japanese emigrants and businessmen have carried it with them to every continent, setting up Nichiren-inspired societies even in such traditionally Buddhist countries as Thailand and Nepal. Their goal is straightforward: to gain peace for the world and salvation for themselves. The two go together; there cannot be one without the other.

Besides the missionary imperative, each Nichiren believer is called to develop his individual potential. This is what 'becoming a Buddha' means to him: he must face the absolute on a one-to-one basis. There is no intermediary between him and the Gohonzon. No esoteric master will initiate him into higher mysteries, no Zen *roshi* guides his progress, and there is no divine or semi-divine saviour to shoulder his problems. Even the holy book, the *Sutra of the Dharma Flower*, only leads him to the door. It is but a symbol, the quintessence of which is contained in its title. Armed only with this Sacred Title, the Nichiren believer is called to emulate the founder and persist until he has attained to Buddhahood. No obstacle can overcome him, no set-back is permanent. Within him lies the power of infinite creativity.

No true Nichiren Buddhist can accept his religion spoon-fed and second-hand. Of course, many nominal believers are content to rely on heavenly Bodhisattvas, charismatic leaders, sacred objects and talismans. Here as everywhere there are more followers than leaders, but individual self-expression always lies just beneath the surface and can burst forth when least expected. The history of Nichiren Buddhism is replete with 'heresies' and spin-off movements. Since everyone must face the Gohonzon one-to-one, the results can be explosive. Strong personalities, from Nikko in the thirteenth century to Guruji in the twentieth, have refused to bow down before any authority except their own conscience.

The real centre for the believer is not his sect but his personal life. Peer organizations like Sokagakkai and other tightly knit societies reinforce what the believer is doing at home and at work by himself. He sets up his own home altar arranged according to the tenets of his particular sect, and this serves as his mystical link with the world of Buddha. It is his personal *kaidan*, the sacred platform where he realizes the Dharma and encounters the Ground of Being. It is here where he changes the quality of his inner life. Normally he performs his devotions twice a day, for about 30 minutes each time, although if he belongs to Nichiren Shoshu he may spend many hours at it.

Whether he is at work or play he puts his whole self into it, changing the quality of this world into Buddha's world. All Nichiren believers chant *Odaimoku*, the Sacred Title, as often as possible throughout the day, whether at home, at work, riding in a bus, or winding up to pitch a baseball. They may give it different interpretations; to some the mantra has magical power, and the more it is recited, the better it will work. For them any problem can be met and overcome through vigorous chanting. For others, it calms and directs the mind by shutting out distractions. For members of Reiyukai, which has its own method of chanting (pronouncing each syllable slowly, beginning softly and ending in a shout), it is a battle cry meaning 'I am going to do my best to make the teachings of the Lotus Sutra come alive in my own life' (*Inner Quest* December 1983, 18).

Another practice common to all Nichiren groups is reciting passages from the *Dharma Flower*. The traditional groups call this the 'secondary practice', but in Rissho Kosei-kai and Reiyukai it is primary. 'It is easy to say that we must know our mind and reform our evil ways,' says a Reiyukai flier, 'but we need a mirror to reflect our mind. The holy sutras are this mirror. By their recitation, we are given a chance to see and contemplate our mind. They guide us to a better knowledge of ourselves' (*The Reiyukai*).

Each denomination has its own favourite scriptural selections, but two are used by nearly all. These are the opening passages of Chapter II, 'Expedients', which introduce the message of the Imprinted Gate that everyone can become a Buddha, and the verses of Chapter XVI, 'The Duration of the Tathagata's Life', the heart of the Original Gate. The latter reveals the essence of the Buddha's original enlightenment: the eternity of all beings as the foundation of universal compassion.

> I am always thinking:
> How shall I cause all living beings
> To enter into the unsurpassed Way
> And quickly become Buddhas, themselves?
>
> (Chap. XVI)

Most groups add other passages at the beginning and end of the recitation. Nichiren Shu now has a fixed service, but advises its members that they may alter it for variety's sake. Chanting is done at a deliberate pace, often to the beat of a drum or wooden clapper. Nichiren Shoshu uses the above two chapters only, repeating them up to five times, and only in the original Chinese;[88] Other groups permit the vernacular or foreign-language translations.

Rissho Kosei-kai recommends private devotional reading or recitation of the entire Threefold Lotus Sutra, generally by taking one chapter a day. No other group places such emphasis on rational understanding of the Sutra and basic Buddhist doctrines. In this way it departs from the Nichiren norm, which sees the Sutra as a means but not an end. Rissho Kosei-kai is the most ecumenical of the Nichiren-derived groups, seeking to balance Mahayana faith with southern Buddhist rationalism. Reiyukai, on the other hand, by refusing to define the absolute and insisting that the believer face the 'spirit world' directly, retains the spirit if not the letter of Nichiren.

In Nichiren Shoshu the study of Nichiren's writings has all but replaced studying the Sutra; doctrinal understanding plays an important role. Doctrine is even more important in Rissho Kosei-kai, where the Sutra is consulted as a guide to daily conduct. This has led Kosei-kai to train its own professional ministry to interpret the Sutra correctly. The same process happened in Hommon Butsuryu-shu, which began as a lay society and ended by ordaining its most qualified participants. Today it draws a sharp line between clergy and laity. For instance, no layman may touch his Gohonzon; if he wishes to clean it, he must call a priest to do it for him.

The *Dharma Flower* is a unique book. Beginning at Chapter XV (the Original Gate), it propounds that the historical Buddha is the eternal Buddha. In *The Lotus Sutra and Religious Realities*, Dr Yensho Kanakura, Member of the Japan Academy, points out that 'the identification of historical existence with eternal existence, in other words, the identification of phenomenon with noumenon, or of reality with ideality, is a very unique thought, not found in other Buddhist sutras or non-Buddhist sutras, including the scriptures of Hinduism. The repeated statement in the Lotus Sutra that this sutra is very difficult to understand, very difficult to believe, may come from the difficulty in understanding this relationship' (2). Since the Ten Worlds including Buddhahood are contained in a moment's thought, this 'identification of historical existence with eternal existence' applies as much to the individual as to the Buddha.

Nichiren was correct when he said that no one before him — not even Chih-i or Dengyo Daishi (Saicho) — had successfully depicted this identification in graphic form. The Sacred Source can be named — 'Eternal Buddha Shakyamuni', for example. The first part of the name is transcendant, the second historical; the two are one Person. However, the name in itself separates the Buddha from our own lives. How can ultimate reality be expressed to show that it is both within us and beyond us?

Nichiren attempts to do this in his Great Mandala-Gohonzon. He depicts ultimate reality as the *relationship* of all beings to each other and to the One Law: *Namu Myoho Renge Kyo*. This One Law brings us, too, into the proper relationship. The Gohonzon is as subtle and profound as the truth it displays; it is both objective and subjective, the many and the one. Nichiren believers find it the perfect manifestation of the Truth 'so difficult to understand'.

It is one thing to expound the 'three thousand things in one mind', as the Sutra does, or to depict it, as Nichiren does; it is more difficult to maintain it. As the old sects became institutionalized, they lost their human touch. The new sects have poured into the vacuum, emphasizing 'heart-to-heart communication', but in stressing 'the many' they risked losing identity with 'the one' — the identity that Nichiren considered crucial. In Reiyukai and Rissho Kosei-kai the Eternal Buddha Shakyamuni is worshipped in the form of a giant statue. As such, he becomes an object of worship distinct from and far above us common mortals.

Helen Hardacre describes the extraordinary theatrics used at Shakaden, Reiyukai headquarters, to present the Eternal Buddha to an adoring public (*Lay Buddhism*, 79):

> The side walls of the auditorium are paneled with very thin, streaked marble, lit from behind. At a signal from the mistress of ceremonies, the audience began to chant the daimoku. As we chanted, the overhead lights began to dim, leaving only the pale green light from behind the marble, and a blue ultraviolet light shining down on something behind the brass doors of the altar. After five minutes or so, eerie music of violins and falsetto voices began, and slowly, as the chanting continued, the great brass doors began to open. Parting, they revealed a huge unpainted wooden statue of Shakyamuni, the right hand raised in the *abhaya*, 'fear not' mudra. Even from the back of the hall, the five-meter high statue evoked audible gasps of astonishment. Gradually the chanting ceased as the audience sat staring at the statue. Some people were crying or praying. Later, people I interviewed said that the statue was alive. A voice was heard, telling the audience to make a vow in the presence of the Buddha on how we would live our lives from that moment on. After an interval of perhaps five minutes more, we began chanting the daimoku again, and the doors closed.

Nearly all the domestic and foreign missions of the Nichiren societies are well financed, enabling them to put on a good appearance before the public. Salaried employees, however, can become entrenched bureaucrats, and the spirit of innovation can get buried in committees. 'Busy-ness' can replace real accomplishment. The calendar of events at a mission headquarters in California, staffed by three or four full-time employees, often reveals less activity than is found at a Protestant church down the street, manned by one hard-working pastor. Sokagakkai International, on the other hand, has demonstrated that missions are most successful when conducted by enthusiastic volunteers, who work in their own time and at their own expense, evangelizing with all their hearts to usher in the happy world of *kosen rufu*.

It is often said that Nichiren was the most intolerant of all Buddhist teachers. 'Nichiren is the pillar and beam of Japan,' he told the officer

come to arrest him and later reiterated in writing. 'If you lose me, you
will be toppling the pillar of Japan! Immediately we will face the
disaster of . . . conflict within the realm and also foreign invasion. Not
only will the people of our nation be put to death by foreign invaders,
but many of them will be taken prisoner. All the Nembutsu and Zen
temples . . . should be burned to the ground and their priests taken out
to Yui beach to have their heads cut off! If this is not done, then Japan
is certain to be destroyed' (MW 3.171). He was a 'monotheist' who
maintained that there could be but one Dharma and one Buddha. His
followers have carried on his militant spirit by challenging all rivals to
public debate. A defeated foe is then expected to drop his old religion
for the true faith.

Nichiren Buddhists, however, have been less willing to give up their
position even after defeat in a debate. They prefer death to compromise, and their stubbornness has sometimes brought persecution down
on their heads. The *Dharma Flower* praises those who are 'willing to
lay down their lives' for the truth. In some cases, outlawed Nichiren
Buddhists will 'go underground', as did the *Fuju-fuse* believers, but
rarely will they renege.

Nichiren Buddhists see themselves as possessing a mandate to save
their country and through it the world. Just how this is to be done is
spelled out most clearly by President Ikeda of Sokagakkai: convert one-
third of the Japanese people, change a second third from enemies into
friends, and then be able to help the final third indirectly. Nearly one-
third of the Japanese people have already been converted. The second
step, he says, is now underway: to earn the respect and friendship of
a second third. This means toning down aggressive *shakubuku*
conversions and replacing them with peaceful methods, such as *shoju*
(conversions by good example). The same 'one-two' tactic must be
launched around the globe. There can be no peace for Japan as long
as the rest of the world is in chaos.

> When all the vehicles of the world are united into the One
> Buddha Vehicle and all the people of the world chant, *Namu
> Myoho Renge Kyo*, the wind will not beleaguer branches nor
> boughs, nor will the rain pour down hard enough to break a
> clod. The world will become as peaceful as in the reign of
> Emperor Fu Hai or Shen Nung. Disasters will be driven from the
> world, man's life will be prolonged, and both the teachers and
> the taught will retain perennial youth and eternal life. This is the
> only way to secure the peace of our present lives in this world.
> (Nichiren, *Nyosetsu-shugyo-sho, Showa-teihon*, 733)

The fire in the lotus is spreading across Japan and over the seas. Its goal
is to ignite the earth.

Appendix 1

How to Practise Nichiren Buddhism

Every morning and evening, the practitioner says *Gongyo*, a service of sutra recitation and prayer, before his *Gohonzon*. Preferably the Gohonzon is a copy of Nichiren's Great Mandala, but if the believer has none, he may use a copy of the Sacred Title, a small statue of the Buddha, or another object on which he can focus his attention. The service may be lengthened or shortened, depending on the circumstances. Other selections from the Sutra or the writings of Nichiren may be added. The following service is recommended by Nichiren Shu. It is similar to that used in other Nichiren sects, but there are differences particularly in the wording of the prayers. The invocations also differ; each sect invokes its own patriarchs.

Primary Practice (Shogyo)

Primary Practice is recitation of the *Odaimoku* or Sacred Title, *Namu Myoho Renge Kyo* (normally pronounced *Nam myo ho den gay kyo*).

Auxiliary Practice (Jogyo)

Recitation of the Lotus Sutra and other devotions constitute Auxiliary Practice. The selections most commonly read are:

1. Prelude (*Kaikyo-ge*)
2. Chapter 2, 'Expedients' (*Hoben-bon*)
3. Chapter 16, 'The Duration of the Life of the Tathagata' (*Nyorai Juryo-hon*), Verses (*Jiga-ge*)
4. Chapter 21, 'The Supernatural Powers of the Tathagatas' (*Nyorai Jinriki-hon*), Verses (*Jinriki-ge*)

5. The Coming of the Buddhas (*Yokuryo-shu*)
6. The Difficulty of Retaining the Sutra (*Hoto-ge*).

Liturgy of Nichiren Shu

Bowing to the Three Treasures

With all our hearts, we bow to the eternal Buddhas of the worlds of the ten directions.

With all our hearts, we bow to the eternal Dharmas of the worlds of the ten directions.

With all our hearts, we bow to the eternal Sanghas of the worlds of the ten directions.

Invocation

Honour be to the Great Mandala, the Perfect Circle of All Honourable Ones, the Ground of Being revealed by our Founder Nichiren.

Honour be to the Eternal Buddha Shakyamuni, our Original Teacher, the Lord of the Dharma, our Great Benefactor, who attained enlightenment in the remotest past.

Honour be to Many-Treasures Tathagata, the Buddha from out of the past who came to this world to bear witness to the truth of the *Dharma Flower*.

Honour be to the Buddhas of the worlds of the ten directions in the past, present, and future, who are all emanations of the Eternal Buddha Shakyamuni.

Honour be to Superior Action, Limitless Action, Pure Action, Steadfast Action, and other Bodhisattvas who are disciples of the Eternal Buddha Shakyamuni.

Honour be to Manjushri, Samantabhadra, Maitreya, Medicine-King, Medicine-Lord, Brave-In-Giving, Wonderful-Voice, World-Voice-Perceiver (Kanzeon), and other Bodhisattvas who are disciples of the historical Buddha Shakyamuni or of Buddhas of other worlds.

Honour be to Shariputra, Maudgalyayana, Kashyapa, Ananda, and other Disciples who have been assured of their future Buddhahood.

Honour be to Great Brahman, Shakra-devanam-Indra, the Guardian Kings of the Four Quarters, and other deities who have vowed to protect the practitioners of the One Vehicle.

Honour be to our Founder, the Great Bodhisattva Nichiren, his Six Senior Disciples, the Nine Senior Disciples of Nichiro, and others who have handed down the teachings to us.

Honour be to Renge-ajari Nichiji, the first overseas missionary.

We now honour all of you. May you come to this hall of enlightenment out of your compassion for us, look at us with the light of your wisdom, and accept our offering of chanting the Sutra!

Prelude

The most profound and wonderful teaching is presented in this sutra. This sutra is difficult to meet even once in thousands and millions of aeons. Now we have been able to see, hear, receive, and keep this sutra. May we understand the most excellent teaching of the Buddha!

The most excellent teaching of the Great Vehicle is very difficult for us to understand. We shall be able to approach enlightenment when we see, hear, or touch this sutra. Expounded is the Buddha's truth. Expounding is the Buddha's essence. The letters composing this sutra are the Buddha's manifestation.

Just as perfume is caught by something put nearby, so shall we be richly benefited by this sutra, even when we are not aware of it; so many merits are accumulated in this sutra!

Anyone can expiate his sin, do good deeds, and attain Buddhahood by the merits of this sutra. It does not matter whether he is wise or not, or whether he believes the sutra or rejects it.

This sutra is the most wonderful and most excellent taught by the Buddhas of the past, present, and future. May we meet and receive it, birth after birth, world after world!

Myo ho ren ge kyo, ho ben pon dai ni: The Sutra of the Lotus of the Wonderful Dharma

Chapter 2: 'Expedients'

Ni Ji Se Son,	Thereupon the World-Honoured One
Ju San Mai,	Quietly emerged
An Jo Ni Ki,	From his samadhi
Go Shari Hotsu.	And said to Shariputra:
Sho Butsu Chi E,	The wisdom of the Buddhas
Jin Jin Mu Ryo.	Is profound and immeasurable.
Go Chi E Mon,	Its gate is difficult to understand
Nan Ge Nan Nyu.	And difficult to enter.
Is Sai Sho Mon,	No Shravaka-Disciple
Hyaku Shi Butsu,	Or Self-taught Pratyekabuddha
Sho Fu No Chi.	Can understand it.
Sho I Sha Ga.	Why is that? [because]
Butsu Zo Shin Gon,	The [present] Buddhas attended on many
Hyaku Sen Man Noku,	Hundreds of thousands of billions
Mu Shu Sho Butsu,	Of [past] Buddhas,
Jin Gyo Sho Butsu,	And practised the innumerable teachings
Mu Ryo Do Ho,	Of those Buddhas bravely and strenuously

Yu Myo Sho Jin,	To their far-flung fame till they attained
Myo Sho Fu Mon,	The profound Dharma
Jo Ju Jin Jin,	Which you have never heard before,
Mi Zo U Ho,	And also because they are expounding
Zui Gi Sho Setsu,	The Dharma according to the capacities
I Shu Nan Ge.	Of all living beings in such ways that the true purpose of their teachings is difficult to understand.
Shari Hotsu.	Shariputra!
Go Ju Jo Butsu I Rai,	Since I became Buddha, I also
Shu Ju In Nen,	Have been expounding various teachings
Shu Ju Hi Yu,	With different stories of previous lives,
Ko En Gon Kyo,	Various parables, and various similes.
Mu Shu Ho Ben,	I have been leading all living beings
In Do Shu Jo,	With innumerable expedients
Ryo Ri Sho Jaku.	In order to save them from attachments,
Sho I Sha Ga.	Because I have the power
Nyo Rai Ho Ben,	To employ expedients,
Chi Ken Hara Mitsu,	And the power to perform
Kai I Gu Soku.	The Paramita of Insight.
Shari Hotsu.	Shariputra!
Nyo Rai Chi Ken,	The insight of the Tathagatas
Ko Dai Jin Non.	Is wide and deep.
Mu Ryo Mu Ge,	They have all the [states of mind
Riki Mu Sho I,	Towards] innumerable [living beings],
Zen Jo Ge Datsu San Mai,	Unhindered [eloquence], powers,
Jin Yu Mu Sai,	Fearlessness, dhyana-concentrations,
Jo Ju Is Sai,	Emancipations, and samadhis. They entered
Mi Zo U Ho.	Deep into boundlessness, and attained the Dharma which you never heard before.
Shari Hotsu.	Shariputra!
Nyo Rai Nyo Shu Ju Fun Betsu,	The Tathagatas divide the Dharma
Gyo Ses Sho Ho,	Into various teachings, and expound
Gon Ji Nyu Nan,	Those teachings so gently and skilfully
Ek Ka Shu Shin.	That living beings are delighted.
Shari Hotsu.	Shariputra!
Shu Yo Gon Shi,	In short, the Buddhas attained
Mu Ryo Mu Hen.	The innumerable teachings
Mi Zo U Ho,	Which you have never heard before.
Bus Shitsu Jo Ju.	No more

Shi,	Will I say,
Shari Hotsu.	Shariputra,
Fu Shu Bu Setsu,	Because the Dharma
Sho I Sha Ga.	attained by the Buddhas
Bus Sho Jo Ju,	Is the highest Truth,
Dai Ichi Ke U,	Rare [to hear] and difficult
Nan Ge Shi Ho.	To understand.
Yui Butsu Yo Butsu,	Only the Buddhas attained
Nai No Ku Jin,	The highest Truth, that is
Sho Ho Jis So.	The Reality of All Things
(Sho I Sho Ho	(In regard to
Nyo Ze So	Their appearances as such,
Nyo Ze Sho	Their natures as such,
Nyo Ze Tai	Their embodiments as such,
Nyo Ze Riki	Their powers as such,
Nyo Ze Sa	Their activities as such,
Nyo Ze In	Their primary causes as such,
Nyo Ze En	Their environmental causes as such,
Nyo Ze Ka	Their effects as such,
Nyo Ze Ho	Their requital as such,
Nyo Ze Hon Matsu Ku	And the equality of these [nine factors]
Kyo To.)	as such.)

(repeat three times)

The Coming of the Buddhas
The Buddhas, the World-Honoured Ones, appear in the worlds in order to cause all living beings to open [the gate] to the insight of the Buddha, and to cause them to purify themselves. They appear in the worlds in order to show the insight of the Buddha to all living beings. They appear in the worlds in order to cause all living beings to obtain the insight of the Buddha. They appear in the worlds in order to cause all living beings to enter the Way to the insight of the Buddha.

The Triple World
> The Triple World is not peaceful.
> It is like a burning house.
> It is full of sufferings.
> It is dreadful.
>
> There are always the sufferings
> Of birth, old age, disease, and death.
> They are like flames
> Raging endlessly.
>
> I have already left
> The burning house of the Triple World.

I am tranquil and peaceful
In a bower in a forest.

This Triple World
Is my domain.
All living beings in it
Are my children.

There are many sufferings
In this world.
Only I can save
All living beings.

Dispatch of Monks and Nuns

If a teacher of the Dharma expounds this sutra
After my extinction,
I will manifest the four kinds of devotees:
Monks, nuns, and men and women of pure faith,
And dispatch them to him
So that they may make offerings to him,
And lead many living beings,
Collecting them to hear the Dharma [from him].
If he is hated and threatened
With swords, sticks, tile-pieces, or stones,
I will manifest men and dispatch them to him
In order to protect him.

The Appearance of a Stupa of Treasures

Thereupon a loud voice of praise is heard from within the stupa of treasures:

Excellent! Excellent! You, Shakyamuni, the World-Honoured One, have expounded to this great multitude the Sutra of the Lotus Flower of the Wonderful Dharma, the Teaching of Equality, the Great Wisdom, the Dharma for Bodhisattvas, the Dharma protected by all the Buddhas. So it is! So it is! Shakyamuni, the World-Honoured One, what you have expounded is all true.'

Myo ho ren ge kyo, nyo rai ju ryo hon, dai ju roku: The Sutra of the Lotus of the Wonderful Dharma

Chapter 16: 'Duration of the Life of the Tathagata'

Ji Ga Toku Butsu Rai — Since I became Buddha
Sho Kyo Sho Ko Shu — It is many hundreds of thousands
Mu Ryo Hyaku Sen Man — Of billions of trillions
Oku Sai A So Gi. — Of *asankhyas* of aeons.

Jo Sep Po Kyo Ke	For the past innumerable aeons
Mu Shu Oku Shu Jo	I have been expounding the Dharma
Ryo Nu O Butsu Do	To hundreds of millions of beings
Ni Rai Mu Ryo Ko.	To lead them into the Way to Buddhahood.
I Do Shu Jo Ko	In order to save [perverted] people,
Ho Ben Gen Ne Han	I expediently show my Nirvana to them.
Ni Jitsu Fu Metsu Do	In reality I never pass away.
Jo Ju Shi Sep Po.	I always live here and expound the Law.
Ga Jo Ju O Shi	Although I always live here
I Sho Jin Zu Riki	With perverted people
Ryo Ten Do Shu Jo	I disappear from their eyes
Sui Gon Ni Fu Ken.	By my supernatural powers.
Shu Ken Ga Metsu Do	When they see me seemingly pass away,
Ko Ku Yo Sha Ri	Make offerings to my relics,
Gen Kai E Ren Bo	Adore and admire me,
Ni Sho Katsu Go Shin.	Become devout, upright, and gentle,
Shu Jo Ki Shin Buku	And wish to see me
Shichi Jiki I Nyu Nan	With all their hearts
Is Shin Yok Ken Butsu	At the cost of their lives,
Fu Ji Shaku Shin Myo	I reappear on Mt. Sacred Eagle
Ji Ga Gyu Shu So	With all my Sangha
Ku Shutsu Ryo Ju Sen	And say to them:
Ga Ji Go Shu Jo	'I always live here.
Jo Zai Shi Fu Metsu	I shall never be extinct.
I Ho Ben Riki Ko	I show my extinction to you expediently
Gen U Metsu Fu Metsu.	Although I never pass away.
Yo Koku U Shu Jo	I also expound the unsurpassed Dharma
Ku Gyo Shin Gyo Sha	To the living beings of other worlds
Ga Bu O Hi Chu	If they respect me, believe me,
I Setsu Mu Jo Ho.	And wish to see me.
Nyo To Fu Mon Shi	You have never heard this;
Tan Ni Ga Metsu Do	Therefore, you thought that I pass away.'
Ga Ken Sho Shu Jo	I see [perverted] people sinking
Motsu Zai O Ku Kai.	In an ocean of sufferings.
Ko Fu I Gen Shin	Therefore I disappear from their eyes
Ryo Go Sho Katsu Go	And cause them to admire me.
In Go Shin Ren Bo	When they adore me,
Nai Shutsu I Sep Po.	I reappear and expound the Law to them.

Jin Zu Riki Nyo Ze	I can do this by my supernatural powers.
O A So Gi Ko	For innumerable aeons
Jo Zai Ryo Ju Sen	I live on Mt. Sacred Eagle
Gyu Yo Sho Ju Sho.	And in all other abodes.
Shu Jo Ken Ko Jin	[Perverted] people think:
Dai Ka Sho Sho Ji	'This world is in a great fire.
Ga Shi Do An Non	The end of the aeon is coming.'
Ten Nin Jo Ju Man.	Really this world of mine is peaceful.
On Rin Sho Do Kaku	It is filled with gods and men.
Shu Ju Ho Sho Gon	Its gardens, forests, and palaces
Ho Ju Ta Ke Ka	Are adorned with treasures;
Shu Jo Sho Yu Raku.	Gem trees have fruits and flowers;
Sho Ten Kyaku Ten Ku	Living beings are enjoying themselves;
Jo Sa Shu Gi Gaku	And the gods are beating heavenly drums,
U Man Da Ra Ke	Pouring music and mandarava blossoms
San Butsu Gyu Dai Shu.	On the Buddha and all assembled beings.
Ga Jo Do Fu Ki	My pure realm is indestructible.
Ni Shu Ken Sho Jin	But [perverted] people think:
U Fu Sho Ku No	'It is full of sorrow, fear and pain,
Nyo Ze Shitsu Ju Man.	And will soon burn away.'
Ze Sho Zai Shu Jo	Because of their evil karmas,
I Aku Go In Nen	Sinful people cannot hear even the names
Ka A So Gi Ko	Of the Three Treasures
Fu Mon San Bo Myo.	For innumerable aeons.
Sho U Shu Ku Doku	To those who have accumulated merits,
Nyu Wa Shichi Jiki Sha	Who are gentle and upright,
Sok Kai Ken Ga Shin	And see me living here,
Zai Shi Ni Sep Po.	Expounding the Dharma,
Waku Ji I Shi Shu	I say: 'The duration
Setsu Butsu Ju Mu Ryo	Of my life is immeasurable.'
Ku Nai Ken Bus Sha	To those who see me after a long time,
I Setsu Butsu Nan Chi.	I say: 'Hard it is to see a Buddha.'
Ga Chi Riki Nyo Ze	This I can do by the power of my wisdom.
E Ko Sho Mu Ryo	The light of my wisdom knows no bounds.
Ju Myo Mu Shu Ko	The duration of my life is forever.
Ku Shu Go Sho Toku.	I obtained this by ages of practices.
Nyo To U Chi Sha	All of you, wise men!
Mot To Shi Sho Gi	Have no doubts about this!
To Dan Ryo Yo Jin	Remove your doubts, have no more!

Butsu Go Jip Pu Ko.	The Buddha's words are true, not false.
Nyo I Zen Ho Ben	The physician, who sent a man expediently
I Ji O Shi Ko	To tell his perverted sons
Jitsu Zai Ni Gon Shi	Of his death in order to cure them,
Mu No Sek Ko Mo	Was not accused of falsehood though living.
Ga Yaku I Se Bu	Likewise, I am the father of this world.
Ku Sho Ku Gen Sha.	I save all living beings from suffering.
I Bon Bu Ten Do	Because they are perverted, I say
Jitsu Zai Ni Gon Metsu	That I pass away even though I do not.
I Jo Ken Ga Ko	If they always see me,
Ni Sho Kyo Shi Shin	They will become arrogant and licentious
Ho Itsu Jaku Go Yoku	And cling to the five desires
Da O Aku Do Chu.	Till they fall into evil paths.
Ga Jo Shi Shu Jo	I know all living beings,
Gyo Do Fu Gyo Do	Who practise the Way and who do not.
Zui O Sho Ka Do	Therefore I expound various teachings
I Ses Shu Ju Ho.	According to the capabilities of all.
Mai Ji Sa Ze Nen	I am always thinking:
I Ga Ryo Shu Jo	'How can I cause all living beings
Toku Nyu Mu Jo Do	To enter into the unsurpassed Way
Soku Jo Ju bus Shin.	And quickly become Buddhas themselves?'

Devotion

The Wonderful Truth expounded in the Sutra whose Sacred Title we now chant is what the past Buddhas taught, the present Buddhas are teaching, and the future Buddhas shall teach. It is the Great Law, true and pure, the propagation of which was entrusted primarily to Superior-Practice Bodhisattva by the Buddha on the Vulture Peak. Once we chant the Sacred Title, *Namu Myoho Renge Kyo*, we shall attain the right view that the three thousand things exist in our minds just as they are; the Pure Land of Tranquil Light shall be made manifest in our sight; our Buddha-nature shall be identified with the Buddha of Three Bodies in One; and, together with all other beings, we shall enjoy living in the Land of Truth.

May the sound of our chanting the Sacred Title permeate the whole world, be offered to the Three Treasures, and bestowed on all beings! May all beings enter the world of the One Reality, the Great Vehicle; may the Buddha-land be adorned and all beings favoured with the merits of our chanting!

Odaimoku Chanting

Namu Myoho Renge Kyo (repeat as often as desired)

Hoto Ge

'The Difficulty of Keeping the Sutra'

Shi-Kyo Nan Ji	It is difficult to keep this sutra.
Nyaku Zan Ji Sha	I shall be glad to see anyone
Ga-Soku Kan Gi	Keeping it even for a moment;
Sho-Butsu Yaku Nen.	So will all the other Buddhas.
Nyo-Ze Shi Nin	He will be praised by all the Buddhas.
Sho-Butsu Sho Tan	He will be a man of valour,
Ze-Soku Yu Myo	A man of endeavour.
Ze-Soku Sho-Jin.	He should be considered
Ze-Myo Ji-Kai	To have already observed the precepts,
Gyo Zu-Da Sha	And practised the *dhuta*.
Soku-I Shit Toku	He will quickly attain
Mu-Jo Butsu-Do.	The unsurpassed Buddha-way.
No O Rai Se	Anyone who reads and recites this sutra
Doku-Ji Shi-Kyo	Will be a son of mine.
Ze-Shin Bus Shi	He shall be considered to live
Ju Jun-Zen Shi.	On the stage of purity and good.
Butsu Metsu-Do Go	Anyone after my extinction
No Ge-Go Gi	Who understands the meaning of this sutra
Ze-Sho Ten Nin	Will be the eye of the world
Se-Ken Shi Gen.	Of gods and men.
U-Ku I Se	Anyone who expounds this sutra
No Shu Yu Setsu	Even for a moment in the dreadful world
Is Sai Ten Nin	Should be honoured with offerings
Kai O Ku-Yo.	By all gods and men.

Prayers

General Prayer (Ippan Eko)

We respectfully dedicate all our merits gathered up now
To the Eternal and True Teacher, Shakyamuni Buddha;
To the Supreme Teaching, the *Dharma Flower*;
To the leader of the Latter Day of the Declining
   Dharma,
Great Master Rissho Daishi, Our Founder, the Great
   Bodhisattva Nichiren;

To those great teachers of the Nichiren Sect
Who have established meritorious acts according to our
   faith;
And to the protective deities of the Dharma.

May all beings under the heavens and within the four
   seas
Convert themselves to the *Dharma Flower*!
May the *Dharma Flower* spread throughout
Ten Thousand years of the Latter Age of the Declining
   Dharma!
May the heaven and earth last forever
And peace permeate this nation!
May the five crops be abundant
And all people enjoy peace and happiness!
May our families live in safety
And live long without misfortune!
May our posterity last forever
And their families be prosperous!
May we cleanse our six senses
And repent all our sins committed from time eternal!

In a land of true Buddhism
Wherein ten thousand people will flourish;
In a family wherein the Sutra is recited daily
Seven calamities will disappear.

We pray for the souls of our ancestors
And for all the souls of the universe;
We pray that they attain enlightenment,
Overcome suffering, and gain happiness;
We pray that they obtain Buddhahood in this world
Through the merits of the Lotus Sutra;
May all beings of the spiritual world be helped equally!
Namu Myoho Renge Kyo!

Memorial Prayer (Tsuizen Eko)

We respectfully dedicate the merits of chanting the *Dharma Flower*
and reciting the Sacred Title in the presence of the Buddha, our
Founder Nichiren, and the Three Treasures to the soul(s) of ____, for
whom we observe the __th memorial service today. May the sound of
our recitation of the *Dharma Flower* and the *Odaimoku* permeate
throughout the spiritual world! May the soul(s) of the deceased
permeate throughout the spiritual world! May the heart of our prayer
permeate throughout the spiritual world! May all our merits go to the
deceased and increase the happiness of the deceased!

   It is said in the *Dharma Flower*, 'Good men or women in the future who hear the Sutra of the Lotus Flower of the Wonderful Dharma with faithful respect caused by their pure minds, and have no doubts, will not fall into hell, the region of hungry spirits, or the region of animals. They will be reborn before the Buddhas of the worlds of the ten directions. They will always hear this sutra at the places of their rebirth. Even when they are reborn among men or gods, they will be given wonderful pleasures. When they are reborn before the Buddhas, they will appear in lotus-flowers.'

May all sentient beings be blessed with these merits, and may we all together attain Buddhahood!

Namu Myoho Renge Kyo!

The Four Great Vows (Seigan)

Shujo Muhen Seigan Do	Sentient beings are innumerable: I vow to save them all.
Bonno Mushu Seigan Dan	Our evil desires are inexhaustible: I vow to quench them all.
Homon Mujin Seigan Chi	The Buddha's teachings are infinite: I vow to learn them all.
Butsudo Mujo Seigan Jo	The Way of the Buddha is unexcelled: I vow to attain the Path Sublime.

Repeat slowly and distinctly:

NA MU MYO HO REN GE KYO

NA MU MYO HO REN GE KYO

NA MU MYO HO REN GE KYO

Notes

If he wishes to recite the Chinese (Shindoku), the practitioner gives but one beat to every character regardless of its number of syllables (i.e., *Ji* takes one beat; *Toku* takes one beat; *Shari-hotsu* takes two beats). The HOTO-GE, however, has a rhythm of its own which is indicated here by the dashes between certain characters.

All vowels are pronounced 'continental' style: *a* as in 'father'; *e* as in 'bet'; *i* as in 'machine'; *o* as in 'oboe'; *u* as in 'rule'. Consonants are similar to English, except *r*, which is pronounced with the tongue and sounds more like the English *d*.

The *Odaimoku* is pronounced 'Nam-myo-ho-den-gay-kyo'. There are various ways to accompany it with a drum beat, the most common being, 'Don-don-don-doku-don-don'.

The service may be shortened or lengthened for variety.

Selections from the *Dharma Flower* or the writings of Nichiren may be used. The initial invocations are often omitted by lay practitioners, who begin instead with the Prelude.

Appendix 2

Statistics _____

Japanese Sects, Branches, and Societies Derived from Nichiren _____

Name, founder and date	Edifices	Clergy	Adherents
1. Nichiren Shu Nichiren; 1251 founded sect; 1274 founded Kuon-ji, Minobu.	5,181	8,030	2,281,368
2. Nichiren Shoshu Nikko; 1288 seceded from Minobu; 1290 founded Fuji Branch.	417	593	16,225,205
3. Kempon (Manifest) Hokke Shu Nichiju; 1384 seceded from Nakayama; 1389 founded Myoman-ji.	221	177	92,576
4. Hokkeshu (Original Branch)* Nichiben & Nisshu (14c), Nichiryu (15c); seceded from Ikegami.	509	683	560,930
5. Hokkeshu (Jin Branch) Nichijin; 1406 seceded from Kempon Hokke.	185	268	161,938
6. Hokkeshu (Shin Branch) Nisshin; 1489 seceded from Nakayama School.	212	309	68,625
7. Hommon Hokkeshu* Nichiryu; 1423 seceded from Ikegami (Shijo) School.	103	327	39,050

8. Nichiren-shu Fujufuse Branch Nichio; 1595 organized without government permission; 1875 legalized.	20	23	28,330
9. Nichiren Komonshu Nichiko; 1666 organized without government permission; 1875 legalized.	8	11	26,213
10. Nichiren Honshu Nichizon; 1333 seceded from Fuji; 1950 seceded from Nichiren Shu.	50	100	54,912
22. Hommon Butsuryu-shu* Nagamatsu Nissen; 1857 lay society; 1947 independent sect.	288	796	512,379
23. Nichirenshugi Butsuryuko* Schism from Hommon Butsuryu-shu, 1947.	9	9	2,173
25. Kokuchukai Tanaka, 1884 organized Rissho Ankoku-kai; 1914 took present name.	70	56	13,770
28. Nihonzan Myohoji Fujii Nichidatsu; 1919 in Manchuria.	149	198	745 †
29. Reiyukai Kubo & Kotani, 1925	17	2,530	2,512,425
30. Myodakai Sahara, 1951	376	2,226	219,240
31. Myochikai Miyamoto, 1951	264	1,715	677,941
32. Bussho Gonenkai Sekiguchi, 1950	9	5,936	1,391,673
36. Rissho Kosei-kai Niwano & Naganuma, 1938	589	7,779	4,704,452

Totals

37 organizations	9,677	34,904	30,579,306
* Eight Chapters branches	900	1,815	1,114,532

† Nihonzan Myohoji counts as members only lay brothers & sisters.

All the ancient sects claim to derive from Nichiren himself, directly or indirectly.

Organizations not mentioned in our text have been omitted from this list.

Numbers 29–37 are derived from Reiyukai.

Source: Japan Buddhist Federation, 1978. Statistics for Homon Butsuryushu are for 1983. All figures were submitted by the individual organizations, which alone are responsible for their accuracy.

According to these statistics, Nichiren Buddhism, with its 30.5 million adherents, is the largest Buddhist school in Japan. It is followed by 2) Pure Land Buddhism, 21 million in 25 branches; 3) Shingon, 11.5 million in 45 branches; 4) Zen, 9.5 million in 23 branches; 5) Tendai, 5.5 million in 20 branches; 6) Nara sects, 4.5 million in 7 branches; 7) two non-classified schools with 200,000 members.

Glossary ⸻

Abbreviations: C: Chinese; J. Japanese; N: Nichiren; NB: Nichiren Buddhism; NS: Nichiren Shu; NSS: Nichiren Shoshu; P: Pali; RK: Reiyukai; RKK: Rissho Kosei-kai; S: Sanskrit. All terminology is Japanese unless otherwise noted.

Amida: contraction of Amitabha and Amitayus (S); Buddha of Infinite Light and Life; Reward-body of the Buddha; the only Object of Worship in Pure Land Buddhism.
Asuras (S): Furious spirits; one of the ten worlds: anger.

Blue Sutra (Aokyokan): RK selections from the Threefold Lotus Sutra with special prayers.
Bodhisattva (S): A future Buddha who devotes his life to helping others; a personified aspect of the Buddha.
Bodhisattvas from (under) the Earth: A vast multitude of disciples of the Original Buddha; the followers of Nichiren.
Buddha (S): An enlightened one. **The Buddha:** The Original Buddha Shakyamuni.
Buddha-nature: Potential for attaining Buddhahood; pure universal essence. The term does not appear in the *Flower Dharma*, but is understood as equivalent to 'the One Vehicle'.
Butsu-dan: Box-like structure containing image of the Gohonzon or Object of Worship; home altar.

Chih-i (Zhi-yi):J: Chigi, 538–97: Chinese Buddhist philosopher who systematized all Buddhist teachings and founded the Heavenly Terrace School (C. T'ien-t'ai; Tan-tai. J: Tendai).

Dai-Gohonzon: Gohonzon inscribed on a plank and enshrined at Taiseki-ji; said by NSS to be the embodiment of the life of Nichiren, who is the manifestation of the Original Buddha.

Dai-mandara or Omandara: The Great Mandala.

Daimoku: Literally, 'title'; The Sacred Title in five (Myo Ho Ren Ge Kyo) or seven (Na Mu Myo Ho Ren Ge Kyo) characters; normally pronounced, *Nam-myoho-renge-kyo.*

Daishonin: 'Great Saint', a title of Nichiren. The Eight Chapters Branch gives this title to Nichiryu also.

Dengyo Daishi: Posthumous name of Saicho (767–822), who introduced the Heavenly Terrace (Tendai) synthesis to Japan; founder of Enryaku-ji on Mt. Hiei, which became the most important Buddhist centre in Japan.

Deva (S): (J: Ten). Heaven; a heavenly being; one of the ten worlds: happiness.

Devadatta (S): Cousin and enemy of Shakyamuni. The Devadatta Chapter (14) of the *Dharma Flower* states that he will become a Buddha in the future.

Dharani (S): Sacred words summing up many meanings; a magical incantation. To 'obtain dharani' is to 'get the point'.

Dharma (S): (J: Ho; P: Dhamma): Law, Norm; Truth; fact; teaching (as in Buddha-Dharma).

Dhyana (S): (J: Zen): Meditation.

Dozen: N's first teacher, a priest of esoteric Tendai (Taimitsu).

Eight Chapters (Happon): Chapters 15–22 of the *Dharma Flower* considered by Nichiryu to be the true Original Gate.

Eightfold Path: 1) Right view, 2) right aim, 3) right speech, 4) right action, 5) right livelihood, 6) right effort, 7) right mindfulness, 8) right contemplation. Basic to fundamental Buddhism and RKK.

Ennin (794–866): Tendai scholar who went to China and returned with esoteric texts and implements in 845. N accused him of having introduced extraneous elements into Tendai.

Esho funi: Unity of outer circumstances and interior life.

Esotericism: Secret teachings and practices derived from Indian Tantra. In Japan, there are two kinds: 1) Shingon esotericism, Tomitsu, introduced by Kobo Daishi; 2) Tendai esotericism, Taimitsu, introduced partially by Saicho and fully by Ennin.

Eternal Original Buddha Shakyamuni: (J: Hombutsu): 'The great life force of the universe' (Niwano) manifesting as the historical Shakyamuni; in Jodo Shinshu, Amida is considered the Original Buddha; in Shingon, he is Mahavairocana. Only in the *Dharma Flower* does the historical Shakyamuni announce that he himself is the Original Buddha.

Expedient Teachings: (J: Hoben) 'As you each live differently, I show you each a different way.' (Sutra of Infinite Meanings); partial truths.

Five Periods of the Buddha's Teaching: 1) Flower Garland (*Kegon*), taught for 21 days; 2) Little Vehicle (*Agon*), 12 years; 3) Provisional Great Vehicle (*Hodo*), 16 years; 4) Prajna-Wisdom Teachings (*Hannya*), 14 years; Complete Great Vehicle of the *Dharma Flower* and Nirvana sutras (*Hokke-nehan*), 8 years, totalling 50 years of ministry.

Five Principles of Nichiren: (*Go-ko*, 'five ropes'): 1) *Kyo*, the doctrine: Daimoku is the name of the ultimate teaching of the Buddha because it reveals what is not found previously, i.e., that both the Little and the Great Vehicles lead to the same goal, Buddhahood, and the historical Shakyamuni is eternal and original; 2) *Ki*: kinds of people; even the degenerate people of the modern age are saved by the *Dharma Flower*; 3) *Ji*: the time, now: the Age of Degeneration; 4) *Koku*: the country, Japan, where all types of Buddhism have already been introduced; 5. *Jo*: order of propagation: previous teachings have prepared the way for the final one.

Five Types of Religious Teachings: 1) *Judo*: Confucianism and Taoism; 2) *Gedo*, the Outer Way: non-Buddhist teachings of India; 3) *Shakugon*: ancient temporal teachings of Hinayana and pre-*Dharma Flower* Mahayana; 4) *Shakumon*: Imprinted Gate of the *Dharma Flower*; 6) *Hommon*: the Original Gate. N insists that these five must not be reversed or mixed in sequence.

Flower Garland (S: Avatamsaka, J: Kegon): a long sutra revealing the enlightened mind of the Buddha; considered second in profundity only to the *Dharma Flower* — second because it excludes Hinayana disciples from ever attaining enlightenment.

Formal Norm Period or Counterfeit Dharma: (*Zoho*): Second historical period in the history of Buddhism, extending from AD52 to 1052, and characterized by academic formalism.

Fourfold Methods of Conversion and Fourfold Doctrines of Conversion: A classification of Chih-i. The four methods are sudden, gradual, secret, and variable; the four doctrines are the Three Baskets of Hinayana, shared doctrines, distinctive doctrines, and the complete doctrine of the Lotus. They are sometimes called the **Eight Teachings**. The teachings are also classified according to contents as combined, sole, contrasted, inclusive, pure, and additional teachings (Nirvana Sutra). By interlocking these components, Chih-i unified Buddhist thought.

Four Great Bodhisattvas who lead the Bodhisattvas from the Earth: Superior-Action (*Jogyo*), Limitless-Action (*Muhengyo*), Pure-Action (*Jyogyo*), and Steadfast-Action (*Anryugyo*). N is considered the incarnation of Jogyo. They symbolize the four qualities of Nirvana: true self, eternity, purity, and happiness.

Four Noble Truths: 1) Suffering is universal; 2) The cause of suffering is ignorant craving; 3) Eliminate the cause to eliminate the suffering; 4) The method is to follow the Eightfold Path.

Four-storied Teaching (Shiju-hohai): 1) pre-Lotus teaching; 2)

Shakumon; 3) Hommon; 4) Observation of our own mind (*kanjin*) as revealed in the 16th chapter of the *Dharma Flower*.

Four Virtues of Mahaparinirvana (Shitoku) as revealed in the Nirvana Sutra: *jo*, permanency; *ga*, self; *raku*, bliss; *jo*, purity. They are equated with the Four Great Bodhisattvas and are the opposites of the Three Signs of Being (impermanence, no-self, and suffering) as well as impurity.

Fu Ssi and Sheng Nun: Mythological Chinese emperors from the Golden Age.

Fujii Nichidatsu (1885–1985): Founder of Nihonzan Myohoji Daisanga.

Fujii Nichijo (1879–1971): Chief Abbot of Kuon-ji and Archbishop of NS.

Fuju-fuse, 'Receive nothing-give nothing': Purist movement begun in 1595 by Nichio, which would neither give to nor receive from the government. Suppressed in 1669, it went underground, re-emerging in 1874 under Shaku Nissho, who was able to get it recognized as a legitimate sect.

Gatha (S): 'Singly raising a chant'; verse form.

Gaya, India: Place where Shakyamuni attained enlightenment.

Gohonzon: 'Fundamental Venerable' (Petzold); 'Supreme Being' (Anesaki). *Hon* is 'root' or 'source'; *zon* is 'honoured'; *go* is an honorific. NS distinguishes three meanings: 1) *Kompon-sonsu Honzon*: that which to worship is the fundamental practice; 2) *Honrai-soncho Honzon*: that which has existed since the beginningless beginning of the past; 3) *Honno-songyo Honzon*: that which is eternal and most honourable.

Gongyo: A religious service; daily practice of believers.

Gosho (*Shimpen Nichiren Daishonin Gosho Zenshu*): Sacred scripture of NSS; a collection of N's writings and 'oral teachings' published in 1951.

Great Beneficient Teacher and Lord Shakyamuni, The Eternal Buddha: Object of worship (Honzon) of RKK.

Great Mandala (Omandara): Graphic depiction of the Sacred Source first shown by N on 8 July 1273, to illustrate its description in his essay, *Kanjin Honzon Sho*. He made many copies later. According to Satomi, it contains all possible forms of worship: theism, nature-worship, serpent-worship, ancestor-worship, demon-worship, king-worship, hero-worship, all subordinated to the One Law (*Japanese Civilization* 83). It is not a person or a deity but the Dharma-world revealed in the *Dharma Flower*: all beings, both benevolent and malevolent, manifesting their intrinsic value.

Great Vehicle; Mahayana: Teachings of northern Buddhism prevalent in China, Korea, Japan, Tibet, and Mongolia.

Hama School: Founded by Senior Disciple Nissho at Kamakura; the most conservative of the N schools, it long maintained friendly ties with Tendai: now a part of NS.

Heavenly Terrace (C: T'ien-t'ai, J: Tendai): Syncretistic school of Mahayana developed by Chih-i and brought to Japan by Saicho (Dengyo Daishi). N was a Tendai monk.

Heian Period (794–1185), when Tendai and Shingon dominated J Buddhism.

Hei-no-Saemon, also known as Taira no Yoritsuna or Hei no Saemon-no-jo Yoritsuna: Minister of War of the Kamakura Regency who ordered the execution of N and later attempted to eradicate NB from Kamakura.

Hieizan, Mount Hiei: Centre of Tendai and long the centre of J Buddhism; N studied there for 10 years.

Hinayana (S): The Lesser Vehicle; Theravada is its only surviving school; it predominates in SE Asia; the term 'Southern Buddhism' is preferred today.

Hojo: Clan ruling Japan from Kamakura at the time of N.

Hoke-kyo: the *Dharma Flower* Sutra; the Lotus Sutra.

Hokkeko: Lay association affiliated with NSS.

Hokke-shu: 'Dharma Flower Sect', meaning either 1) Tendai, 2) NB in general 3) a Shoretsu sect which formerly used the name, or 4) a confederation formed in 1952 of three Shoretsu sects. N described himself as belonging to the Hokke-shu.

Hokke-shu-hon-monryu: 'Dharma Flower Sect, Original Branch'; founded by Nichiryu in 1423; an Eight-Chapters (*Happon*) sect.

Hokke-shu-jin-monryu: 'Dharma Flower Sect, Jin Branch', formerly called Hokke-shu; founded by Nichijin in 1406.

Hokke-shu-shin-monryu: 'Dharma Flower Sect, Shin Branch', formerly called Hommyo-hokke-shu; founded by Nisshin in 1489.

Hommon: The second half of the Lotus Sutra revealing the eternal life of the Buddha Shakyamuni; the Original Gate.

Hommon-butsu: The Buddha revealed in *Hommon*: the Original or Eternal Buddha.

Hommon Butsuryu-shu: Originally a lay society founded by Nissen Nagamatsu in 1848 within the Eight-Chapters Branch; became an independent sect after World War II.

Hommon-hokke-shu: 'Original Gate Dharma Flower Sect'; An Eight-Chapters sect with headquarters at Myoren-ji, Kyoto.

Hommon-ji, Ikegami, Tokyo: Great Head Temple and Administrative Headquarters of NS. N died there in 1282.

Hommon-ji, Kitayama, Shizuoka Prefecture: Temple founded by Nikko in 1291; long a head temple of the Komon (Nikko) branch, it is now affiliated with NS.

Hommon-no-daimoku: The Sacred Title of the Original Gate.

Hommon-no-honzon: The Sacred Source of the Original Gate, generally as manifested in the Great Mandala. See **Gohonzon**.

Hommon-no-kaidan: The True Ground of the Original Gate, where one receives it and puts it into practice.

Honen (1133–1212): Founder of the Pure Land Sect (*Jodo-shu*), which reduced all Buddhism practice to one: reciting the Name of Amida Buddha (*Nembutsu*). He was strongly criticized by N.

Honzon: Principal object of veneration in a Buddhist temple; symbol of the highest reality, the guardian deity, or the patron saint. See **Gohonzon**.

Hoza: In RKK, a 'Dharma Circle' of believers to discuss personal problems and seek Buddhist remedies.

Ichinen Sanzen: Three thousand things in a single moment of thought; all of reality and all possibilities are potentially within every existing thing.

Ikeda, Daisaku (1928–): Third president of Sokagakkai.

Ikegami School: founded by Senior Disciple Nichiro at Ikegami near Tokyo; also called Hikigayatsu School; now a part of NS.

Imprinted Gate; Realm of Trace (Shakumon): Teachings of the historical Buddha in the first half of the Lotus Sutra; all living beings contain the Buddha-nature. This teaching was transmitted from Shakyamuni to Medicine-King Bodhisattva (S: Bhaisajyaraja, J: Yakuo), thence to Chih-i, Dengyo, and Nichiren.

Infinite Meanings Sutra (*Muryogi-kyo*): Introductory sutra to the *Dharma Flower*.

Inner Trip: RK term for spiritual introspection and/or a pilgrimage to Japan.

Itchi-ha: Unity or Harmonious Branch of NB, holding that all Buddhist teachings and practices harmonize and find their culmination in the Original Gate. NS and Fuju-fuse hold this view. In 1879 this branch was authorized by the government to change its name to the Nichiren Sect (*Nichiren Shu*), Fuju-fuse calling itself, 'Nichiren Sect, Fuju-fuse branch'. Compare **Shoretsu**.

Izu Peninsula: Site of N's first exile, 1261–63.

Jisso: 'The true aspect'; reality; *Jisso-ron*; phenomenology of Tendai as opposed to *engi-ron*, production by causation as taught by Kegon; *Shoho jisso*: all things are the truth; itself; the variety of phenomena expresses the real state of the universal and eternal truth (*Dharma Flower*, Chap. 2).

Jodo: A Pure Land.

Jodo Shinshu: 'True Pure Land Sect' founded by Shinran, 13th century.

Jodo-shu: 'Pure Land Sect', founded by Honen, early 13th century.

Jojakko-do: 'The Land of Eternally Tranquil Light'; the Pure Land of Dharmakaya which Nichiren Buddhists hope to manifest on this earth.

Kaidan: Place for receiving the precepts of Buddhist discipline and the ability to live up to them; ordination platform subject to government supervision.

Kaikyo-ge: Verses (recited) on opening the Sutra; the first stanza is of unknown origin and is common to many Buddhist schools; the others were composed by Udana Nichiki (1800–59) for use in NS.

Kakocho: Book containing posthumous names of one's ancestors, relatives, and friends.

Kalpa: An aeon.

Kamakura: City near modern Tokyo which became the de facto capital of Japan under the Hojo Regency, 1185–1335.

Kamikaze: Divine wind which destroyed two Mongolian invasions.

Kanjin: To observe or contemplate the mind, especially to see the truth of *ichinen sanzen*, 'the great white doctrine among the great white doctrines'; in NB, the Diamoku.

Karma: 'action'; conditions in the present were caused in the past; conditions of the future are caused in the present.

Kegon: 'Flower Garland'. *Kegon-shu*: Sect based on the Flower Garland Sutra; one of the Nara sects.

Kempon Hokke-shu: 'Manifest Dharma Flower Sect'; *Shoretsu* sect founded by Nichiju at Kamakura in 1381; maintains that the Original Gate is found only in Chapter XVI.

Kobo Daishi: Posthumous name of Kukai.

Komeito: 'Clean Government Party' founded by Sokagakkai.

Komon-ha: Nikko Branch of NB, also called the Fuji Branch; it consists of several sects, the largest of which today is NSS. Some of the sects now belong to NS, some to NSS, and others are independent.

Kosen-rufu: Worldwide propagation of NB.

Kotani, Kimi (1901–71): Sister-in-law of Kakutaro Kubo, co-founder and second president of RK, and guardian of the third president.

Kiyozumi: Site of Seicho-ji, the temple where N began his studies.

Kubo, Kakutaro (1892–1944): Founder of Reiyukai.

Kubo, Tsugunari (1936–): Son of the above; President of RK.

Kukai, Kobo Daishi (774–835): Founder of Shingon, Japanese esotericism.

Kumarajiva (334–413): Missionary from Kucha to China; translator of the *Dharma Flower*.

Kuon: The remotest past; eternity.

Kuon-ji: Founder's Temple (*Sozan*) built by N at Mt. Minobu; the spiritual centre of NS. N was the first Chief Abbot, Niko the second; between the death of N and the installation of Niko, it was supervised by Nikko and other disciples in rotation.

Lotus Sect: See **Hokke-shu**.

Lotus Sutra: Common English rendering for *Hoke-kyo*, the *Dharma Flower Sutra*.

Mahayana: The Great Vehicle which excludes no one. Because some Mahayana sutras do exclude some people, they are called 'provisional Mahayana' as distinct from the *Dharma Flower*, which is 'true Mahayana'.

Makiguchi, Tsunesaburo (1871–1944): Founder of Soka Gyoiku Gakkai, precursor of Sokagakkai.

Mandala (S): Graphic design, usually circular, depicting spiritual truth; used in esotericism as an aid to meditation.

Mantra (S) **(J: Shingon):** A syllable, word, or verse manifesting a sound which can effect spiritual or even physical results.

Many-Treasures Buddha, Abundant Treasures Buddha (J: Tahonyorai, S: Prabhutaratna): A Buddha from the distant past who appears to testify to the truth of the *Dharma Flower*. He is enclosed in a great Treasure Tower or stupa, and cannot be seen until Shakyamuni reveals him. The stupa is made of the 'seven treasures', representing the seven words, *Na Mu Myo Ho Ren Ge Kyo*. Chih-i says that Many-Treasures Buddha represents objective Truth and Shakyamuni the subjective Wisdom to perceive it. These two are one in the Daimoku.

Mappo: Period of the Decline of the Dharma, beginning approximately 2,000 years after the death of Shakyamuni and lasting 10,000 years; the modern age.

Mara: 'Murderer'; Lord of the Realm of Desire, who reigns, not from hell, but from the highest heaven of desire.

Meditation on Bodhisattva Universal Virtue Sutra (Kanfugengyo): Supplement to the *Dharma Flower*.

Meditation on Eternal Life Sutra (*Kanmuryoju-kyo*): One of the three sutras of Pure Land Buddhism.

Michibiki: Witnessing; converting others; a term used in RK and RKK.

Middle Path: The path between the extremes of self-mortification and hedonism; the Eightfold Path; for Tendai and N, it also means the 'true state' (*jisso*) of both emptiness and temporality. See **Three Truths**.

Minobu, Minobuzan: Mountain where N retired; site of Kuon-ji, Founder's Temple, and centre of Minobu School of NS.

Mirokusan: Mt. Maitreya, spiritual retreat centre of RK.

Mount Hiei: Seat of Tendai Buddhism near Kyoto; the head temple is Enryaku-ji.

Muni (S): Sage.

Muryogi-kyo: Sutra of Infinite Meanings; introduction to the *Dharma Flower*.

Muryoju-kyo: Sutra of Eternal Life; principal sutra of Pure Land Buddhism.

Myoko Naganuma (1889–1957): 'Mrs Myoko', vice-president and co-founder of RKK.

Nagamatsu, Seifu (1817–90); also called Nissen Shonin; Eight Chapters priest who founded Hommon Butsuryu-ko in 1857.

Naga (J: *ryu*, 'dragon'): Serpent water god; elephant; a noble person. The Naga Princess is the daughter of Sagara, 'the ocean'. Her enlightenment in Chap. 14 of the *Dharma Flower* symbolizes that all beings, human and non-human, male and female, young and old, can attain Buddhahood.

Nagarjuna (J: Ryuji): Indian philosopher of 2nd or 3rd century, considered the founder of eight schools of Mahayana.

Nakayama School: Founded by Toki Jonin (Nichijo); now part of NS.

Nambu Sanenaga, Lord of Minobu: Offered hospitality to N, but later disagreed with Nikko and made him leave Mt. Minobu.

Namu Myoho Renge Kyo: The Sacred Title, 'I devote myself to the Sutra of the Lotus Flower of the Wonderful Dharma'; generally pronounced, 'Nam-myoho-renge-kyo'. The first word is from S, serving as an honorific for the 'Five (C) Letters', *Miao-fa lien-hua-ching* in their J pronunciation. *Renge* represents the law of causality: the lotus-fruit (*ren*) and flower (*ge*) blossom together. This is the wonderful law (*myoho*) of the three thousand things in one moment's thought. *Kyo* is sutra, the teaching.

Nara: Japanese capital before the founding of Kyoto (Heian); seat of the first national kaidan.

Nembutsu: Practice of calling on the name of Amida Buddha (*Namu Amida Butsu*) for a happy rebirth in his Pure Land.

Never-Despising Bodhisattva (Jo-fukyo): in the *Dharma Flower* he is persecuted for despising no one, claiming that all his tormentors will become Buddhas; N says that his gospel is different in words from that of Jo-fukyo, but the same in spirit.

Nichiji (1250–?): Sixth of the six Senior Disciples; first NB missionary to foreign shores.

Nichijin (1339–1419): Founder of Hokke-shu-jin-monryu and early champion of the *fuju-fuse* principle.

Nichiju (1318–96): Founder of Kempon Hokke-shu; insisted that he alone really understood N.

Nichio (1565–1630): Founder of Fuju-fuse Branch.

Nichiren (1222–82): founder of NB; the name means 'Sun Lotus'.

Nichiren Shoshu: 'Orthodox Nichiren Sect', name adopted in 1913 by the Fuji Branch; before 1900 the Fuji Branch was part of the Komon Branch; Taiseki-ji in Fujinomiya, Shizuoka Prefecture, is its head temple. It maintains that Nichiren, not Shakyamuni, is the Original Buddha, and the Gohonzon at Taiseki-ji is his physical embodiment. Sokagakkai is affiliated with this sect.

Nichiren Shoshu-no-Yoshinkai: Organization founded in 1980 by Nittatsu Hosoi, former High Priest of Taiseki-ji, in opposition to Sokagakkai.

Nichiren Shu: Nichiren Sect. In the broad sense, all NB sects except the Nikko Branch. In the narrow sense, name adopted in 1876 by the former *Itchi-ha*; claims to have been founded by N in 1253; spiritual centre: Kuon-ji, Founder's Temple on Mt. Minobu; administrative centre: Ikegami Hommon-ji, Tokyo, where N died; other important temples at N's birthplace; sect's birthplace at Kiyosumi, Toki Jonin's Hokekyo-ji; Nikko's Kitayama Hommon-ji; etc.

Nichiro (1243–1320): Second of the six Senior Disciples of N; first abbot of Hommon-ji, Ikegami, Tokyo.

Nichiryu (1384–1464): NB reformer; founder of the Eight Chapters Branch (Happon-ha).

Nichizo (1267–1342): Missionary who successfully introduced NB to the capital of Kyoto.

Nikkan (Nichikan) (1665–1726): High Priest of Taiseki-ji, who systematized the distinctive doctrines of NSS.

Nikko (1245–1333): Third of the six Senior Disciples of N; founder of Komon Branch; founder of Taiseki-ji and Hommon-ji temples in Shizuoka Prefecture.

Niko (1253–1314): Fourth of the six Senior Disciples of N; superintended Kuon-ji after the departure of Nikko.

Nipponzan Myohoji Daisanga: Missionary order founded by Nichidatsu Fujii in Manchuria, 1919.

Nisshin 'the Pot-Wearer' (1407–88): Outstanding NB missionary.

Nitcho (1422–1500): Chief Abbot of Kuon-ji on Mount Minobu who did much to advance the primacy of his see. Another **Nitcho** (1252–1317) was the fifth of the six Senior Disciples.

Nirvana (S) (P: Nibbana; J: Nehan): Extinction; release from the bondages of time, space, and conditioned existence; the *Dharma Flower* teaches that Nirvana is universal, so there can be no individual Nirvana. **Parinirvana:** Complete extinction, often meaning the death of Shakyamuni Buddha.

Nittatsu Shonin: High Priest of NSS; broke with Ikeda and Sokagakkai.

Niwano, Nichiko (1938–): Son of Nikkyo Niwano; became 'President Designate' of RKK in 1960.

Niwano, Nikkyo (1906–): Founder and President of RKK.

Odaimoku, Omandara: Honorific forms of Daimoku and Mandara (Mandala).

O-eshiki: Annual festival commemorating the death of N, 13 October.

Ogasawara, Jimon: NSS priest who advocated harmonizing NSS with State Shinto during World War II.

O-kuji: A mystical practice of RK generally associated with healing.

On: Chinese characters with a Japanese pronunciation.

One Vehicle (S: Ekayana; J: Ichijo): The two Hinayana Vehicles (ways to enlightenment) of the Disciples and Buddhas-for-themselves (S: pratyekabuddhas) plus the Mahayana vehicle of the Bodhisattvas are really one, the Buddha Vehicle.

Original Buddha (Hombutsu): the absolute; in Tendai and NS,

Shakyamuni is the O.B. perfectly manifesting the unity of the One with the temporal. In NSS, the O.B. is Nichiren, 'the oneness of Person and the Law'.

Original Enlightenment: A Japanese development in Tendai and Shingon which became widespread after the 12th century; since we are 'originally enlightened' just as we are, there is no distinction between good and evil, right and wrong, truth and error, etc. 'Naturalness' (*jinen*), advocated by the Tendai philosophers Kakucho (960–1034) and Chujin (1065–1138), was developed in Shin, Jodo, and Zen Buddhism. NB also felt its influence.

Original Gate (Hommon): Revelation of the eternal life of the Buddha as revealed in the second half of the *Dharma Flower*, especially Chap. 16.

Original Vow: 'The altruistic impulse deeply rooted in human nature, perhaps in the cosmos, itself' (Suzuki), to save all beings. The Original Vow of Amida is the basis of Pure Land Buddhism. N vowed to become the pillar, eyes, and great vessel of Japan (*Kaimoku Sho*).

Oya: Parent; in RK and RKK, the spiritual parent who introduces one to the faith.

Pali: 'Text'; ancient language of western India combining several dialects, and since 28 BC serving as the international written language of southern Buddhism.

Paramita (S): 'Reaching the other shore (of Nirvana)'; the six practices to attain that goal: generosity, morality, patience, vigour, meditation, and wisdom. In Mahayana these practices often replace the Eightfold Noble Path.

Prajna (S): Transcendental wisdom.

Pratyekabuddha (S): Self-enlightened one who achieves enlightenment by and for himself; an enlightened non-Buddhist.

Pure Land (Jodo): According to the Original Vow of Amida, anyone can be born after death in his Pure Land if he but repeats the Name 'up to ten times'. Certain sinners, however, are excluded. According to N, the only eternal Pure Land is that in the pure mind of Shakyamuni. This fundamental Pure Land of the Lotus is called the Land of Eternally Tranquil Light.

Rencho: Original monastic name of Nichiren.

Reiyukai: Independent lay Buddhist organization conceived by Kakutaro Kubo and Chise Wakatsuki (1884–1971) in 1919 and organized by them in 1925. Around 1927, Kubo, his brother, and his sister-in-law started a new group in Akasaka, Tokyo, from which descends the modern RK.

Reverse relationship (*gyakuen*): To react negatively to the *Dharma Flower* is to cause adverse conditions in the future. Nevertheless, this is considered preferable to no relationship at all — like one brief instant of searing pain which heals compared to aeons of dull throbbing pain which accomplish nothing. Once any kind of relationship to the Sutra has been established, it can never be broken and will lead inevitably to Buddhahood.

Rissho Ankoku Ron, 'Establish the Right Law and Save our Country': Treatise composed by N, in 1269–70 and presented to the Kamakura government.

Rissho Daishi: Honorary title given to N by the Emperor in 1922 at the instigation of Chigaku Tanaka and the chief abbots of all the Nichiren sects. It means 'Great Teacher for the Establishment of Righteousness'.

Rissho Kosei-kai: Independent lay Buddhist organization founded by Nikkyo Niwano in 1938.

Ritsu (S. Vinaya): Rules of discipline for monks and nuns.

Ryokan: A Shingon-ritsu priest, contemporary of N, well known for his acts of charity.

Saddharma Pundarika Sutra (S): The Sutra of the Lotus Flower of the Wonderful Dharma; *Myoho Renge Kyo.*

Sacred Title or Formula: Odaimoku: Namu Myoho Renge Kyo.

Sado: Island of NW Japanese coast were N was exiled, 1271–4.

Saha (J. Shaba): The world where Shakyamuni preaches the Dharma; this world.

Sakyamuni, Shakyamuni (J. Shakamuni): 'Sage of the Shakyas'; usual J name for Siddhartha Gautama, the historical Buddha (563–483BC).

Saicho: Dengyo Daishi.

Sandai-hiho: The Three Great Secret Dharmas: Hommon-no-Honzon, Hommon-no-Daimoku, and Hommon-no-Kaidan.

Sandai-hiho-sho: 'Treatise on the Three Great Secret Dharmas, said to have been written by N shortly before his death, but the authorship is disputed.

Sangai (J): Triple World: Realms of Desire, Form, and Non-form.

Sangha (S): Order of Buddhist monks; in NS, all followers of N; in NSS, all followers of Nikko.

Sariputra, Shariputra (S): Said to have been the wisest of Shakyamuni's disciples .

Senzo Kuyo: Ancestor remembrance; a daily obligation in RK and RKK.

Shakaden: Great meeting hall at RK Headquarters, Tokyo.

Shakubuku-shoju: To subdue evil and promote good; two methods of propagation: aggressive and by good example.

Shichimen Daimyojin: Goddess identified with Benzaiten (S. Sarasvati) or Kichijoten (S. Shrimahadevi). Her sacred mountain is located next to Mount Minobu. Sometime between 1616 and 1623, the mountain was donated to Kuon-ji Temple, Mt. Minobu, and since then she has been considered the protecting deity of NS. The new religion of Bentenshu (1952), which derives from Shingon, is dedicated to her worship.

Shin Buddhism: Properly, *Jodo Shinshu*, but the term is sometimes used loosely to mean all groups practising the Nembutsu.

Shin-bukkyo: 'New Buddhism' from the Kamakura period (1185–1333), including Nichiren, Jodo, Jodo Shinshu, and Zen; not the same as the 'new religions' of the 20th century.

Shingon: 'True Word', esoteric school founded by Kukai (Kobo Daishi). S. *mantra*.

Shingon-ritsu: Sect combining Shingon with traditional monastic precepts.

Shimizu, Ryozan (1865–1928): N philosopher; identified the Japanese Emperor with Original Buddha.

Shimizu, Ryuzan (1870–1943): N scholar; criticized Ryozan for chauvinism; compiled a N Bible with original texts and modern J translations (1923) and edited a shorter version for the common reader (1932).

Shinran (1173–1262): Founder of the True Pure Land Sect (Jodo Shinshu).

Shinto: Indigenous J religion revived in 19th century to foster nationalism.

Shobo: Period of True Dharma, when there is true doctrine, practice, and attainment; first 1000 years (or 500) after death of Shakyamuni. In the second period there is doctrine and practice, but not attainment; in the final period there is doctrine only.

Shonin: 1) A saint or holy man; a Buddha or Bodhisattva; 2) (written with a different first character) a superior person; honorary title given to a priest of high rank.

Shoretsu: contraction of *Hon-sho-shaku-retsu*, or 'Hommon Superior, Shakumon Inferior'; a number of N sects maintain this doctrine, but differ from each other in particulars; NSS, Hokke-shu, Hommon Butsuryu-shu, and others are Shoretsu; NS supports the opposing *Itchi* theory of harmony between superior and inferior portions of the *Dharma Flower*.

Showa-teihon-Nichiren-shonin-ibun (Showa Standard Edition of Nichiren's Writings): Four volumes with topical index, compiled at Rissho University, 1952.

Shuju Ofurumai Gosho ('On the Buddha's Behaviour'): Autobiographical material of N, but so elaborated upon by subsequent editors that it is no longer reliable as a historical document; it contains many interesting anecdotes not found elsewhere.

Siddhartha Gautama: The historical Shakyamuni Buddha.

Six Senior Disciples: Shortly before his death, N entrusted his mission to six monks. In order of seniority, they were Nissho, Nichiro, Nikko, Niko, Nitcho, and Nichiji.

Sokagakkai (Value Creation Society): Lay Buddhist organization affiliated with NSS; founded by Makiguchi in 1930; suppressed during the war, it was refounded and renamed by Toda in 1945. Today it is the largest religious lay organization in the world.

Sokaimyo: Scroll with symbolic characters and family names, used in RK and RKK. Traditional *kaimyos*, as used in many J Buddhist sects, contain only the name of a deceased individual.

Stupa: Tower or pagoda, originally for enshrining relics.

Sravaka, Shravaka (S) (J: Shomon): A disciple of the historical Buddha, generally meaning a Hinayana follower.

Superior-Action or Practice, Eminent Conduct (S: Visista-caritra, J: Jogyo): Leader of the Four Great Bodhisattvas from (under) the Earth; N is considered his manifestation.

Sutra (S): Scripture containing teaching attributed to the Buddha.

Tanaka, Chigaku (1861–1939): Prominent NB philosopher and militant; claimed N should rule Japan, and Japan should rule the world; founded *Kokuchukai*, 'Pillar of the Nation Society' in 1914; it is now headed by his grandson, Koho Tanaka.

Tathagata (S): Translated in J as *Nyorai*, 'the Thus-Come-One', who has arrived from and gone to *tathata*, 'suchness', but the real original of the term is unknown; an epithet of the Buddha.

Tatsu-no-Kuchi: Execution grounds outside Kamakura where N miraculously escaped death.

Ten Factors of Existence (*junyoze*): 1) appearance, 2) inner quality or nature, 3) embodiment, 4) potency, 5) function, 6) inner cause, 7) environmental cause, 8) effects, 9) retribution, 10) inseparability of the nine (*Dharma Flower*, Chap. 2).

Ten Worlds or Realms of all living things (*jikkai*): hell, hungry spirits, animals, humanity, heavenly beings, *asuras* (furious spirits), disciples of the Buddha, *pratyekabuddhas* (solitary sages), Bodhisattvas, and Buddhas; each contains all the others potentially; each interacts with its own environment; all exist in the one mind.

Tendai (Heavenly Terrace): J sect founded by Dengyo Daishi (Saicho) based on C T'ien-t'ai, with additional elements drawn from Pure Land, and esotericism. Chih-i is often called, 'Tendai the Great'.

Tengu-fudo: Type of esoteric Buddhism derived from Shingon.

Theravada: 'Way of the Elders'; only surviving Hinayana sect, dominant in SE Asia.

Three Bodies of Buddha (S: Trikaya; J: Sanjin): 1) Truth-body (Dharmakaya/Hosshin), being-in-itself, 'suchness'; 2) Reward-body (Samboghakaya/Hojin), truth comprehensible or idealized; Manifest or Action-body (Nirmanakaya/Ojin), the historical Buddha. According to N, when we chant Odaimoku, our body is the Truth-body, our mind is the Reward-body, and our behaviour is the Manifest-body.

Three Categories Differing Living Beings (*San-seken*): Individual make-up, social environment, and location in space/time.

Three Signs of Being or Seal of the Three Laws (samboin): 1) All things are impermanent; 2) Nothing has a ego; 3) Nirvana is quiescence.

Three Truths (Santai): *Ku*, emptiness, all existence is non-substantial; *ke*, all existence has transient reality; *chu*, middle way transcends this dichotomy. *En-nyu-san-tai*, 'Complete combination of the Three Truths': The universal (*ku*) apart from the particular (*ke*) is an abstraction; the particular apart from the universal is unreal; the universal realizes its true nature in the particular, and the particular derives its meaning from the universal; the middle path (*chu*) unites these two aspects of the one reality. Each of the three consists of all three.

Three Poisons: Desire, animosity, and delusion.

Three Thousand Things (Worlds) in the Momentary Existence (Ichinen-sanzen): All possible existences are contained on one thought; the figure of 3,000 is obtained by combining the Ten Factors, Ten Worlds (10×10 since each contains all the others potentially), and the Three Categories.

Three Treasures (Sambo): Buddha, Dharma, and Sangha. In NS, the Eternal Buddha Shakyamuni is the Buddha, the Sacred Title is the Dharma, and Nichiren and his followers are the Sangha. In NSS, Nichiren is the Buddha, the Sacred Title is the Dharma, and Nikko and his followers are the Sangha.

Threefold Lotus Sutra: Sutra of Innumerable Meanings (*Muryogi-kyo*), Lotus Sutra (*Myoho Renge Kyo*), and Meditation on the Bodhisattva Universal Virtue (*Kanfugen-gyo*).

Toda, Josei (1900–58): Disciple of Makiguchi and founder of Sokagakkai.

Toki Jonin (1216–99): Most prominent lay follower of N; ordained himself with the name of Nichijo; founder of Nakayama School.

Transmission of Shakyamuni's Teachings: External transmission from Shakyamuni to Medicine-King Bodhisattva (Bhaisajya-raja/Yakuo), to Chih-i, to Saicho, to Nichiren; Internal transmission from Shakyamuni to Superior-Action Bodhisattva (Visista-caritra/Jogyo), to Nichiren.

Twelve-fold Chain of Dependent Origination: Ignorance, actions, consciousness, body and mind, senses, contact, sensations, desire, clinging, existence, birth–old age–death.

Void, Emptiness (S: shunya, shunyata; J: ku): Relativity; absence of any permanent sub-stratum; infinite potentiality.

Vulture Peak, (S: Grdhrakuta), Mount Sacred Eagle (J: Ryojusen): High hill near Rajagriha, India, where Shakyamuni preached many sutras including the *Dharma Flower*.

Williams, George (Masayasu Sadanaga): Director of Nichiren Shoshu of America.

Notes

1. The Five Periods are 1) the Flower Garland, 2) the Deer Park, 3) the Expanded Teachings, 4) the Wisdom Teachings, and 5) the Lotus and Nirvana Sutras. The Four Doctrines of Conversion are 1) Tripitaka ('Three Baskets', the Hinayana doctrines), 2) Shared, 3) Distinctive (Mahayana), and 4) Complete. The Four Methods of Conversion are 1) Sudden, 2) Gradual, 3) Secret, and 4) Variable. Most modern students have questioned the temporal sequence. In 1965 the eminent Tendai scholar Shindai Sekiguchi pointed out that Chih-i himself never used the term 'Five Periods', but spoke of 'Five Flavours'. Dengyo Daishi, who introduced Chih-i's teachings to Japan, did not use the term either. 'Five Flavours' does make more sense. The Flower Garland Sutra, for instance, may have the 'flavour' of Shakyamuni's enlightenment, but that does not necessarily mean that it was written first or even preached first. Any of the 'five flavours' could have been taught at any time depending on the capacities and needs of the listeners. See Chappell, 36ff. However, in these pages we have used the traditional Five Periods as a convenient method of classifying Shakyamuni's teachings. Chinese and Japanese writers have done the same at least since the days of Chih-i's great disciple Chan-jan (Zhan-ran, also called Miao-lo, 711–82).
2. Japanese, *Kegon*, Sanskrit, *Avatamsaka*. See note 1.
3. Not all Buddhists agree that this 'harmless concentration may be practised by any person irrespective of religious beliefs'. All the steps of the Eightfold Path should be practised concurrently, and this involves commitment. Meditation done by itself for 'peace of mind' may lead to harmful self-absorption. There are Buddhist sutras that claim that wrong meditation is worse than no meditation. One such case is cited by Nichiren in his *Essay on the Teaching, Capacity, Time and the*

Country (Kyoki Jikoku Sho). See also Christmas Humphreys, 'Should Buddhists Meditate?', *Exploring Buddhism*, 170 ff.

4. In Southern Buddhism (Hinayana), the term 'Bodhisattva' generally refers to Shakyamuni himself, before he became the Buddha. The 'four infinite virtues' of a Bodhisattva are the same in both traditions: loving-kindness, compassion, sympathetic joy, and equanimity.

5. See Kukai, *Major Works*, translated by Yoshito S. Hakeda (New York: Columbia University Press, 1972). There is no English translation of the three esoteric sutras.

6. English translations of these texts can be found in *The Shinshu Seiten: The Holy Scriptures of Shinshu.*

7. Kukai, 'The Difference between Exoteric and Esoteric Buddhism', *Major Works*, 151 ff. 'It was indeed on this occasion (when the Buddha preached Chap. 16 of the Lotus Sutra) that the final truth, the long cherished plan, was proclaimed; it was on this day that all gained completely the unsurpassed truth' (207).

8. A little known translation is by the Christian missionary Timothy Richards, who was fascinated by what he saw as parallels between the *Lotus* and the Gospels. He titled his work, *The New Testament of Higher Buddhism* (Edinburgh: T. and T. Clark, 1910).

9. Selections from this version will be found in E.A. Burtt, *The Teachings of the Compassionate Buddha*, 141–61.

10. Edward Conze, Introduction to D.T. Suzuki, *On Indian Mahayan Buddhism*, 14.

11. S.F. de Silva, 'The Expansion of Buddhism', *2500 Buddha Jayanti Souvenir* (Colombo: The Landa Buddha Mandalaya, 1956), 28.

12. *Samantapasadika*, a Hinayana text, and the Mahayan *Nirvana Sutra.* The *Ajatasatru Sutra* tells the same story, but concentrates more on the suffering king than the queen.

13. The Sanskrit text used by Kern consists of 27 chapters, the 11th and 12th being joined as one. There are some other differences in various versions. See Murano, *The Lotus Sutra*, Introduction and Translator's Notes; *The Threefold Lotus Sutra*, Introduction.

14. The Four Qualities of Nirvana are the opposites of the four basic conditions of human life: true self as opposed to non-self; eternity as opposed to constant change; purity as opposed to impurity; happiness as opposed to suffering.

15. *Shingyo Hikkei: A Handbook for Members of the Nichiren Sect*, 96. These vows are to be recited twice daily.

16. This may be a mistranslation. The Sanskrit *Sadaparibhuta* means 'Always Despised'.

17. Four kinds of devotees: monks, nuns, laymen, and women.

18. Chih-i chose Chapters 2 ('Expedients'), 14 ('Peaceful Practices'), 16 ('Duration of the Life of the Tathagata'), and 25 ('The Universal Gate of the World-Voice-Perceiver Bodhisattva') as the most important chapters of the Sutra. Nichiren revised the selection to Chapters 2, 13 ('Encour-

agement for Keeping the Sutra'), 16, and 21 ('Supernatural Powers of the Tathagatas').

19. Mizuno, *Buddhist Sutras*, 27. For a translation, see Vincent A. Smith, *Asoka: The Buddhist Emperor of India*.

20. Shoson Miyamoto, 'Studies of Buddhism and the Lotus Sutra,' Kanko Mochizuki (ed.), *Recent Developments of Japanese Buddhism Based on the Lotus Sutra*, 2. The author goes on to say, 'This was not a mere idealistic protest against class and racial discriminations; it was a direct, earnest voice, accordant with reality. Shakyamuni was the world's first great humanist, who clarified principles of equality and order in racial problems and professional classifications. Many know him as the founder of Buddhism, but very few appraise him in this light. Among a few Western scholars, who extol Shakyamuni's revolutionizing spirit, tribute is paid to his protests against the caste system, but none have elaborated on the logical ground on which it was made.'

21. Teresina R. Havens in her *Buddhist and Quaker Experiments with Truth*, culminates in the message of the *Lotus*, and quotes a Nichiren priest as saying, 'All of us are Buddha's children and have his nature. As fathers and mothers love their children, so the Buddha loves the many people of the world. No Japan, no China, no India. Buddhism is one family. All people become Buddha' (78).

22. For a helpful diagram, see Chappell, 31.

23. *Madhyamika Shastra.* For Madhyamika as developed in China, see Hsueh-li Cheng, *Empty Logic: Madhyamika Buddhism from Chinese Sources.*

24. A translation is given by Dwight Goddard, *A Buddhist Bible* 437 ff. The contents, however, which imply strict monastic seclusion, hardly seem suitable for a busy army officer. Most likely this work, like others attributed to Chih-i, is a collection of lecture notes.

25. For charts, see C.B. Dharmasena.

26. One can be reborn as a human being when 'the five virtues and the five precepts are practiced. The five virtues are benevolence, righteousness, propriety, wisdom, and faithfulness. The five precepts are no killing, no stealing, no adultery, no lying, and no drinking of alcoholic beverages. By practicing these ten deeds to a moderate degree, the fate of this rebirth is received.' Chappell and Chegwan, 87.

27. *Lotus Sutra* Chap. II 28–9. This is called the One Great Purpose Why the Buddhas Appear in the World: to open, reveal, awaken, and penetrate. See Chappell 79–81.

28. Neo-Confucianism, like Hinduism in India, borrowed certain ideas from Buddhism, used them to modify the ancient traditions of Confucianism and Brahmanism respectively, and then turned them successfully against Buddhism. On Neo-Confucianism, see Arthur W. Wright, *Buddhism in Chinese History* 86ff. On the Buddhist influence on Hinduism, see Lal Mani Joshi, *Brahmanism, Buddhism and Hinduism* (Kandy: Buddhist Publication Society, 1970).

29. Miao-lo is the name of his temple. His given name was Chan-jan (Zhan-ran). He is also called the Great Teacher Ching-hei after his birthplace. It is a widespread custom to name important Buddhist priests after the monastery where they taught or the town of their birth. Chih-i is often known as 'the Greek Teacher T'ien-t'ai (Tian-tai)'. Chang-an (Zhang-an) is called Kuan-ting after his place of birth.

30. In the *Shoku Nihongi* there is the following entry dated 788: 'There had been no rain since last winter — a full five months. Reservoirs were already dried up. Everybody was in despair. In the morning, the emperor took a bath and went out to his yard to pray, himself. Eventually, the sky became dark with clouds and it began to rain heavily. All the courtiers started dancing and shouting, "Banzai!" [Attendants] over the fifth rank were given new clothes. They felt that the prayer for rain was fulfilled because of the sincerity and virtue of the emperor.' Zensho Asaeda, 'Historical Significance of Saicho's Establishment of Japanese Tendai School', (Honolulu: International Conference on the Lotus Sutra in Japanese Culture, 1984). 2–3.

31. Tendai, the Japanese for T'ien-t'ai, refers to the sect founded by Saicho. It differs from Chinese T'ien-t'ai, however, in that it incorporates many elements not found in Chih-i and the Chinese masters, especially esoteric rituals and initiations.

32. Both the nature and history of early Tantra are still controversial subjects. Recent studies by Jeffrey Hopkins, Reginald Ray, and L.A. Seigel will be found in *Buddhist–Christian Studies*, V (1985), 159 ff.

33. Jacob Needleman, *The New Religions: The Teachings of the East — Their Special Meaning for Young Americans* (New York: Pocket Books, 1972), Chap. 7: 'Tibet in America'.

34. The theoretical difference between Shingon and Tendai eso-tericism is that Shingon claims a special revelation from the Dharma-body of Buddha, called Vairocana or 'Great Sun' (*Dainichi*), who permeates the universe. Shakyamuni is only one of his manifestations. Tendai esotericism, following the *Dharma Flower*, believes the Three Bodies are one Buddha; Vairocana is just a name, not a distinct entity. All sutras which teach the One Vehicle are called esoteric and equal 'in theory'. Those which teach mystical *mudras* (gestures) and *mantras* (incantations) are called superior 'in practice' This esotericism of Tendai is called Taimitsu; that of Shingon is known as Tomitsu.

35. Kazuo Kasahara, 'The Shin Sect in the Kamakura Period', *Dharma World* XIII (July 1986), 47–8.

36. Article II of the Nishi Hongwanji Constitution reads: 'The funda-mental teaching of the Jodo Shinshu is to hear and to have faith in the Holy Name of Amida and to give thanksgiving to his Great Compassion — this is called the Absolute Truth (*Shintai-mon*). To obey the laws of morality and to be loyal to one's country — this is called the Secular Truth (*Zokutai-mon*). Therefore, all of the acts of morality by the Shin devotee are not for the sake of accumulating merit for the sake of

rebirth, but are to be considered as thanksgiving to Amida Buddha for His Love and Mercy.' *Buddhism and Jodo Shinshu* (San Francisco: The Buddhist Churches of American, 1955), 135.

37. Kencho-ji at Yamanouchi, built for Rankei Doryu of the Rinzai Zen Sect.

38. Senchu Murano, 'A History of Buddhism, XCV', *The Young East*, XV (Autumn 1966), 9.

39. *Myoho-Renge-Kyo* is the Japanese pronunciation of the Chinese, *Miao-fa-lien-hua-ching*, which is the title of the Chinese translation of the *Saddharma-pundarika-sutra* by Kumarajiva. *Saddharma* means 'true law' (dharma), and *pundarika* 'white lotus'. The Chinese translation is a little different in meaning from the original one because *miao* means 'wonderful' and *lien-ha* 'lotus flower'. *Namu* comes from the Sanskrit *namas*, which means 'Honour be to'. The optative mood of the word was lost when it was translated into Chinese as *kuei-ming* (*kimyo* in Japanese), which means, 'I devote myself to'. Senchu Murano, 'An Explanation of the Great Mandala' (University of Hawaii, International Conference on the Lotus Sutra in Japanese Culture, 1984).

Contrary to popular opinion, Nichiren did not invent the formula *Namu-Myoho-Renge-Kyo*, which had been used in Tendai Buddhism. Nichiren, however, made it central, not peripheral. Senchu Murano, 'The Lotus Sutra and Nichiren' 30 April 1984; privately printed), 1.

40. Many authors say that Nichiren criticized all the Japanese sects in his first sermon. There is no historical transcript of the sermon, so all such accounts are imaginary. In the *Rissho-Ankoku-ron*, which was written seven years later (1260), Nichiren limited his criticisms to the Nembutsu. Not until his exile on Izu (1261-2) do his recorded works broaden their criticisms to include other sects.

41. *Kai Shu E* (Nichiren Order of America), Leaflet No. 5.

42. Christensen 51. The verses will be found in Murano, *The Lotus Sutra*, 269 and 216.

43. Toki Jonin (1216-99?). We give his name in the usual Japanese order: family name first (Toki) followed by his Buddhist name (Jonin). The family temple is now Nakayama Hokekyo-ji, a Head Temple of the Nichiren Order and repository of many valuable documents written by Nichiren.

44. Zen was promoted in Kamakura by such teachers as Eisai and Dogen, who had travelled to China, and Rankei Doryu (Lan-ch'i Tao-lung), a native Chinese, who convinced Nichiren not to bother going to China. It was supported by the Hojo clan, especially Tokiyori. Shingon-ritsu and Shingi Shingon were recent break-offs from Shingon.

45. Endo Asai, 'Sokagakkai', *Recent Developments of Japanese Buddhism Based on the Lotus Sutra* 12. Also 'Sandaihiho-sho: An Essay on the Three Great Mysteries', *Journal of Nichiren Buddhism*, Vol. III and IV, 1983.

46. These ideas are set forth in many of Nichiren's writings, especially

in his long essay 'Selection of the Time', MW 3: 79–184.

47. Yoshifumi Ueda, 'The Lotus Sutra and the Development of Mahayana Buddhism', Yensho Kanakura (ed.), *The Lotus Sutra and the Development of Buddhist Thought*, 15.

48. Pao-chang, *Biographies of Buddhist Nuns*, tr. Li Jung-hsi (Osaka: Tohokai, Inc., 1981).

49. I.B. Horner, *Women in Early Buddhist Literature* (Kandy: Buddhist Publication Society, 1961) 19.

50. Junko Oguri, 'Views of Women's Salvation in Japanese Buddhism'. The quotation is from Nichiren's *Gessui gosho*.

51. 'All laws and phenomena are included in the five characters, *myo-ho-ren-ge-kyo*'. *Hokekyo Daimoku sho*. See *Lotus Sutra*, Chap. 19, 256.

52. Also called Taira no Yoritsuna; Taira and Hei are written with the same Chinese character.

53. Robert N. Bellah, *Tokugawa Religion*, 35. Mitsuyuki Masatsugu, *The Modern Samurai Society: Duty and Dependence in Contemporary Japan*, *passim*.

54. Some scholars believe that Abutsu, or Abutsu-bo, as Nichiren generally called him respectfully, was a native of Sado.

55. 'Sandaihiho-sho: An Essay on the Three Great Mysteries', *Journal of Nichiren Buddhism*, III (1983), 42.

56. John Carpenter, 'Calligraphy in Japanese Buddhism,' *Dharma World* XIV (March/April 1987), 39.

57. These remarks were directed to Nanjo Tokimitsu, a staunch supporter who later helped Nikko establish Taiseki-ji Temple.

58. Copies of this beautiful print are sometimes mislabelled 'Nichiren in the Snow on Sado'.

59. Ikegami Hommon-ji, on the outskirts of modern Tokyo and administrative headquarters of the Nichiren Order (*Nichiren-shu*), is not the same as Kitayama Hommon-ji, which was founded by Nikko in the Fuji area. The latter was for many centuries a Head Temple of the Nikko Branch, but since 1941 has been affiliated with the Nichiren Order.

60. Sandra Seki, 'Introducing Nichiren Temples: Sogenji', *Nichiren Shu News*, No. 35 (1985), 4, and *Kuon-ji* (Kuon-ji: Minobusan, n.d.), 20.

61. The following name changes took place in 1898 and then in 1950: Kommon-ha (founded by Nikko) became Hommon Shu. (In 1900 Taiseki-ji and its dependent temples withdrew from Kommon-ha, calling themselves Nichiren-shu Fuji-ha; in 1913 this name was changed to Nichiren Shoshu. Yobo-ji seceded from the merged Hommon Shu and Nichiren-shu in 1950, naming itslf Nichiren Honshu.) Myomanji-ha (founded by Nichiju) became Kempon Hokke Shu and retained this name in 1950. Honjoji-ha (founded by Nichijin) became Hokke Shu and then Hokke Shu (Jin Monryu). Happon-ha (founded by Nichiryu) became Hommon Hokke Shu and then Hokke Shu (Hon Monryu). Nisshin Monryu became Hommyo Hokke Shu and then Hokke Shu (Shin Monryu). The terms *monryu* and *ha* both mean 'branch'.

62. Kitayama means 'northern hill'.

63. According to Nichiren Shoshu, the epistle *Shonin Gonan Ji*, which they translate as 'On Persecutions Befalling the Buddha', contains 'the sole reference to his inscription of the Dai-Gohonzon as the purpose of his life' (MW 1: 243). However, this epistle makes no specific mention of a Gohonzon.

64. The Nichiren Shu understanding is given in its official handbook, *Shingyo Hikkei*: 'Our faith is to obtain the world of peace and tranquility by reciting the *Odaimoku* while facing the *Gohonzon*. The *Gohonzon* is the Eternal Buddha, who embraces us with His rays of wisdom and compassion when we put our complete faith in Him. The *Gohonzon* as shown in Chapter 16 of the Lotus Sutra is the relationship between the Eternal Buddha Shakyamuni on the one hand, who is calling us and trying to save us all, and ourselves on the other hand, who pray with all our hearts to be saved and help others to be saved. Therefore, we revere Shakyamuni Buddha as the *Gohonzon*. The *Omandara* represents the enlightenment of the Eternal Buddha and the very heart of the Buddha, and therefore it is a graphic representation of Shakyamuni's spirit, itself' (4–5).

65. '*Nam-myoho-renge-kyo*' is called the original Law of *kuon ganjo*, meaning the Law which has existed since time without beginning. Unlike the other Buddhas who awakened to this Law, Nichiren Daishonin is originally enlightened to the Law; in other words, his life is originally one with the Law from the infinite past or *kuon ganjo*. Therefore, the Daishonin is called the original Buddha of *kuon ganjo*. Borrowing the imagery of the Lotus Sutra's ceremony in the air, he inscribed his enlightened life — which is one with the law of *Nam-myoho-renge-kyo* — in physical form as a mandala, which he established as an object of worship. In those days the Shingon sect used pictures of Buddhas and Bodhisattvas as mandalas, but these were merely symbols of the people's reverence for these sacred beings. Nichiren Daishonin chose to use the ceremony in the air described in the Lotus Sutra in order to express his enlightenment, but the mandala he inscribed is not a symbol; it is the embodiment of the life of the original Buddha, which is at the same time the eternal Law of *kuon ganjo*. On 12 October 1279 Nichiren Daishonin established this mandala, called the Dai-Gonhonzon (literally supreme object of worship) as the basis of faith for all people everywhere' (Kirimura, *Outline of Buddhism* 75–6).

66. Taiseki-ji, like some other temples, counts Nichiren as its founder even though he never set foot there. This is considered justified if the actual founder was personally converted by Nichiren. It is not uncommon in Japan to name a distinguished predecessor as the honorary founder of a temple. Nichizo, for example, who struggled so hard to open the door for Nichiren Buddhism in Kyoto, gave the credit not to himself but to his Master Nichiro, who never went to Kyoto.

67. *Dictionary of Buddhist Terms and Concepts* 482–3. The term *kuon jitsujo* is found in Chapter 16 of the Lotus Sutra (*Nen ga jitsu jo-butsu irai kuon nyaku shi*: 'In reality I became the Buddha in the remotest past as previously stated') and is used by Nichiren Shu. The term *Kuon ganjo* is not used in the Sutra but was invented by Nichiren Shoshu theologians to distinguish between Shakyamuni's 'remotest past' and Nichiren's 'beginningless past'. Murata, 65–6.

68. This idea appeals to the prominent biologist Hisatoki Komaki, who writes: 'Quite recently I came to know that Nichiren Daishonin revealed that "Nam-myoho-renge-kyo" is the ultimate true entity of the Law of Life that vibrates in infinite and eternal harmony throughout the Universe. At first, I regarded the chanting of "Nam-myoho-renge-kyo" as merely one of the most powerful methods of controlling our mind or regulating our life-rhythm in a very desirable and natural (healthy) rhythm. By regarding [it] so, I interpreted the Buddhist word "kudoku" [religious merits] as the "improvement" of our daily life as the result of excluding the "noise" of our life-rhythm by chanting [the] strongest invocation, "Nam-myoho-renge-kyo". Recently, however, I realized that my understanding was the recognition of [only] half of the truth. I realized that the chanting of the Daimoku (Nam-myoho-renge-kyo) is not only the most powerful method of tuning our mind in[to] the rhythm of the Universe, but [is] also the Rhythm of the Universe, itself. I realized that [this] is the very reason why the chanting of "Nam-myoho-renge-kyo" is the most effective [means for] clarifying and strengthening our "life pattern"'. Hisotaki Komaki, *The Selected Works*, Vol. III: Scientific and Philosophical (The British Hisotaki Komaki Foundation, Plymouth, England, and the American Hisotaki Komaki Foundation, Norwalk, USA, 1980) 97.

69. Unless otherwise noted, all 20th century Japanese names are rendered in the Western style: given name followed by family name.

70. In some Nichiren groups mystical experience is normative. Helen Hardacre questioned members of Reiyukai and found that 79.2 per cent reported that they had experienced *kuji*, which in Reiyukai means a transcendental experience in the broad sense or spiritual healing power in the narrow sense. (Hardacre, 244)

71. Schecter, *The New Face of Buddha*, 261–2; Brannen, *Soka Gakkai: Japan's Militant Buddhists*, 101; Fujiwara, *I Denounce Soka Gakkai*, 89.

72. In his historical novel *The Human Revolution*, Daisaku Ikeda gives Jimon Ogasawara the name, 'Jiko Kasahara'.

73. *World Tribune*, interview with Akron, Ohio, theatre manager Wayne Alley after the 1973 General Meeting.

74. For Nichiren Shoshu in Britain, see Richard Causton, *Nichiren Shoshu Buddhism*, 270ff. The headquarters of NSUK are at Taplow Court, Berkshire. Its motto is 'Trust through Friendship, Peace through Trust'.

75. The words are not actually Kubo's, but come from an article in the official Reiyukai magazine, *Reiyukaiho*, No. 134 (12 April 1941). Cited by Hardacre, 49.

76. Thomsen, 109. Fifteen groups originating from Reiyukai, their dates and founders, are listed by Hardacre, 49.

77. Thomsen 110–11; Hardacre, 46–7.

78. Maitreya (Pali, *Meteyya*; Japanse, *Miroku*), 'Benevolent': the clan name of the future Buddha. His given name is Ajita, 'Invincible'.

79. Niwano, *Travel to Infinity* 122–6. In *Lifetime Beginner*, a later and more detailed autobiography, Niwano does not mention that Rissho Kosei-kai was once affiliated with Nichiren Shu.

80. The 'divine revelations' reported by Niwano bear a close resemblance to the 'demonic voices' studied by psychologist Wilson Van Dusen, *The Natural Depth of Man* (New York: Harper and Row, 1972), Chapter 10: 'Hallucinations'.

81. *Myoho-Renge-Kyo: The Sutra of the Lotus Flower of the Wonderful Law*, tr. Bunno Kato, rev. W.E. Soothill and Wilhelm Schiffer (1971); *Muryogi-Kyo: The Sutra of Innumerable Meanings and Kanfugen-Gyo: The Sutra of Meditation on the Bodhisattva Universal-Virtue* (1974); *The Threefold Lotus Sutra* (1975). The latter combines the contents of the other two with some minor revisions.

82. *The Lotus Sutra: Life and Soul of Buddhism* (1971); *Buddhism for Today: A Modern Interpretation of the Threefold Lotus Sutra* (1976); *A Guide to the Threefold Lotus Sutra* (1981).

83. *Travel to Infinity* (1968); *Lifetime Beginner* (1976).

84. Masahiro Mori, *The Buddha and the Robot: A Robot Engineer's Thoughts on Science and Religion* (1981); Kogen Mizuno, *Buddhist Sutras: Origin, Development, Transmission* (1982), *The Beginnings of Buddhism* (1980), and *Basic Buddhist Concepts* (1987); Bunsaku Kurata and Yoshiro Tamura, (eds.), *Art of the Lotus Sutra* (1987).

85. The monthly *Dharma World* replaced *Seikyo Times* in 1974; it increased in size and became bi-monthly in 1986.

86. By 1988 there were Rissho Kosei-kai churches in Okinawa, Honolulu, Kona, and Maui in Hawaii, Los Angeles, San Francisco, Seattle, Chicago, and New York and societies in Britain and Australia.

87. Lotus Sutra, Chap. 3. Kato's translation reads, 'All these living creatures are my sons to whom I will equally give the Great-vehicle, so that there will be no one who gains an individual nirvana, but all gain nirvana by the same nirvana as the Tathagata' (90). Hurvitz reads, 'He gives the Great Vehicle equally to all, not allowing any of them to gain passage into extinction for himself alone, but conveying to them all the extinction of the Thus Come One' (63).

88. There are sets of five recitations in the morning and three in the evening. In each set the entire 16th chapter is read once; otherwise only the verses. The pace is as rapid as possible.

Bibliography

Akiya, Einosuke, *Guide to Buddhism* (Tokyo: The Seikyo Press, 1968).

Anesaki, Masahuru, *Nichiren the Buddhist Prophet* (Gloucester, Mass.: Peter Smith, 1966).

Argüelles, José and Miriam, *Mandala* (Berkeley and London: Shambala, 1972).

Bellah, Robert N., *Tokugawa Religion* (Boston: Beacon Press, 1970).

Benz, Ernst, *Buddhism or Communism: Which Holds the Future of Asia?* (New York: Doubleday, 1965).

Blofeld, John, *Bodhisattva of Compassion: The Mystical Tradition of Kwan Yin* (Boulder: Shambala, 1978).

Bloom, Alfred, 'Historical Significance of Nichiren's Buddhism'. *Young East*, XIV (Autumn 1965), 2–6, 28.

——, *Shinran's Gospel of Pure Grace* (Tucson: The University of Arizona Press, 1965).

Buddhadatta Mahathera, A.P., *Concise Pali-English Dictionary* (Colombo: U. Chandradasa de Silva, 1968).

Buddha-Dharma, New English edn. (Berkeley: Numata Center for Buddhist Translation and Research, 1984).

Buddha's World (Tokyo and Los Angeles: The Reiyukai).

Buncie, William K., *Religions in Japan: Buddhism, Shinto, Christianity* (Rutland/Tokyo: Charles E. Tuttle Co., 1955).

Burtt, E.A. (ed.), *The Teachings of the Compassionate Buddha* (New York: A Mentor Religious Classic, The New American Library, 1955).

Brannen, Noah S., *Soka Gakkai: Japan's Militant Buddhists* (Richmond: John Knox Press, 1968).

Campbell, Joseph, *The Hero with a Thousand Faces* (Princeton University press, second edn, 1968).

——, (ed.), *Myths, Dreams and Religion* (Dallas: Spring Publications, Inc. 1970).

——, with Bill Moyers, *The Power of Myth* (New York: Doubleday 1988).

Causton, Richard, *Nichiren Shoshu Buddhism* (San Francisco: Harper & Row, 1989).

Chappell, David W. (ed.), Ichishima, Masao (compiler), *T'ien-T'ai Buddhism: An Outline of the Fourfold Teachings* recorded by Korean Buddhist Monk Chegwan (Tokyo: Daiichi-Shobo, 1983).

Cheng, Hsueh-li, *Empty Logic: Madhyamika Buddhism from Chinese Sources* (New York: The Philosophical Library, 1984).

Christensen, J.A., *St. Nichiren* (Tokyo: Nichiren Shu Betsuin, 1981).

Circle (The International Reiyukai Quarterly Magazine) (Tokyo: The Reiyukai).

Conze, Edward, *Buddhism: Its Essence and Development* (New York: Harper Torchbooks, 1959).

——, *Buddhist Meditation* (London: George Allen and Unwin, 1956).

——, *Buddhist Scriptures* (Harmondsworth: Penguin, 1959).

——, *Buddhist Texts Through the Ages* (New York: Harper Torchbooks, 1964).

Cowell, E.B. (ed.), *Buddhist Mahayana Texts* (New York: Dover Publications, 1969).

Daihoko, Hommon Butsuryu-shu.

Dator, James A., *Soka Gakkai: Builders of the Third Civilization* (Seattle: University of Washington Press, 1969).

De Bary, W. Theodore, (ed.), *The Buddhist Tradition in India, China and Japan* (New York: The Modern Library, 1969).

——, *Sources of Chinese Tradition*, vol. I (New York: Columbia University Press, 1960).

——, *Sources of Indian Tradition*, vol. I (New York: Columbia University Press, 1958).

——, *Sources of Japanese Tradition*, vol. I (New York: Columbia University Press, 1958 (1964)).

Dharma World (Tokyo: Rissho Kosei-kai).

A Dictionary of Buddhist Terms and Concepts (Tokyo, Nichiren Shoshu International Center, 1983).

Discovery (Los Angeles: Reiyukai America).

Dykstra, Yoshiko K. (tr.), *Miraculous Tales of the Lotus Sutra from Ancient Japan (Dainihonkoku hokekyoenki of Priest Chingen)* (Hirakata City: The Kansai University of Foreign Studies, 1983).

Earhart, H. Byron, *Japanese Religion: Unity and Diversity* (2nd edn) (Belmont, California: Wadsworth Publishing Co., 1974).

Eidmann, Karl Philipp, *The Unimpeded Single Way* (San Francisco: Bureau of Buddhist Education, 1963).

Einstein, Albert and Infeld, Leopold, *The Evolution of Physics* (New York: Simon and Schuster, 1942).

Ellwood, Robert S., *The Eagle and the Rising Sun* (Philadelphia: Westminister Press, 1974).

Fujii, Kyoyu, *Nichiren Shonin Eden* (Minobusan Kuonji, 1973).

——, (ed.), *The Pictorial Life of Saint Nichiren*, painted by Chokusai Uenaka (Tokyo: Nichiren-shu Asian Buddhist Friendship Association, 1986).

Fujii, Nichidatsu, *Buddhism for World Peace* (Tokyo: Japan-Bharat Sarvodaya Mitrata Sangha, 1980).

Fujimoto, Ryukyo, *An Outline of the Triple Sutra of Shin Buddhism*, vol. II (Kyoto: Hyyaka-en Press, 1960).

Fujiwara, Hiroshi, *I Denounce Soka Gakkai* (Tokyo: Nisshin Hodo Co., 1970).

Getty, Alice, *The Gods of Northern Buddhism* (New York: Dover Publications, 1988).

Guenther, Herbert V., *The Tantric View of Life* (Boulder and London: Shambhala, 1976).

Goddard, Dwight (ed.), *A Buddhist Bible* (Boston: Beacon Press, 1970).

Groner, Paul, *Saicho: The Establishment of the Japanese Tendai School* (Berkeley: Berkeley Buddhist Studies, 1984).

Hakeda, Yoshito, *Kukai: Major Works, translated, with an Account of his Life and a Study of his Thought* (New York: Columbia University Press, 1972).

Hardacre, Helen, *Lay Buddhism in Contemporary Japan; Reiyukai Kyodan* (Princeton: Princeton University Press, 1984).

Havens, Teresina R., *Buddhist and Quaker Experiments with Truth* (Philadelphia: Religious Education Committee, Friends General Conference, n.d.).

A History of Nichiren Buddhism in Hawaii (Honolulu: Nichiren Mission of Hawaii, 1982).

Holton, D.C., *Modern Japan and Shinto Nationalism* (New York: Paragon Book Reprint Corp., (rev edn), 1963).

The Honolulu Advertiser, 'Bishop Breaks the Buddhist Mold', *The Sunday Star-Bulletin & Advertiser*, (30 August 1981).

Hosino, Eiki, 'Some Characteristics of Japanese Buddhism in Hawaii', *Young East*, vol. 9, no. 1 (Winter 1983), 29–35.

Hoshino, Eisen and Murano, Senchu, *The Lotus Sutra and Nichiren* (Jitsujoji Temple, 1968).

Htoon, U Chan, *Buddhism and the Age of Science* (Kandy: Buddhist Publication Society, 1967).

Humphreys, Christmas, *Buddhism* (Harmondsworth: Penguin, 1955).

——, *Exploring Buddhism* (Wheaton, Ill.: Theosophical Publishing House, 1974).

Hunter, Louise H., *Buddhism in Hawaii: Its Impact on a Yankee Community* (Honolulu: University of Hawaii Press, 1971).

Hurvitz, Leon, *Scripture of the Lotus Blossom of the Fine Dharma (The Lotus Sutra)* (New York: Columbia University Press, 1976).

I Devote Myself to the Lotus of the True Law (Tokyo: The Reiyukai, 1975).

Ichishima, Masao, 'Lotus Debates between Tendai and Hosso Schools

Concerning the Attainment of Buddhahood', (University of Hawaii: International Conference on the Lotus Sutra in Japanese Culture, 1984).
——, 'The Teachings of the Tendai Sect', *Young East*, vol. XV (Summer 1966), 22–4.
Ienaga, Saburo, *The Pacific War: 1931–1945* (New York: Pantheon Books, 1978).
Iida, Shotaro, 'Seven Hundred Years After Nichiren', (International Conference on the Lotus Sutra in Japanese Culture, University of Hawaii, 1984).
Ikeda, Daisaku, *Buddhism, Its First Millennium* (Tokyo: Kodansha International Ltd., 1977; first pb edn, 1982).
——, *The Human Revolution*, vol. IV (Tokyo: The Seikyo Press, 1968).
——, *Lectures on Buddhism*, vol. IV (Tokyo: The Seikyo Press, 1967).
——, *Science and Religion* (Tokyo: Sokagakkai, 1965).
Inner Quest (Tokyo: The Reiyukai).
Inagaki, Hisao, *A Dictionary of Japanese Buddhist Terms* (Kyoto: Nagata Bunshodo, 2nd edn, 1985).
Inner Trip Friends (Los Angeles: The Reiyukai).
Itohisa, Hoken, 'The Development of the Nichiren Sect in Kyoto: Formation of "Monryu" or Subsects and Their Organizational Structure' (International Conference on the Lotus Sutra in Japanese Culture, University of Hawaii, 1984).
Iwamoto, Yutaka, 'Kanzeon', *Young East*, vol. 8, no. 2 (Spring 1982), 14–34.
Japanese–English Buddhist Dictionary (Tokyo: Daito Shuppansa, 1965).
Journal of Nichiren Buddhism (New York: The Institute of Nichiren Buddhism).
Ju-Ryo-Hon (Tokyo: Nipponzan Myohoji, 1978).
Kaihatsu, Reiyukai America Association.
Kanakura, Yensho (ed.), *The Lotus Sutra and the Development of Buddhist Thought* (Kyoto: Heirakuji Shoten, 1970).
Kato, Bunno (tr.), *Myoho-Renge-Kyo: The Sutra of the Lotus Flower of the Wonderful Law* (Tokyo: Kosei Publishing Co., 1971).
Kern, H., *Saddharma-Pundarika or The Lotus of the True Law* (New York: Dover Publications, 1963). First published by Clarendon Press, Oxford, 1884.
Kirimura, Yasuji, *Fundamentals of Buddhism* (Santa Monica: World Tribune Press, 1982).
——, (ed.), *Outline of Buddhism* (Tokyo: Nichiren Shoshu International Center, 1981).
Kitagawa, Zencho, 'Characteristics of Nichiren's Interpretation of the Lotus Sutra', *Osaki Gakuho*, no. 138, (February 1985).
Kosei Times (Tokyo: Rissho Kosei-kai).
Kubo, Katsuko, *Reflections in Search of Myself* (Tokyo: Sangaku Publishing Co., 1976).

Kubo, Tsugunari, 'The Dawn of New Buddhism'. (Tokyo: *Circle Quest* and *Inner Quest*, The Reiyukai).

——, *The Development of Japanese Lay Buddhism* (Tokyo: The Reiyukai, 1986).

——, *Inner Trip* (Tokyo: Sankei-Shinbun, 1972).

——, *The Philosophical Foundation of the Lay Buddhist Practice of the Reiyukai as depicted in the Lotus Sutra* (Tokyo: The Reiyukai, 1988).

——, *The Reiyukai Movement as an Interreligious Philosophy* (Tokyo: The Reiyukai, 1987).

Kyoden: Selections from the Threefold Lotus Sutra (Tokyo: Rissho Kosei-kai, 3rd rev edn, 1979).

Layman, Emma M., *Buddhism in America* (Chicago: Nelson Hall, 1976).

Lectures on the Sutra: Hoben and Juryo Chapters (Tokyo: Nichiren Shoshu International Center, rev edn, 1984).

Legge, James (tr.), *A Record of Buddhistic Kingdoms: Being an account by the Chinese Monk Fa-Hien of his travels in India and Ceylon (A.D. 399–414) in search of the Buddhist Books of Discipline* (New York: Paragon Book Reprint Corp; Dover Publications, Inc., 1965).

Lotus Sutra: see Murano, *The Sutra of the Lotus Flower of the Wonderful Law.*

The Liturgy of Nichiren Shoshu: The Taisekiji Version, 1979.

The Major Writings of Nichiren Daishonin (Tokyo: Nichiren Shoshu International Center, vol. I, 1978, vol. II, 1981, vol. III, 1985, vol. IV, 1986).

Malalasekera, G.P., *Aspects of Reality as Taught by Theravada Buddhism* (Kandy: Buddhist Publication Society, 1968).

Masatsugu, Mitsuyuki, *The Modern Samurai Society: Duty and Dependence in Contemporary Japan* (New York: American Management Associations, 1982).

Matsunami, Kodo, 'Buddhism in the World Today: An Overview', *Young East*, vol. 7, no. 4 (Autumn 1981), 6–30.

McFarland, H. Neill, *The Rush Hour of the Gods* (New York: Macmillan, 1967).

The Middle Way (London: British Buddhist Association).

Minobusan Kuonji (Minobusan, 1982).

The Miroku Sutra (Tokyo: The Reiyukai, 1974).

Mizuno, Kogen, *The Beginnings of Buddhism* (Tokyo: Kosei Publishing Co., 1980).

——, *Buddhist Sutras: Origin, Development, Transmission* (Tokyo: Kosei Publishing Co., 1982).

Mochizuki, Kanko (ed.), *Recent Developments of Japanese Buddhism Based on the Lotus Sutra* (Kyoto: Heirakuji Shoten, 1968).

——, Suzuki Ichijo, and Shioda Gison, *The Nichiren Sect, Part 1* (Tokyo: The Young East Association, 1958).

Montgomery, Daniel B., *The Eye of the Sutra* (Tokyo: The Reiyukai, 1974).

——, 'The Lotus Sutra and the New Religions: The Lotus Comes West' (International Conference on the Lotus Sutra in Japanese Culture, University of Hawaii, 1984).

Murano, Senchu, 'An Explanation of the Great Mandala' (Honolulu: International Conference on the Lotus Sutra in Japanese Culture, 1984).

——, *A History of Buddhism*, vol. XCIV, 'The Kamakura Government and Buddhism': vol. XCV, 'Nichiren and the Nichiren Sect', *Young East*, vol. XV (Autumn 1966), 5–14.

——, 'Nichiren's Writings', (privately printed, 1982).

——, *An Outline of the Lotus Sutra* (Tokyo: Nichiren Shu Headquarters, 1974).

——, 'The Sokagakkai and the Nichiren Sho Sect', *Young East*, vol. XV (Summer 1966), 2–8.

——, (tr.), *The Sutra of the Lotus Flower of the Wonderful Law* (Tokyo: Nichiren Shu Headquarters, 1974).

Murano, Senchu and Montgomery, Daniel B., *The Sutra of the Lotus Flower of the Wonderful Dharma* (Tokyo: Nichiren Shu Headquarters, 1990).

Murata, Kiyoaki, *Japan's New Buddhism: An Objective Account of Soka Gakkai* (New York & Tokyo: Walker/Weatherhill, 1969).

Muryogi-Kyo: The Sutra of Innumerable Meanings and Kanfugen-Gyo: The Sutra of Meditation on the Bodhisattva Universal-Virtue (Tokyo: Kosei Publishing Co., 1974).

Myoko Ichiza (Hommon Butsuryu-shu. 1986).

NSA Quarterly (Santa Monica, CA: World Tribune Press).

NSA Seminar Report, 1968–1971 (Santa Monica: World Tribune Press, 1972).

Narada Thera and Bikkhu Kassapa, *The Mirror of the Dhamma* (Kandy: Buddhist Publication Society, 1963).

Nezu, Masuo, 'Comparisons of Honzons of Rissho Kosei Kai and Soka Gakkai in Relation to Nichiren Buddhism' (privately printed, September 1972).

——, 'Nichiren's Thought on Jingi Shinko' (privately printed, June 1972).

Nichiren, *Hoon-jo*, Taikyo Yajima (tr.) (Tokyo: Nichiren Shu Overseas Propagation Promotion Association, 1988).

——, *Kaimoku-sho*, Kyotsu Hori (tr.) (Tokyo: Nichiren Shu Overseas Propagation Promotion Association, 1988).

——, *Nyorai Metsugo Go Gohyakusai Shi Kanjin Honzon Sho or The True Object of Worship for the First Time in the Fifth of Five-Century Periods after the Great Decease of the Tathagata*, Senchu Murano (tr.) (Tokyo: The Young East Association, 1954).

——, *Rissho Ankoku Ron or Establish the Right Law and Save Our Country*, Senchu Murano (tr.) (Tokyo: Nichiren Shu Headquarters, 1977).

——, *Senji-sho*, Kyotsu Hori (tr.) (Tokyo: Nichiren Shu Overseas Propagation Promotion Association, 1989).

Nichiren Shoshu Sokagakkai (Tokyo: The Seikyo Press, 1966).

Nichiren Shoshu International Center, *Lectures on the Sutra* Tokyo, (rev. edn, 1984).

The Nichiren-shu (Tokyo: Asia Buddhist Friendship Association, Nichiren-shu, 1985).

Nichiren Shu Jiten (The Encyclopedia of the Nichiren Sect) (Tokyo: Nichiren-shu Shumuin, 1982).

Nichiren Shu News (Tokyo: Nichiren Shu Shumuin).

Niwano, Nichiko, *My Father, My Teacher* (Tokyo: Kosei Publishing Co., 1982).

Niwano, Nikkyo, *Buddhism for Today: A Modern Interpretation of the Threefold Lotus Sutra* (Tokyo: Kosei Publishing Co., 1976).

——, *A Guide to the Threefold Lotus Sutra* (Tokyo: Kosei Publishing Co., 1981).

——, *Honzon: The Object of Worship in Rissho Kosei Kai* (Tokyo: Kosei Publishing Co., 1969).

——, *The Lotus Sutra: Life and Soul of Buddhism* (Tokyo: Kosei Publishing Co., 1970).

——, *The Richer Life* (Tokyo: Kosei Publishing Co., 1975).

——, *Travel to Infinity* (Tokyo: Kosei Publishing House, 1968). (Japanese *Mugen e no tabi*, 1963).

Nomura, Yosho (ed.), *The Lotus Sutra and Religious Realities* (Kyoto: Heirakuji Shoten, 1976).

Oguri, Junko, 'Views on Women's Salvation in Japanese Buddhism', *Young East*, vol. 10, no. 1 (Winter 1984), 3–11.

Osaki Gakuho: The Journal of Nichiren Buddhism (Tokyo: Rissho University).

Parks, Yoko, 'Nichiren Shoshu Academy in America: Changes During the 1970s', *Journal of Nichiren Buddhism*, vol. 3, Winter 1983.

Petzold, Bruno, *Buddhist Prophet Nichiren: A Lotus in the Sun* (Tokyo: Hokke Journal, Inc., 1978).

——, *Tendai Buddhism* (Yokohama: International Buddhist Exchange Center, 1979).

——, 'Tendai Buddhism as Modern World View', *Young East*, vol. IV (8 October 1929), 281–304.

A Phrase A Day (Tokyo: Nichiren Shu Overseas Propagation Promotion Association, 1986).

Practice: Awareness, Action, Development (Tokyo: The Reiyukai, n.d.).

Prebish, Charles S., *American Buddhism* (North Scituate, MA: Duxbury Press, 1978).

Quest (Tokyo: The Reiyukai).

Reiyukai: Awareness, Action, Development (Tokyo: The Reiyukai, n.d.).

Reiyukai: Its Aims and Practices (Tokyo, n.d.).

Reiyukai: People Promoting Friendship and Awareness (Los Angeles: Reiyukai America, n.d.).

Reiyukai and Social Services (Tokyo: Reiyukai, 1958).

Reiyukai Today (Tokyo: Reiyukai, n.d.).

Reichelt, Ludwig, *Truth and Tradition in Chinese Buddhism: A Study of Chinese Mahayana Buddhism* (New York: Paragon Book Reprint Corp., 1968. First published in Shanghai, 1928).

Religion is Life: Guide for New Members (Tokyo: Rissho Kosei-kai, 1987).

Rissho Ankoku (Tokyo: Nichihonzan Myohoji, 1979).

Rissho Kosei-kai (Tokyo: Kosei Publishing Co., 1966).

Rissho Kosei-kai: For Our New Members (Tokyo: Kosei Publishing Co., 1972).

Rodd, Laurel Rasplica, *Nichiren: A Biography* (Occasional Paper no. 11: Arizona State Unversity Center for Asian Studies, 1978).

——, *Nichiren: Selected Writings* (Honolulu: Asian Studies at Hawaii, no. 26, University of Hawaii, 1980).

Sakamoto, Yukio (ed.), *The Lotus Sutra and Chinese Buddhism* (Kyoto: Heirakuji Shoten, 1972).

Sashida, Nikki, *A Guide to a New Believer* (Kyoto: Hommon Butsuryu-shu, 1978).

Satomi, Kishio, *Japanese Civilization: Its Significance and Realization* (London: Kegan Paul, Trench, Trubner & Co. Ltd., 1923).

Saunders, E. Dale, *Buddhism in Japan* (Philadelphia: The University of Pennsylvania Press, 1964).

Schecter, Jerrold, *The New Face of Buddha: Buddhism and Political Power in Southeast Asia* (New York: Coward-McCann, Inc., 1967).

Seikyo Times (Tokyo: Sokagakkai International).

Shingyo Hikkei: A Handbook for Members of the Nichiren Sect (Tokyo: Nichiren-shu Shumuin, 1978).

Shinsekai, no. 2, 1985 (Tokyo: Nichiren-shu Shumuin).

The Shinshu Seiten (Honolulu: The Honpa Hongwanji Mission of Hawaii, 1955).

Shobo (The Right Dharma), Nichiren-shu.

Skinner, Clarence R., *A Religion for Greatness* (Boston: Universalist Publishing House, 1945).

Smith, Vincent A., *Asoka: The Buddhist Emperor of India* (Oxford: Clarendon Press, 1901).

Soothill, William E., *The Lotus of the Wonderful Law* (Oxford: Clarendon Press, 1930).

Soothill, William E. and Hodous, Lewis, *A Dictionary of Chinese Buddhist Terms* (New York: Paragon Books, 1970).

Suzuki, Beatrice Lane, *Mahayana Buddhism* (London: George Allen and Unwin, 1959).

Suzuki, D.T., *On Indian Mahayana Buddhism* (New York: Harper Torchbooks, 1968).

——, *Zen Buddhism* (New York: Doubleday Anchor Books, 1956).

Takakusu, Junjiro, *The Essentials of Buddhist Philosophy* (Honolulu:

University of Hawaii Press, 3rd edn, 1956).

Tamura, Kwansei, 'Nichiren's Appeal to the Present Age', *Young East*, vol. 8, no. 3 (Summer 1982), 10–13.

Tamura, Yoshiro, 'Interaction Between Japanese Culture and Buddhism: The Thought of Original Enlightenment', *Osaki Gakuho* no. 238 (February), 1985.

Tanabe, George, 'Tanaka Chigaku: The *Lotus Sutra* and the Body Politic' (International Conference on the Lotus Sutra in Japanese Culture, Honolulu: University of Hawaii, 1984).

Tanaka, Chigaku, *What is Nippon Kokutai?* (Tokyo: Shishi-o bunko, 1937).

Tanaka, Junichi, 'Distinguished Disciples of Nichiren', *Nichiren Shu News*, no. 3 ff.

Tanaka, Koho, 'Chigaku Tanaka as a Modern Japanese Buddhist Reformer' (International Conference on the Lotus Sutra in Japanese Culture, Honolulu: University of Hawaii, 1984).

Tannisho: a Primer, tr. Dennis Hirota (Kyoto: Ryukoku University, 1982).

The Teaching of Buddha (Tokyo: Bukkyo Dendo Kyokai, 93rd and rev edn, 1984).

Thera, Narada and Kassapa, Bikkhu, *The Mirror of the Dhamma* (Kandy: Buddhist Publication Society, 1970).

The Threefold Lotus Sutra: The Sutra of Innumerable Meanings, The Sutra of the Lotus Flower of the Wonderful Law, The Sutra of Meditation on the Bodhisattva Universal Virtue (New York/Tokyo: Weatherhill/Kosei, 1975).

Thomsen, Harry, *The New Religions of Japan* (Rutland: Charles E. Tuttle Co., 1963).

Toda, Josei, *Lecture on the Sutra* (Tokyo: The Seikyo Press, 3 edn, 1968).

Tsunoda, Shoko, Shoka Masunaga and Kenryo Kamata, *Buddhism and Jodo Shinshu* (San Francisco: The Buddhist Churches of America, 1955).

Turner, Tina, *I, Tina* (New York: Avon Books, 1987).

2500 Buddha Jayanti Souvenir (Colombo: The Lanka Bauddha Mandalaya, 1965).

Watanabe Hoyo, *Watakushi-tashi no Nichiren-shu* ('Our Nichiren Sect') (Tokyo: Sosaku Shuppan-sha, 1980. English translation by Michael E. Sheahon, *Nichiren Shu News*, no. 32 ff).

——, 'Nichiren's Thought Appearing in the Rissho Ankoku Ron and Its Acceptance in the Modern Age', *Osaki Gakuho*, no. 138 (February 1985), 11–20.

Watanabe, Shoko, *Japanese Buddhism: A Critical Approach* (Tokyo: Kosukai Bunka Shinkokai, 1968).

Watts, Alan W., *Nature, Man and Woman* (New York: Pantheon Books, 1958).

Webb, Russell, *An Analysis of the Pali Canon* (Kandy: Buddhist Publication Society, 1975).

Williams, George M., *NSA New Members' Handbook: The Basics of Nichiren Shoshu Buddhism* (Santa Monica: Nichiren Shoshu Soka Gakkai of America, 1983).

World Tribune (Santa Monica: Nichiren Shoshu of America).

Wright, Arthur F., *Buddhism in Chinese History* (Stanford: Stanford University Press, 1959; rev 1971).

Yamamoto, Kosho, *The Other-Power* (Ube: The Karinbunko, 1965).

Yamasaki, Taikyo, *Shingon: Japanese Esoteric Buddhism* (Boston and London: Shambhala, 1988).

Zimmer, Heinrich, *Philosophies of India* (New York: Meridian Books, 1956).

Index